Thinking About Psychopaths and Psychopathy

Thinking About Psychopaths and Psychopathy

◆

Answers to Frequently Asked Questions
With Case Examples

Edited by Ellsworth Lapham Fersch

iUniverse, Inc.
New York Lincoln Shanghai

Thinking About Psychopaths and Psychopathy
Answers to Frequently Asked Questions With Case Examples

Copyright © 2006 by Ellsworth Lapham Fersch

All rights reserved. No part of this book may be used or reproduced by any means, graphic, electronic, or mechanical, including photocopying, recording, taping or by any information storage retrieval system without the written permission of the publisher except in the case of brief quotations embodied in critical articles and reviews.

iUniverse books may be ordered through booksellers or by contacting:

iUniverse
2021 Pine Lake Road, Suite 100
Lincoln, NE 68512
www.iuniverse.com
1-800-Authors (1-800-288-4677)

ISBN-13: 978-0-595-41544-1 (pbk)
ISBN-13: 978-0-595-85891-0 (ebk)
ISBN-10: 0-595-41544-X (pbk)
ISBN-10: 0-595-85891-0 (ebk)

Printed in the United States of America

Contents

About the Book. xi
About the Contributors. xiii
Introduction xvii

Frequently Asked Questions

CHAPTER 1 Characteristics of and relations among psychopathy, sociopathy, and antisocial personality disorder. 3

Is psychopathy a legal term, a psychological term, both or neither?. 3
What are the characteristics of a psychopath? 3
What is the Hare Psychopathy Checklist? 4
What are the differences between the psychopathy definitions designed by Hare and by Cleckley? 5
Do the varying degrees of psychopathy indicate that it is a continuous rather than a categorical construct? 6
Has the term psychopathy been used in legal contexts? 7
Are all psychopaths the same or are there subtypes? 7
What are the most relevant diagnoses defined in the American Psychiatric Association's Diagnostic and Statistical Manual of Mental Disorders? 8
What is antisocial personality disorder? 8
What is a manic episode? 9
What is conduct disorder? 9
What is oppositional defiant disorder? 10
What is narcissistic personality disorder? 10
What are borderline and histrionic personality disorders? 11
What is sociopathy? 11

How are children with psychopathic symptoms categorized? 11
How do the terms psychopathy, sociopathy, and antisocial personality disorder differ? 12
Is psychopathy defined by personalities, behaviors, or inclinations? 13
Is there a difference between being psychopathic and being psychotic? 14
What capacities does the psychopath lack? 14
Are psychopaths considered rational? 15
Which psychological disorders are most commonly comorbid with psychopathy? 15
Why is psychopathy not included as a diagnosis in the Diagnostic and Statistical Manual of Mental Disorders? 16
Is psychopathy linked with promiscuity? 16
Is there a notion of psychopathy in all cultures? 16
What are some common misconceptions about psychopaths? 17
Because the law defines the corporation as a person can it also be diagnosed as a psychopath? 17
Are there other disorders that are often comorbid with psychopathy? 18
Is sociopathy just an excuse? 18
Are individuals with antisocial personality disorder really antisocial or just radically pro-self? 19
Are psychopaths numb to their socially unacceptable behavior or do they simply exhibit problems with impulse control? 20
If not an aversion to societal norms or an overall disillusionment with society, how else would one explain the causes of psychopathy? 20

Chapter 2 Psychological, biological, gender-related, and other theories of causation. 22

How significantly is psychopathy a product of nurture versus nature? 22
Have any genes associated with diseases or conditions been identified that may cause psychopathy? 23
What neurological dysfunctions have been linked to psychopathy? 23
How can neurobiology help identify a cause for psychopathy? 24
What physiological peculiarities do psychopaths possess? 25
Are there neurophysiological differences between successful and unsuccessful psychopaths? 26
How does the environment affect psychopathy? 26

What characteristics might a psychopath express as a child? 27
Is there a specific economic class from which a majority of psychopaths tend to come? 28
Are psychopaths deficient in cognitive skills? 28
What is the IQ range in psychopaths? 29
Are persons in academia any more or less likely to be or become psychopaths? 29
Is there evidence supporting a cycle of abuse with relation to the spread of psychopathy? 30
Are psychopaths aware of their behavior? 30
Does the psychopath want to be a psychopath? 31
Do particular ethnic or social groups show a higher prevalence of psychopathy? 32
Do the antisocial acts performed by psychopaths increase in severity over time? 32
Are there any common concomitants to psychopathy that help diagnosis? 33
Are criminal acts of the psychopath caused by some sort of uncontrollable impulse? 33
What is the relation between attachment and psychopathy? 34
Are rates of psychopathy different across the genders? 35
Is our current model of psychopathy gender-biased? 35
What is Functional Magnetic Resonance Imaging? 36
What are the physiological and biological differences between male and female psychopaths? 37
Are certain psychopathic personality traits more prone to occur within one gender than the other? 38
Which comorbid mental disorders are most common among female psychopaths? 38
Does psychopathy appear to be more heritable in males than in females? 38

CHAPTER 3 Psychological and psychiatric forms of treatment and their use and effectiveness 40

Where are psychopaths generally treated? 40
Which response is more effective, sentencing psychopaths to prison or admitting them to mental hospitals? 41
What is the recidivism rate of criminal psychopaths? 41
What effect do Therapeutic Communities have on psychopaths? 42

What is considered a successful outcome of therapy?	43
What is the improvement rate of psychopaths in prisons?	43
Is psychopathy curable?	43
What parts of the psychopathic personality can potentially change?	44
How useful are traditional forms of psychotherapy for treating psychopathy?	44
Can drugs treat psychopathy?.	45
Can selective serotonin reuptake inhibitors, which may reduce aggression, at least reduce antisocial behaviors in psychopaths?.	45
Can surgery correct psychopathy?	46
Can Cognitive Behavioral Therapy be effective for psychopaths?	46
Are there any effective stay-at-home treatments for psychopathy?	47
How much does it cost to incarcerate or to treat a psychopath?	47
Is there a prevention program for psychopathic behavior?	48
What is therapeutic pessimism and how does it relate to the treatment of psychopaths?.	48
Why are psychopaths considered untreatable?	49
Is evil a psychological concept?.	50

Chapter 4 Media portrayals of and legal responses to psychopaths … 51

Do books and movies such as American Psycho, Red Dragon and The Silence of the Lambs accurately portray the psychopath?	51
While the news media usually portray psychopaths in a negative light, are books or movies more sympathetic to the psychopath?	52
How do theatrical productions deal with psychopaths?	52
Do movies, literary, and other works depicting psychopaths in the form of serial killers prevent society from recognizing other categories of psychopaths, including friends and white-collar psychopaths?	53
Can violence and selfishness in such media as television, films, and video games lead to psychopathy?.	54
Has corporate culture, with its levels of materialism and competition seeming to reward patterns of behavior that could be considered psychopathic, increased the number of psychopaths?	54
Have media representations of the psychopath gone so far as to impact jury decisions at trial?.	55

How often are enemies of a political establishment labeled psychopaths and how fair are these labels? 55

Does psychopathy differ cross-culturally? 56

What were the first laws to refer to psychopathy? 56

How do courts and legislatures address psychopaths, considering that psychopathy is not listed in the Diagnostic and Statistical Manual as a disorder? 57

Are there laws to warn communities of psychopaths' release from confinement or presence in the community, like the Megan's Laws that alert people about sex offenders? 57

Does the fact that psychopaths are rationally aware affect the legal standards to which they are held? 58

Does a psychopath's awareness of his psychopathy affect the legal standards to which he is held? 59

How often do psychopaths employ the insanity defense? 59

Are psychopaths ever successful when they represent themselves during a trial? 60

Are psychopaths more likely than nonpsychopaths to receive the death penalty? 61

Can psychopaths feel right and wrong? 62

Case Examples

CHAPTER 5   Collective Cases..65

   Dick Hickock, Perry Smith, In Cold Blood, and Truman Capote..............65

   Kenneth Lay, Jeffrey Skilling, Andrew Fastow, and Enron 101

CHAPTER 6   Case Studies 129

   Frank Abagnale, Jr...129

   Marshall Applewhite and Jim Jones...................................140

   Velma Barfield 151

   Patrick Bateman, Bret Easton Ellis, and American Psycho..................166

   Whitey and Billy Bulger 181

   Ted Bundy 199

   The Corporation..207

   Saddam Hussein..222

   Ted Kaczynski and Henry Murray 234

Devin Moore and Grand Theft Auto............................... 242
Scott Peterson 251
Gary Ridgway 262
Martha Stewart 273

Bibliography 281

About the Book

This volume grew out of my Harvard seminar on Psychopaths and Psychopathy in which the contributors participated by discussing these topics and cases and by writing these materials. Some had previously taken one or more of my courses: lectures on Psychology and Law, seminars on The Insanity Defense and Confining the Sexually Dangerous. Profiles of all appear in About the Contributors.

This volume is modeled on the earlier ones that answered approximately one hundred frequently asked questions and presented over a dozen case studies. This book follows that general organization. Because the answer to each question is self-contained and because readers may choose to explore the book in various ways, some materials are repeated where necessary to answer each question. For simplicity, the masculine pronoun has been used throughout when both males and females may be involved. On some occasions, a plural accompanies a singular to make the same point.

In addition to the questions and answers, to which everyone contributed, this volume also includes a number of case examples. As the members of the seminar began to explore their own potential cases, they realized that the topic is often examined elsewhere in too narrow a manner. Only the most extreme conventional criminals tend to be labeled as psychopaths. This volume reflects an expansion from a more narrow psychological and legal focus on ordinary street crime and criminals to include non-conventional white-collar crime and criminals as well and the problems of morality, and political and social policy which accompany those white-collar psychopaths.

Each contributor then explored a case illuminating an important aspect of the broader topic of psychopathy and wrote an individual study about it. These Case Studies are arranged alphabetically. Their subtitles reflect the nature of the primary issue each addresses. In addition, the participants in the seminar explored collectively two case examples. The first involved two conventional criminals and the author who wrote about them, and the second, a corporation and the individuals within it, as well as the related professionals and organizations, many accused of non-conventional white-collar offenses against individuals and society itself.

Although this volume includes an extensive Bibliography, it does not refer specifically to each listing within the text itself. Intended for the general reader and not for the researcher or the scholar, this volume assists that reader in thinking about psychopaths and psychopathy by presenting varying approaches to the materials. At the same time, it provides a comprehensive list of references for those who may wish to examine further some aspect of the topic. All involved with this volume urge those who read it to explore at length these other works for their interpretations and particular styles. It is the hope of everyone who contributed to *Thinking About Psychopaths and Psychopathy* that this volume will encourage all readers to pursue further the many cases and concepts about which we hear and see so much.

Because the contributors conducted no interviews, clinical or otherwise, with any of the subjects in these cases, and because attempts to describe and to label the subjects depend on and thereby reflect what others have said and written, a strong cautionary note is in order about the material in this book. The inclusion of any individual or organization is not meant to imply that the diagnostic label of psychopath or psychopathy is necessarily applicable. The inclusion, instead, is meant to signal that this volume attempts to explore as broadly as possible the important topic of psychopaths and psychopathy and its legal, psychological, moral, and social relation to psychoforensic issues.

About the Contributors

Christopher Benway concentrates in Biology at Harvard University, where his areas of interest include genetics and molecular biology. He has worked with Dr. Alan Michelson's *Drosophila* laboratory at Harvard Medical School, and plans to further explore *Drosophila* development and to investigate the relationship between genetic control, behavior, and memory with Dr. Sam Kunes' laboratory at Harvard's Biology Laboratories. He enjoys recreational soccer and basketball and is a member of the Harvard Republican Club. For this book, he contributed the case study on Ted Bundy and addressed questions concerning the biological and genetic aspects of psychopathy. He resides in Milton, Massachusetts, and is an avid Boston Red Sox fan.

Alexander Blenkinsopp concentrated in Social Studies at Harvard University and is pursuing further study in Criminology at the University of Oxford. While at Harvard, he worked as a research assistant for Frankfurter Professor of Law Alan Dershowitz and was Executive Editor for the *Harvard Crimson*. His thesis on the civil commitment of sex offenders and the legal rights associated with punishment won the twenty-five-hundred-dollar Thomas Temple Hoopes Prize. He also contributed to and was the Associate Editor of the earlier Harvard seminar books, *Thinking About the Insanity Defense* and *Thinking About the Sexually Dangerous*. He was Associate Editor of this entire book.

Marina Bontkowski studies Psychology in conjunction with the Mind, Brain, and Behavior Interdisciplinary Initiative at Harvard University. She has worked in Professor Daniel Schacter's laboratory on the neuropsychology of aging where she aided in research on baseline memory functions of older adults. A member of the Radcliffe varsity crew team, she also assists with statistics for the varsity men's and women's hockey teams. She wrote the Frank Abagnale, Jr. case study and contributed primarily to the section on theories of causation.

Jane Brinkley concentrates in Psychology at Harvard University where she has worked for Professor Todd Pittinsky's social psychology laboratory at the Kennedy School of Government's Center for Public Leadership. Her areas of interest include abnormal psychology and social psychology. She has worked on the technical crew of The Hasty Pudding Theatricals and also helped address issues facing women on Harvard's campus as a member of The Seneca. For this book, she contributed the case study on Gary Leon Ridgway, the Green River Killer. Hailing from Seattle, Washington, she found this case to be particularly interesting. She also contributed to several of the frequently asked questions.

Irene Choi concentrates in Psychology, with an interest in legal issues, and is pursuing a foreign language citation in Spanish at Harvard University. An active member of student government and an all-girl rock band she has also played violin in the Harvard-Radcliffe Orchestra and the Mozart Society Orchestra. She has hosted an underground rock radio show for the Harvard radio station and has done volunteer work for the Small Claims Advisory Service. She also contributed to the earlier Harvard seminar book, *Thinking About the Sexually Dangerous*. For this book, she wrote the Martha Stewart case.

Ellsworth Lapham Fersch has taught at Harvard University in the Medical and Extension Schools and in the College since receiving his J.D. in law and his Ph.D. in clinical psychology there. He has been a visiting faculty member at various colleges and universities, including Boston University, Yale University, and the University of Massachusetts. A licensed clinical psychologist and member of the Massachusetts bar, he served as a long-time director of the Massachusetts Court Clinic. As General Editor of this volume, he guided its preparation in his seminar, contributed material, and wrote the Introduction. He was also General Editor of the other volumes in this series: *Thinking About the Insanity Defense* and *Thinking About the Sexually Dangerous*.

Alexander Gordon concentrates in Psychology at Harvard University where he has also pursued music studies. He counts Bach and Thelonious Monk among his primary musical influences. He directed the music for a spring production of *Chicago* in the historic Agassiz Theater and played in the Harvard Jazz Band as well as in jazz clubs and with groups in the Cambridge area. A resident of Norwell, Massachusetts, he will be a non-resident music tutor in John Winthrop House and plans to pursue further music studies at the University of Massachusetts Boston. He spent a year studying and practicing Tibetan Buddhism at the Gampo Abbey in Nova Scotia. For this book, he wrote the Ted Kaczynski and Henry Murray case, contributed to the collective cases, and to the frequently asked questions.

Christine Mathieson concentrates in Psychology at Harvard University where her interests range from social psychology to psychopathology. She has worked in the Professor Daniel Wegner Laboratory aiding in the research of ideas surrounding mental control. On the board of Pleiades Society, a Harvard women's group, where she is the head of a non-profit community service branch, she is a Leverett House senior gift agent. She was also a part of the NCAA Championship Radcliffe crew team. She spent a semester abroad at the University of St. Andrews where she became interested in the theoretical perspectives of psychology. She also contributed to the earlier Harvard seminar book, *Thinking About the Sexually Dangerous*. For this book, she wrote the Scott Peterson case study, and contributed to the characteristics and legal response sections in the frequently asked questions.

Erin McGuirk concentrates in English and American Literature and Language at Harvard University, where she is pursuing a foreign language citation in French. She has been a member of the cross-country and track teams and has volunteered at St. James Homeless Shelter through the Phillips Brooks House Association. She plans to pursue a career in journalism, and also has a special interest in screenwriting. For this book, she wrote the case study on the Whitey and Billy Bulger brothers, and contributed to the frequently asked questions and the collective case studies. She is a resident of Boston, Massachusetts.

Olivia Milian-Rodriguez concentrates in Psychology at Harvard University where her primary focus is on psychopathology, particularly self-destructive behaviors. She has worked in Professor Matthew Nock's Laboratory as a research assistant studying self-injury in adolescents and has done additional coursework in computer programming. She is an active member of the Harvard Anime Society. She contributed the case study of Velma Barfield and answered several of the frequently asked questions. She was born and raised in Miami, Florida.

Mark Musico concentrates in Philosophy and is part of the Mind, Brain, and Behavior Interdisciplinary Initiative at Harvard University. His philosophical interests span philosophy of mind, including accounts of rationality, disjunctivism, epiphenomenalism, and evolutionary ethics. He has studied music perception and cognition under Dr. Mark Tramo. His non-academic endeavors include volunteer work with the Small Claims Advisory Service, which provides legal assistance to greater Boston residents, and service as accompanist and music director for theatrical productions at various regional theaters. At Harvard, he has directed *Carousel* on the mainstage of the Loeb Drama Center as well as productions in many other locations. For this book, he wrote the Saddam Hussein case study, contributed to the frequently asked questions on neurobiological research into psychopathy, and edited the frequently asked questions on statutory, judicial, and legal responses to psychopathy. He was Associate Editor of this entire book.

Cindy Nguyen concentrates in Psychology at Harvard University where her academic and research interests include the cognitive interface between bipolar disorder and creativity, the biological causes of schizophrenia, and psychological and legal issues involved in recovered memories. She has worked for female empowerment through a domestic violence clinic and for enabling disadvantaged communities through self-education. She enjoys Victorian literature. For this book, she wrote the case study on The Corporation. She also contributed to the frequently asked questions and the collective cases.

James P. Sharp concentrates in Psychology at Harvard University, where his academic interests have revolved around psychopathology and he has focused heavily on all aspects of psychopathy. He has worked in Professor Richard McNally's Laboratory for the research of people who believe they have recovered memories from past lives. He is the Chairman of the Quincy House Committee and Director of the Quincy Collective both of which are responsible for a wide variety of social events in Harvard's Quincy House. He is also a Director of the Cambridge Youth Enrichment Program, one of the Summer Urban Programs in the non-profit organization Phillips Brooks House. For this book, he wrote the Patrick Bateman, Bret Easton Ellis, and *American Psycho* case study and contributed to the treatment section of the frequently asked questions and to the collective cases. He was Associate Editor of this entire book.

Jonathan Spiker concentrates in Psychology at Harvard University, where he has served as a research assistant in Professor Daniel Wegner's Social Psychology Laboratory and in Professor Jesse Snedeker's Developmental Laboratory. He plans to pursue study in business school in order to start his own company. For this book, he wrote the Marshall Applewhite and Jim Jones case study and contributed to the frequently asked questions and the collective cases. He also contributed to the earlier Harvard seminar book, *Thinking About the Sexually Dangerous*. Jonathan hails from Honolulu, Hawaii, where he was a four time undefeated state high school wrestling champion and a member of the National Honor Society.

HaNhi Tran concentrates in Psychology at Harvard University where her areas of interests include drug and criminal policy and criminal behavior. She is devoted to working for refugee and immigrant groups and other underprivileged communities. In the future, she hopes to be able to work for various marginalized communities throughout her professional career. For this book, she wrote the Devin Moore and Grand Theft Auto case study and contributed to the frequently asked questions and the collective cases.

Introduction

This volume addresses a topic that leads the news, informs documentaries and profiles, moves from reportage to entertainment and back again, and concerns everyone who cares or writes about the harm that some do to others. Whether that harm is on an individual or a broader scale, whether it occurs down the street, across the country, or in a continuing television drama or a film, everyone knows about people scammed or injured or killed, put out of work or deprived of retirement funds, lied to or otherwise deceived, and about those people and organizations that do it to them without remorse or guilt. Yet there is also much confusion in society, in the media, even among specialists within the legal and the psychiatric and psychological communities, about the topic.

That confusion starts with the very terms psychopath and psychopathy. While they occur in the popular literature, and are deeply embedded in the public imagination, they appear only indirectly in the official scientific literature. The index to the authorized list of psychological and psychiatric illnesses, as defined by the American Psychiatric Association in its *Diagnostic and Statistical Manual of Mental Disorders*, does not contain the word psychopath at all. The *Manual* does say in its general discussion of antisocial personality disorder that the pattern of disregard for, or violation of, the rights of others has also been called psychopathy, sociopathy, or dyssocial personality disorder. In so doing, the *Manual* equates the four terms. But the *Manual* only authorizes the use of antisocial personality disorder for diagnostic, treatment, insurance, legal, and other purposes.

So in my own courses over the years, when I have shown all or part of a documentary about serial killers which labels them psychopaths, I have without any consideration of differences, simply told students that the term psychopath is interchangeable with sociopath and antisocial personality disorder and that they can use any one in answering questions, writing exams, and thinking about the issues. Until this seminar I have not considered the differences to any great extent.

Even more confusing to students and to the public at large are the connotations of the word antisocial. Many who hear the word antisocial think of the person who does not interact successfully with others, stays to himself at gatherings, appears either too shy or dismissive of others to be part of something larger than he is. Yet the *Manual* says, to the contrary, that the individual with antisocial personality disorder may exhibit the superficial charm of someone with the traditional label of psychopath.

To add further to the confusion, the diagnosis of antisocial personality disorder requires the labeled individual to be at least eighteen years old and to have had a diagnosis of conduct disorder before the age of fifteen. And conduct disorder also focuses on behavior rather than personality. It requires that an individual display three of four criteria: aggressivity toward people or animals, property destruction, theft or lying, serious rules violations. Because of these requirements, the label of antisocial personality disorder does not fit some who engage in that pattern of disregard for others. According to the *Manual*, their criminal behavior is not accompanied by the required personality characteristics, and so they can only be considered as individuals with adult antisocial behavior.

As the *Manual* lists them, the diagnostic criteria for antisocial personality disorder are behaviors rather than personality characteristics. The diagnosis requires three or more of seven which include repeatedly performing acts that are grounds for arrest, using aliases or lying to gain profit or pleasure from others, failing to plan ahead, engaging in many physical fights or assaults, showing a reckless disregard for one's own or others' safety, failing to sustain consistent work or to honor financial obligations, being indifferent to and lacking remorse for damage done to others. It is behavior rather than personality that determines this diagnosis.

Thus the behavior-based diagnostic criteria listed in the *Manual* are different from the paragraphs preceding them which describe the disorder and elaborate on personality characteristics. And the *Manual*'s statement that antisocial personality disorder appears to be associated with low socioeconomic status and urban settings conflicts with the analysis presented first in 1942 by Hervey Cleckley, MD, in his work, *The Mask of Sanity: An Attempt to Clarify Some Issues About the So-called Psychopathic Personality*. He described the characteristics of nonconventional white-collar as well as conventional street psychopaths and illustrated his principles with significant case materials.

More recently, Robert Hare, PhD, registered his disagreement with, even disapproval of, the American Psychiatric Association handling of the issue. He noted that while the diagnostic criteria in the *Diagnostic and Statistical Manual of Mental Disorders* focus on behavior, the accompanying explanatory material focuses as well on personality, including the superficial charm, failure of empathy, and grandiosity which the *Manual* admits have been elements of psychopathy. Hare's research and writings argued that the disjunction between the diagnostic criteria presented in the *Manual* and the accompanying explanatory material demonstrates that psychopathy and antisocial personality disorder are not the same. In his *Without Conscience: The Disturbing World of the Psychopaths Among Us*, he argued that research on psychopathy showed that it was more complex and nuanced than antisocial personality disorder. It included, he determined, two explicit factors, the first of which is only implicitly presented in the *Manual*'s discursive essay material.

As opposed to the *Manual*'s seven limited diagnostic criteria, Hare operationalized twenty in his Psychopathy Checklist-Revised, the PCL-R. He described the first factor as an emotional one. It refers to the selfish, callous, and remorseless use of others. With information obtained from files and from semi-structured hour-and-a-half to two-hour interviews, it includes eight items: glibness and superficial charm, a grandiose sense of self-worth, pathological lying, manipulativeness, a lack of empathy, and of remorse, shallow affect, and a failure to accept personal responsibility. He described the second factor as a behavioral one. It refers to a chronic, unstable lifestyle. With information gathered from files and other ancillary sources it includes ten items: proneness to boredom, with accompanying need for stimulation, parasitic lifestyle, poor behavioral control, early behavioral problems, including juvenile delinquency, and failure to succeed with lesser forms of sanction, lack of realistic long-term goals, impulsivity, and irresponsibility. Two items, promiscuous sexual behavior and many short-term marital relationships, though they are used, do not load on either factor. And he concluded that while reliable diagnoses of psychopathic personality disorder can be made based solely on extensive file and ancillary material, interviews alone do not lead to reliable diagnoses.

The consequences of the label psychopath extend far beyond a limited diagnostic purpose. Use of the results of the diagnostic labeling occurs in the legal as well as in the mental health system. Because many practical decisions, involving diagnosis, treatment, sentencing, classification, confinement, even death, require the drawing of lines separating the degrees of psychopathy, the PCL-R scoring system accommodates that effort. Scoring each factor as 0, 1, or 2, an individual's total can range from 0 to 40. Lines then have generally been drawn at scores of 30 or more for psychopaths, 21-29 for possible or partial psychopaths, and 20 or less for non-psychopaths. Research has shown that the overall difference among these groups is highly significant.

Hare stated that what the American Psychiatric Association *Manual* did not do directly in its diagnostic list of criteria for antisocial personality disorder but only by indirection in its paragraphs explaining the diagnosis, he did directly for psychopathy. He differentiated it from antisocial personality disorder; he gave it specificity; he examined the research he and others conducted concerning it; he demonstrated that most psychopaths fit criteria for antisocial personality disorder, but most people with antisocial personality disorder are not psychopaths; and he argued for a revision of the psychiatric nomenclature to take all this into consideration.

Beyond descriptions of the psychological disorder for use in diagnosis and treatment in the mental health system are consequences which flow from a diagnosis of psychopathy in the legal system. Those consequences have considerable importance. The diagnosis impacts the determination of criminal guilt as questions arise about the insanity defense or diminished responsibility. It enters into determinations of sentencing, in terms of severity and of length, and of civil liability, as both may involve intent, mental illness, background factors, standing in the community, personality as well as behavior. Jurors and judges often seek indications of remorse, for example, to help them determine the appropriate consequences for damaging behavior. And when the perpetrators are white-collar and non-conventional, more affluent, perhaps more educated, and generally respected in all other areas of their lives, jurors and judges may assess them differently from conventional offenders who fit the stereotypical lower class, perhaps minority, less educated parameters. And yet both may be psychopaths. More recently, efforts to commit offenders to mental hospitals following completion of their criminal sentences may involve determinations of their psychopathic potential. Finally, questions of executability may involve predictions of future behavior based on labels such as psychopathy. Though all these legal proceedings examine the relation among psychological, familial, social, economic, and racial determinants, society often finds psychological and psychiatric factors the most compelling.

Many commentators have reflected on these matters. In the psychoanalytic literature, Adelaide Johnson wrote in 1949 about superego lacunae in those who commit offenses: their consciences have gaps or holes as does swiss cheese. In the criminologic literature, James Q. Wilson wrote in 1985 about those who are tempted by illegal or immoral behavior and watch to see if anything happens to others who engage in such conduct: lack of enforcement, he argued, breeds further disrespect for and violation of the law. In the behavioral psychological literature, Stanton Samenow revised in 2004 his explorations of criminal thinking patterns, which are now termed cognitive distortions. And in the increasing neuroscientific and biological literature, the influence of genes on behavior has gained added relevance.

A revealing interaction between antisocial behavior and insanity occurred in the two trials of Andrea Yates who methodically drowned her five children in the hour when she was alone with them. In the first trial, the psychiatric testimony of Dr. Park Elliott Dietz appeared influential in convincing the jury that Yates' behavior was antisocial, perhaps psychopathic, rather than the result of psychosis. He concluded that she was not out of touch with reality; in fact, he argued that she had planned their deaths, had waited for an opportune time when she was alone, had called police immediately afterwards to say she had done wrong. The jury found her guilty and she was sentenced to prison. On appeal, her conviction was overturned because of Dietz's inadvertent or deliberate misstatement concerning a television program about someone who drowned her children and then pleaded insanity which program had not even aired. On retrial, a different jury, hearing almost the same evidence and experts, found her not guilty by reason of insanity. The earlier jury had implicitly found her acts to be antisocial, perhaps psychopathic, but not the result of psychosis; the later jury found her acts to be the consequence of her psychotic mental state.

In the psychiatric literature, the American Psychiatric Association asked in its 1982 *Statement on the Insanity Defense* whether the legal standards in use concerning the insanity defense should be modified. It concluded that the insanity defense ought not to be available for persons primarily diagnosed with personality disorders such as antisocial personality disorder, which it also termed sociopathy. To do so, it maintained, would not accord with modern psychiatric knowledge or beliefs, and it concluded that offenders with antisocial personality disorders should be considered criminally responsible for heuristic reasons if for no other. The American Psychiatric Association determined that only serious disorders, such as schizophrenia or bipolar disorder, should lead to acquittals by reason of insanity.

But a different response followed Yates' second trial. In an editorial arguing for reform, the *Boston Herald* responded to the second jury's verdict finding Andrea Yates not guilty by reason of insanity in the planned drowning deaths of her five young children by advocating a guilty but insane model. It said that such a verdict would provide a balance between mercy and justice because convicted offenders could receive mental health treatment until their recovery at which time they would finish their sentence in prison. In essence, it argued that a person could be both guilty as a psychopath or antisocial personality would be, and insane as a seriously mentally ill person would be. Yet the two words contradict each other.

This conflict between the words guilty and insane appears unresolvable, and in the Yates case unnecessary, for the solution the *Herald* sought was exactly what was happening after the first jury found Andrea Yates guilty of murder in 2002. Though sentenced to prison, she was spending most of the time in a prison mental health facility. In other words, the sentence imposed after the first trial found her guilty, as would the guilty part of guilty but insane, but confined her first to a mental health facility, as would the insane part of that verdict, where she would be treated until she was ready, if ever, to enter the prison setting itself.

The idea of guilty but insane has been around for a considerable time. Years ago a professor at Harvard Law School argued for the same thing as the *Boston Herald* did in response to the Yates case. He advocated the new verdict of guilty but insane to express the psychiatric truth that the offender's mental illness played a significant role in his acts. He advocated turning to modern psychiatry for essential help. But as I wrote then and more recently in *Thinking About the Insanity Defense* and to the *Boston Herald*: Why turn only to modern psychiatry for help in determining what contributed to a defendant's criminal behavior? What about modern religion and economics and sociology and philosophy and politics and literature as well as old-fashioned common sense? Why should a term like insane, related to psychology though a legal not a psychological or psychiatric term, be added to the word guilty when no other word is added?

Partly insanity has been accorded special status among the excuses or explanations for antisocial conduct because it seems to negate the intent necessary to commit a criminal act; yet Yates intended to kill her children and said shortly afterwards that she knew it was wrong to do so. Partly it has, because psychology is defined as a science of the mind; yet the directly opposing testimony of forensic psychiatrists and psychologists in the Yates' and other trials suggests some lack of scientific precision. And partly it has, because ours has become a psychological society.

Yet some argue that the special status accorded insanity is actually too narrow. Given the chance, their reforms might enumerate the many factors that make it difficult or perhaps impossible in their view for an individual to conform conduct to the requirements of law. Beyond guilty but insane the expansionists might add guilty but fanatically religious, economically disadvantaged, sociologically anomic, philosophically existentialist, politically radical, literarily superior, extremely infatuated, or jealous, or even very, very sorry. They might even argue that these excuses should mandate a finding of innocent. Yet that is what psychopaths argue as they attempt to escape personal responsibility for their acts which have harmed others. The efforts of psychopaths and of defenders of the mentally ill or seriously troubled appear more similar than some might wish to acknowledge.

Others, however, would restrict the excuses that the mentally disordered or the psychopathic could offer, excluding even insanity. Their reform would return to two verdicts, guilty and innocent, so that society can determine through the criminal law what is morally tolerable and what is not. Seriously wounding or killing someone in self-defense may well be tolerable; intending to and killing one's children ought not to be. And, they say, it is unnecessary to add words to the verdict, especially if their only purposes are to make juries more likely to convict and to mandate the place for initial confinement of the defendant.

And now again, in this book about psychopaths and psychopathy, it can be noted that while psychology and psychiatry, and other fields, can help in understanding events which involve the law, the real reform is the courage to take seriously the individual's explanations and to weigh them and the acts in the balance of moral acceptability or unacceptability. That provides justice. Once the verdict is in and the sentence imposed, then every offender ought to receive the help that common sense, or psychology or religion or any other specialty, can offer to help him become better and to deter future offending. That provides mercy. This book details those efforts to understand motives, acts, and consequences through a series of case examples and a series of answers to frequently asked questions.

The cases include both ordinary street and white-collar offenses and both conventional and non-conventional offenders, who range from the completely psychopathic to the potentially or marginally psychopathic to the less psychopathic to the non-psychopathic. In some instances, cases are included simply because one or more commentators have labeled individuals or institutions as sociopathic or psychopathic or antisocial. The cases cover the widest variety of individuals and institutions, from serial killers, to imposters, to governmental officials, to a professor and his student, to corporate executives, to a literary creation, to writers and their subjects, to a video game and its player, to corporations, and cults, and their leaders. The cases attempt to examine the full array of those to whom the label of psychopath has been affixed.

These case analyses, together with the responses to frequently asked questions, are designed to help readers think more clearly about psychopaths and psychopathy. Because of psychopaths' high profile in, and their damage to, society, the effort to understand the legal, psychological, moral, and social significance of psychopaths, and of the larger topic of psychopathy itself, remains especially important.

Frequently Asked Questions

1

Characteristics of and relations among psychopathy, sociopathy, and antisocial personality disorder

Is psychopathy a legal term, a psychological term, both or neither?

Psychopathy is a term used in both psychological and legal settings. While not listed as an official disorder by the American Psychiatric Association in its *Diagnostic and Statistical Manual of Mental Disorders*, it is widely viewed as a useful diagnosis. In law, the diagnosis of psychopathy can be used as an aggravating factor in a person's sentencing. Since researchers have shown that recidivism rates are extremely high in psychopaths, psychopaths are often given longer prison sentences than nonpsychopathic offenders and are more readily sentenced to death than nonpsychopaths. In addition, though sexual psychopath laws have fallen out of favor, their replacement laws in some states permit the civil commitment of sex offenders at the completion of their prison sentences on the similar theory that they are more likely to reoffend.

What are the characteristics of a psychopath?

Psychopathy was initially described by Hervey Cleckley, M.D., in 1942, as a form of personality disorder. He did not operationalize his general description though he did present numerous case examples of both conventional street offenders and non-conventional white-collar and other offenders. In 1980, Robert Hare, Ph.D., did operationalize the term in his Psychopathy Checklist (PCL), which was later revised in 1985 as the Psychopathy Checklist-Revised (PCL-R). The checklist consists of twenty items which are considered valid character traits of psychopaths.

What is the Hare Psychopathy Checklist?

The Hare Psychopathy Checklist-Revised, or PCL-R, is a diagnostic tool used to rate a person's psychopathic tendencies. The PCL-R consists of a twenty-item symptom rating scale that allows trained examiners to assess a subject's degree of psychopathy. It is accepted by many in the field as the best method for determining the presence and degree of psychopathy in a person. The PCL-R is used for diagnosing psychopathy in individuals for clinical, legal, or research purposes.

The PCL-R contains two parts, a semi-structured interview and a review of the subject's history. During the evaluation, the clinician scores twenty items that measure elements of psychopathy. The material covers two key factors that help define the psychopath: selfish and unfeeling personality and an unstable and antisocial lifestyle. The interview portion of the evaluation covers the subject's background, but because psychopaths lie frequently and easily, the information they provide must be confirmed by the documents in the subject's case history. The twenty traits assessed by the PCL-R score are glibness and superficial charm; a grandiose sense of self-worth; need for stimulation and proneness to boredom; pathological lying; conning and manipulating; lack of remorse or guilt; shallow affect; callousness and lack of empathy; parasitic lifestyle; poor behavioral control; promiscuous sexual behavior; early behavior problems; lack of realistic long-term goals; impulsivity; irresponsibility; failure to accept responsibility for own actions; many short-term marital relationships; juvenile delinquency; revocation of conditional release; and criminal versatility. When scored, the PCL-R provides a total that indicates how closely the test subject matches the score that a prototypical psychopath would receive. Each of the twenty items is given a score of zero, one, or two based on how well it applies to the subject being tested. A prototypical psychopath would receive a maximum score of forty, while someone without psychopathic traits or tendencies would receive a score of zero. A score of thirty or above generally qualifies a person for a diagnosis of psychopathy.

What are the differences between the psychopathy definitions designed by Hare and by Cleckley?

By studying and observing countless numbers of social deviants, Hervey Cleckley extracted the sixteen traits he thought were most central to his concept of a psychopath. He created no concrete test or point system to determine whether one could officially be diagnosed as a psychopath. Cleckley simply described the actions and intentions of psychopaths so that the term psychopath would have some reference point to explain what was meant when using the term. Cleckley did not anticipate the use of psychopathy as a clinical construct with quantitative measures for dangerousness assessment and prediction. It was merely an idea derived from his clinical practice which he presented in his book *The mask of sanity*.

Hare used this conceptual description of psychopathy to create the Psychopathy Checklist, or PCL, and later the PCL-R, which was an attempt to refine and quantify the original idea. The PCL-R incorporated the degree to which a person possesses a given quality and, using the sum of the specific traits, the degree to which a person is generally psychopathic. This scale captures the concept that people can be more or less psychopathic, represented by a numerical value. Although Cleckley's original sixteen traits may have been altered in the translation to the PCL-R, Hare's new construct allowed for a degree of scientific study and classification previously unattainable by the mere existence of a set of descriptors.

It is instructive to examine the differences between Cleckley's and Hare's lists of traits. Cleckley required that psychopaths be free of delusions or anxiety. Hare eliminated that requirement. According to Hare's checklist, a diagnosis of psychosis, which is usually marked by delusions or hallucinations, or any other mental disorder is compatible with psychopathy. Essentially, those other disorders might indeed be present, but they are not considered when assessing psychopathy; they are not part of the PCL-R score. Hare also dispensed with Cleckley's requirement that suicide threats rarely be carried out. The PCL-R is designed primarily to evaluate living individuals, so one can ever know whether someone will commit suicide in the future; therefore, suicide completion is irrelevant at the time of the test. Finally, Hare eliminated Cleckley's mentions of alcohol consumption. The rest of Cleckley's list was simply reworded to make them more concise and contemporary.

The largest change stems from Cleckley's descriptor of inadequately motivated antisocial behavior. Hare, in designing the two-factor system of the PCL-R, extrapolated upon the broad trait of antisocial behavior seen in psychopaths. He turned that one label into a series of more specific antisocial acts that encompass an individual's entire life, such as juvenile delinquency, parasitic lifestyle, poor behavioral controls, and criminal versatility. It is this expanded weight of antisocial behavior that best defines the leap from Cleckley's to Hare's conceptualization of psychopathy.

While most psychopaths probably fit both Cleckley's and Hare's set of criteria, there are also probably a number of individuals who fit one definition but not the other.

Do the varying degrees of psychopathy indicate that it is a continuous rather than a categorical construct?

The term categorical in this context implies that a mental condition or disorder exists on a completely different plane from what is considered average. People either have the condition or they do not have the condition; there is no scale or gray area. For instance, many genetic disorders are categorical: either someone has Turner's syndrome or he does not have it. Mental disorders are typically categorized as either present or not present in the *Diagnostic and Statistical Manual of Mental Disorders*, but many are viewed as continuous in nature.

Hare's Psychopathy Checklist Revised, or PCL-R, suggests that if a subject scores thirty or above out of forty on the scale, it is enough to diagnose this person as a psychopath. However, because the scale is simply a sum of psychopathic traits, it implies that scoring higher on more items indicates an individual is increasingly psychopathic, regardless of his relation to the arbitrary cut-off value of thirty points. A score of forty is considered more psychopathic than thirty-one, which is more psychopathic than ten, which is more psychopathic than four.

Cleckley highlighted the diverse nature of psychopathy by creating categories many psychopaths may likely fall into, such as the businessman, the gentleman, the man of the world, the scientist, the psychiatrist, or the physician, to suggest that not all psychopaths are merely criminals. Every person's personality is unique unto himself, and although a psychopath may exhibit an excess of superficial charm or degrees of callousness, the extent to which one behaves in these manners certainly varies from fellow psychopaths.

Hare's PCL-R was designed as a continuous scale. Individuals can score anywhere on a scale from zero to forty, denoting a spectrum of psychopathy. In other words, people can be more or less psychopathic than other people. The cutoff values for what is deemed psychopathy are somewhat arbitrary and often vary depending on the context. As with most personality disorders, taxometric analyses, tests to determine how many distinct curves from a variable exist in a population, support the fact that psychopathy exists on a single continuum. Psychopaths simply represent an extreme set of attributes that are present in the general population.

Antisocial personality disorder, on the other hand, may be categorical. There is less research available, but taxometric analysis revealed that people with antisocial personality disorder are potentially distinctly different from average individuals. Of course, the disorder is a behavior-oriented construct, so it is logical that any given person either commits antisocial acts or does not. There is less gray area in analyzing behavior. Psychopathy's emotional and interpersonal characteristics are not uncommon attributes in humans; it is simply a matter of how many a specific person possesses simultaneously and how severe those qualities are. With that in mind, psychopathy's spectrum can be visible in any sample population. Even criminals with antisocial personality disorder will exhibit a spectrum of psychopathy scores, albeit with a higher average score than other populations.

Has the term psychopathy been used in legal contexts?

Various states and nations have enacted statutes relating to psychopathy, and in their statutes have defined psychopathy in their own terms. The Washington State Legislature, for example, defined psychopathic personality as a genetic or acquired condition which affects the individual's emotional and behavioral functions, such that it is difficult or impossible for the individual to integrate into normal society. A 1939 California statute defined psychopath as any child sexual offender. The United Kingdom's Mental Health Act defined psychopathic disorder as a chronic condition which leads the individual to act aggressively and irresponsibly.

Are all psychopaths the same or are there subtypes?

There is considerable debate as to whether the group of individuals labeled psychopaths is homogeneous or whether there are distinct distinguishing factors among them that justify creating subtypes. There are several benefits to identifying subtypes of psychopaths, pertaining primarily to potential treatment options or simply in terms of refining a clinician's or prison official's notions of what kind of person they are dealing with.

Several different ways to classify psychopaths have been proposed in recent years. One proposal is that psychopaths can be characterized across four subtypes of psychopathy: a narcissistic variant, a borderline variant, a sadistic variant, and an antisocial variant. The subtypes are based on observed differences in the interpersonal relationships, patterns of crime, and institutional behavior of psychopathic persons. The narcissistic variant consists of characteristics consistent with pathological degrees of grandiosity, entitlement, and callous disregard for the feelings of others. The borderline variant is generally linked to affective instability and self-destruction. The sadistic variant encapsulates many of the well-known, highly disturbing serial killer cases. Sadistic psychopaths are able to recognize the suffering of others and derive great pleasure from inflicting pain. The antisocial variant is the most pure form of the psychopath as described by Cleckley and many others. This subtype of psychopath is the criminal who is unable to control his behavior or refrain from acting on his impulses. The antisocial psychopath is a parasite who is in constant need of stimulation. These four subtypes are only one recommendation for dividing a heterogeneous population. More useful categories may be designed in the future.

What are the most relevant diagnoses defined in the American Psychiatric Association's Diagnostic and Statistical Manual of Mental Disorders*?*

Antisocial personality disorder is most closely aligned by the Association with psychopathy and is said to be interchangeable as a diagnosis with sociopathy as well. Other related diagnoses include conduct disorder, narcissistic personality disorder, borderline personality disorder, and oppositional defiant disorder. Other disorders, which need to be addressed in the context of psychopathy, are schizophrenia and bipolar disorder.

What is antisocial personality disorder?

The official *Manual* describes antisocial personality disorder as a persistent disregard for the rights of others which begins by age fifteen and continues into adulthood, though it cannot be diagnosed before age eighteen. It says other terms for the disorder are psychopathy and sociopathy. While individuals with antisocial personality disorder do appear to have an aversion to complying with societal norms, their behavior involves more aggression towards society than withdrawal from society. They not only exhibit disregard for the rights of others, they violate them for their own benefit. Their lawless behavior is usually persistent. They may react with indifference when caught, often blaming their victim and offering no compensation.

Antisocial personality disorder is a condition in which an individual completely ignores the rights of others. To receive this diagnosis, an individual first has to show at least three of the following behaviors: repeated acts that result in arrest such as theft or assault, regularly lying or conning, inability to plan ahead, high levels of physical aggressiveness, engaging in activities that endanger others, inability to hold onto a job, and lack of remorse for causing harm to others. Additionally, the individual must have a history of conduct problems in childhood or adolescence, preferably with a diagnosis of conduct disorder. Finally, the diagnosis of antisocial personality disorder can only be given to adults. Due to the emphasis on aggression and criminal behavior, the disorder is often underdiagnosed in females. Although the term is often used interchangeably with psychopathy, there are differences between this disorder and psychopathy.

Though antisocial personality disorder is often comorbid with a number of other disorders, it cannot be diagnosed if the symptoms only occur during a schizophrenic or manic episode. Although many psychopaths have all the markers of antisocial personality disorder, most of those diagnosed with antisocial personality disorder are not psychopaths because psychopathy is considered a smaller, stringently defined subpopulation of antisocial personality disorder. While most psychopaths satisfy the criteria for antisocial personality disorder, most of those diagnosed with antisocial personality disorder are not psychopaths.

What is a manic episode?

A manic episode is a distinct period, lasting at least a week, of abnormally and persistently elevated, expansive, or irritable mood, characterized by three or more of these: grandiosity, greatly decreased need for sleep, pressure to talk, racing thoughts, distractibility, significantly increased activity or agitation, pleasure-seeking in activities that may prove painful.

What is conduct disorder?

Conduct disorder is a psychological disorder normally diagnosed in children or adolescents. It is a condition in which an individual consistently behaves in a manner that ignores other people's basic rights or major age-appropriate rules of conduct. These behaviors include three of four major criteria: higher than average levels of aggression to people or animals, such as bullying or fighting; the destruction of property, such as starting fires; a tendency toward lying and stealing; and other serious violations of rules, such as truancy or running away. While many children occasionally display some of these behaviors, children diagnosed with conduct disorder behave this way so consistently that they are generally unable to function well socially or academically. The behavior found in conduct disorder is more severe than in oppositional defiant disorder, but not as severe as in antisocial personality disorder. Even though it is normally a diagnosis given to children, adults who do not quite meet the diagnostic criteria for antisocial personality disorder can be given a diagnosis of conduct disorder.

What is oppositional defiant disorder?

Like conduct disorder, oppositional defiant disorder is normally diagnosed in children or adolescents. Oppositional defiant disorder is defined by consistently negative, hostile, and defiant behavior for six months in at least four of eight categories. Specific behaviors found in this condition include frequent loss of temper, regularly arguing with adults, refusing to obey rules, deliberately annoying other people, and spitefulness or vindictiveness. When reading this list of behaviors, it seems like a description of common childhood behavior, but a diagnosis of this disorder only occurs when the behavior occurs more often than is normal for an individual's age group, and the behavior is severe enough to impair the individual's ability to function in school or in social relationships.

What is narcissistic personality disorder?

This disorder refers to a pervasive pattern of grandiosity, need for excessive admiration, and lack of empathy, present in at least five of nine contexts, including, among others, exaggerated self-importance, preoccupation with fantasies of greatness, a feeling of being special, a sense of entitlement, interpersonal exploitation, lack of empathy, and arrogant, haughty behavior or attitudes.

What are borderline and histrionic personality disorders?

Borderline personality disorder refers to a pervasive pattern of instability of interpersonal relationships, self-image, and affects, with marked impulsivity, and five or more of these: great fear of abandonment, unstable intense relationships, identity disturbance, impulsivity, suicidality, severely reactive mood, feelings of emptiness, undue anger, transient paranoid ideation. Histrionic personality disorder refers to a pervasive pattern of excessive emotionality and attention-seeking behavior, consisting of five or more of these: demand to be the center of attention, focus on physical appearance, provocative interactions, shifting shallow emotions, vague speech, self-dramatization, suggestibility, misperception of relationships as intimate.

What is sociopathy?

Robert Hare noted that sociopathy and psychopathy are often used interchangeably, presumably because this use makes it is less likely to confuse these terms with psychoticism or insanity. Hare pointed out a slight difference in thinking. Syndromes of sociopathy are believed to be caused entirely by social forces and early experiences. Sociopathy has also been used to refer to antisocial personality disorder.

Although in 1952 sociopathic personality was used in place of psychopathic personality, it seems that the term is falling into disuse. While the idea of sociopathy may have some validity, there is no current measure for testing sociopathy as there is for psychopathy and antisocial personality disorder, thereby preventing its use as a clearly defined, technical term.

How are children with psychopathic symptoms categorized?

Children cannot be diagnosed with any kind of personality disorder until they are eighteen years old because their brain, and by extension their personality, are not considered fully developed. Instead, if they display symptoms similar to psychopathy or antisocial personality disorder, they are diagnosed with conduct disorder. To be diagnosed with conduct disorder, children must repeatedly display a certain number of particular behaviors that violate social norms and have very little regard for the rights of others. The peculiarity about children with conduct disorder is that little seems to effectively modify their undesirable behavior.

Although children cannot be formally diagnosed with psychopathy, prevalence rates of antisocial behavior among the general adolescent population range between two percent and six percent, which represents between 1.3 and 3.8 million youth. These children are sometimes referred to as fledgling psychopaths. Several studies have found that conduct disorder may be an antecedent to psychopathy and antisocial personality disorder later in life, but there is currently no reliable test that can be administered to children to predict whether they will develop into adult psychopaths. There are a handful of youth psychopathy measures that have been recently designed, such as the PCL-R: Youth Version, the Antisocial Process Screening Device, and the Child Psychopathy Scale. The latter two are self-report measures, so their reliability is intrinsically under question, and the PCL-R:YV has surprising difficulty predicting future psychopathy and maintaining construct validity. Much more research in early detection is necessary in order to pinpoint at-risk youth effectively.

How do the terms psychopathy, sociopathy, and antisocial personality disorder differ?

Although the *Diagnostic and Statistical Manual of Mental Disorders* lists the terms psychopathy and sociopathy as other terms for antisocial personality disorder, the three terms do differ. The source of this confusion is most likely due to the behavioral overlaps among the three disorders. While antisocial personality disorder is characterized by behaviors psychopathy is based both on behaviors and personality traits. The American Psychiatric Association purposely based antisocial personality disorder on behaviors because they believed it would be easier to quantify. Because the diagnosis is based on behaviors, however, the term does not seem so useful since it can simply be thought of another term for criminality. There are estimates that nearly eighty percent of individuals in prison could be classified as having antisocial personality disorder. The field of criminology tends to treat antisocial personality disorder as synonymous with criminality, and as a result many criminologists refer to it as a wastebasket category.

Individuals with antisocial personality disorder are a diverse group. Psychologists consider the juvenile version of it to be conduct disorder, and individuals must have had conduct disorder before they can be diagnosed with antisocial personality disorder. The main characteristic is a complete and utter disregard for the rights of others and the rules of society. Those with the disorder rarely show anxiety or feelings of guilt. It is positively correlated with psychopathy but they are not terms that can be used interchangeably.

Sociopathy is another term often used interchangeably with psychopathy. There is no recognized checklist for sociopathy as there is for psychopathy. There is a general sense that sociopathy is a less severe term than psychopathy and thus the hope for a cure for sociopathy. Sociopathy is often characterized as a dysfunctional conscience. Sociopaths are often characterized as only caring about fulfilling their own needs and desires. The term sociopath is sometimes used by experts in referring to people whose bad character is due principally to parental failures rather than an inborn temperament. Four subtypes of sociopathy have been identified: common, aggressive, alienated, and dissocial. One researcher claimed that some common sociopathic traits are egocentricity, callousness, impulsivity, conscience defect, exaggerated sexuality, excessive boasting, risk taking, inability to resist temptation, antagonistic, deprecating attitude toward opposite sex, lack of interest in bonding.

Psychopathy is often considered a more serious disorder than sociopathy. It is a constellation of behavioral, affective, and interpersonal characteristics. The general public tends to associate psychopathy with what they consider psycho serial killers, whereas they may consider a sociopath to be a heartless and callous businessman. These ideas are public conceptions and do not have scientific support.

As a final distinction research suggests that those with antisocial personality disorder often age out of crime, whereas sociopaths and especially psychopaths who are criminal do not, and are at a very high risk of recidivism.

Is psychopathy defined by personalities, behaviors, or inclinations?

More detailed than the standard two-factor perspective, it is possible to divide psychopathy into three conceptual factors: interpersonal, affective, and lifestyle. These factors may manifest as personality traits, behavioral characteristics, and patterned decision-making inclinations. The interpersonal factor involves how the individual interacts socially with other people, such as whether the individual is glib or grandiose, or pathologically lies to and cons others. The affective factor involves the emotional picture of the individual, such as whether they have shallow emotions, a lack of empathy, a lack of guilt, or a lack of remorse. The lifestyle factor involves how the individual decides to carry out their life, such as whether they are impulsive, irresponsible, parasitic, nomadic, or lacking goals.

Is there a difference between being psychopathic and being psychotic?

Yes, psychopathy and psychosis are two different psychological phenomena. Psychopathy is defined as a cluster of personality and behavioral characteristics such as being charming, glib, superficial, irresponsible, and manipulative. Often, the psychopath is sane, rational, and even quick-witted. When they are brought into hospitals for evaluation of competency, criminal responsibility, or commitment, they are routinely declared sane and competent. They do not suffer from delusions or hallucinations. Psychosis, on the other hand, is a psychological illness in which a person's thinking becomes irrational and disturbed. It is essentially an altered perception of reality. Often, psychotic individuals may have hallucinations in which they see or hear things that do not exist and they are, therefore, unable to distinguish between the real world and the mental world they inhabit. Schizophrenia and bipolar disorder, as well as schizophrenic or manic episodes are examples of psychotic states. Although they sound similar, psychopathy and psychosis are two very different psychological conditions.

What capacities does the psychopath lack?

Psychopaths are often described as having a shallow range of affect. In other words, they tend to lack certain feelings, or may not experience them to such a strong and profound extent as others might. These feelings include, but are not limited to, empathy, guilt, remorse, disgust, and fear. Many experts indeed believe that although psychopaths are able to reproduce the so-called pantomime of emotions, they do not necessarily experience the emotions themselves. Any display of emotion on their part would thereby simply be the product of imitation. Other experts argue that psychopaths may actually be hypersensitive to certain emotions. This idea is supported by the fact that they often have very low tolerance for frustration.

Psychopaths also often have a grandiose sense of self-worth and do not understand the need or purpose of social norms and moral obligations. In turn this leads them to act selfishly and irresponsibly, with no regard for the consequences of their actions. They are thus often described as lacking a conscience and sensitivity for others' feelings or wellbeing.

Are psychopaths considered rational?

In one sense, psychopaths are exceptionally rational. They do not suffer from delusions or hallucinations. They often possess keen analytical skills and intelligence above the average level. They present themselves as being cool, collected, and lucid. They are able to figure out what serves their own best interests with remarkable efficiency.

Yet in another sense, psychopaths are irrational in that they do not value the basic rights of others. By not accepting the value of human life, free from suffering, psychopaths display a fundamental deficiency in rational thought. Some philosophers would claim that it is not rationality they lack but rather a moral sense. However, in psychopathy's full manifestation, the moral sense is lacking to such an extreme degree that one would be hard-pressed to call these individuals rational. Modern psychology has demonstrated how much of what we consider rational behavior is predicated on a multitude of implicit social judgments, each of which has a moral component. Without this moral calculus, the psychopath lacks a deep, fully rational understanding of life.

Which psychological disorders are most commonly comorbid with psychopathy?

Because the characteristics and behavioral patterns of psychopaths are relatively similar to those with antisocial personality disorder and sociopathy, these two disorders have a very high comorbidity with psychopathy. Persons in all three conditions exhibit disregard for the rights of others, and regularly violate the rights of others through deceit and manipulation for their own benefit. Their lawless behavior is usually compulsive, and they often react with indifference when caught, often blaming their victim and showing no remorse.

Psychopaths are commonly comorbid with borderline, histrionic, and narcissistic personality disorders, all of which are characterized in varying degrees by a grandiose sense of self. Psychopaths also may engage in reckless sexual behavior, reckless driving habits, and substance abuse, and often feel anxiously intolerant of boredom. Many of these behaviors can also be found in anxiety disorders, mood disorders, substance-related disorders, somaticization disorder, pathological gambling, and other disorders of impulse control.

Why is psychopathy not included as a diagnosis in *the* Diagnostic and Statistical Manual of Mental Disorders?

The American Psychiatric Association made the decision that behaviors are more easily and reliably quantifiable than affective and interpersonal traits. Because psychopathy requires evaluation of affective and interpersonal factors as well as of antisocial behaviors, the Association has chosen to include only antisocial personality disorder which can be diagnosed solely on the basis of the antisocial behaviors.

Is psychopathy linked with promiscuity?

Promiscuous behavior is specifically listed as a characteristic of the psychopath by Hare in his checklist. Psychopaths commonly have a shallow view of sexuality. Their sexual relations are frequent but lack substantive content.

One possible explanation for psychopaths' promiscuity is their impaired impulse control. Most members of society feel sexual desire. Most, however, are able to restrain themselves from acting on their urges unless certain situational factors exist. The psychopath is unlike the ordinary individual with respect to sexual discretion. Believing his sexual prowess to be superior to others, the psychopath engages in sexual activity with whoever happens to be available.

Is there a notion of psychopathy in all cultures?

Current anthropological evidence indicates that psychopathy is known to all cultures of all times, although it is known by many different names, and it appears in many different forms. One book goes to the root of the question, analyzing the very origin of violence in primitive primates, mankind's progenitors, and Cleckley stated that documented cases of psychopathy nearly three millennia old have been discovered.

Different sources claim different statistics on worldwide psychopathy. One study surveyed one hundred black students from Africa, administering the psychopathy checklist to all. The study concluded that psychopathy is, on average, equally prevalent in America as it is in this small subsection of the African population. However, another study found a higher percentage of psychopaths in North America than in Europe.

Given that psychopathy is a culturally defined condition, it is logical that there may be some variance in its prevalence throughout the world.

What are some common misconceptions about psychopaths?

Common misconceptions about psychopaths often stem from fictional literature and the media. These often use terms such as schizophrenia, psychosis, and psychopath interchangeably despite the fact that there are fundamental differences among them. Hollywood's traditional psychopaths are often portrayed as calm, charming, calculating, and highly intelligent, when in truth psychopaths are more likely to be impulsive, disorganized, and short tempered because they have very little tolerance for frustration. In literature and film and the media, they are also often attributed extraordinary abilities, such as foresightedness, when in fact they often lack insight into the consequence of their own actions. Finally, psychopaths are often presented in novels or movies as having experienced some sort of trauma or abuse during their childhood when that is not a necessary factor contributing to their mental disorder.

The most glaring misconception about psychopathy is the conflation of psychopathy and insanity. This misconception leads to the general image of psychopaths as hallucinatory, schizophrenic, and subject to many other psychoses to which they are actually not. A further misconception is that psychopaths are all street criminals and serial killers. Psychopaths may include politicians, popular figures, businessmen, and the seemingly average next-door neighbor. Most individuals probably have no idea that psychopathy is an actual psychological term. It is important to remember that there are rigorous guidelines in diagnosing psychopaths. It is important to distinguish psychopathy from antisocial personality disorder and sociopathy. It is important to realize that calling people psychopaths is not synonymous with calling them crazy.

Because the law defines the corporation as a person can it also be diagnosed as a psychopath?

The corporation was viewed as a person as early as 1793 when a corporate scholar defined it as a collection of many individuals who unite to form one body that can act in many ways as an individual might act.

Because the corporation is composed of many individuals with varying degrees of executive responsibility and is itself a person, the question arises when a corporation commits an illegal or antisocial act, who should be held responsible for the behavior, the various participating individuals alone, or the corporation as well.

Since the end of the nineteenth century, the corporation has enjoyed legal personhood and court protection of its rights. Because this corporate person has many of the same rights and obligations as natural persons, corporations themselves have been diagnosed, as have individuals, as psychopaths. A book and film, for example, have advanced the thesis that the corporation is a psychopath in its single-minded pursuit of profit and power.

Are there other disorders that are often comorbid with psychopathy?

A recent study on a group of patients in a high security hospital facility found that those who diagnosed with psychopathy had a higher than average incidence of other personality disorders, particularly antisocial personality disorder. Other personality disorders with high frequency of comorbidity with psychopathy included narcissistic, histrionic, and borderline personality disorders. Psychopathy has also been found to co-occur with substance abuse and schizophrenia. A study on female adolescents who met criteria for psychopathy found high comorbidity with substance abuse, attention deficit hyperactivity disorder, and depression. Other disorders were also found in these groups, though in lower percentages, and it was found that individuals with psychopathy were significantly more likely than normal individuals to show multiple psychological disorders. It is important to note that this data came from individuals who were forcefully committed to hospitals or imprisoned due to criminal behavior or for presenting some sort of danger to themselves and others. It may be the case that imprisoned or hospitalized psychopaths are those that have some other condition exacerbating the effects of their psychopathy on their behavior.

Is sociopathy just an excuse?

Some argue that the sociopath is not responsible for his antisocial or illegal actions because, by the very definition of his disorder, society is to blame. In other words, they contend that sociopaths are merely the products of their upbringing, and their poor behavior therefore cannot be their own fault. Sociopaths commonly use this tactic, for their tendency is to blame their actions on anybody or anything except themselves.

The label sociopath, as opposed to psychopath, first gained popularity in the 1950s. This was a time when social constructivism was the dominant paradigm, and individuals were understood to be products of their social environment. From this perspective, crime was understood as a normal response to unnatural conditions. The sociopath was thus excused from his own wrongdoing. Where the sociopath could once claim the devil made him do it, he could now claim society made him do it, and thereby escape punishment with little more than a stern rebuke.

Since the age of sociopathy, psychologists and others moved on to the more modern term of psychopathy. This change implied an internal, psychic etiology, rather than an external, social etiology. But now psychology has moved beyond interpersonal relationships to concerns with interneural connectivity. And while this psychological focus may suggest that the psychopath escapes culpability, the law has moved toward enhanced punishment for psychopaths. They are sentenced to longer prison terms, may be civilly committed once their prison sentence has ended, and have a greater likelihood of receiving a death sentence where capital punishment exists.

Are individuals with antisocial personality disorder really antisocial or just radically pro-self?

Narcissism, egotism, and arrogance are all typical traits of individuals who suffer from antisocial personality disorder. They tend to think of themselves, and of their own personal gain, at the expense of those around them. However, it is difficult for us to know whether people with the disorder inflict suffering on others for their own sake, or whether in their antisocial actions they merely regard others as means to their own ends.

The preponderance of evidence points to the former condition, that causing suffering in others is a worthwhile goal in itself for individuals with this disorder. There are many instances where they go out of their way to cause pain and discomfort in others, without gaining anything in particular for themselves. The young child who tortures cats does so for purely sadistic enjoyment, not because it advances status or brings wealth. Some individuals with antisocial personality disorder will go out of their way and risk great harm to themselves in order to cause harm in another.

Ultimately, antisocial personality disorder often involves a combination of both narcissistic self-absorption and antisocial tendencies that go beyond selfish needs and desires. Either one cannot be simply reduced to the other.

Are psychopaths numb to their socially unacceptable behavior or do they simply exhibit problems with impulse control?

The question presents a disparate binary which characterizes the complex psyche of the prototypical psychopath. Generally, psychopaths can control their impulses in social situations. However, a sense of control is clearly lacking at those times when they violate the law or otherwise violate social norms. While psychopaths act in ways most normal human beings do not, any problems with impulse control do not then lend themselves to remorse for the asocial action, as psychopaths are generally lacking emotional concern for others. Hare contended that while psychopaths understand that society has moral rules, they do not possess an emotional understanding of morality.

When tested against normal control subjects, psychopaths exhibit no greater tendency to respond incorrectly, to disregard cues suggesting they change their behavior, or to solve problems impulsively. Intelligence level, however, actually contributes to one's ability to control impulses in both psychopaths and normal control subjects. While Hare regarded the psychopath's tendency to act irrationally as a lack of inhibition and self-control, he also maintained that psychopaths do not lose control and are always capable of understanding exactly how they are behaving. They also understand what recourses their behavior will have. In short, psychopaths understand laws and rules, but often do not feel any moral obligation to follow them.

If not an aversion to societal norms or an overall disillusionment with society, how else would one explain the causes of psychopathy?

The indifference with which the prototypical psychopaths regard societal norms does not stem directly from an aversion towards society. Instead, their behavior results from an ignorance of the emotional reasons underlying the moral fiber of these norms. All psychopaths share some degree of abnormality in the brain's limbic system, which lends itself to intellectual processing of emotions, at the expense of actually feeling the corresponding emotion. Therefore, psychopaths do not act out of a disillusion with society, but rather they merely lack the emotive qualities which would enable them to care about what they do wrong. Psychopaths share a propensity toward intellectualizing and rationalizing what others would feel emotionally. When breaking the law or acting against some other societal norm, psychopaths understand the implications and ramifications of their behavior, which they carry out more for their own pleasure and personal gain than out of a distaste for society. While understanding that their actions are against the law, psychopaths will follow through with their intentions, and later rationalize their reasons for doing so. The emotional relevance of societal norms, then, holds no power in dissuading psychopaths from acting as they please, and elicits no sense of remorse after the act is committed.

2

Psychological, biological, gender-related, and other theories of causation

How significantly is psychopathy a product of nurture versus nature?

There is no simple answer to this much-debated question. Different scholars have contended that their research supports each of the two possibilities. Some find that criminality is genetically determined regardless of the family or other environment the individual encounters; others find that criminality is taught by families or peers or others. The answer is probably different from the implication in the question. Instead of one cause, the combination of nature and nurture seems most likely to produce psychopathy. Some studies, for example, have discovered brain abnormalities, or serotonin levels, which contribute to aggression and perhaps to psychopathy. Other studies have discovered that dysfunctional family life and antisocial peers, with various forms of physical or sexual abuse contribute to antisocial emotions and behaviors. Because large numbers of those genetically predisposed and of those environmentally determined do not become psychopaths, it is most likely an interaction between the two that causes psychopathy. In other words, an individual genetically predisposed who grows up in a positive environment becomes a moral, considerate individual, while an individual genetically predisposed who grows up in a negative, exploitative, aggressive, sexual, or antisocial environment becomes a psychopath. The interaction produces psychopaths.

Have any genes associated with diseases or conditions been identified that may cause psychopathy?

As of yet, there are no human genes specifically associated with psychopathy. However, studies on animals suggest that genes contribute to some components of temperament, including affect and aggression. Therefore, it is possible that homologues of these genes might have similar association in humans. Researchers have identified mutant knockout mice expressing elevated aggressive behavior that lack brain nitric oxide synthase. Another strain lacks the gene encoding for the 5-HT1b receptor. Such findings from loss of function experiments do not unambiguously identify the genes for aggression, yet their role in mice suggests that human homologues could help characterize the pathology of human antisocial personality disorder.

What neurological dysfunctions have been linked to psychopathy?

Psychopaths seem not to have any major functional neuropsychological problems. They perform on par with nonpsychopaths in various basic verbal, auditory, and visual tests that usually distinguish individuals with brain lesions or neurological defects. In short, psychopaths are not impaired in daily sensory-motor operations. There have been no consistent findings showing any physical abnormalities in their brains. Psychopaths' uniqueness lies more in the detailed functioning of the neurological pathways instead of in larger structural aspects.

Some of the brain regions that have received the most attention in research are the amygdala, the orbitofrontal cortex, and the anterior cingulate. The most prevalent modern views of the neurology of psychopaths focus upon their emotional peculiarities and their lack of empathy. These facets seem to be central to the psychopath construct. In repeated studies, psychopaths exhibit a normal physiological reaction to stimuli that directly threaten them, such as a gun pointed at them, but an extremely attenuated reaction to stimuli that indicate others are distressed, such as someone crying. This is a representation of the lack of empathy that Cleckley and Hare stressed. Psychopaths can feel fear and anxiety when things directly threaten them, but they lack the normal response to seeing others in similar situations. Where in the brain can this trait be attributed?

The amygdala is known as the locus for fear and empathy. However, individuals with lesions in the amygdala can still accurately recognize emotions in others.

That leads to the theory that the amygdala is not essential for the recognition of emotion, but for the analysis of emotion. Psychopaths can tell if someone is sad or happy or scared, but they do not truly understand how that person feels.

Positron Emission Tomography Imaging has revealed how psychopathic brains function in emotional memory situations. Healthy controls generally use their anterior and posterior cingulate, inferior frontal gyrus, amygdala, hippocampus, and the ventral striatum when remembering words with emotional significance. Psychopaths do not remember the words any less well and they have no memory deficits, but the brain regions used during memorization are different from those used by healthy individuals. The inactive regions in the psychopaths are important limbic system structures, all implicated in various emotions, implying that the sensation of feeling the emotion is absent in this process. In order to memorize emotional stimuli as well as anyone else, they tend to use alternative neural pathways such as the bilateral inferior lateral frontal cortex. By using alternate cognitive pathways, psychopaths mimic the manner in which normal individuals handle affective material, but do not feel the emotion themselves.

The more that Functional Magnetic Resonance Imaging and Positron Emission Tomography Imaging are used in the study of psychopathy, the more researchers will know about the abnormal functioning of the psychopathic brain. Studies are constantly being conducted to refine and expand the current knowledge in this field. The information here represents the most replicated and consistent findings on the neurology of psychopaths, but it is by no means the absolute truth or all that is currently known.

How can neurobiology help identify a cause for psychopathy?

Because behavior and learning are controlled in most part by the brain and nervous system, it is no great leap to imagine that neurobiology or neuroscience might lead to a complete understanding of the personality. Whether genetics or environment plays a greater part in the advancement of the disorder may eventually be determined through neuroscience. And research may similarly discover the method by which it progresses. For instance, with advanced imaging technology and understanding of the operations of neurotransmitters at the synapse, the centers for emotional response in the brain can be identified. With comprehensive examination of clinical psychopaths a specific protein or chemical deficiency characteristic of the disorder might be identified. Further genetic and developmental study might identify a mutation responsible for the deficiency. If an individual's environment is determined to be largely responsibly for the disorder, neuroscience might characterize the environment's physiological effect on the brain. For example, some studies suggest that in the psychopathic population the amygdala, which plays a key role in the processing of emotions, is reduced compared to healthy individuals. Using neurobiological techniques it has been shown that psychopaths exhibit a reduced response to emotional stimuli.

Many researchers have found neurobiological explanations for many of the traits of psychopathy. For example, impulsivity, recklessness and irresponsibility, hostility, and aggressiveness may be determined by abnormal levels of neurochemicals including monoamine oxidase, serotonin and 5-hydroxyindoleacetic acid, free-thyroxine, testosterone, cortisol, and adrenocorticotropic hormone, among other things. Features such as sensation seeking and incapacity to learn from experiences might be linked to cortical under arousal. Researchers have also found that sensation seeking could be related to low levels of monoamine oxidase and cortisol and high concentrations of gonadal hormones, and reduced prefrontal grey matter volume. Because of this research, psychopaths can be considered, at least to a small degree, as suffering from neurobiologically determined behavioral abnormalities. There is still, however, evidence that social factors do play a role in the development of psychopathy and that even if a person has biologically predetermined factors that would make them a psychopath their environment would play a role to the degree to which these factors play out in his personality.

What physiological peculiarities do psychopaths possess?

In 1957, a researcher set up an experiment in which participants would hear two distinct tones, A and B, repeated over a period of time. Near the end of tone A, a machine applied a small shock to the participant. After the participant sat through a number of trials, being shocked after each application of tone A, he measured the skin conductance of the participant while applying tone A without the shock in order to evaluate the anticipatory arousal conditioned by the shocks. The psychopathic sample had a significantly lower anxiety response than the nonpsychopathic sample. The researcher presumed that this physiological distinction was due to a lack of emotional involvement in the aversive condition. He linked this ability to avoid the conditioned effects of punishment to social development. He proposed that the natural fear of consequential negative punishment prevents antisocial behavior in most individuals. Normal people are socialized this way whereas psychopaths lack the ability to acquire fear for any punishment; therefore, this fearlessness causes a disruption of the normal socialization process, causing the individual to act antisocially. However, there is quite a conceptual gap between a conditioned fear response and poor fear conditioning being the basis for antisocial behavior. Nevertheless, this physiological characteristic of psychopathy is truly remarkable and spurred further research of the theory.

A more recent study measured skin conductance of psychopathic and control participants while presenting them with pictures of neutral, distressing, and threatening cues. Psychopaths and controls had similar responses to the neutral cues, but significantly different reactions to the distressing signals. Psychopaths showed only a very slight increase in anxiety when exposed to pictures of anguished individuals compared to a drastic jump in skin conductance reported in the control group. Equally interesting is the fact that psychopaths scored comparably to controls when presented with threatening cues; their skin conductance increased. This evidence suggests that psychopaths are able to be affected by threats or feel fear, which is in direct opposition to the earlier theory.

Are there neurophysiological differences between successful and unsuccessful psychopaths?

Brain studies of psychopaths have showed deregulation of and abnormal connectivity to emotional centers in the brain. These studies have stressed the importance of the limbic system, superior temporal lobe, corpus callosum, and amygdala. There are, however, neurobiological differences between psychopaths as well. Recent studies have shown that ninety-four percent of unsuccessful psychopaths have an asymmetrical hippocampus. This is striking compared to finding the abnormality in less than fifty percent of psychopaths who were never arrested prior to the study. While all psychopaths exhibit shallow emotional responses, it is thought that the hippocampal abnormality prevents the unsuccessful psychopaths from fear conditioning that would help understand what actions would get them arrested.

How does the environment affect psychopathy?

The etiology of psychopathy is far from concrete. There is an idea of what neurological dysfunctions and antisocial behavior psychopaths may exhibit, but how those traits originate is largely unknown. Through experience, psychologists generally agree that psychopathy fits the etiological pattern of most mental disorders:

a set of innate characteristics combined with specific environmental situations and events during development causes one to form a psychopathic personality. Although the biological bases have garnered the most modern attention for psychopathy research, psychologists recently like to stress the idea that for any one person, reaching psychopathy might require a different set of circumstances and heritable traits than another. In other words, some cases of psychopathy might be largely genetic in nature while other cases might be largely developmental.

That being said, what are the specific conditions that could possibly foster a psychopath? Psychodynamic theories, although outdated, state that psychopathy stems from poor parent-child interaction, stunting the growth of the superego. This is the apparent lack of conscience seen in psychopaths. More modern behaviorists suggested that psychopathy comes from modeling and conditioning. In essence, this theory suggests that psychopaths were children who received reinforcement at improper times, desensitizing them to emotion in general. Mid-twentieth century sociological theory believed that psychopaths simply have a role-playing deficit in which they cannot understand or anticipate others' feelings. More modern psychologists believe attachment theory may be able to explain psychopathy. It states that low socioeconomic status and neglectful, punitive, or inconsistent parenting may lead to antisocial behavior. This theory provides the most plausible, research-supported environmental contribution to etiology. It also gives hope for prevention measures through education and intervention programs for at-risk youth.

Although nothing is certain, it seems that a detrimental childhood environment might contribute to the development of psychopathy to some degree. It also must be remembered that many children who are raised in very similar environments turn out to be very different people. It is a unique combination of innate traits and reactions to environmental stimuli that forms personality.

What characteristics might a psychopath express as a child?

Some believe that a psychopath can display signs as early as age three. From then on he would show possible warning signs of future psychopathic tendencies such as lying, fighting, stealing, bullying, bad judgment, cheating, cruelty to animals, vandalism, manipulation skills, truancy, sexual activity, fire setting, substance abuse, and running away from home.

Is there a specific economic class from which a majority of psychopaths tend to come?

Although there are few studies regarding the interactions between economic class and psychopathy, there have been studies done on IQ, which has been found to be directly related to financial success. In European and African communities there have been no interactions found between IQ and psychopathy, suggesting that it is not the economic situation of a person that would make them more likely to be a psychopath. It is possible that the environment of financially successful persons is one of great stress and criticism that may lead to developing psychopathy. It is more likely, however, that persons of lower economic status become psychopaths based on findings on antisocial personality disorder. It has been found that antisocial personality disorder may be linked to problems within the family, such as parental antisocial attitudes, broken homes, physical punishment, inconsistent discipline, and childhood separations. Though these characteristics are not exclusive to persons of lower socioeconomic status, they are more prominent within this group.

Are psychopaths deficient in cognitive skills?

Some cognitive abilities are impaired in the psychopath. For example, long-term planning is difficult for the psychopath due to his impulsive behavior. Although it is common for the psychopath to speak grandly of his life ambitions, this amounts to little more than groundless braggadocio. It is also difficult for the psychopath to think about emotions. Because of their own emotional poverty, they do not understand the role that feelings play in human lives. They are able to function in society only through empty mimicry of emotion. Neurological experiments have demonstrated evidence of a neural impediment to socialization that may be at the heart of this deficiency.

In other ways, psychopaths are as cognitively competent as others are. They suffer from no delusions or neuroses. Their intelligence ranges consistently with the average population. They can be quite witty and charming in everyday interactions. Neuropsychological testing has found psychopaths to be generally in command of their analytical capacities.

Hare conducted a series of experiments in which psychopaths were shown to respond to emotional words just as quickly as neutral words, whereas most people process emotional words more quickly. In another experiment involving Magnetic Resonance Imaging, the limbic system of the psychopath showed considerably less excitation when the subject was exposed to negative emotional words, compared to normal limbic system activity levels. These results imply that the psychopath suffers from a deficiency in emotional processing.

Yet another experiment conducted by Hare and others demonstrated that psychopaths are also deficient in processing abstract words and concepts. Perhaps this accounts for the psychopath's inability to comprehend the meaning of concepts such as love, empathy, or remorse.

What is the IQ range in psychopaths?

Cleckley noted that psychopaths can often exhibit intelligence greater than the average individual's. Cleckley never reported any empirical evidence to support his theory, however. He simply designed the construct based on his observations. A psychopath is a more compelling figure often romanticized in the media. It is also probably quite evident that they use their intelligence very differently from the average person, which is why it may have come to Cleckley's attention. It also must be remembered that IQ is only one measure of intelligence. There are other characteristics about psychopaths that Cleckley may have meant when calling them intelligent. On the other hand, a criminal is often thought to have a below-average IQ. That image, of course, is of the common criminal, not psychopaths.

Nevertheless, recent studies found that there is no difference in intelligence between psychopaths and nonpsychopaths. Furthermore, IQ has no valid correlation to violence in any individuals, psychopathic or not. Psychopathy may predict violence, but IQ adds no effective contribution to such models. These findings are quite clear, but there is little effort to find other facets of psychopathy that IQ may affect. Although characters such as Hannibal Lecter in *The Silence of the Lambs* may promote the exciting image of the highly intelligent killer, psychopathy and patterns of violence are on average unrelated to intelligence.

Are persons in academia any more or less likely to be or become psychopaths?

Although psychopaths can be intelligent like anybody else, this does not mean they tend toward academic professions more than the average individual. Theoretically, psychopaths could be found in any profession should they desire to pursue it, but there currently are no exact statistics on psychopaths' occupations. In looking at the proposed criteria for psychopathy indicated by Cleckley, however, it is understandable that psychopaths might be academically inclined. They are cunning. They are also often described as intelligent, narcissistic, clever, witty, and manipulative. Basically, they know how to manipulate people. They can study and interpret people. While this often takes intelligence, it also is necessary for psychopaths to understand their victims in order to use them. Ultimately, the Hannibal Lecter stereotype of the academic psychopath is largely a romanticized view designed by the media. This does not mean that psychopaths cannot be geniuses or academics, but there is no evidence to support the notion that psychopaths have an inclination to study academic topics intensely.

Is there evidence supporting a cycle of abuse with relation to the spread of psychopathy?

Childhood abuse is often thought to lead to behavioral problems in children. If a parent is abusive towards his children, it may be due to a biological factor within the parent. This biological factor could be genetically transferred to the child, which may help explain why abusive parents have a greater likelihood of having children with antisocial behavior than nonabusive parents. However, a study of twins suggested that as much as twenty percent of the population variation in antisocial behavior can be attributed to direct environmental factors after genetic factors are controlled. While the empirical data is lacking, there does appear to be a correlation between abuse suffered during childhood and the development of conduct disorder and adult psychopathy. Many violent psychopathic criminals were in abusive or neglectful households. Yet most people abused during their youth do not exhibit psychopathic characteristics. It is only when an abusive childhood environment interacts with innate biological peculiarities that the combination can give rise to psychopathy.

Are psychopaths aware of their behavior?

The inner world of psychopaths will likely remain a mystery to us, for their own subjective report is commonly unreliable, and medical science does not yet possess a means for divining the experienced reality of another individual without their cooperation.

That said, it seems likely that psychopaths are perfectly well aware of their behavior. Most are able to remember their actions in exquisite detail, and are sometimes known to brag about their deeds to others in a manner that suggests full awareness of the crimes committed or acts performed. Despite this, psychopaths will frequently claim they have no recollection of having committed their crimes, as their legal defense. This could be considered another example of psychopathic chicanery. Psychopaths undoubtedly are aware just as anybody else is aware, but they often fail to reflect upon their actions or bother to analyze themselves.

If psychopaths are not aware of some aspect of their behavior, that aspect would be the moral implications of their actions. They are often caught by surprise when confronted about their conduct. They simply seem not to understand what the problem is.

Does the psychopath want to be a psychopath?

Psychopathy is an extremely complex phenomenon and psychological construct, and thus it is difficult to ascertain if the psychopath really desires to be psychopathic. Surely, as Hare and Cleckley note, the people in psychopaths' lives often make numerous attempts to rehabilitate them and to help them financially. Even when they are offered many opportunities, psychopaths eventually return to their former habits and leading lives of deception, manipulation, remorselessness, without any clear goals or guiding principles. In this way, it could be interpreted as purposefully deciding upon psychopathy as a lifestyle choice. To add to this, most psychopaths fail to see their lifestyle decisions or personality deficits as disordered. Like most personality disorders, psychopathy is an egosyntonic disorder. If psychopathy were egodystonic, somehow opposed to the individual's sense of self and experienced as the cause of the individual's personal suffering, there might be enough distress to foster a search for treatment. But because there is only the distress the world beyond the individual psychopath may impose on him, psychopaths do not seek such treatment. In other words, psychopathy partially describes a person just as a healthy individual's personality defines him. This is a major part of the reason why rehabilitation programs for psychopaths have such low success rates. In light of emerging biopsychological research in psychopathy, however, it is becoming clear that psychopathy has many biological correlates and this implies that psychopathy is more than simply a decision on the part of psychopaths to act and live in certain ways.

Do particular ethnic or social groups show a higher prevalence of psychopathy?

Little rigorous research has been done to determine if different ethnic or social groups have different rates of psychopathy. One study done on psychiatric patients found that African Americans scored slightly higher on the psychopathy checklist than Caucasian subjects. That same study also found that men scored slightly higher on the psychopathy checklist than women. However, the differences in scores were minor. Another study directly looking at differences between African American and Caucasian subjects found no significant difference in levels of psychopathy. One study comparing rates of violent crime between Asian Americans and Caucasian subjects found that incidence of psychopathy seemed slightly lower in the Asian American population. A major problem with these studies is that the subjects tend to be either prison inmates or hospital patients. Differences in scores might simply reflect different crime rates between groups. Also, differing crime rates are affected by factors other than prevalence of psychopathy, such as economic and social conditions. It appears that if any differences exist between groups, the differences are small.

Do the antisocial acts performed by psychopaths increase in severity over time?

As with many other questions about psychopathy, most information comes from prison inmates and hospital patients. Thus, answers may not be accurate for the general population of psychopaths. From what is known, it appears that antisocial acts of psychopaths do increase in severity over time and then the incidence of antisocial acts appears to taper off towards middle age. For example, a psychopath might engage in petty theft at first, and then move on to forgery. For many psychopaths, however, it appears that their behavior spontaneously improves towards middle age. The explanations for this change are varied. It is possible that psychopathy is the result of very slow maturation of the brain, so the psychopaths' mental development might eventually reach a level approaching normal. Alternatively, the psychopath might simply grow tired of his activities or of being incarcerated and decide to stop committing crimes. It is also possible that they simply get better at concealing their actions and do not get caught as often. It is important to note that the serial killer generally showed signs of violent antisocial behavior before they ever killed, but not every violent psychopath becomes a serial killer.

Less data is available on noncriminal psychopaths. It is possible that they follow a similar pattern. There are cases where partners of possible psychopaths report that the difficult behaviors abate as they grow older, but this might reflect an improved ability to handle the difficult individual rather than an actual improvement in behavior.

Are there any common concomitants to psychopathy that help diagnosis?

There are many concomitants to psychopathy, though none like the auditory hallucinations that accompany schizophrenia. Psychopathy is often accompanied by alcohol or narcotic dependence. Psychopaths also have tendencies toward excess gambling. Regarding drug dependence, it remains unclear whether drug use is causal or symptomatic in psychopathy, as it is known that alcohol and narcotics can result in impulsive, aggressive features similar to those witnessed in psychopaths. Nonetheless, these activities may be easily detectable signs to aid a psychopathic diagnosis. As is often the case, a concomitant to psychopathy may be other personality disorders. Psychologists refer to this phenomenon as comorbidity.

Are criminal acts of the psychopath caused by some sort of uncontrollable impulse?

The Psychopathy Checklist recognizes the psychopath as a social deviant, and uses the label impulsive to refer to poor behavioral controls. However, the checklist does not specify whether impulsivity is a manifestation of psychopathy or a contributing factor to its development.

Researchers at the Adult Forensic Mental Health Services from the University of Manchester in the U.K. have found what may be a biological component to impulsive behavior in psychopaths. In offender samples, researchers found a negative correlation between the impulsive antisocial component of psychopathy and serotonergic neurotransmission. That is, the more impulsive psychopaths were found to have lower levels of brain serotonin. Again, this correlation should not be interpreted to mean that decreased serotonin in the brain causes impulsive behavior in psychopathy. However, it does provide a biological perspective from which to understand psychopathy and its core component of impulsivity.

With these biological research findings in mind, the question arises as to whether psychopaths can truly control their impulsive behavior. If impulsivity has something to do with their innate neurotransmission, then it would seem that their biology, and thus their impulsivity, is beyond their control. However, at least some psychopaths seem to be able to control when they exhibit impulsive, antisocial behavior and when they keep these impulses in check, as demonstrated by successful psychopaths. Thus, it might appear that these impulses can be reined in though all thoughts and behaviors are impacted by biological neurotransmission. The issue of the conflict between scientific determinism and the law's reliance on the concept of free will remains the subject of much debate. As more research emerges, it appears that impulsivity is not simply a matter of biology or personality or environment, but most likely a combination of them all.

What is the relation between attachment and psychopathy?

Attachment styles refer to the way in which humans view close personal relationships, and how they cope with attachment and loss of such relationships. There are four classifications for attachment in adults. Secure individuals are comfortable opening up to and becoming close to other people. They do not fear abandonment, and they act in a healthy manner when they face rejection or loss. Avoidant individuals are uncomfortable opening up to others and becoming close to them; they fear intimacy with others for fear of abandonment or rejection, and thus are dismissive of attachment-related experiences and downplay their significance. Anxious or ambivalent individuals worry that their attachment figures do not love them and display this insecurity towards their partners. They are preoccupied with the thought of rejection and are often are dependent on their partners and want to merge completely with the other person.

One study found no correlation between psychopathy score and attachment classification. However, they did find some evidence that highly psychopathic individuals were more likely to be dismissive of attachment-related experiences than individuals who were less psychopathic. This study suggested that psychopaths do not form the same intimate bond with other human beings as normal individuals do.

Researchers have suggested that psychopaths have deficient attachment because they lacked attachment-related experiences due to the fact that normal individuals, including their parents, were unwilling or unable to form close relationships with them. Furthermore, it is speculated that psychopaths possess biological features that prevent them from experiencing any emotional depth and thus they are unable to become attached to any individual. Even if provided with sensitive parents and a nurturing home environment, psychopathic children might still develop deficient attachment styles.

Are rates of psychopathy different across the genders?

While there is little hard data to confirm the actual prevalence of psychopathy across men and women, it is speculated that psychopathy is significantly more common among men than women. Hare has estimated that approximately one percent of the population is psychopathic. This means that almost three million people in the United States are psychopaths. The American Psychiatric Association has reported that approximately three percent of men and one percent of women are psychopathic. Estimates from an author who has had extensive experience in working with victims of abuse are as high as thirty percent for men and ten percent for women. Those figures, however, are likely describing a less technical form of the construct, such as people who have even a small number of psychopathic traits. Taken together, the figures suggest that the ratio for male to female psychopaths is approximately three to one. However, these estimates may be biased by the fact that research concerning psychopathy is usually conducted among male prison inmates, where the number of psychopaths is high.

Is our current model of psychopathy gender-biased?

There is some debate among experts about whether women truly have fewer psychopathic tendencies. Some researchers have contended that the traits measured by the Psychopathy Checklist might be gender-biased and not account for variations of the disorder that exist among women. For instance, men are typically more aggressive than women. Although aggression is not part of the definition of psychopathy, studies have found a strong relationship between aggression and psychopathy. Because women are characteristically less aggressive than men, it may be that the model for psychopathy is skewed toward including more men.

In general, male and female psychopaths differ dramatically in terms of their expression of psychopathy, which suggests that women and men experience the dysfunction differently. It is possible that two different conceptions of psychopathy should be developed to account for the significant gender differences in the manifestation of the disorder. If a new model is formed for women, a higher prevalence of psychopathy among females may be visible.

Furthermore, there is some suggestion that because most of the literature concerning psychopathy is written by males and focused on males, it would seem natural to suspect that there are more male psychopaths than female psychopaths. Most psychologists, criminologists, and police officers are male and this may be a factor in why there are more male psychopaths than female psychopaths. Likewise, most sample groups consist of convicts, who are much more likely to be men than women. In some ways, the material on psychopathy reflects the state of psychological research before Carol Gilligan wrote her work specifically focusing on women and girls. Before her work, psychology and psychological research had been the province of males. Perhaps in a similar fashion, psychopathy is now in that province.

What is Functional Magnetic Resonance Imaging?

Functional Magnetic Resonance Imaging is a technique for determining which parts of the brain are activated by different types of physical sensation or activity, such as sight, sound, or the movement of a subject's fingers. This brain mapping is achieved by setting up a scanner in a special way so that the increased blood flow to the activated areas of the brain shows up on fMRI scans.

The changes in brain activation or metabolism are not directly observed, but only indirectly measured. The effects of local increases in blood flow and microvascular oxygenation are mapped. This allows researchers to examine spatial and temporal changes in a wide range of brain functions, such as how we see, feel, move, understand each other, and generate memories. Because the technique is safe, many scans can be repeated over time. Also, the technique has led to hypotheses concerning many different brain pathologies, some of which, like gambling and drug abuse, show no structural brain changes. Further, researchers have found areas of the brain associated with reward and punishment and have studied the relation between the magnitudes of the brain activation and of rewards and punishments received. They hypothesized that damage to the brain may prevent individuals from judging behaviors and consequences. Efforts continue to discover anomalies in the way psychopaths process information.

What are the physiological and biological differences between male and female psychopaths?

Recent studies suggest that men and women display patterns of behavioral and cognitive differences that reflect varying hormonal influences on brain development. It is well understood that there are subtle differences in the way male and female brains process language, information, cognition, and emotion. Males, human and nonhuman, typically demonstrate higher aggressive tendencies than females. Males appear to be better at spatial and navigational tasks whereas females appear to express greater empathy and greater verbal and social skills. Often these differences have been attributed in large part to the environment. More recent evidence, however, suggests that the effects of sex hormones on brain organization occur so early after birth that environmental stimuli are acting on vastly different brains in males and females.

Other researchers have associated personality disorders, such as psychopathy, with the male tendency to act out versus the female tendency to internalize. Some critics argue that these characterizations only typify the stereotypes of gender roles. Often, men with borderline personality disorder who act impulsively and aggressively tend to be seen as having psychopathy.

In studying the effects of androgens like testosterone on rats, scientists have revealed that the respective behaviors expressed by males and females are largely influenced by hormones. For instance, male rats deprived of androgens immediately after birth will exhibit reduced expression of male specific sexual behaviors. Likewise, females supplemented with androgens after birth exhibit increased male sexual behaviors.

Two hormones that have been studied are cortisol and testosterone. Males with higher testosterone levels exhibit more aggressive behavior than males with lower testosterone levels, and females with higher testosterone levels exhibit lower aggressive behavior than females with lower levels of testosterone. Females with higher cortisol levels exhibit higher aggressive behavior than females with lower cortisol levels, and males with higher cortisol levels exhibit less aggressive behavior than males with lower cortisol levels.

From these studies, and further studies that identify differences between the male and female hypothalamus, it is clear that male and female brains are indeed very different and that there is an important connection between these differences and the different expressed behaviors. It is generally understood that on average males and females differ in personality; it is likely, therefore, that such differences can explain the very unbalanced ratio of male to female psychopaths. The natural difference in expression of empathy expressed by males and females will be of particular interest to this inquiry.

Are certain psychopathic personality traits more prone to occur within one gender than the other?

Many personality differences have been noted between female and male psychopaths. Women tend to exhibit more histrionic, melodramatic, self-dramatizing behavior patterns than men. Male psychopaths typically display more antisocial and narcissistic behavior. Two researchers found that women scored higher on the Psychopathy Checklist items of deceitful and of poor behavior control, whereas men scored higher on the items of adolescent antisocial behavior and of adult antisocial behavior. Additionally, other studies have found that males are markedly resistant to treatment, whereas female psychopaths do not express an unwillingness to be treated. Female psychopaths tend to have later onset of childhood behavioral problems and later age of onset of aggression than boys. Female psychopaths tend to engage in sexual promiscuity more often than their male counterparts. With respect to promiscuity, male psychopaths tend to view their romantic partners as objects to be dominated, whereas females tend to adopt a more passive attitude.

Which comorbid mental disorders are most common among female psychopaths?

In general, psychopathy has been found to be highly correlated with drug abuse, anxiety, and depressive disorders. For females, studies have supported the strongest link between psychopathy and histrionic personality disorder. Histrionic personality disorder is characterized by excessive emotionality, attention seeking, obsession with one's own physical appearance, and dramatic behavior. Other studies have reported high rates of comorbid psychiatric disorders like depression, anxiety, and suicidal behavior in females.

Does psychopathy appear to be more heritable in males than in females?

Some research has suggested that male psychopaths are more susceptible to environmental factors while female psychopaths have a greater genetic predisposition to the disorder. Psychologists have found that the offspring of female psychopaths are more vulnerable to the disorder than those of male psychopaths. The perspective of sociobiologists is consistent with this theory, arguing that male psychopaths are less likely to reproduce due to a penchant for riskier lifestyles compared to female psychopaths.

3

Psychological and psychiatric forms of treatment and their use and effectiveness

Where are psychopaths generally treated?

There are various facilities to which psychopaths may be sent, such as juvenile facilities, correctional facilities, prisons, and hospitals. Yet there are no centers specifically dedicated to the rehabilitation of psychopaths. The reason is twofold. First, younger psychopaths who have been arrested and sentenced are serving time in a juvenile institution and older psychopaths in jails and prisons. Even when there are rehabilitative programs in these facilities, psychopaths generally do not respond well to these treatments. Second, psychopaths who have not committed serious offenses may be sent to hospitals instead of prisons, where they are psychologically evaluated. Doctors routinely declare them sane and competent and psychopaths soon demand release, a right to which they are legally entitled.

Many psychopaths frequently get in trouble with the law, but there are rarely specific programs which the court can mandate they attend. Even if there were such programs, change is extremely difficult because psychopaths rarely acknowledge their disorder, and because changing a personality defect such as a lack of emotional affect, a lack of remorse, or a lack of interpersonal empathy is an extremely time-consuming, difficult, and poorly understood endeavor.

Recently, there has been a greater shift from a rehabilitative focus to a more punitive emphasis due to the lack of responsiveness in rehabilitation programs and the high recidivism rate of psychopathic offenders. Various states are passing statutes that increase the sentences of psychopaths to prison, require their commitment to in-patient psychiatric facilities upon completion of their prison time, even facilitate the imposition of the death penalty given prescribed circumstances. The aim of all these measures is to reduce these psychopaths' exposure to society.

Although this approach seems only to forestall inevitable offenses among those who are returned to society, there simply are not many successful models available for rehabilitating the psychopath. Some emphasis has been placed on prevention. An approach to youth intervention and screening for antisocial behavior in adolescence has been suggested as a preventive measure. If prevention is possible, it may hold the key to dealing with psychopathy as a psychological disorder and as a societal problem.

Which response is more effective, sentencing psychopaths to prison or admitting them to mental hospitals?

From the research, it appears that neither response is particularly effective beyond the incapacitation that some form of incarceration provides. That incapacitation prevents the psychopath from further harm to society and to individuals. The theory for placing the psychopath in a mental hospital is that treatment will reduce the likelihood of reoffending. But the drawback of commitment to mental institutions is that there are not many studies proving the efficacy of treatment programs and often those institutions providing therapy are reluctant to treat psychopaths because they are difficult, insidious patients. And both institutions and treaters know that psychopaths can be good at speaking the language of treatment without incorporating any of the changes treatment is designed to promote.

What is the recidivism rate of criminal psychopaths?

Researchers have estimated that the recidivism rate, the rate at which psychopathic offenders re-offend after their incarceration or other sanction, is approximately twice that of nonpsychopathic offenders. Not all psychopaths are criminals, but a substantial number of criminals are psychopaths. Depending on the sample, estimates vary from eighteen percent to forty percent of the criminals in prison are psychopaths. Researchers have also found that upon parole release, psychopaths were four times more likely to violate parole compared to nonpsychopathic offenders. Three years after follow-up, eighty percent of psychopaths had failed parole guidelines.

What effect do Therapeutic Communities have on psychopaths?

Therapeutic community can refer to a program for prison inmates, both mentally disordered and healthy. Such a therapeutic community is run primarily by the inmates themselves, focusing on creating positive social and interpersonal skills. There is generally minimal professional contact between therapists and patients. The convicts are simply guided to perform a variety of skill-building activities and to enforce a simple punishment and reward system. When an inmate exhibits marked behavioral improvement and an understanding of proper social interaction, he can be released on parole.

Therapeutic communities have become less used in recent years, but they were common places for convicted psychopaths in the 1960s, 1970s, and 1980s. As expected, psychopaths spent much longer in therapeutic communities and were much more difficult to manage than the average criminal. A retrospective review of one therapeutic community concluded that psychopaths committed more violent or antisocial behavior after spending time in it than after spending time in prison. The possible explanation for this phenomenon states that the therapeutic community may have provided an environment for psychopaths to learn from each other and to sharpen their techniques. In that sense, the community was perhaps a more sophisticated example of the prison as teacher. Psychopaths eventually deceived therapists into thinking that they had improved in order to be released, ready to commit more crimes.

More recent investigations into therapeutic communities have focused on their limitations. Rather than sites for skill building, many simply dispensed such drugs as methedrine, LSD, scopolamine, and alcohol in order to calm the participants. Also, in many instances professional therapists did very little personally to attend to the participants' needs. Finally, the follow-ups found that on average only one quarter of the participants exhibited extended behavioral improvement after conditional release.

Because of these factors, these communities have become a less common form of therapy for both common criminals and psychopaths. Regardless of their therapeutic value, they played a significant role in the history of treatment for psychopathy.

What is considered a successful outcome of therapy?

The baseline measure of success is recidivism rates: how many individuals commit crimes after release, and, of those, how many commit violent crimes. In the case of non-criminal psychopaths, effectiveness of treatment is determined by the program's ability to guide the psychopath toward a prosocial lifestyle. That would include interpersonal and behavioral improvements or emotional progress.

What is the improvement rate of psychopaths in prisons?

A meta-analysis, a study that combines findings from a multitude of previous studies, concluded that an average of twenty percent of psychopaths in prison exhibited improved behavior once released.

Is psychopathy curable?

Past treatment programs for psychopaths have had low success rates due to methodological inefficiencies, inappropriate emphases, and noncompliance on the part of psychopaths. Because psychopathy includes enduring personality characteristics, many treatment programs for psychopaths focus on personal change rather than psychological cure. Among psychopaths in correctional facilities, risk management has emerged as a core component in treatment programs. Risk may be managed through the improvement in the offender's self-regulation, and through the monitoring and avoidance of high-risk situations in the offender's community. Even with the emergence of risk management treatments and improved methodology, the recidivism rate of psychopaths remains elevated. Because of psychopaths' penchant for rule breaking and remorseless personality, they are often resistant to treatment programs that appeal to their conscience or sense of morality.

In spite of treatment ineffectiveness, there may be hope in responsivity treatment programs, which emphasize personal and matched approaches to treating various psychopaths. For example, if one psychopath is interpersonally deficient and another is lacking in emotional language skills, each should receive different treatment goals. This approach has proven somewhat beneficial for nonoffending psychopaths and may hold the promise of rehabilitating psychopathic offenders. The main goal is to improve the psychopath's interactions and social behavior.

What parts of the psychopathic personality can potentially change?

Hare and his colleague found a great deal of promise in targeting cognitive features that are modifiable within the mind of a psychopath. There are about seven or eight features of psychopathy that can potentially change with age, such as impulsivity, irresponsibility, and the need for stimulation. Furthermore, many of these factors have a biological basis. Testosterone clearly correlates with aggression; therefore, biologically targeting these components may help to accelerate the process of change that occurs with age. While lack of empathy and egocentricity are features that remain fairly stable, therapies that analyze psychopaths' tendency to appeal to rationality to justify their actions, rather than emphasize their feelings, might have some benefit.

How useful are traditional forms of psychotherapy for treating psychopathy?

There is no sure treatment for psychopaths. Much research shows that psychopathy does not improve with traditional psychotherapy treatment and may become worse because that therapy gives the psychopath more practice as he deals with a therapist, who often does not have the means or interest to verify what he is told; and that practice can lead to the psychopath's becoming better at lying and trickery. This does not necessarily mean that psychopaths are untreatable; it just means that traditional therapy does not work for them and the task to rehabilitate them is more difficult than for nonpsychopathic individuals. Hare has said that although no treatment has worked especially well thus far, this does not mean that there will not someday be a treatment for psychopathy. He likens this to the idea that polio was once untreatable. Hare has stated that even if psychopaths' core personalities cannot be changed there will be a way to reduce their propensity for antisocial behavior. Because there is evidence that psychopathic individuals become less psychopathic as they get older, there is hope that researchers can discover why this is the case and that they can attempt to accelerate this progression.

Can drugs treat psychopathy?

No medication can cure psychopathy, though a wide variety of pharmaceutical interventions can treat various symptoms. All such medications have their primary function in some domain other than psychopathy, yet find great practical use for the psychopath.

Neuroleptics have a tranquilizing effect, minimizing tension, anger, and anxiety. In addition to treating depression, antidepressants can also reduce aggressive behavior in some cases. Commonly used to stabilize mood swings, lithium can be effective in reducing impulsive, explosive, and emotionally unstable behavior. Benzodiazepines are useful in curbing aggressive states and inducing sleep. Having increasingly been used to treat schoolchildren for attention deficit and hyperactivity disorders, psychostimulants such as Ritalin and Dexedrine are sometimes effective in reducing impulsive and uncontrollable behavior in psychopaths. Anticonvulsants have been observed to mollify angry outbursts.

Can selective serotonin reuptake inhibitors, which may reduce aggression, at least reduce antisocial behaviors in psychopaths?

Serotonin is an important neurotransmitter in the human brain. It regulates a great number of mental processes. Many symptoms of mental disorders can be reduced by increasing serotonin transmission throughout the brain. Selective serotonin reuptake inhibitors block the reuptake of serotonin between synapses, causing more serotonin to travel across to the post-synaptic terminal and continue transmission to the next neuron. Inhibitors such as Prozac, Zoloft, and Paxil can affect mood, anxiety, and motivation through this process.

Little research has been done on the effects of selective serotonin reuptake inhibitors on psychopathy. There is some evidence that they may improve behavior in individuals with antisocial personality disorder, and some individuals find that they reduce their aggression and irritability. Without controlled tests, it is difficult to answer this question. Selective serotonin reuptake inhibitors might improve the behavior of psychopaths. The real problem, however, is getting the psychopath to comply with the treatment long enough for the drugs to help.

Can surgery correct psychopathy?

Frontal lobe and limbic system damage have been implicated as a possible cause of psychopathy. If this hypothesis is correct, then perhaps a physical alteration of the brain structure might restore normal function. This view supports the practices of electroconvulsive therapy and psychosurgery.

Electroconvulsive therapy is the practice of sending eighty- to one-hundred-and-ten-volt electric surges through electrodes attached to the patient's temples, causing generalized convulsions. This has been a remarkably successful tool in the treatment of resistant depression. It is unclear whether it has any significant effect on psychopathy.

Psychosurgery began with the lobotomy, in which the prefrontal lobes were partially removed from the rest of the brain. This procedure was very much in vogue through the 1940s, despite the drastic consequences on the personality of the patient. It effectively stopped erratic, destructive behavior of antisocial individuals, but destroyed their personalities and individuality in the process. Modern psychosurgery is more sophisticated, with so-called fractional operations destroying small portions of brain tissue in strictly localized areas. The neural circuit connecting the amygdala and the hypothalamus is sometimes cut, as a common operational procedure. Lobotomies, however, may be regarded as unethical, and modern surgery is only used as a last-ditch effort, after all other possible options have failed.

Can Cognitive Behavioral Therapy be effective for psychopaths?

Cognitive behavioral therapy is the revolutionary technique developed by a psychologist in the 1960s. It has been proven highly effective in treating a wide variety of mental disorders, including schizophrenia, and depressive and obsessive-compulsive disorders. The treatment is based on the interrelationship between cognition, emotion, and action. By examining his own defective cognitions, or thoughts, a person can identify and correct distortions that lead to negative emotions and maladaptive behavior.

A crucial factor in the process is that patients recognize that they have a problem that needs to be addressed. While the psychopath can be quite adept at convincing a therapist that he has seen the error of his ways and has reformed, he rarely takes this fundamental step in a genuine way. This puts greater pressure on the therapist and can lead to therapeutic pessimism and burnout.

This does not mean that cognitive behavioral therapy is of no use in the treatment of psychopaths. Rather, it points specifically to the aspect of the therapeutic process that needs the most attention when dealing with the psychopath. Therapists must aid them in recognizing that their behavior is maladaptive and leads to mainly negative consequences for themselves. The therapist for such a person must be unusually perceptive and skilled at ferreting out phony confessions and sham progress, for the psychopath's tendency will be to talk about and to mimic therapeutic progress. Because psychopaths genuinely believe there is nothing wrong with themselves, the therapist's task is to help them understand and accept that society's reactions are appropriate ones for their socially unacceptable behavior.

Are there any effective stay-at-home treatments for psychopathy?

While they may sound like self-help tools, the *Self-Appraisal Questionnaire* and the *Guidelines for a Psychopathy Treatment Program*, published in 2005, are actually designed for use by trained psychologists. In fact, the existence of any sort of guidelines for psychopathy treatment is a relatively new development in the field. Prior to their efforts, psychopathy treatment mostly revolved around ineffective drugs or forums in which psychopaths reinforced their deceptive tendencies.

How much does it cost to incarcerate or to treat a psychopath?

If a psychopath were convicted in Massachusetts of a violent crime, and sentenced to a number of years in a high-security state prison, his incarceration would be costly. In Massachusetts, annual prison expenses total almost forty thousand dollars per inmate. In the federal system, prosecuting a criminal costs roughly fifty-five thousand dollars per regular trial and over two hundred and eighteen thousand dollars per death penalty trial.

Cognitive behavioral therapy prices range widely, but even with a most rigorous treatment schedule, say four sessions per week for an entire year, the total cost of this schedule would be less than half the cost of keeping an inmate in prison for the same length of time.

Is there a prevention program for psychopathic behavior?

Because psychopathy and antisocial personality disorder are extremely difficult to treat effectively, there has been increasing effort to minimize developmental and environmental risk factors. Programs have been used to deal with the family environment for children and adolescents at risk. Parents learn effective discipline and supervision of their children. Studies have shown that family intervention is successful in some cases where the child improves his academic performance and becomes less likely to engage in drug abuse or with delinquent peers. Family intervention at the earliest age is more successful that at an adolescent age.

The FAST Track program, an acronym for Families And Schools Together, is an example of a family and school intervention program employed in inner-city areas where children are at risk for developing psychopathic behavior as they grow up in poor neighborhoods and associate with older delinquent children. The principal aims are interpersonal conflict management, emotional awareness, and self-control. Teachers and parents are taught how to manage disruptive behavior in children and there is constant communication between the parent and teacher regarding the academic curriculum of the child. Children in FAST track have developed better social skills and shown improved academic achievements, which may deter them from engaging in psychopathic behavior.

What is therapeutic pessimism and how does it relate to the treatment of psychopaths?

Therapeutic pessimism refers to a therapist's belief that a patient is virtually incurable or that he is uncertain about his ability to rehabilitate the patient. This term pertains to many diseases and disorders thought to be incurable, including psychopathy. Psychopaths are commonly believed to be extremely difficult to treat, if they can be treated at all. The idea that therapy for psychopathic individuals is a waste of time affects how a therapist treats a psychopathic patient and how the psychopathic patient receives treatment. Therapeutic pessimism is pervasive among individuals who work on rehabilitating psychopaths and this therapeutic pessimism is often thought to undermine motivation to find viable treatment options for psychopaths.

Why are psychopaths considered untreatable?

Cleckley's initial definition of psychopathy was an effort to describe the most insidious of individuals. He succeeded in his effort because psychopath remains the label of choice for the most dangerous, elusive, chaotic, and frustrating individuals. Psychopathy is thought by many to encompass the worst of the worst. In order to logically complete that idea of the worst imaginable person, Cleckley promoted the notion that psychopaths were unresponsive to treatment or punishment. In 1992, researchers retrospectively evaluated the outcome of psychopathic and nonpsychopathic patients who participated in a therapeutic community from 1968 to 1972. The results indicated a mild reduction of the recidivism rates and a significant reduction of violent recidivism rates among nonpsychopaths in comparison to a control group that spent an equal amount of time in prison. However, the psychopaths in the therapeutic community violently recidivated more frequently than those in the control group. These results seemed to indicate that the treatment made the antisocial behavior of the psychopaths worse. This was taken as confirmation of the pointlessness of treating psychopaths.

Though researchers generally attributed most treatment failures to the shortcomings of the treatment itself, in this instance the researchers placed the reason for failure on the psychopaths. Only two years later did the authors of the study question the therapeutic community system instead of the psychopath, but for those who wanted to find psychopaths unworthy of treatment attention, the study itself had already provided enough evidence.

The therapeutic community is just one example of the difficulty of treating psychopathy. Psychopaths are commonly placed in treatment for one or more of the many problems that tend to plague them, but rarely are they treated primarily for psychopathy. Psychologists studied female psychopaths receiving treatment for substance abuse. Psychopaths and nonpsychopaths participated in either a therapeutic community or a heuristics system, which is a common rehabilitation program for inmates. As expected, the researchers described the psychopathic participants as noncompliant, violent, and disruptive. Psychopaths had shorter program retention, more avoidances of urinalysis, and much poorer therapist ratings than did nonpsychopaths. This was expected because the psychopath was clearly defined as the type of individual who will be deceptive, violent, and noncompliant. The problem in many of these instances is that by treating psychopaths for a comorbid condition the psychopathy remains unaddressed and the treatment for the comorbid issue is stunted as well. Psychopathy interferes with any other attempted treatments.

A variety of common psychological treatments have proven reasonably successful in curbing psychopathic behavior, but because no extensively researched treatment program effectively cures or improves all or most psychopaths, it is quite possible that some psychopaths are indeed immune to treatment. Perhaps that impervious group within the general category of psychopathy embodies the true idea of psychopathy that Cleckley wanted to capture when designing the construct. Those individuals might be the truly evil ones that most people envision when they think of psychopaths. Unfortunately, no research exists that tracks specific psychopaths through various treatment programs in order to see if one treatment succeeds where another failed in the same individual. However, current research supports the fact that psychopaths are far from untreatable. As a group, they are resistant to treatment, but they are not immune.

Is evil a psychological concept?

The index to the *Diagnostic and Statistical Manual of Mental Disorders* does not contain the word evil. Only within the last few years has the word evil increasingly surfaced as a label for psychopathic and criminal behavior and as a suggestion for its cause. In a Frontline documentary on two serial killers some years ago, a prominent University of California at Berkeley psychologist diagnosed them as sexual psychopaths, and then concluded with her view that they might simply be evil. A psychologist hired by the court to examine them for competency to stand trial and criminal responsibility sometime later declared that they were evil and that only an exorcism might be effective with them. In the discussion of the terrorists who downed the World Trade towers or those who committed other suicide and homicide bombings the effort to label them as psychopaths and to describe their psychopathy has often resulted in widespread use of the word evil. How that religious, philosophical, and political concept will integrate with psychological, psychiatric, and societal efforts to understand, prevent, punish, and reform emotionally and behaviorally disordered individuals remains to be seen.

4

Media portrayals of and legal responses to psychopaths

Do books and movies such as American Psycho, Red Dragon *and* The Silence of the Lambs *accurately portray the psychopath?*

Fictional psychopaths such as Hannibal Lecter and Patrick Bateman are often based upon real-life psychopaths but exhibit many characteristics atypical of the average psychopath. Indeed, authors of crime-thrillers balance elements of realism and romanticism to create an intriguing and engaging plot and often accuracy is sacrificed for literary effect. Though characters like Hannibal Lecter are spellbinding and capture the audience's imagination, it is unlikely that a true psychopath would necessarily fit the model that is the Hollywood psychopath. First, only very few psychopaths become serial killers or murderers. Movies rarely display the interpersonal harm psychopaths are capable of committing in everyday contexts. And, though psychopaths may in fact be very engaging people, often very persuasive and convincing liars and manipulators, it is more likely that an actual psychopath would be more impulsive, disorganized, and short-tempered than the calm and enigmatic Hannibal Lecter. The lack of empathy and remorse that is characteristic of the psychopath, however, is greatly demonstrated by Lecter.

In Alfred Hitchcock's *Psycho*, Norman Bates does not appear to fit the mold of a psychopath. His entire grasp on reality is distorted, which is especially made apparent by the fact that he dresses up as his mother to kill people. Norman Bates may suffer something closer to a psychotic disorder or dissociative identity disorder which was formerly termed multiple personality disorder. Bates' expression of private remorse when he snaps out of his mother personality also indicates that he is not a psychopath.

While the news media usually portray psychopaths in a negative light, are books or movies more sympathetic to the psychopath?

It may be true that the news media generally show contempt towards the psychopath, but the attention given to psychopaths in film and literature seems often to glorify them. Books and their movies, such as *The Silence of the Lambs* and *American Psycho*, do not specifically condemn the behaviors of psychopathic killers. Rather, the literary psychopath often becomes the protagonist who is to some extent sympathetic. Hannibal Lecter is often cheered as a most intriguing villain, not condemned for his deplorable and revolting actions, and his final comment about fava beans and chiani is recalled by everyone and applauded by many. The tables have been turned and Lecter becomes an individual about to mete out justice to a doctor who has demeaned him during his incarceration. Video games in which players take the role of a psychopathic criminal or killer promote further sympathy. In light of such glorification, it is no great surprise that even the most contemptuous criminal psychopaths, such as Ted Bundy, were received with an almost cult-like fan following.

How do theatrical productions deal with psychopaths?

Arguably the most famous, or at least most obvious, theatrical psychopaths are Sweeney Todd and Mrs. Lovitt, stars of the musical *Sweeney Todd*. Mrs. Lovitt is the unassuming steward who makes meat pies from the clients slaughtered by Todd, the Demon Barber of Fleet Street. Todd goes to London to avenge the death of his wife. Despite his rage, Todd charms the locals, who constantly come to Todd's shop for a shave, or a pie. The story comes from Thomas Pest's *The String of Pearls: A Romance*, and originally an actual psychopath, Sawney Bean. Bean was known as the Man-eater of Scotland because he killed passers-by and ate their corpses. Despite several accounts that more closely parallel the story of the demon barber, no police records have been found, and the stories can probably be attributed to popular lore of the time. It is interesting how the horror of the real-life story can be glamorized in the protagonists of the musical.

Other notable theatrical psychopaths include Don Juan in Moliere's *Don Juan*, Hedda Gabler in Ibsen's *Hedda Gabler*, the assassins in Sondheim's *Assassins*, and the six ladies of the Cell Block Tango in Kander and Ebb's *Chicago*.

In fact, the Six Merry Murderesses of the Cook County Jail, characters from the award-winning stage and movie musical *Chicago*, are classic examples of psychopaths. All have been jailed for allegedly killing their boyfriends or husbands. Yet through their song and characters, they appear to be engaging and humorous. And, as they tell their tales in the song Cell Block Tango, there is no effort to make them victims, not even of battered woman syndrome. Instead, it becomes increasingly apparent that they killed in cold blood, without remorse. With most, there was minimal provocation for the killings. For example, Liz fired two shotgun blasts into her husband's head because he was popping his gum. Annie had a better reason: her boyfriend was secretly keeping six wives. Yet her colloquial glib remark that some guys just can't hold their arsenic reveals her psychopathic side while at the same time amusing the audience. One of the women makes little attempt to conceal the brutality of her deeds. She claims her husband ran into her knife ten times. The lead character adopts a common tactic among psychopathic defendants. She maintains that she blacked out completely and remembers not a moment of her boyfriend and sister's demise, only that she did not do it. The Six Merry Murderesses are effective on a dramatic and comic level precisely because of the depth of their depravity, the totality of their psychopathy.

Do movies, literary, and other works depicting psychopaths in the form of serial killers prevent society from recognizing other categories of psychopaths, including friends and white-collar psychopaths?

Some argue that Hollywood's representation of psychopaths as serial killers misdirects society's impression of the common psychopath. As individuals are increasingly exposed to the media's version of psychopathy, they may be unaware that their lover who borrows money from them and leaves without notice for days at a time may represent the more common form of psychopathy. Individuals tend to be surprised to learn that psychopaths are capable of appearing to be normal members of society. The greatest danger of the media's tendency towards representing the psychopath as a serial killer may be that it can blind individuals to psychopathic traits within the people they interact with daily.

Can violence and selfishness in such media as television, films, and video games lead to psychopathy?

Experts are divided on how much media can affect the behavior of those who spend time with it. Many researchers have shown that viewing violence in the media can be a factor in the perpetration of antisocial acts. Children are the most vulnerable to such media since they are the most malleable and often do not have sufficient understanding to differentiate between real life and fantasy in the media. There have been cases of children imitating what they see in the media and this can have dangerous results. Media may have an impact on a person's actions but there is no evidence that it can cause psychopathy. Since psychopathy is a disorder that comprises both behaviors and personality, media may have an effect on a person's behaviors but there is no evidence that they can change a person's fundamental personality. There is no scientific proof that media can in any way cause psychopathy, although there is evidence that they can be a factor in a person's carrying out antisocial acts.

Has corporate culture, with its levels of materialism and competition seeming to reward patterns of behavior that could be considered psychopathic, increased the number of psychopaths?

Without a solid estimate of what percentage of the population is psychopathic and without data on what percentage of the population was psychopathic before the rise of the American corporation, it is impossible to determine whether or not corporations have affected the number of psychopaths. It has been suggested, however, that corporations have made it easier for psychopaths to blend in and to succeed. It is also possible that corporations offer many more opportunities for criminal acts by nonconventional white-collar psychopaths than smaller businesses would, and that the relatively light consequences for financial crimes might encourage individuals to engage in behavior they would not in a stricter system. In that event, corporations might be encouraging antisocial behavior in a specific context. Psychopaths thrive where there are suitable victims. Corporations may provide an abundance of such victims making those with psychopathic personalities more ready to engage in acts of victimization.

Have media representations of the psychopath gone so far as to impact jury decisions at trial?

It is difficult to categorize the various biases that may influence a jury. Certainly the many lay definitions and misconceptions of psychopathy will influence a jury. Serial killer Ted Oswald was awarded a second trial due to jury bias, though this was likely due to the large volume of media coverage rather than representation of his alleged psychopathy.

It is helpful to frame the question of jury impact more specifically. When would media representations of psychopathy impact the jury at all? One obvious answer is in cases where the insanity defense is employed. The general bias the public seems to have assumes that many people are crazy, insane, and psychopathic; the average jury member, bombarded by media representations, would likely be confused about technical legal meanings. Yet trial precedents, including the cases in this book, show that these media representations often have little impact on jury decisions. Only about one-quarter of insanity pleas are successful, and very few plead insanity in the first place. Media impact is probably much more detrimental through excess exposure to the case rather than skewed representations of psychopathy.

Another clear answer is in matters of sentencing. Because juries are now frequently forced to consider psychopathy as an aggravating factor, especially where the death penalty is possible, media representations of the disorder may play a significant role in influencing their deliberations and conclusions.

How often are enemies of a political establishment labeled psychopaths and how fair are these labels?

A review of news reports provides a generally clear indication of how frequently psychopathy is used as an indictment of political enemies. United States' labels of Saddam Hussein, Osama Bin Laden, Kim Jong Il, and various terrorists as psychopaths have become common in speech. Yet the extent of such labeling goes beyond these world figures. Some members of the federal government called Cindy Sheehan, who opposed the War in Iraq after her son's death, a psychopath and added the term nutcase as well. Enemies of all sorts and at all levels of government are branded as psychopaths. Paul Craig Roberts, former associate editor of the *Wall Street Journal* and former Assistant Secretary of the Treasury, retaliated against the executive branch's labeling of others as psychopaths by issuing a warning that the U.S. government was in the hands of psychopaths. More striking was the widespread publication of this news by Iraq supporters. America became the target of labeling as the enemy of the Iraqi political establishment. Psychopathy is defined according to social norms and labels of psychopathy firmly pit one side against another, deeply rooting an us-versus-them mentality.

Does psychopathy differ cross-culturally?

Psychologists have tested the Revised Psychopathy Checklist, or PCL-R, cross-culturally. Studies in Sweden supported the PCL-R as possessing strong internal consistency and significant predictive validity. There, psychopaths were twice as likely as nonpsychopaths to recidivate. Also, the PCL-R proved to be a better predictor of future violence than substance abuse, conduct disorder, previous convictions, age, socioeconomic status, type of previous sentence, or any combination of these factors. This idea of substantiating the PCL-R's validity in other nations was expanded to encompass England, Belgium, Germany, Portugal, Spain, Norway, Denmark, and Scotland. All of these nations have effectively adopted the PCL-R into their cultures. The types of crimes seem to vary slightly depending on culture. What is deemed antisocial can be different, but the psychopaths remain the same in that they tend to break whatever norms exist in any given culture. One caveat to this supposed universality of the PCL-R is that the nations that have accepted the checklist are primarily Caucasian, western nations. There have been no complete studies of psychopathy in developing nations and non-western cultures. However, there is the possibility that psychopathy is not even tested equally across racial lines here in the United States because the majority of psychopaths recorded are white males. Results to date have varied in their conclusion, so this concept has yet to be conclusively studied.

What were the first laws to refer to psychopathy?

The earliest statutes that were created in the United States that contained the word psychopath were sexual psychopath statutes. Until the 1930s, those who committed crimes involving sex were usually held morally culpable for their crimes and imprisoned. In the 1930s, psychiatrists introduced a therapeutic perspective that viewed sex offenders as suffering from a psychological pathology. As this view gained strength, the legislatures responded. Michigan passed the first sexual psychopath law in 1937. Criminals diagnosed as sexual psychopaths were confined indefinitely, until psychiatrists declared them safe to reenter society.

Between 1937 and 1950, twelve states and Washington, D.C. had enacted similar laws. That number had grown to twenty-nine states by 1970. In 1970, a few more than half the states had adopted sexual psychopath laws. These statutes were typically promulgated in the aftermath of particularly lurid sex crimes that captured public attention. Most have now been abandoned while some states have adopted new laws for the civil commitment, after their release from prison, of sex offenders.

How do courts and legislatures address psychopaths, considering that psychopathy is not listed in the Diagnostic and Statistical Manual *as a disorder?*

Courts and legislatures rarely use the term psychopath on their own. They usually use the term in conjunction with sexual offenders, labeling offenders as sexual psychopaths when the individual has demonstrated high recidivism rates. Courts also informally utilize the term psychopath to refer to criminals who have demonstrated particularly heinous criminal acts. Again, the term is used informally, though lawyers and judges often use the term liberally.

In one interesting case that came before the U.S. Court of Appeals for the Seventh Circuit in 2000, an inmate in a Wisconsin prison wanted to participate in a sex offender treatment program in order to increase his chances of receiving parole. A psychologist diagnosed the inmate as a psychopath, and stated that psychopaths do not benefit from such treatment programs. As a result, the inmate was not allowed to participate. The inmate then sued; he accepted his diagnosis as a psychopath, and then claimed that his exclusion violated the Americans with Disabilities Act and several other laws. The Court of Appeals ultimately dismissed the inmate's arguments, noting that it is not clear that psychopathy is actually a disease or disability.

Are there laws to warn communities of psychopaths' release from confinement or presence in the community, like the Megan's Laws that alert people about sex offenders?

There are not such laws. It would seem important to a community to know when a psychopath moves in next door, as it would be for them to know that a sexual offender moved in. Even though psychopathy predicts recidivism to a great degree, much more so than a sexual offense, there are no laws in place to warn a community of a psychopath's release. This situation is likely caused by the fact that psychopathy is not a concretely identifiable concept. Whereas sex offenders are deemed sex offenders when they are convicted of a sex offense, no conviction automatically leads to the conclusion that one is a psychopath. There would also be controversy about what level of the Psychopathy Checklist would make someone eligible to fall under a statue defined purely by psychopathy, rather than some mix of psychopathy and sexual offenses. In addition, there is the logistical problem that not all convicts are tested in prison to determine whether they are psychopathic.

Does the fact that psychopaths are rationally aware affect the legal standards to which they are held?

Psychopaths' awareness does affect the legal standards to which they are held. The insanity defense is one example of that. A rule commonly used in insanity defense cases in the United States is the M'Naghten rule. Under the M'Naghten rule, a defendant employing an insanity defense must clearly prove that he was suffering from such a defect of reason that he either did not understand the nature and quality of the act he committed, meaning that he did not know what he was doing, or did not know that it was wrong. Psychopaths are rationally aware of their actions, as well as whether their actions are considered right or wrong. In fact, one study found that psychopathic criminals judged conventional and moral transgressions to be more wrong than their nonpsychopathic counterparts. Whether or not the psychopaths agree with the judgment that committing such transgressions is bad is not addressed. It is clear, however, that psychopaths are able to judge whether society has deemed an action right or wrong. It appears that a psychopath, however, ignores these judgments of right and wrong. It is likely that psychopaths have a deficit that interferes with their ability to feel the moral importance of rules and laws, but they generally prove capable of understanding the definitions and demands of laws nevertheless. Psychopaths may believe that the laws should not apply to them but this does not mean that they do not know that there are laws even though they may do such horrific things that people often say that only an insane person could such a thing. Psychopaths may have different drives and impulse controls than normal individuals but most fully understand the legal difference between right and wrong. They do not hallucinate and they are not delusional. They fully understand what is going on around them and choose to act the way they do. Thus in the legal sense, a psychopath is sane.

Does a psychopath's awareness of his psychopathy affect the legal standards to which he is held?

If psychopaths are aware that they are behaving psychopathically, it seems they make the choice to continue their antisocial behavior and to refrain from treatment. This would become a significant issue if the Durham test, a previous standard in insanity defense cases, were still commonly used. The Durham rule was based on the question of whether the defendant's behavior was the product of mental disease or defect. If it was, then the defendant was not criminally responsible for his otherwise unlawful actions. Although the Durham test has fallen into disuse, it appears that it would exempt psychopaths from legal responsibility if their psychopathy were considered a mental defect that produced an illegal action. Note the stark contrast to the M'Naghten test for insanity defenses, which would hold a psychopath legally accountable if he knew what he was doing and knew that it was wrong. Further research into the first-personal experiences of psychopaths is essential to resolve this important legal issue.

How often do psychopaths employ the insanity defense?

Often, the psychopath is sane, rational, and even quick-witted. When they are brought into hospitals, they are routinely declared sane and competent to stand trial. They do not suffer from delusions or hallucinations. Psychosis, which is almost always a requirement for employing the insanity defense, defines a psychological illness in which a person's thinking becomes irrational and disturbed. Often, the person has hallucinations in which he perceives sensory stimuli that may not even exist, or delusions, or both, and is therefore unable to distinguish between reality and imagination. Psychopaths do not suffer from psychosis. The definition of psychopathy does not include criteria for how rational or irrational one must be. Furthermore, because the *Diagnostic and Statistical Manual of Mental Disorders* does not include a definition of or criteria for psychopathy, expert psychoforensic witnesses do not frame their responses in an insanity defense case in terms of psychopathy. Thus psychopathy does not become a mental disease that can excuse the perpetrator of criminal acts. The legal tests of insanity used in the United States, whether the M'Naghten rule or the American Law Institute rule, include the requirement that at the time a person commits his act, he is not able to appreciate the wrongfulness of his action due to a mental disease or defect. Usually, psychopaths who commit crimes are declared by psychiatrists to be mentally sound and therefore, sane.

Even though the general public notion is that attorneys fall back upon the insanity defense in a large number of cases, one study has shown that the insanity defense was used in only one percent of all felony cases. The same study found that for all cases in which the insanity defense was used, defendants were only successful in one quarter of those cases. Furthermore, as most criminals are not psychopaths, one may conjecture that the incidence of insanity with regards to a psychopath is actually extremely low. The insanity defense prevents the law from punishing a person who does not understand that his behavior was wrong. Although criminal psychopaths may not truly understand why their behavior is deemed unacceptable, they generally fully grasp that their behaviors are illegal and punishable. Whether or not they care about the ramifications of their actions is irrelevant.

In the rare cases in which the insanity defense is used, the defense will not acknowledge psychopathy as the cause of insanity. Instead, if the client has other comorbid disorders, such as schizophrenia or bipolar disorder, the defense will allude to those disorders, which are officially listed in the *Diagnostic and Statistical Manual of Mental Disorders*, as the mental disorders that substantially confirm insanity in the legal sense.

Are psychopaths ever successful when they represent themselves during a trial?

Defendants are provided the right to waive their right to outside counsel and to serve as their own attorney by the Sixth Amendment to the U. S. Constitution. There are several stipulations to this right, including that the defendant must be deemed by a judge to be competent to stand trial and to represent himself. Competency does not imply normal mental functioning. Instead, the defendant must understand the judge's warning about the disadvantages of self-representation, have knowledge about the charges and possible punishments and some awareness of the rules of evidence and the roles of court personnel and procedures, and understand both the risk of an unsuccessful defense and the difficulties of acting as his own counsel. Because psychopaths have a grandiose sense of self, it is easy to understand why a psychopath would elect to represent himself during a trial despite the improbability of success. Even though very few notorious criminals have successfully defended themselves in a court of law, many have tried. Ted Bundy, Charles Manson, the Sunset Murderer Douglas Clark, and many others failed in their attempts to win over their juries. In many of these cases, the criminals' mask of normalcy slipped and juries were able to detect their hidden sinister nature.

H.H. Holmes was the first murderer to defend himself in a U.S. court. Holmes was a notorious scam-artist who tortured and killed dozens, possibly hundreds, of people he tricked into staying at a building he opened as a hotel in 1893. He performed quite well as an attorney until he called for a lunch break immediately after the corpse of his victim was described in grisly detail, exposing his lack of empathy.

Ted Bundy defended himself in the trial of the so-called Chi Omega murders. Though unqualified, Bundy was confident that he would dazzle the courtroom and jury with his charm. He would frequently flash smiles at his audience. However, Bundy's attempts did not help his case. When interrogating witnesses he encouraged them to recount the most gruesome details. Jurors said he seemed to delight in reliving the murders, especially to relish in the description of his crimes during police testimony.

It appears that the very nature of the disorder of psychopathy makes it difficult for psychopaths to convince juries of their innocence. Psychopaths' inability to react appropriately to the details of their heinous crimes, and their exaggerated belief in their own ability to understand the sophisticated aspects of a trial have thus far ultimately doomed their efforts.

Are psychopaths more likely than nonpsychopaths to receive the death penalty?

When psychopaths and the legal system collide, as they often do, several issues arise. For most mentally disordered criminals, the existence of mental illness either removes or mitigates criminal responsibility. However, in the case of a diagnosis of psychopathy, the legal system is apt to be quite harsh. Seen not as impaired, but as lacking any desirable qualities and untreatable and eager to resume their criminal behavior, psychopaths are more likely than nonpsychopaths to be given the death sentence for comparable offenses. Unlike mental disorders that make people feel and act unlike themselves, psychopathic behavior is egosyntonic. In other words, what a psychopath does is representative of his personality. In fact, Psychopathy Checklist-Revised scores are now incorporated into the sentencing phase of capital murder trials in order to evaluate the likelihood or unlikelihood of a moral reformation. Psychopaths are highly likely to violently recidivate when released from prison; consequently, jurors tend to see them as unredeemable cases, individuals too cruel for anyone to harbor hope for a brighter future. In fact, mock jury members have found anyone diagnosed as psychopathic more dangerous than nonpsychopaths, even when they are explicitly told that the psychopath is not violent and the nonpsychopath is violent. The label psychopath itself is sufficient even in spite of evidence to the contrary.

Legally, an individual should only be tried and sentenced for what he has done, not what others think he will do. However, in the case of the violent psychopath, the proven rates of violent recidivism are almost impossible for jurors and judges to ignore. When a psychopath has an exceedingly likely chance of seriously reoffending and of then returning to prison after release, the legal system has increasingly chosen not to benignly watch the inevitable occur. It has instead decided to step in to prevent future violent crimes. Thus it is that the law has acted and psychopaths are more likely to be sentenced to death.

Can psychopaths feel right and wrong?

It is important to realize that this question is distinct from asking whether psychopaths know or understand right and wrong. Although they clearly understand the definitions in the law, they cannot comprehend the values underlying the law. While they can understand morals, they have an inability to implicitly feel morals. Cross-culturally, children as young as thirty-nine months can recognize the distinction between moral transgressions and conventional transgressions. The latter are the result of rules of behavior which maintain civil order but are not among the essential principles of life; rules can change and do from time to time. The former are the result of those essential principles which are constant and which forbid harming others. In various studies, psychopaths have shown difficulty compared to nonpsychopath controls in moral-conventional distinction tasks, failing to understand, for example, that if laws prohibiting murder were lifted, murdering would remain wrong. In general, psychopaths can comprehend the written laws, but they do not attach meaning to them. They lack what has been called a moral sense.

Case Examples

5

Collective Cases

Dick Hickock, Perry Smith, *In Cold Blood*, and Truman Capote

Two conventional street criminals and the author who wrote about their lives and executions

Abstract

Dick Hickock and Perry Smith were conventional street criminals. Both have been called psychopaths. They met and became friends in prison while both were serving sentences. Each had been incarcerated in 1956, Smith for a robbing a store, Hickock for writing bad checks. Smith, troubled with headaches, a problem leg, and later diagnosed with a more serious mental disorder, bragged to Hickock that he had previously murdered a man. Hickock, diagnosed later as a psychopath, had heard from another prisoner about a Kansas farmer, for whom he had once worked, who kept considerable amounts of money in a safe in his house. Hickock, released before Smith, contacted Smith following his release from prison so that they could work together to rob the Clutters of their ten thousand dollars.

They met and drove to the Clutter farm, intent on robbing the family. Hickock had declared that they should leave no witnesses behind. Once there, they tied up Mrs. Clutter and the two teenage children who were home, and ordered Mr. Clutter to open the safe. He told them there was no safe, and that he had very little money in the house. At that point, the family were all killed. Mrs. Clutter was shot, as were daughter Nancy and son Kenyon. Mr. Clutter's throat was cut and he was shot. Hickock and Smith left the house and traveled to Mexico, to Florida, and through the southwest.

Hearing about the murders, Hickock's former fellow prisoner reported the earlier conversation about Clutter and the safe to authorities, and Hickock and Smith were later arrested in Las Vegas. Tried and convicted for murder, both were sentenced to death by hanging. Appeals took five years after which the sentences were carried out.

Truman Capote, already an established writer and a social figure in New York City, was about this time searching for an idea for his next book. When he saw a brief newspaper notice of the Kansas murders, he spoke with his editor at *The New Yorker* and then headed to Kansas with his long-time childhood friend Harper Lee, whose book *To Kill a Mockingbird*, would soon appear. Once there, with Lee's invaluable assistance and against what would have initially seemed great odds, he became friendly with investigators, townspeople, and especially with Smith, who detailed for him the events leading up to the killings, as well as the actual murders themselves. Capote wrote much of his book, and told others about it, but could not complete it until the sentences were carried out. He attended the executions, and just before he was hung, Smith kissed Capote on the cheek. Capote's book, *In Cold Blood*, established what he called the non-fiction novel. It became and remains an exemplary literary work, for style and content, and depth of analysis, and it formed the basis for an outstanding and faithful film, directed by Richard Brooks. Further, Capote's efforts, with Lee's help, to win over investigators and townspeople and Smith himself became the focus for another award-winning film, *Capote*, directed by Bennett Miller. The latter film and the related biography of Capote on which it was based raise the question of whether he engaged in psychopathic behavior with the killers and especially with Smith in order to complete the book, which required, he concluded, their executions to be carried out.

This case examines many of the significant issues in psychology, criminal justice, and society that are raised by the defendants' actions before, during, and after the murders, and by the author's efforts to reconstruct the events of the night of the murders, the lives of the victims, and the lives and personalities of the killers. Among those issues are the extent to which each of the three exhibited some characteristics of the psychopath, though two were conventional criminals, and one was an acclaimed writer and if anything, a less-conventional, white-collar psychopath.

Background of Smith and Hickock

How did Perry Smith's early life affect his behavior and attitude in his later life?

Perry Smith was the son of two rodeo performers and was born on October 27, 1928 in Huntington Valley, Nevada. His parents were Florence Julia Buckskin and Tex John Smith. Perry Smith was the youngest of four children and his early childhood was spent traveling all over the western United States while his parents competed on the rodeo circuit. In 1933, Smith and his family settled in Reno, Nevada. A few years later, Smith along with his siblings moved to San Francisco with their mother after she had a violent fight with her husband. Florence and Tex would later divorce and their marriage was marked with violence, adultery and alcoholism. A short time later Florence became an extreme alcoholic and Smith along with his siblings were placed in foster homes. This is when his problems began. His first arrest came at eight years old and after living in several detention centers and foster homes he returned to Reno, Nevada to live with his father.

Smith attended school until the third grade and then moved all over the Western United States with his father. They eventually settled in Alaska in search of gold. At age sixteen, Smith joined the Merchant Marines. He would eventually join the army and receive a bronze star for his duties in Korea. Before he left the army in 1952, he broke his left leg in five places in a motorcycle accident. Smith also alleges that he was assaulted physically and sexually while in the army.

Without a doubt, Perry Smith had a troubled first twenty-three years of his life. He seemed to always be out of place and incongruent with society. The unstable relationships, lack of parenting, motorcycle accident, abuse and death of his mother all affected his sense of well being and identity. His mother died drunk and destitute. Eventually his older sister would die from falling off a window and being run over by a taxi all while she was extremely intoxicated. Smith's brother committed suicide following an argument with his wife in which she committed suicide first. Tex died from a self-inflicted gun shot to the head in 1986. It seems as if the Smith family was destined for disaster and catastrophe. Dorothy, the sister who did not have any of the misfortunes of her family, wanted nothing to do with anyone in her family.

Perry Smith never seemed to fit in anywhere. Truman Capote wrote that he believed that Smith's dysfunctional childhood and watching his parents especially his mother ruin their lives turned him into a monster. The Smiths were once a happy, loving family but eventually everything fell apart. Perry Smith experienced first hand the falling apart of a loving family and this must have devastated him. His childhood was loose and disorganized. He often wrestled with mixed emotions of guilt and sympathy. This tremendous emotional pain that he felt was exacerbated and became physical pain when he was injured in a motorcycle accident. Smith became addicted to aspirin as a way to cope with his physical pain but aspirin also represented a way to bury his emotional pain and problems.

Smith's later life of serious crime was an adult extension of his childhood criminal activities. His criminal record was a natural extension of the strange and difficult environments that he was a product of. He had bittersweet emotions about his mother and father. The wonderful images of riding horses with his mother and father brought him relief and joy from the real world. Thoughts of being a Las Vegas headline singer brought him an escape into a fantasy world. But when he snapped back into reality he realized that his world was falling apart and that his capabilities were limited. No matter how hard he tried to do good and resist temptation, he always fell back into his old criminal ways.

It is a highly regarded theory that childhood trauma can lead to difficulties with functioning as an adult. In fact, some people have a hard time adjusting to and fitting in society after a serious traumatic event. Perry Smith was no different. His traumatic youth left him unable to function normally in society and led at least in part to his killing of the Clutter family. Despite his lack of education, he was a seemingly smart person who was very artistic and skilled at playing the guitar. He had grander plans for his future but because he knew nothing better than crime, he could not escape the grasp crime had over him.

What was Perry Smith's childhood like?

Perry Smith's childhood was very difficult and traumatic. He was the youngest of four children. His mother, a Cherokee Indian, and his father, a Caucasian, were both rodeo performers. He spent his early life traveling with his family across the country for rodeos. Life for Smith seemed happy at the beginning but quickly declined. His mother ultimately became a prostitute and on at least one occasion Smith and his siblings witnessed her servicing a client. His father was abusive and continually beat his wife, once so terribly that she took the children and left him. When he was six, his mother took him and her other children away from their father, moving them to San Francisco. Smith's mother became an alcoholic and Smith said that alcohol was particularly destructive to her because she was a Cherokee and that she had no tolerance for it. When he was still a very young boy, his mother died when she suffocated on her own vomit. He went into foster care and various orphanages. He was grievously abused by his various caregivers and in the orphanages in which he was raised. He lived for a short while with his father. He and his father had lofty dreams of finding gold and striking it rich and moved to Alaska to do so. However, his father was abusive and eventually kicked him out of their home, leaving all of his belongings outside. Smith was never able to receive any sort of substantial education although he desired one. He only attended school through the third grade. He clearly wanted to learn and was interested in complex matters. Capote brought him books in prison, such as the works of Thoreau, which Smith greatly enjoyed. He was always interested in art and music; he painted pictures and played the guitar.

His troubling upbringing not only affected him and his later actions but also his siblings. Two of his three siblings committed suicide. It is clear that Smith had a troubled childhood that may well have played a significant part in turning him into a criminal and killer.

What role did Smith's childhood experiences play in his psychopathic behavior?

It is possible that the life-threatening event in which Smith's father held a gun to his head resulted in posttraumatic stress disorder, a psychiatric disorder that can occur following the experience of life-threatening events, such as natural disasters, serious accidents, or violent personal assaults like rape. While most survivors of trauma eventually return to normal, some people will have stress reactions that do not go away on their own. These individuals may develop posttraumatic stress disorder. People who suffer from it often relive the experience through nightmares and flashbacks, have difficulty sleeping, and feel detached or estranged, and these symptoms can be severe enough and last long enough to impair a person's daily life significantly.

There were other events in his life that also could have contributed to the disorder. His older sister died from falling off a window and then being run over by a taxi. His brother committed suicide following an argument with his wife, at which time she committed suicide. Additionally, Smith broke his left leg in five places in a motorcycle accident. These events and more could have contributed to his rampage. Smith in fact had flashbacks on several occasions. He also had trouble sleeping, although this may be attributable to the pain caused by his leg.

If Smith had posttraumatic stress disorder, it was likely a cause of his killing rampage. It is also possible that Smith experienced childhood trauma and did not develop the disorder. There were also a series of unstable relationships in Perry's life that could have lead to his irrationality. It has also been suggested that Perry suffered from paranoid schizophrenia.

With such a series of events early in his life, it seems easier to understand Smith's committing these crimes. He never seemed to have any friends and he never found a niche in life. Truman Capote wrote that he believed that Smith's dysfunctional childhood turned him into a monster. For Smith, his once happy childhood became tangled and complex. His parents often fought with each other and eventually separated. There is support for the theory that the instability in his family and lack of attention he received caused emotional pain that eventually manifested itself in his heinous acts.

Did Smith's family upbringing contribute to his criminal acts?

Smith had three siblings, an older brother named Tex, Jr., or James, and two older sisters named Barbara and Fern, who later changed her name to Joy. Both of Smith's parents were considered alcoholics. His parents also fought constantly over little things, and Smith's father was abusive towards his wife and to the children. Smith's father reportedly almost beat his wife to death after he caught her having an affair with a sailor. In 1935, Smith's mother left her husband and took the children to live in San Francisco. While growing up in San Francisco, Smith spent most of his time on the streets in order to avoid his drunken mother. He associated with the neighborhood street gangs, got into trouble, and spent much of his time in detention homes. His father eventually gained custody of Smith, and together they both traveled doing odd jobs.

Smith's family upbringing certainly influenced his criminal turnout. Both his parents were substance abusers, and his father made illegal alcohol in his home. His father had a propensity for violence. The cycle of abuse theory suggests that Smith could have developed an inclination towards violent and abusive behavior because he grew up seeing that this was common behavior. His parents also neglected him for a large portion of his childhood, and this led Smith to hang with street gangs. Furthermore, since his parents neglected him, Smith failed to be socialized towards acceptable behavior. He probably never internalized the gravity of criminal behavior since his parents as well as peers participated in similar antisocial activities.

Did Hickock's family upbringing contribute to his criminal acts?

Hickock's youth was for the most part free from delinquent behavior. He was a fair student and graduated from high school in 1949. Hickock married a woman named Carol Bryan and had three sons with her. Hickock actually worked hard as a full-time mechanic for Mark Buick Company and at night as an ambulance driver. Things began to go awry when the couple overspent and found themselves in financial debt. Hickock then impregnated another woman by the name of Margaret Edna and went to live with her; his wife divorced him. Hickock began to write bad checks, and he was incarcerated in 1956 for his crime. While in prison, Edna divorced him. He was paroled on August 13, 1959, and he was convicted of no other crimes until the Clutter murder.

Hickock seemed to have a relatively normal upbringing, and none of his immediate family members committed any notable criminal acts. Trouble started for Hickock once he fell into financial debt with his first wife. Hickock resorted to writing bad checks to try to make ends meet. It seemed like he pursued the Clutter murder not out of a penchant for violent crimes, but for the money.

What were the similarities and differences in Perry Smith's, Richard Hickcock's, and Truman Capote's relationships with their fathers?

Of the three figures, Richard Hickock's relationship with his father is least unusual. His father was known to be firm with his children, but not abnormally so. Hickock lived a relatively normal childhood. He was a high school icon and athlete, giving his father the right to be proud.

Perry Smith's case was less normal. His alcoholic mother took him away from his father because he was an alcoholic. Yet she would provide him little relief; he became a gang member and spent time in a number of detention homes. At age sixteen, Smith was reunited with his father. He dreamed of joining his father on Alaskan mining prospects. Despite the joy of that time, he remained plagued by antagonistic images of his father beating him and approaching him with a shotgun.

Truman Capote's reminiscence of his own father is similarly morbid. In the movie *Capote*, Truman likened a morbid skeptic of *In Cold Blood* to his father, insinuating that his father was unsupportive of his work. George Plimpton, who wrote an oral biography of Capote, confirmed the antagonism he faced from both his real father and his stepfather.

Did Perry Smith and Richard Hickock have a sexual relationship?

In Cold Blood and *Capote* included many scenes that contributed to the thesis that Perry Smith and Richard Hickock had a sexual relationship, or at least some form of homoerotic and substantial emotional attachment. Hickock's general dominance over Perry was illustrated in his diminutive names for Smith, including baby and honey. Other indications can be tracked throughout their relationship. While in the Clutter house, Smith became enraged with Hickock for his wanting to rape Nancy Clutter. Some might claim Smith was merely trying to prevent further harm than taking money, but rape seems insignificant next to murder. There must have been some further motivation to stop Hickock, and it has been suggested that that was the jealousy of seeing him with someone else, with a woman. A similar instance occurred in Mexico, where Smith refrained from sharing in Hickock's promiscuity and became immensely disturbed by Hickock's relations with prostitutes. Finally, Smith showed Capote disdain for his giving Hickock pornography magazines in prison. All of these attempts to restrain Hickock's sexuality showed that Smith had some stake in Hickock's sexuality. The relationship must have been more than merely psychological; it was likely sexual.

Unfortunately, there is little factual corroboration for these events. Why, then, would one be interested in whether Hickock and Smith actually had a sexual or homoerotic relationship? Some commentators have argued that understanding Hickock and Smith's sexual relationship is the only way to fully understand what happened the night the Clutter family was murdered. One commentator, for example, took Hickock and Smith's claim that they only intended to rob, not murder, the Clutters to be sincere. He hypothesized the only thing that could have driven the two to kill was tension between them. He interpreted Hickock's intention to rape Nancy Clutter as the source of this tension. Under his hypothesis, an apparently irrelevant sexual relationship became one of the primary reasons the Clutters were killed. He also believed this was part of the reason that Smith took responsibility for all four of the murders. Despite lashing out with vicious murders, Smith could not bear to incriminate his lover.

Another point of interest is exploring what bearing such a sexual relationship might have had on the Hickock and Smith's psychological state. Hervey Cleckley, in *The Mask of Sanity*, commented on the relationship between homosexuality and psychopathy. Cleckley, while making it clear that homosexuality in no way implies psychopathy, stated that psychopathy does often involve deviation from sexual norms. This deviation might include same-sex relations. He also noted a common homosexual desire for people who are unavailable. The relation between Smith and Hickock seemed to describe a situation that would serve his hypothesis. Smith's display of this typical longing, in tandem with Hickock's promiscuity, might have contributed to the Clutters' deaths.

The killings

Would Perry Smith have murdered the Clutter family if Richard Hickock had not been involved?

Many people argued that Richard Hickock's role as the dominant male in his relationship with Perry Smith was strong evidence that he was the instigator of the murders. Furthermore, the Perry Smith that Capote developed in his novel was a very sympathetic character with whom Capote felt a strong kinship, which he made apparent when he revealed to Harper Lee that he felt as if he and Smith grew up in the same house. How could a man as seemingly kind and pathetic as Perry Smith murder an entire family, if indeed he were the one who killed them all? Some believed the Richard Hickock played an important role in the tragic events.

It was Hickock's idea to go to the Clutter household, and he easily convinced Smith to go there. He told Smith of the information he had received from his cellmate. The night of the murder Smith told Hickock to turn back but Hickock did not listen. Instead, he entered and the pair proceeded to look for the safe they never found. Once Smith realized that the money was not there and that they were lied to, he again insisted that they leave the household. He even said that Mr. Clutter was a nice man, but Hickock instructed Smith to tie up Mr. Clutter and his son. Smith did this and after Hickock left, Mr. Clutter complained about the ties being too tight and that he was cold, so Smith untied Mr. Clutter and put him on a mattress. Smith also had to prevent Hickock from raping the Clutter girl. During this time Smith bonded with the girl by looking at her trophies and sharing stories of his childhood. He went downstairs shortly thereafter and told Hickock how crazy they were for only finding a mere forty-three dollars.

In order to answer the question of whether Smith would have committed the murders without Hickock, it is necessary to analyze his psychological state before and while he committed the Clutter family murders. Prior to the Clutter family killings, Smith had been jailed and paroled for robbery. His background suggested a lifetime of minor criminal acts that may have been a reaction to his home environment. In the movie version of *In Cold Blood*, Smith had several flashbacks to his mother, siblings, and father. All of these scenes involved drinking, and some involved abuse. For example, when at the hotel with Hickock he had a flashback of his mother drinking in front of him and his siblings. Completely drunk, she began to take off her clothes and have sexual relations with a male caller.

Perry Smith may have suffered from posttraumatic stress disorder. According to the *Diagnostic and Statistical Manual of Mental Disorders*, this disorder is characterized by diminished responsiveness to the external world, estrangement from other people, reduced ability to feel emotion, and outbursts of anger. Regarding the traumatic event, the sufferer is often plagued by nightmares or startling images of the event, despite constant effort to put it out of mind. The night of the Clutter murder, Smith had a flashback to his father confronting him with a gun pointed in his face, and his father saying that he would be the last living thing that his son would ever see. Fortunately the gun was not loaded and Smith walked away and never looked back. He stated to the minister before his death that the only thing he would miss in the world is a poor old man and his hopeless dreams. It seems as though Smith's brush with death may have been a cause of posttraumatic stress disorder. It was clearly a moment he never forgot.

Additionally, it is important to note the significant role that Hickock played in manipulating Smith's behavior before the murders. This is seen in various instances, such as when Hickock took Smith shopping for a suit. Hickock was able to convince Smith to steal from a store, suggesting that he was easily manipulated and that Hickock played a strong role in his life. Considering Smith's lack of family and jail time, it is reasonable to conclude that the reason Hickock played such an important role in his life was because Smith had no other friends.

Smith's actions toward Mr. Clutter and Kenyon suggest that he felt sympathy for the Clutters and thus it did not make sense that he would want to kill them. However, the events after he untied Mr. Clutter provide insight into Smith's mental state: It is possible that when Hickock came toward Smith this caused him to have a flashback to his father standing over him holding a gun in his face. It is also likely that this flashback triggered Smith's rampage. Smith stated, after the killing, that he did not know what happened in that brief span of time. He said that the killing had nothing to do with the family, only that they happened to be there. However, it is also important to keep in mind that he would not have been there in the first place if it were not for Hickock.

Smith had several traumatizing childhood experiences, flashbacks of his father nearly killing him, and he felt alone in the world. Capote even sympathized with him for his sincerity and trustworthiness. It is difficult to comprehend why a man of Smith's intelligence and personality could find the courage to rampage against an entire family when he could not even stand up to his friend. Again, it is important to note that there were several instances when Smith tried to convince Hickock to leave. While it is unlikely that Smith would have been in that household were it not for Hickock, it is also likely that he would have had such a flashback without the presence of Hickock. Thus, while Perry may not have found himself in the same situation without the help of Hickock, Hickock probably could not have controlled the events that triggered Perry's rampage.

Robert Hare refers to Richard Hickock and Perry Smith in his book *Without Conscience* as an example of a bizarre criminal partnership with elements of psychopathy. He recognized Hickock as a smooth-talking and manipulative psychopath and referred to Smith as borderline psychotic, or as Capote has related in his novel, a paranoid schizophrenic. It is likely that apart from one another neither would have had the will to commit the Clutter murders. Though he put on a show of masculinity and bravado, Hickock had never murdered anyone before. His previous crimes were limited to theft and check fraud. Likewise, although probably more prone to violent outbursts, Smith had never murdered before that night in Holcomb. But with Hickock's remorseless resolve steering the fragile, malleable mind of Perry Smith, they were able to commit vicious and cold-blooded criminal acts. In interviews, Hickock admitted to masterminding the crimes and said he had recruited Smith because he thought he was a natural born killer.

This mastermind-accomplice relationship has been suggested by Hare in other contexts. Hare admits that it is rare that two psychopaths would get along very well, as one egocentric and callous person would find it difficult to stand another. However, as psychopathic personalities may vary like normal personalities, one can imagine two personalities with complementary interests fitting together quite nicely. For instance, one especially glib and manipulative psychopath may take the role of the talker, and orchestrate a pair's crimes and behaviors. His complement is the doer, a particularly antisocial psychopath who lacks the extroverted characteristics of his partner but is equally devoid of empathy or remorse. He has no trouble executing the orders of the talker.

One commentator, who himself spent many years in prison, denied Capote's claim that Smith's killings were the result of some schizophrenic dissociation. Rather, he suggested that the crimes were a consequence of a sexual and psychological relationship between Smith and Hickock. Upon discovering Hickock attempting to rape young Nancy Clutter, he argued, Smith felt slighted and contested Hickock's façade of manliness. He knew that Hickock did not have it within himself to carry out his plans about leaving no witnesses, so he forcefully killed Herbert Clutter in spite of him. Though an intriguing and imaginative explanation, this argument required far more evidence concerning Hickock's and Smith's relationship than was available. We might speculate as to any number of reasons why Perry Smith acted out suddenly and violently, but there is no concrete evidence backing up this hypothesis.

Why did Smith go through with the murders when he said that he did not want to hurt the Clutters?

A number of explanations suggest why Smith ultimately went through with the killings. One refers to the hypothesis that Smith suffered from paranoid schizophrenia. Though he was never formally diagnosed, Capote claimed that the psychiatrist who evaluated Smith would have given him that diagnosis. It is possible that the stress of not finding the expected money added to Hickock's repeated pressure to leave no witnesses will have set off a psychotic episode. Smith did claim to experience a sort of blackout or flashback just prior to killing the Clutters, and the evaluating psychiatrist was unable to determine whether Smith was aware of his actions during the crime.

It is also possible that Smith was not psychotic but just gave into his anger. Smith felt victimized and often blamed his problems on outside sources. The Clutters may have represented everything he wanted but could not have. He may have snapped and lashed out against the closest victims. From the description of the killings, it did appear that rage could have fueled his actions.

Still another possible explanation was that Smith was a victim of circumstances rather than a cold-blooded monster. In many ways, Capote presented Smith as a sympathetic character. However, Smith's sister refused to have anything to do with him, and it is quite possible that she understood Smith better than Capote did. Smith's sister was not surprised to find out her brother was charged with murder. It is possible that Smith was in effect a time bomb, and if he had not murdered the Clutters, eventually he might have killed someone else. When he claimed he did not want to hurt the Clutters, he may have just been saying what Capote wanted to hear.

It may have been one or a combination of the factors listed above or it may have been something else entirely. We will, of course, never really know what went through his mind just before he committed the murders.

Why did Perry Smith have flashbacks before he killed the Clutter family?

Perry Smith was a dreamer. He often had dreams and flashbacks of happy times and supposedly happy futures. Due to his troubled life, flashbacks served as a way to reminisce about the past and use those thoughts to hope for a better future.

Smith often reminisced about the few and only wonderful times he had with his family. Whenever he had these flashbacks, he would always smile and take a minute to enjoy his thoughts and visions.

Perry Smith may have had flashbacks before he killed the Clutter family because he consciously knew it was wrong to kill the Clutter family but could not overcome himself and killed the family anyway. He constantly wrestled with thoughts of right and wrong in his mind but seemed to end up doing wrong. Pleasant flashbacks served as a way to remember and create a happy thought in his mind therefore allowing him to feel comfortable and secure for a minute or two. Supposedly with a comfortable and secure feeling, Perry would have realized that killing the Clutter family was not the right thing to do. Instead, no matter how many positive flashbacks he had, he could not control himself and ended up killing the Clutter family. Perhaps for other criminals and people, flashbacks serve as a way to deter one from committing a crime. Having flashbacks were the only source of joy in Perry's life.

Did Perry Smith and Dick Hickock enjoy killing the Clutters?

Smith and Hickock may have experienced a kind of rush, an exhilaration in the act of killing. Having been primed by the expectation of finding money, they were in a highly excited state. Both Smith and Hickock described the thrill of dominating the Clutter family, of subjugating them with gags and guns.

It is also possible that the two did not particularly enjoy killing the Clutters. Perry described his affection for the family on several occasions. He said that he thought Herb Clutter was a fine gentleman, right up to the moment he slit Clutter's throat. He declared that he protected Nancy from sexual abuse by Hickock because he had taken a liking to the girl. Furthermore, both killers showed some concern for Herb and Kenyon by placing the former on a mattress and propping up the latter with a pillow, before slaughtering them both. However, these are relatively small acts of compassion. Any declaration of affection from these killers seemed insincere, considering fully the brutality of their actions.

Both Smith and Hickock described some feelings of regret, but it was not the kind of positive regret one might hope for. To be specific, Perry once announced that his greatest regret was that his sister Barbara was not in the Clutter house on that night. Hickock laughed upon hearing this and agreed to the sentiment, although he would have chosen his ex-wife. As shallow as their notion of guilt may have been, there is a sense that they felt they had somehow made a mistake.

In a more complex sense, these two murderers might have harbored mixed feelings about killing the Clutter family. While having enjoyed the thrill of criminal behavior, there may have been some conscience that later caused them some psychological difficulty.

Did Smith have any surviving family members at the time the Clutter murder?

While being interrogated by the police about the Clutter murder, Smith claimed that he was in Ft. Scott trying to visit his sister on the day of the murder. This was of course an alibi. It was reported that Smith's father was believed to be deceased at the time of the Clutter murder, but no information was released about his other family members. Even so, Smith believed that he had no surviving family members, and decided to take the blame for all the Clutter murders for Hickock.

Did Hickock have any other surviving family members at the time of the Clutter murder?

Both of Hickock's parents were believed to be alive and living in Olathe, Kansas at the time of the murder. There is no mention of any other family members.

The victims

How does the portrayal of the Clutters differ in the movie version of In Cold Blood from the book itself?

The book devoted a large amount of space, in alternating chapters, to detailed portraits of each member of the Clutter family, showing their lives and personalities and relationships and routines and hopes. Capote depicted them in their innocence and contrasted that with the flawed backgrounds of Smith and Hickock. The movie of *In Cold Blood* removed most of these details and presented a much more limited description of the family. Its focus was on the killers. The movie *Capote* focused on the author, his friend Harper Lee, the Kansas law enforcement officers, and the two killers. The Clutters were only mentioned in passing as the family that was murdered.

How did the residents of Holcomb and local surrounding areas, who were also victims of the violence in their community, react to the murders?

Holcombe was a very small town scattered across a broad stretch of the Kansas plains. Its inhabitants were mostly farmers, Republicans, and devout Methodists.

For fun, residents enjoyed 4-H Club meetings and family picnics, and an occasional visit to nearby Garden City. They had a strong moral code and a rich sense of community. They lived a quiet, ordinary life in the middle of the United States. Thus, one can imagine their grief and rage in response to the murders.

In a more specific sense, the locals varied greatly in their reactions to the murders. The first witnesses to the scene later described their sense of disbelief, their initial numbness. Then there was Mrs. Myrtle Clare who matter-of-factly informed her mother that the four Clutters were dead. Soon thereafter the news went out from church pulpits, over telephone wires, and over the radio waves announcing a tragedy, unbelievable and shocking beyond words. At Hartmann's Café the small space was crowded beyond capacity with frightened gossips. The locals' reactions tended to be more in line with Mother Truitt's response than Mrs. Clare's. Bobby Rupp, Nancy's boyfriend, heard of his loved one's death from Mr. Ewalt. Upon hearing this, Rupp was at first polite, then non-responsive as he stared out at the landscape behind his house. Finally he took off running to the Clutter house, where he was astonished to learn that he was a suspect.

Detective Alvin Dewey of the Kansas Bureau of Investigation adopted an attitude of grim resolve in response to the gruesome killings, investing himself personally in the investigation. He took it upon himself to find the killers, and worked nonstop day and night to accomplish this task. Floyd Wells, an inmate at a prison in Lansing, Kansas, upon hearing the news of the Clutters' murders, felt compelled to report his former fellow inmate, Richard Hickock. This information would eventually lead Dewey to the killers.

How accurate is Truman Capote's portrayal of the Clutter family murders in In Cold Blood?

By writing *In Cold Blood*, Truman Capote created the genre of the nonfiction novel. He wove the plot using factual material, but it read like an intense fictional murder story. Most of the objective facts of the case align perfectly with Capote's interpretation. However, within that general outline, he undoubtedly brought bias and subjectivity into the story in order to make it more interesting to a reader. One major problem in attempting to determine the accuracy of *In Cold Blood* compared to the actual events is that the novel is the only complete, public account of the events. Because the supposedly nonfiction novel was released shortly after Smith's and Hickock's executions, no one bothered to compile the objective case information into a concrete account. So with no standard against which to compare *In Cold Blood*, there can only be speculation about the validity of Capote's perspective.

Further, Truman Capote used an entirely different approach in interviewing the subjects. While interviewing, he never used a recorder or a notepad to collect information. Instead, he relied on his memory which he said was extraordinary. He made a point of letting others know he had ninety-four percent recall of all conversations that he heard. If this was true, then he probably recorded all the events and all the dialogue that he encountered reasonably accurately. Through his conversations with Perry Smith, he was able to portray Smith's history and his actions as Smith told them himself. But there was no way to verify Smith's account, so there were many opportunities for the original events to be recreated with bias. Furthermore, much of the dialogue that Capote included in the novel must have been invented because Capote did not personally witness most of the described events. He often simply knew what happened, then put words into the characters' mouths in order to create the desired scene. No one can tell how accurately the dialogue recaptured actual situations.

Finally, Capote deliberately portrayed Perry Smith as a sympathetic character who was in the wrong place at the wrong time. Hickock appeared to be the psychopath and Smith seemed to have been a good person who did a bad thing. These conclusions are not evident by simply looking at the case evidence. Though Smith was apparently the one who shot the Clutter family, Capote outlined the anguish that the murders caused him. The tone of the novel indicates this bias toward Perry, with whom Capote had spent much intimate time. Perhaps Perry Smith was a psychopath, though. Perhaps Smith seduced Capote and put on a mask of weakness and sorrow. Capote may have fallen into the trap and given Smith what he wanted, an extended life before execution and immortal image as a figure who probably should not have been hanged.

Psychology and law in the trial

What are the forensic personality diagnoses for Perry Smith and Richard Hickock?

Throughout the trial, the issue of the defendants' psychological state was crucial. Early in the proceedings the accused requested to be moved to the state's mental hospital for a comprehensive psychological evaluation, but the judge denied the motion and relied on the local general practitioner's examination. Smith and Hickock pled temporary insanity but the general practitioner declared them sane. The case drew attention from expert psychiatrist Dr. W. Mitchell Jones who testified that Hickock was sane at the time of the crime. He was, however, unable to evaluate conclusively Smith's sanity at the time of the crime.

The state of Kansas used the M'Naghten test of insanity. That formulation was a fairly narrow one. A defendant could be found insane if he did not know the nature and quality of the act he was committing or did not know that it was wrong. A successful insanity defense would have resulted in a verdict of not guilty, though the defendant would nonetheless have been committed to a state hospital for the criminally insane, usually to spend the rest of his life there as a consequence of his brutal acts.

Truman Capote carefully analyzed the personalities of Richard Hickock and Perry Smith. Though psychoforensic professionals who evaluated the defendants only testified about their ability to tell right from wrong, or their sanity, much more can be extrapolated from Capote's interviews and evaluations. Witnesses' discussion was constrained by the M'Naghten rule legal standard, which left little room for any analysis beyond the conclusion as to whether a defendant was insane or not at the time of his actions. Still, Capote gave a detailed account of what psychiatrist W. Mitchell Jones, who because of that rule testified in effect against Hickock and Smith, might have said were he allowed to testify in greater detail and with complete candor in court. Capote presumably interviewed Dr. Jones outside of the court's proceedings to learn more of his views.

Richard Hickock was a lifelong con man and petty thief. Jones found him highly intelligent, charming, and very persuasive. Though raised in a stable environment, he developed criminal tendencies, primarily check fraud and petty theft. He displayed many of the characteristic mannerisms of the psychopath: lying, egotism, manipulation, grandiose self-worth, and lofty goals. Indeed, when Hervey Cleckley's diagnostic criteria for psychopathy are applied to Hickock, he scores highly. Jones's evaluation revealed that Hickock showed no signs of mental confusion or brain damage. Rather, he was very well organized and logical. Jones also recognized in Hickock indications of emotional abnormality. Although fully aware of what he was doing, he committed the crimes against the Clutters, devoid of any remorse or sorrow. Jones also cited Hickock's impulsiveness, short-temper, and low-self esteem as character traits. Jones said that although Hickock professed normal moral standards, he seemed obviously uninfluenced by them. In conclusion, Jones diagnosed Hickock with what he called a severe personality disorder. Subsequent commentators, even textbooks, have labeled Hickock as a classic psychopath.

When asked for an opinion on Perry Smith's sanity, based on his conversations and examinations with him, Jones testified that he had no opinion. Before defense attorney Arthur Fleming could question why he had formed no opinion, prosecutor Logan Green objected. However, Capote again submitted what Jones would have testified. Jones contended that Perry Smith demonstrated definite signs of severe mental illness. His childhood was a brutal one, Jones concluded, one without love, direction, or a fixed set of moral values. Though poorly educated he exhibited fairly high intelligence and a natural propensity for art and music. Jones identified two distinct features of Smith's personality. First was his paranoid orientation. Smith was immensely suspicious and untrusting of others and very sensitive to criticisms others made of him. Jones concluded that Smith's mental projections of what others thought of him dominated the actual intentions or feelings of others. The other feature of his personality was what Jones described as the early signs of a disorder in his thought process. Unlike Hickock, Smith exhibited poor ability to organize his thinking and often seemed to disregard reality. He further demonstrated emotional detachment and did not easily form emotional relationships with other people. Dr. Jones concluded therefore that the personality structure of Perry Smith was very nearly that of a paranoid schizophrenic. And other commentators have noted that the qualifying words very nearly leave open the question of whether Perry Smith also had a personality disorder, psychopathy.

While the current psychoforensic view is that psychopaths' actions are not those of insane people because psychopaths understand society's rules and the difference between right and wrong, they are nonetheless emotionally unattached to those consequences. As research in neuroscience uncovers more about the cognitive nature of the psychopath, some evidence has begun to suggest to some researchers that psychopathy may be more of a mental deficiency than originally believed. Cleckley, after all, called it the mask of sanity. Despite this, the disordering of mental and moral capabilities does not amount to the disorganization of the schizophrenic brain.

Would Truman Capote's emotional relationship with Perry Smith strongly counter the argument that Smith was a psychopath?

A hallmark characteristic of psychopathy is shallow emotional affect. Psychopaths usually are not able to sustain long-term friendships because of their lifestyle choices and pathologic characteristics. They are incapable of experiencing emotional depth and are not moved by such things as truth, love, or tragedy. Yet Smith seemed able to achieve emotional connection with Capote as Capote with him. If an argument were made that Smith was indeed a psychopath, such a strong emotional link might counter that contention. Part of the connection derived from Capote's persuasive and friendly statements, compounded by his initial efforts to obtain a lawyer to argue for an extended execution date, which quickly gained Smith's trust. At the end of all of Smith's letters to Capote, Smith signed as Capote's amigo. In addition, Smith acted genuinely betrayed when he found out that the title of Capote's book would be *In Cold Blood*. Such emotional reactions add credence to the notion that Capote and Smith had a very intimate emotional, if not physical, relationship. But as many have noted, Capote's insincere approach to the relationship may even imply that Capote was a psychopath while Smith was not.

Why were both Hickock and Smith sentenced to death and hanged when Smith took the full blame for killing the Clutter family?

Perry Smith and Richard Hickock were tried in 1959 for the murders of the Clutter family and both were found guilty and sentenced to death. It remains unclear which of the two men actually killed Nancy and Bonnie Clutter, but Perry Smith assumed full responsibility. Under Kansas's law, both men could be given the death penalty, but it was also possible for Hickock to receive a sentence of life imprisonment instead, as it could not be proved he killed anyone. However, the jury did not choose to grant Hickock mercy, and both men were executed on April 14, 1965.

Not all states allow the death penalty and crimes that can result in receiving the death penalty vary from state to state. In some states, only those people who actually commit murders are eligible for the death penalty. Kansas does not follow that policy. Kansas, like many other states, has a felony murder rule. This means that all individuals involved in a capital crime can receive the death penalty, not just the ones directly responsible for the deaths.

Even though Hickock did not confess to taking part in the murders, and Smith took the full blame, under Kansas's law Hickock could be sentenced to death because he was involved in the crime. Though it is impossible to know exactly what made the jury decide to extend the death penalty to Hickock, several factors might have contributed to that decision. First, during the trial it was revealed that Hickock wanted to rape the Clutter's youngest daughter. Though Smith did not allow Hickock to rape the girl, the fact that he was willing to do such a thing may have prejudiced the jury against him. Further, Smith initially claimed that he killed the two men, while Hickock killed the two women. He later retracted this and took the blame for all four murders. Smith claimed he did this because Hickock had family while he did not. This uncertainty may have also encouraged the jury to extend the death penalty to both men.

A third factor to consider is that Smith had never killed prior to this incident, and it appears that he would not have killed the Clutters without Hickock's encouragement. This would suggest that Hickock contributed significantly to Perry's mental state at the time of the crime. Moreover, Hickock could be seen as responsible for the murders because he provided the information and motive for the Clutter killings as well as transportation to the home. And Hickock, present at the murders, did nothing to stop or prevent them from happening. Additionally, he fled the scene of the crime with the Smith and aided him in hiding until the police tracked them down later. Finally, Hickock was a career criminal. If the jury had been aware of this, they may have been less inclined to see him as redeemable.

Whatever reasoning the jury followed, in the end under Kansas's law, both men could be given the death penalty for their actions, and the jury decided that Hickock did not deserve clemency.

What were the bases for their appeal for stays of execution?

Hickock's and Smith's many appeals for stays of execution focused on their legal representation, which they claimed was inadequate, and upon the judge's denial of their transfer to the state hospital for proper psychological evaluation. Attorneys Joseph P. Jenkins and Robert Bingham contended that their clients had been unjustly convicted because legal counsel had not been appointed to them until after they had confessed and waived preliminary hearings. Furthermore, the attorneys contended that Smith and Hickock had not been competently represented at trial and that key evidence, the shotgun and knife taken from the Hickock home, was seized without a search warrant. The defendants had also moved to transfer the venue of the trial, as the small community was already largely affected by and opinionated about the crimes. This motion was denied, and the judge noted that several ministers in the allegedly biased area were preaching against capital punishment.

If Capote had tried once again to find Perry Smith and Richard Hickock a lawyer to make their appeal, could the lives of Hickock and Smith been spared?

Capote ultimately refused to answer Smith's requests for help in obtaining a proper lawyer for their appeal to the Supreme Court. Capote had been assisting Hickock and Smith in their pursuit of a proper appeal for many years. It appears this relationship was established primarily because Capote wanted the men to live long enough for them to confide in Capote about the details of the murders. Once Smith did reveal the events of that night, Capote ceased responding to the telegrams he received from the men, presumably because he wanted an appropriate ending to his story, which would only be possible if the men were executed.

While it is unclear whether Capote could have helped spare Smith and Hickock, several theories are suggested based on legal elements of the case and an analysis of possible legal precedents. For instance, it could be argued that intervention from Capote could have helped the two murderers avoid the death penalty. Capote's earlier support for Smith and Hickock, particularly with respect to finding them better lawyers to represent them in their appeals, did prove to be successful in temporarily delaying their execution. It is possible that if Capote had succeeded once again in helping them find adequate representation, the Supreme Court would have accepted their argument that their previous lawyers were unfit. Previous courts had accepted an appeal like this in the past, so it was possible that it could happen again. Also, Capote was a wealthy and well-connected individual who probably had the resources to seek out a competent and successful lawyer.

However, the likelihood is small that Smith and Hickock would have ultimately been saved from the death penalty. As Judge Pickett of the Court of Appeals for the Tenth Circuit stated after denying Hickock and Perry's appeal, the right to legal counsel does not suggest that miracles will be performed. And as several other judges noted, the confession to the crimes was not disputed. The fact remained that Smith and Hickock brutally murdered a well-respected family, a crime that essentially guaranteed a death sentence in Kansas.

Most likely, if Capote had continued to support Smith and Hickock in seeking appeals, their execution would have simply been temporarily delayed for a few more years. Many criminals sentenced to death remain on death row for decades until their appeals run out or they ultimately die in jail. Smith and Hickock might have been able to survive a few more years waiting on their appeals, but their death sentences would most likely have been upheld.

Could Capote be considered partially responsible for the execution of Smith and Hickock?

Prior to their final appeal, Capote cut off contact with Hickock and Smith. He did not respond to their requests for help in finding an attorney. He more or less abandoned them to their fate. His initial efforts on their behalf were fueled by his need to keep them alive long enough to gather the material for his book, and when their continued existence made it impossible for him to finish the book, he pulled away. It is probably not possible that if Capote had helped them locate a good attorney, they might have won their final appeal and been granted life imprisonment instead of the death sentence. At the very least, his assistance could have protracted the appeals process and kept them alive longer. Capote had influence and he might have been able to make a difference.

On the other hand, by that point Capote's book had been well publicized, and its title gave the world a very clear and negative image of the killers. Though the contents would treat them somewhat sympathetically, the public did not yet have full access to the book. Capote may have inadvertently altered public perception of Hickock and Smith negatively. The case had been well publicized by that point, so an appeal would have proven difficult, and without good legal assistance it would not have been possible for them to win. In the end, Capote's decision to withdraw his support may have sealed their fate.

Prison

What is the significance of Perry Smith reading Thoreau while in prison?

In both the movie version of *In Cold Blood* and in *Capote*, Perry Smith is seen with works by Henry David Thoreau. The intent to portray Smith as a thoughtful person, even an intellectual, should be obvious. While this portrait of Smith is a bit heavy-handed, the issue of IQ is by no means irrelevant to the issue of psychopathy. Studies have shown that a high percentage of violent psychopaths have a low IQ. One might claim that Perry Smith's intelligence contradicts this data, proving that more intelligent psychopaths can be just as vicious as the less so. One might, however, also use this claim as one piece of evidence in the argument that Perry Smith was probably not a psychopath.

How would those who contended that Smith was a psychopath interpret his academic tendencies? One way would be to interpret Smith's acts as civil disobedience. A proposed defense of Timothy McVeigh in the Oklahoma City Bombings included citations of Thoreau's *Civil Disobedience* and likened McVeigh to John Brown. The lines between intranational terrorism, civil disobedience, and psychopathy are certainly blurred and, at the very least, far from mutually exclusive. If Smith's case is taken to be similar, his avid reading ceases to be such an impressive intellectual feat; it is possibly the case of a psychopath frantically searching for a convincing defense at his next appeal.

There are a few important factors to keep in mind when distinguishing psychopathy from civil disobedience. Psychopaths are not necessarily criminals, whereas civil disobedience, by definition, involves illegal activity. Neither psychopathic behavior nor civil disobedience necessarily involves violent action. Illegal activity on the part of a psychopath is often the result of lack of internal control and lack of emotion. But perhaps most importantly, a psychopath may be goal-directed in his illegal activity, but will rationalize the situation only after the fact. Civil disobedience involves antecedent beliefs, rational thought, and purposeful action, certainly supported by more emotion than the average psychopath possesses. Here is where the argument that Smith was searching for a civil disobedience defense falls apart. Both Hickock and Smith admitted that their only premeditated action involved finding the Clutter family safe and escaping with the money. If murder had not been part of the original plan, construing the murders as a commentary on social injustice would have been, to say the least, far-fetched.

The alternative was that Smith was an intellectual, sensitive to and thoughtful about many complex issues. Truman Capote, when describing his interactions with Smith, noted his particular taste for philosophers George Santayana and Thoreau. The choice of these philosophers should not be taken as mere coincidence. Both write on intensely personal, ethical issues. Perry Smith was not reading *Civil Disobedience* as had been suggested. Instead he was reading *On Man and Nature*, the emotional and spiritual depth of which seems an unlikely topic of interest for an emotionally shallow psychopath. Actual interpretation of the content of Santayana and Thoreau's works, though, remains unclear. Santayana and Thoreau both emphasize that there is no universal good; they encourage free spirits. This again appears to be material Smith might have used to justify his actions. Santayana is probably most famous for arguing that human good is finite. The limiting mark of a person's goodness does not depend on some fixed standard, but instead on the conditions of one's environment. Rather than looking for justification for his actions, Perry Smith probably sought only an explanation. He desired to know, in a more personal way than any psychologist, how the deeply emotional person he thought himself to be could commit an action that would become known only as one of the most famous instances of cold-blooded murder in history.

Conclusions gained from Smith's reading, as opposed to his behavior, are obviously limited. As Truman Capote provided personal insight into Smith's character, a certain narrative distance was maintained. Capote provided an account that, until the moment he died, Smith was allegedly quoting the likes of Thoreau and Santayana. The director of Kansas state penal institutions at the time of Smith's execution, provided first-hand confirmation. More than a cold-blooded killer searching for reprieve in an intellectual loophole, the prison official said that Smith was a deeply thoughtful and caring person. In both *In Cold Blood* and *Capote*, Smith is often seen in or on the verge of tears. These moments seem unbelievable because they are cast so perfectly as dramatic moments in a novel or film. But the director again confirmed that these stories, as perfectly theatrical as they may be, were true. If his reading habits and his thoughtful conversation about ethics are alone insufficient to prove Perry Smith's emotional depth, perhaps they are sufficient proof in tandem with deeply emotional behavior.

As a novelist who was merely after details for his story, should Capote have been allowed so many private meetings with Perry Smith?

Capote should not have been allowed to tamper so much with the legal proceedings surrounding the Clutter case. Truman Capote visited Perry Smith and Richard Hickock as an author with an agenda, to produce a great literary work. He was not allowed into their jail cells in any legal capacity and actually had no business interfering in the case's legal proceedings as he was not a legal representative for either one of the murderers. It seemed that his friendship was a ploy for personal gain. It was not out of friendship that he funded the new lawyers who negotiated the appeal. This gesture of kindness was a stall tactic, so that he could receive further information while the executions were postponed, not once, but several times.

Through persistence and manipulation, Capote was allowed many hours inside the jail cell of Perry Smith, and was able to probe the depths of his mind and largely influence the path his case took. An uneducated and vulnerable drifter, Perry Smith was at the mercy of Capote's influence and his lawyer's success. Hickock had fallen out of his previous position of power, no family members surfaced to offer Smith support throughout the trial, and even Capote began to wane in his devotion once the appeals threatened to prevent the execution. In fact, Capote withdrew support from the case after the lawyers got a new appeal, for if the executions did not occur, Capote knew his novel's ending would not be as successful, and his book's value would decline substantially.

Truman Capote

Why did Truman Capote become so fascinated by the murders?

Around the time of the Clutter murders, Truman Capote had been experimenting with a new kind of writing, which he termed the non-fiction novel. With this style he hoped to unify the precise factuality of non-fiction with the dramatic theatricality of the novel. Therefore when he read of the quadruple slayings in Holcomb, he recognized the opportunity to play the role of investigative journalist, much like the private eye of the contemporaneous film noir genre. Murder, being dangerous, dark, and sexy, made for the ideal theme of this new writing.

Capote's intelligence was legendary; he scored two hundred fifteen on an IQ test administered in high school. Many wondered why such a formidable intellect would be attracted to such a gruesome scene. A philosopher and historian offered one explanation when he conjectured that intelligence might be evil. Another possible explanation was that Capote regarded the criminal mind as constituting one of the foremost engaging mysteries of his time. Insight into what caused Smith and Hickock to kill that night might be intractably difficult, but it would had a tremendously worthwhile payoff, as understanding and predicting criminal behavior would save society from much harm. Undoubtedly Capote recognized the many possibilities an investigation of the criminal mind would present.

How did Capote use his upbringing to further the research and writing of In Cold Blood?

Capote was born in 1924, and was raised mainly by poor relatives in Monroeville, Alabama, because his parents neglected him. His father, Arch, was frequently otherwise occupied, concocting one get-rich-quick scheme after another. His mother, Lillie Mae, was deeply embarrassed by Truman's girlish ways and so distanced herself from him, devoting less attention to him than to her quest for social prominence. This campaign turned out to be astonishingly successful. Changing her name to Nina, Lillie Mae divorced Arch, wed a Cuban businessman named Capote, and ended up living on Park Avenue in New York City. This social climbing life took its toll. Capote's mother was an alcoholic, and she committed suicide in 1954.

It appeared that Capote emphasized and embellished his own unhappy childhood to create a bond with Perry Smith, whose early years were traumatic. Capote used the fact that his mother was alcoholic to bond with Perry Smith whose mother was also an alcoholic. Capote may well have felt a genuine connection between himself and Perry because of the similar tribulations of their childhoods, but it is clear that Capote intentionally played these up so that Smith would feel a bond with him and would therefore be more likely to open up to him. Capote's plan worked and Smith wound up telling Capote everything he needed to know to write a best-selling book.

How did writing In Cold Blood *affect Truman Capote?*

Writing any story about the murder can be life altering for an author. Imagine spending years of one's life immersed in the details and events surrounding the deaths of innocent people. For most nonpsychopathic individuals, the process of putting all the emotion, action, loss, gore, and cruelty of murder into writing is a draining process. That is the process that Truman Capote undertook when writing *In Cold Blood*, except that the events he penned were real. In fact, they were unfolding as he wrote the book. The process of researching, communicating closely with Perry Smith, and recording his understanding of the situation had a tremendous effect on Capote's life that manifested itself in a variety of manners.

Capote first began the writing process with a rather aloof attitude about the murders he had read about in the paper. He initially addressed the police chief in charge of the case by saying that he did not care much about the victims; he just wanted to know about the killings and killers. Capote wanted fodder for an exciting best-selling novel, and he was not afraid to make sure people knew that. This attitude prevailed for much of the writing process and often surfaced to dominate his actions, but things became slightly different when Perry Smith and Richard Hickock were apprehended.

Truman Capote immediately became fascinated with Perry Smith and saw him as containing the wealth of information necessary to write his book. Capote had never interacted with a murderer before. He was probably surprised by what he encountered. Expecting to find an unsympathetic brute, he instead witnessed a scared, ashamed man asking for medication for a painful leg injury. Intrigued by how such a disconnect existed not only between Hickock and Smith, but also between his expectations and Smith, Capote began formulating his novel based on regular, intimate discussions with Perry Smith. From this time onward, Capote exhibited a shocking dual identity.

On a superficial level, Capote grew quite fond of Smith and spent a lot of time catering to his needs and desires. He helped Smith be productive in prison and found him lawyers to help with some of his appeals. It seemed that by meeting Perry Smith and spending time with him, Capote's initial detachment from the story dissolved and he began to sympathize with the criminal. On the other hand, Capote proved that he grew even more disconnected from the personal story of the crime when discussing the writing process with his editor and his closest friends. He helped Smith get a lawyer in order to get more information from him and later he wanted Smith quickly executed so that could finish the novel. To his friends, this was a new side of Capote. He had always been blunt, but wishing death upon another for selfish reasons was quite extreme.

Writing the novel dominated Capote's entire life and it seemed to his friends that all he ever spoke about during this time period was the case. Capote's relationship with his own partner became increasingly strained during this period when he was rarely home, repeatedly cancelled vacations, and single-mindedly focused on the case, which marred even the little bit of time they spent together.

Capote drank heavily during the writing of the book and also had a drug problem. He was so consumed by the subject matter of the book that he showed little regard for the lives and achievements of those close to him. At unrelated parties and events, such as the premiere party for *To Kill A Mockingbird*, an important event for the author, his friend Harper Lee, he spoke only about himself, complaining bitterly about his book-related troubles. He showed a similar lack of concern when his partner's book was published. It is likely that Capote had an innately selfish, narcissistic personality and tended always to talk a lot about himself but the writing and research for *In Cold Blood* dramatically exacerbated this. The execution of Perry Smith had a seemingly strong impact on Capote. He was seriously worn out after having spent six years of his life on the case but he also seemed to have been depressed by Smith's death. By the end of the case and the book, he was in such a profound depression that he could not even get out of bed. It is clear that writing the book wreaked havoc on Capote's mental health.

However, one final, severe shift occurred in Capote's perspective while he worked to finish *In Cold Blood*. He traveled to witness the execution of Smith and Hickock. In his last interaction with Smith before his death, Capote broke down in apparently genuine fashion. It is difficult to infer what exactly caused those tears, but they were likely a combination of guilt over his selfishness and the realization that he truly cared about the individual who was going to die. It may even have been possible in his capacity as a showman to fake the act, but there is no motive to tell lies to someone who will die shortly. Furthermore, after witnessing the hanging and finishing *In Cold Blood*, Capote dealt with depression and alcoholism. When the book was published, it was very successful and Capote received much praise and fame. He had written two other successful novels before *In Cold Blood*, *Breakfast at Tiffany's* and *Other Voices, Other Rooms*. But *In Cold Blood* catapulted him to even greater level of recognition and also made him a wealthy man. He was paid an estimated two million dollars in immediate magazine, book and film payments. In this respect, *In Cold Blood* affected Capote positively. Yet his life began to go progressively downhill. During the years after *In Cold Blood* was published, Capote consumed increasing quantities of tranquilizers with alcohol. His writing also began deteriorating, and by the middle of the 1970s he was doing virtually no writing at all. His drinking spun out of control and he made headlines when he fell off a stage, drunk, while giving a speech in 1977. Capote died on August 26, 1984, of liver disease complicated by phlebitis and multiple drug intoxication. It is impossible to know whether his psychologically and emotionally taxing work caused his drug and alcohol problems but it is certainly likely that it was a major contributing factor.

Without the help of an autobiography, it is nearly impossible to speculate on what plagued him for so many years. It could have been guilt over Smith's death or how he abused his relationship with Smith. Perhaps it was simply the powerful nature of writing the novel on the subject. He might have been confused about the conflicting feelings surrounding the murders because he liked Perry Smith as a person, but could not forget that he had killed the Clutter family.

Why did Truman Capote reveal personal stories to people he had recently met?

In many ways Truman Capote was a narcissist. He cared primarily about himself and his goals, which is exemplified by his relationship with his partner as well as his relationship with Perry Smith. Capote manipulated even his friends to get them to do or say what he wanted. In Kansas, Capote seized every opportunity to take advantage of the persons closest to the Clutter family and to the investigation in order to manipulate them. He did this to create the best story he could. One method of getting the interviewees to open up was to relate to them. Though he appeared open, Capote seemed disconnected from the people he relied on. But by relating a personal story to the person he was interviewing, Capote was able to make this person feel more comfortable in discussing with him what happened. He used his personal stories to get information for his novel. Capote realized that relating personal stories, regardless of their degree of truth, enables people to develop a relationship even with someone they do not know. In gathering material for his novel, Capote was able to relate to townspeople, law enforcement officials, and to Smith himself in order to learn the full details of the night the Clutters were murdered, what led up to the killings and what happened afterwards. While those who surrounded him in Kansas were very different from those with whom he associated in New York, Capote's capacity for story telling served him well as he investigated the murders and wrote his novel.

Why did Perry Smith choose to confide in Capote?

In *Capote*, Smith and Hickock seemed quite adamant against speaking to anyone about the murder after they had been captured, convicted, and incarcerated. While Hickock was still vocal and obnoxious to the wardens and to anyone willing to speak to him, Smith remained relatively mute, speaking only when necessary, and appearing very unresponsive and unfriendly. When Capote first met Smith, Smith seemed sullen-faced and in pain, and did not respond to Capote's attempts at small talk. He only spoke to ask Capote if he had any painkillers for his headache. This interaction differed markedly from their interaction years later, where Smith considered Capote his only friend and requested that he be present at his execution. Capote was able to get Smith to confide in him by making him feel that he truly cared about him, when no one else did, and that Capote had Smith's best interest in mind. Smith felt that Capote was the only person that truly cared for him and therefore revealed his thoughts to Capote.

Capote manipulated Smith to speak to him during interactions in the local jail. Capote often surprised Smith by bringing him painkillers. This act pleased Smith because it showed him that there was someone out there who actually listened to his concerns, kept him in mind, and took the effort to get him what he needed. Another instance when Smith felt that Capote aided him when no one else would was when Capote visited Smith at the federal prison one month after Smith and Hickock had been sentenced to death. Smith had not eaten or spoken to anyone for a month. When Capote arrived, Smith was bedridden and very near death. Since Smith could not eat solid food, Capote bought baby food and hand fed him. Capote nursed Smith back to health. In a sense, Smith felt that Capote saved his life. Beyond this, Smith felt that Capote was earnestly fighting to save his life and believed that Capote was making a real effort to overturn Smith and Hickock's death sentence by hiring lawyers to appeal it. To Smith, Capote appeared to be a savior, and Smith might have felt obligated to reciprocate Capote's generosity by responding to his questions and revealing his life.

Smith might have also confided in Capote because of Capote's status. Capote was a world-renowned writer. He could be anywhere and with anyone in the world, but in Smith's mind, Capote chose to be with him when he visited him. Smith felt honored, and perhaps he felt obligated to speak to this important man. Furthermore, Capote also revealed personal facts about his own life, and again Smith might have felt he needed to reciprocate. Finally, Smith might have wanted to talk to Capote so that he could tell his story. Here was Capote, a well-renowned writer who was offering to write a story about Smith and Hickock.

Therefore, Smith might have confided in Capote completely out of his own volition and out of his own desire for fame.

What methods and strategies did Capote use to get Smith to talk to him?

Capote manipulated Smith and was able to get him to speak by making Smith feel obligated to reciprocate his actions. Capote went out of his way to save Smith's life, first by visiting him at the prison and nursing him back to life, then by offering to appeal Smith and Hickock's death sentence by paying for a lawyer. Because Capote gave him so much, Smith felt obligated to repay him in some way. Since Capote wanted Smith to reveal his past and his thoughts, Smith felt obligated to do so.

Smith also admired Capote, and he did not want to disappoint him. Therefore, he tried to please him in every way, in large part by talking to Capote, revealing details about the murder. Capote made a point to emphasize his own importance, making Smith understand how lucky he was to have Capote's time. Capote oftentimes mentioned how he could be at certain functions, meeting certain famous people, but instead he chose to be with Smith.

Capote also confided in Smith, leading Smith to believe that Capote considered him his close friend. Capote made Smith feel special and unique. This again made Smith feel obligated to open up to his best friend. Even though Smith considered Capote his only true friend, Capote certainly did not feel the same way about Smith. Capote only used these tactics to manipulate Smith into giving him facts and ideas for the book that he was going to write. However, he could not tell Smith that he was merely using him. Therefore, he had to lie to him about how he actually viewed Smith and Hickock. For example, Capote would not tell Smith that the title of the book was *In Cold Blood*. Though Capote had promised that Smith and Hickock would be able to tell their true story through the book, Capote lied to Smith in order to get him to continue revealing details so that he could write his book.

Why did Truman Capote take a special liking to Perry Smith?

Besides interviewing Perry Smith so he could write *In Cold Blood*, Truman Capote took a special liking to Smith because Capote could relate to Smith, felt sorry for Smith, and may have been in love with him. Truman Capote was a very flamboyant, eccentric and open homosexual, who had experienced a troubled and rough youth. He was never shown any love by his parents and was a very lonely individual. Capote's mother constantly complained that he was not masculine enough for a male. Perry Smith had a difficult childhood that was marked by his parents' divorce, a criminal record, placement in multiple foster homes and detention centers, his mother's death, and being a victim of sexual and physical assault. Capote was well aware of Smith's disruptive and disordered childhood and could not only relate to Smith but also felt some compassion and sympathy for him. Partly as a result of this, Capote was nice and open with Smith. And they shared a similar experience at moving out on their own. Both Capote and Smith left home at early ages to pursue their careers. Capote began working at the *The New Yorker* at age seventeen, while Smith enrolled in the Merchant Marines at sixteen. They both grew up without much parental guidance and had to learn to take care of themselves.

As a result of being candid with and close to Smith, Capote obtained a great deal of valuable information from Smith about the murders that Smith and Hickock committed. Capote would often spend hours at a time sitting and talking to Smith. Some have suggested that Smith and Hickock were homosexual lovers and that once incarcerated Smith then became a lover of Capote. FBI agent Harold Nye claimed that Capote bribed prison guards with large sums of money and ordered them to give him extra time in the cellblock with Smith and ordered the prison guards to go around the corner whenever he visited Smith. It was alleged that this was when sexual activity between Smith and Capote took place. Smith and Hickock spent five years in jail before they were executed, giving Smith and Capote a considerable amount of time to get to know each other and to develop a firm relationship.

Undoubtedly Capote also took an extra liking to Smith because Smith was willing to reveal more about the murders than Hickock, and because Smith was considered to be the one who killed the family. Smith was lonely in jail and needed a friend. Smith felt guilty about his actions and needed to tell someone about it to relieve himself. Capote was the friend whom Smith could confine in. By being specially nice to Smith, Capote was able to get the entire account of the murders. In one sense Truman Capote saw a mirror image of himself in Perry Smith. Both were men interested in intellectual matters and from troubled childhoods. As Capote at one point suggested, it happened that he took the better path in life while Smith took the worse one.

Was Truman Capote's friendship with Perry Smith genuine?

Truman Capote was most likely not being entirely genuine in his interactions with Perry Smith. This is apparent because of the many contradictions in

Capote's comments to Smith. For example, Capote stubbornly maintained that he had no title for his book, even after Smith discovered that the title was *In Cold Blood*. At various points in their visitations, Capote assured Smith that he would defend his reputation, while he was simultaneously painting a chilling picture of psychopathy. He humored Smith by discussing literature with him, even as he presented Smith's lack of education to the world in his book. And late in the lives of Smith and Hickock, Capote claimed he was searching for a lawyer for their appeal, when he was in fact doing no such thing.

Capote had compelling reasons to take a contradictory attitude towards the killers. On the one hand, he had a vision of a new kind of literature that he was to invent, a type of journalism that would appeal more directly to the senses and the emotions. The image of Smith and Hickock as cold-blooded killers fit perfectly into this model of writing. The reader would be drawn into the criminal minds of the killers, which Capote documented very vividly. It would not be a pretty picture, but Capote needed to win their trust and affection if he was to coax them into divulging their stories. As a journalist, Capote knew the value of a first-hand narrative in reporting. Therefore he sought to befriend Smith and Hickock rather than to grill them in an antagonistic fashion. He lied to them about his true intentions to win their favor. Capote was glib, untruthful, and manipulative towards Smith. He told Smith what Smith wanted to hear, and later when Smith was reluctant to give Capote details about the murders, Capote resorted to emotional blackmail to get the material he needed. Capote's empathy for Smith seemed to extend only so long as Smith did not interfere with Capote's goal. Smith was the topic Capote chose for his literary endeavor. Had the case not presented Capote with such an opportunity, Capote would never have bothered to befriend Smith.

Eventually, the conflict of interest became too great for Capote. As the killers awaited hanging, they begged him for help to stave off the inevitable. Capote, who made empty promises to them, increasingly avoided contact with them. On the one hand, he wanted to be perceived as an authentic friend, but on the other hand, he really wanted them to die so he could finish his book. As this conflict intensified, Capote descended into an alcoholic depression.

On some level, Capote probably did come to care for Smith and Hickock. They bared their souls to him, however twisted those souls might have been. As evidenced by his eventual breakdown, Capote did feel some compassion for these criminals. Capote's initial motivation to get close to Smith was entirely selfish. He saw an opportunity and he took advantage of his position to exploit it. Later, he may have started to see Smith as a person instead of as a possible bestseller, but his behavior towards Smith remained questionable. Much of Capote's behavior towards Smith could be considered psychopathic in nature. Some of his behavior showed genuine emotional attachment, but in the end Capote placed the goal of finishing his book over any attachment he felt for Smith.

Did Truman Capote maliciously use Perry Smith for his own benefit or were his priorities simply naively ordered?

Truman Capote was using the entire situation of the Clutter family murder to write a book, make money, and gain further notoriety and immortality. There was clearly a deep, personal interest in the subject matter, but Capote knew that writing a story about murders and the killers' lives was a unique and promising line of work. What contributed to the success of the material was the fact that Capote was able to interact privately with Perry Smith on a regular basis. He was able to form a trusting relationship with the killer, who sat in prison awaiting execution. Smith was a lonely person in his life. He had a dysfunctional family; his mother was an alcoholic and his father rejected him for his failures. Truman Capote gave him the companionship that he had not felt in a very long time. Smith embraced the enthusiasm with which Capote visited him and asked about his life story. No one had ever been so interested in him before, and because he was in a very difficult position with his hanging imminent, he clung to every bit of hope that Capote brought him.

Capote was not afraid to admit to his friends that the purpose of his visits was to gather information in order to author his nonfiction story of the Clutter family murders. Smith, too, knew that Capote was writing a book about the situation, but because of Capote's friendly demeanor, Smith believed that the book was about the injustices done to him by the criminal justice system. In essence, Smith misconstrued his newly found friend as a warrior for the rights of the accused who would write a powerful report calling for Smith's death sentence to be reconsidered. Capote kept this idea alive by initially finding Smith new lawyers to appeal his case and to prolong execution. Unbeknown to Smith, Capote was admittedly doing this in order to spend more time with Smith and to extend research for his novel. Capote told Smith that he cared about him and that he wanted him to live, but he was not afraid to tell others that he simply needed more time to uncover material for the novel.

The motive for Capote's lying to Perry Smith appeared not to be to protect Smith from being hurt about the reality of his situation but to give him a false sense of security so that he would volunteer more information. At one point, Smith found out that the title of the book Capote was writing was *In Cold Blood*.

Such a title clearly connoted a negative view of the criminals, which ran counter to Smith's preconceptions about the work. Capote smoothly laid the blame on the publishers and said that the title was not his own and that it would change. That lie assured Smith that someone was still on his side, but Capote's motive for the lie was that he had not finished gathering information from Smith and needed the criminal to remain on pleasant terms in order to continue the investigation. Taken in this light, Capote's use of Perry Smith was psychopathic in nature. Capote manipulated him, lied to him, and abused their relationship in order to achieve selfish goals. In one sense it is difficult to label the use of Smith as malicious because Capote's selfish acts worked simultaneously to make the inmate happy and feel loved in a time of need. For a while both Smith and Capote derived benefit from the falsehood.

When Capote had finally retrieved all the information he needed, however, he abandoned the relationship he had formed with Smith. Then he only wanted Smith executed so that he could finish the book. He stopped communicating with Smith. One cannot accurately conclude whether Capote felt guilty about doing that, but it was extremely hurtful to Smith. Like a true psychopath, Capote got what he needed and then left.

Why did Capote experience an intense wave of emotion following the news that Perry Smith and Richard Hickock had lost their final appeal?

This question is particularly perplexing in light of Capote's behavior prior to the news that Hickock and Smith were to be executed. Capote received multiple telegraphs from the pair of prisoners requesting that he assist them in finding a lawyer, but he did not respond to their messages, let alone assist them. His reasons for ignoring the cries for help were selfish. He needed an ending for his book and knew the only way he could find this closure was if the two men died. His decision not to help Smith and Hickock was motivated by this need. In the past, Capote's intervention in finding the men a lawyer had helped to extend their lives. Therefore, Capote knew well that he was capable of assisting the men and in not doing so, he was playing an integral part in their deaths. With this information, it was surprising for Capote to be devastated by the news of their upcoming execution.

From this perspective, it is possible that Capote's wave of emotion arose from a sense of guilt or responsibility for not answering Smith's frequent requests for support. Having been abandoned by most of his remaining family, Smith's connection to Capote was an extremely important element of his life in prison.

Capote failed Smith where a family member or good friend would have helped. It is possible that Capote realized his selfishness in not hiring a lawyer in order to finish his book.

On the other hand, Capote's expression of grief may have been insincere. Throughout their time together, Capote constantly lied to Smith in order to give the impression that he was a caring friend who had Smith's interests in mind, as when he told Smith that he had not yet chosen a title for his book and then continued to lie after Smith confronted him. Capote took advantage of Smith's vulnerability on numerous occasions, which cast doubt on the sincerity of his investment in their relationship. From this perspective, it appeared that Capote's sadness was a face-saving mechanism in which he seemed to feel anguish in order be consistent with his façade as a loyal friend. Capote's insistence that he did everything in his power to help them was obviously not the case and should lead one to question Capote's sincerity.

Yet it might be possible that Capote's tears were at least partially genuine. He disclosed to many of his friends that he felt a strong sense of connection to Smith. If one chose to believe him, then it could be that he felt a tremendous loss once the execution date of Smith and Hickock was final.

The novel

Did In Cold Blood *change the public's view of Hickock and Smith?*

By the time *In Cold Blood* was published, Hickock and Smith had already been dead for just under a year. The Kansas family murder was a very high profile case that drew enormous media coverage and attention. Although Capote was initially interested in turning the story into another news article, he felt that he would use the story to create a nonfiction novel, which is what he did. His research took five years. Having interviewed the murderers and the townspeople of Holcomb, Kansas, and all the relevant participants in the entire case, and having attended court hearings, and followed police investigations and the appeals process, Capote had assembled about eight thousand pages of research over those years. Because of the extensive media coverage that had occurred by the time *In Cold Blood* was released, many members of the public were aware of details of the case. But in writing his book, Capote had carefully chosen which details of the story to include. His close relationship with the murderers allowed him to portray Hickock and Smith as in a deeper and more full fashion than a mere recital of their ruthless crimes would allow. In discussing many details about their personalities, backgrounds, and lifestyles, and while not diminishing the viciousness of their crimes or stating any of his own opinions directly, Capote was able to portray the killers as humans whose unfortunate life experiences played a significant role in their crimes. To the public, *In Cold Blood* seemed to trace a series of unfortunate circumstances that occurred not only to the Clutter family, but also to the murderers.

To what extent, then, was Capote a psychopath?

At one point in the film *Capote*, the author said to his friend Harper Lee that he felt that he and Perry Smith grew up in the same house but he went out the front door and Smith went out the back door. It may not be too much to add, though he does not, that Smith went through the trap door, while Capote opened the door to destructive behavior and personal deterioration. At another point Capote said to Lee that he could not have done anything to save Smith and Hickock and she responded by pointing out to him the truth as she saw it, that he simply did not want to save them. In his grandiosity about his invention of an entirely new form of writing, his manipulativeness in Kansas and beyond, his selfish use of Smith and others, his lying to Smith about the book itself, his shallow affect toward the end of the killers' lives, and his failure to accept any personal responsibility for his failure to try to help delay or prevent execution, he exhibited the emotional characteristics of a psychopath. While he had been successful before the book and the book brought him even greater levels of success, his failures afterward, in his increased substance abuse, his deteriorated relations with others, and his failure to complete another writing project characterized an individual with an increasingly unstable lifestyle. Whether that fits the behavioral characteristics of the psychopath may be a matter for some conjecture. But there is enough to suggest that Capote was at least a partial nonconventional psychopath who was using two more conventional psychopaths for his own personal ends. And yet the influence of his book for over half a century demonstrates the benefits that can flow from that interactional psychopathy.

Notes about sources

This case study relied on Truman Capote's *In Cold Blood* and the initial film based on it, directed by Richard Brooks. It also benefited from the film *Capote*, directed by Bennett Miller, and the book on which it was based, *Capote: A Biography* by Gerald Clarke; from materials at *crimelibrary.com*, and in *the New York Times* and the *Lawrence Journal-World* and other news media; and from commentaries on the books and the films and the events that informed them.

Kenneth Lay, Jeffrey Skilling, Andrew Fastow, and Enron

Nonconventional white-collar criminals, those who helped them, and a corporation that failed

Enron's rise

In July 1985, Enron was born through a merger between two natural gas pipeline giants, Internorth Inc. and Houston Natural Gas Corporation. The merger resulted in the creation of the longest pipeline network in America. Kenneth Lay was the chairman of the Houston Natural Gas Corporation and played a critical role in bringing about the merger between the two natural gas companies. In 1986, after the creation of Enron, he was named its chairman and chief executive officer.

Early in 1987, problems at Enron started appearing. Despite the possibility that some executives at Enron had engaged in financial wrongdoing at Enron's oil-trading unit in Valhalla, New York, Kenneth Lay allowed them to stay at the company. After several months, the same executives committed a number of illegal acts that cost the company about a billion dollars worth of losses. As of April 2006, prosecutors argued that they should be permitted to present evidence concerning the Valhalla scandal in order to demonstrate that Lay had a pattern of tolerating financial wrongdoing.

Before Jeffrey K. Skilling arrived to work for Enron in 1988, he was a senior partner at McKinsey & Company. At McKinsey, Skilling managed the company's energy business and also consulted Enron as a client in natural gas trading. Skilling was fascinated by the workings of market systems and was especially interested in the creation of new systems.

Andrew Fastow was hired in 1990 by Skilling to be the manager of Enron's new finance division. Fastow was an expert in the booming business of structured finance. Companies used this technique to acquire new capital by selling off parts of the companies' risk through off-books dealings and partnerships.

In 1993, Sherron Watkins, who would become a key figure in the case against Enron, joined the company.

Enron's persistent efforts in lobbying for deregulation led Congress to pass legislation opening up electricity sales to marketers. Not long after, Enron was among the first companies to receive official approval from Congress to sell electricity at market rates. In 1994, Enron began trading electricity and quickly took control of the American energy market.

In 1996, Skilling was named the president and chief operating officer, making him second-in-command at Enron. Since joining Enron, Skilling had huge financial successes in trading natural gas and electricity. The unit's labor force increased from two hundred employees to two thousand.

Its revenues likewise skyrocketed from two billion dollars to seven billion dollars. By 1996, Fastow was committing crimes through off-book financial dealings for personal profit.

In its bid to gain national recognition as the country's dominant electricity retailer, Enron advertised itself during the 1997 Super Bowl. That same year, Fastow created Chewco, a partnership that sought to buy the University of California's stake in a joint venture called JEDI. However, Chewco circumvented several of the requirements necessary for these deals to be put on its ledgers and removed from Enron's books. This was the first of many similar financial maneuvers to conceal debt and exaggerate profits which led to Enron's final collapse.

In 1998, Enron's financial foundation began to weaken as a result of several business ventures, such as an effort in the water business and the purchase of an electricity plant in Brazil. These ended in huge losses for the company.

After careful deliberation of internal and external candidates, Fastow was named chief financial officer of Enron in 1998. In 1999, Enron's board of directors set aside the matter of conflicts of interest and permitted Fastow to continue off-the-books partnerships with companies that did business with Enron.

Many believed that around 1999, Enron began to employ complicated accounting techniques in order to maintain its high share price and raise investments. The purpose was to keep the public impression of Enron as a reputable and thriving company for as long as possible.

In 1999, Fastow created a partnership with LJM. The alleged reason was to buy Enron's weak assets, but the true motive was to hide Enron's increasing debt and continue to exaggerate its profits. Enron's board of directors continued to allow Fastow to be its chief financial officer while he also headed other companies that were financially invested in Enron. Two persons were assigned to oversee the company's financial interests in such deals, Richard Causey, chief accounting officer, and Rick Buy, chief risk officer.

Enron's decline

In 2000, California suffered from an energy shortage that caused the price of electricity to skyrocket. Enron profited immensely from this situation. Enron was eventually accused of being responsible for the shortage.

On February 12, 2001, Lay left his position as chief executive of Enron and Skilling took his place. On August 14, Skilling resigned, citing personal reasons. Lay became chief executive again. The next day Sherron Watkins, one of Enron's vice presidents, contacted Kenneth Lay after noticing irregularities in Enron's accounting practices. Watkins met with Lay on August 22 and restated her concerns. Meanwhile, Enron's stock prices began to fall. Several deals designed by Fastow to hide Enron's massive losses were supported by Enron's stock. With prices falling, those deals began to unravel. On October 16, Enron's partnerships could no longer support the losses and Enron reported a loss of six hundred eighteen million dollars. A few days later, on October 22, Enron announced that the Securities and Exchange Commission had begun to investigate the situation. Two days later, Fastow was removed from his position. Lay spent the last few days of October requesting help from government officials, but his efforts produced no results. On November 9, Enron's board and the board of Dynergy, one of Enron's main competitors, agreed to a merger. By November 20, Enron's stock, which had once reached a high of ninety dollars a share, was down to less than seven dollars. Dynergy called off the merger on November 28. Enron ran out of options. On December 2, 2001, Enron filed for bankruptcy protection.

On January 9, 2002, the Justice Department formed a task force to investigate Enron's collapse. A few weeks later, on January 23, Kenneth Lay resigned from Enron. On February 2, a report from Enron's board implicated several executives in manipulating the company's profits. On August 21, Michael Kopper, one of Fastow's aides, pled guilty to money laundering and gave evidence against Fastow. Fastow was finally arrested on October second. He faced charges of money laundering, fraud, and conspiracy.

On February 5, 2002, Cliff Baxter, Enron's former vice chairman, committed suicide. Also in 2002, Arthur Anderson was charged with obstruction of justice for destroying documents relevant to the Enron scandal.

On May 1, 2003, eleven of Enron's executives and Fastow's wife were arrested for assisting Fastow. On September 10, Ben Glisan, Enron's treasurer, pled guilty to fraud. With evidence mounting against him, Fastow pled guilty and was sentenced to ten years in prison. On January 22, 2004, Richard Causey, another executive implicated in the conspiracy, pled not guilty. On February 19, Skilling was indicted and he pled guilty to thirty-five charges. On July 18, Kenneth Lay was indicted and pled not guilty. On December 28, 2005, Richard Causey agreed to testify against Skilling and Lay in exchange for a reduced sentence.

On January 30, 2006, Lay and Skilling's trial began. On March 28, the prosecution finished presenting its case and the defense began to present counterarguments. On May 25, 2006, both Skilling and Lay were convicted. Both faced possible sentences of over twenty years in prison. On July 5, 2006, Lay died of a heart attack.

The major players

Kenneth Lay

Kenneth Lay was indicted on July 7, 2004 by a grand jury in Houston, Texas, for a total of eleven counts, including securities and wire fraud, making false statements, and misleading the public and Enron investors. Lay was chairman and chief executive officer of the Enron Corporation from 1986 to 2002. He was an integral part of the merger that created Enron and was at the helm of the corporation when it sank. He is accused of earning hundreds of millions of dollars by dumping shares in Enron's highly inflated stock, selling before investors and other shareholders caught wind of Enron's actual dilapidated state. All the while he convinced them to have confidence in the company.

Lay grew up in rural Missouri, son of Omer Lay, owner of a general store. Omer however had the unfortunate habit of gambling the family's savings on entrepreneurial escapades, like the buying and selling of chickens. One particular gamble failed miserably and left the Lay family with little more than their religion and their dreams. Young Ken Lay helped make ends meet by working any odd job he could find. Eventually the family moved to Columbia, Missouri, so the eldest daughter, who was attending the University of Missouri, could live at home. Lay too would attend the University of Missouri, where he enthusiastically discovered the field of economics and how to make money.

Out of college, equipped with a master's degree in economics, Lay was eager to start working. He took an economist job with a company that would later become part of Exxon and began to climb the ranks in the pipeline industry. As the Vietnam War was waged in the 1960s, Lay felt compelled to join Navy's officer candidate school in Rhode Island. He then became an economist for the Pentagon, analyzing the economic effects of military spending. Thereafter, he would take several senior positions at pipeline companies such as Florida Gas, Transco, and Houston Natural Gas. He did some impressive work with Transco and revolutionized the industry by introducing a spot market for gas. These achievements, however, were meager in comparison to the merger he initiated between Houston Natural Gas and InterNorth, the merger that would form Enron.

Lay led the company until 2001, helping it become a top rated American enterprise. By 1999 Enron was the world's largest energy trader with foreign investments and assets valued at over twenty billion dollars. In December 2000, Enron reported that it had tripled its revenues since 1998. Lay handed the chief executive officer title to Jeffrey Skilling in February 2001. Soon thereafter, blaming California's rolling blackouts, Enron shocked the world by reporting a loss of six hundred thirty-eight billion dollars in the third quarter of the fiscal year. Internal turmoil and increasing pressure from the Securities and Exchange Commission saw Enron stock prices plunge. Suddenly, one of the world's most formidable companies was filing for the largest Chapter 11 bankruptcy protection in U.S. history.

Lay faced charges for his role in what is now understood to be something more than a business venture gone badly. The case against Lay relied heavily on the fact that he was chief executive officer. Lay knew that things were going poorly for Enron, the government claimed, but helped officers Skilling and Fastow cover up losses from investors and lied about the company's status. Lay contended that he was in fact the victim, for he was unaware of the mischievous deeds of Andy Fastow, Enron's chief financial officer.

Fastow testified that he had briefed Lay, who reclaimed the chief executive officer position after Skilling's short term, about the off balance partnerships he had created. He testified that he had informed Lay that even if Enron performed outstandingly and they did not make any mistakes, he could not imagine the company surviving the next five years. He claimed that Lay, knowing the poor condition of Enron, asserted to investors that Enron was stronger than ever, thus misleading them.

On May 25, 2006, a jury found Lay guilty on all counts. He died of a heart attack before he received his sentence.

Ken Lay seemed rather unlike the typical psychopath. He was indeed ambitious, a driven man with innovative ways to succeed in the pipeline industry. But his ambition seemed to clearly stem from his meager background. Of all the players accused in the indictment, Lay seemed the most genuine. He has been described as kind, cordial, and even grandfatherly. When he addressed the public after his arrest, the sorrow he expressed about Enron's collapse seemed heartfelt. Enron was his creation and career's work. Lay's testy and combative attitude during his trial, however, blemished his reputation. Analysts said that Lay's actions in court were more typical of Skilling's behavior than of his own. Some might interpret Lay's not guilty plea and subsequent blaming of Fastow and Skilling as shifting the responsibility, a characteristic common in psychopaths. It is unlikely that Ken Lay would have scored very high if clinically tested for antisocial personality disorder or psychopathy, but certain aspects of his personality and behavior certainly contributed to Enron's total psychological profile.

Jeffrey Skilling

Jeffrey Skilling was destined for big things in life and a bright future. The man who would become chief executive officer of Enron was born on November 25, 1953, in Pittsburgh, Pennsylvania. He was the second of four children. While growing up in Aurora, Illinois, Skilling was very ambitious and at age thirteen he became the chief production director for a public access cable television station. After graduating from West Aurora High School, Skilling enrolled in Southern Methodist University where he earned a bachelor's degree in applied science in 1975. Four years later, he earned a Masters of Business Administration degree from Harvard Business School. Skilling was a very bright and highly motivated student, graduating in the top five percent of his class. After graduating, Skilling was hired as a consultant in the energy and chemical division for McKinsey & Company, an impressive first appointment.

In 1987, while working with Enron as a McKinsey consultant, Skilling impressed Enron chief executive officer Kenneth Lay so much that Lay offered him a job. Skilling became the chairman and chief executive officer of the Enron Finance Corporation in 1990. Skilling also became a close friend of Lay. Skilling continued to work hard and worked his way up the Enron ladder. In 1997, Skilling was named president and chief operating officer of Enron. On February 12, 2001, Skilling was named chief executive officer of Enron. As chief executive officer, he verbally assaulted analysts and was faulted for his strange accounting practices. Skilling would not last long as a chief executive officer. He abruptly resigned from his post on August 14, 2001, citing personal reasons, and then quickly sold all his Enron shares, which had a net worth of sixty million dollars. In November 2001, Enron declared bankruptcy. The collapse of Enron meant that investors, employees, and anyone else who had a share in Enron lost most or all of their money and savings. The amount of money lost was estimated to be in the billions.

Skilling and other high-ranking Enron executives were charged with several counts of fraud and insider trading. Skilling faced dozens of counts for fraud, insider trading, and related crimes. He pled not guilty to these charges. He was found guilty on nineteen counts, and was found not guilty on nine other counts.

Jeffrey Skilling was an interesting psychological case. He came from a humble background and through hard work was able to make millions of dollars. He appeared to be a psychopath as well as a greedy liar. Once Skilling came into a lot of money, he seemed to have lost control and became driven by money and greed. In April 2004, he had a breakdown in New York City. After a night of excessive alcohol consumption, Skilling began screaming and running up to people on the streets whom he claimed were FBI agents. He then began ripping open their clothes to reveal their supposed wires. This breakdown was probably due to all of the pressure and stress that Skilling faced at the time.

Skilling possessed the traits of a corporate psychopath. He was manipulative, glib, superficial, egocentric, shallow, and impulsive, and he lacked guilt, remorse and empathy. Skilling had the nerve to ruin thousands of people's lives by committing insider trading and fraud. Billions of dollars were lost overnight, including retirement and life savings. Furthermore Skilling claimed to be innocent and said he was the victim. Since Skilling was a high executive at Enron, he knew that illegal business practices were going on and could have easily stopped or reported them. Instead, he became so carried away that he could not stop his illegal activities. In court Skilling told lie after lie. Convicted nonetheless, he faced decades in prison.

Andrew Fastow

Andrew Fastow was Enron's chief financial officer. He was born in Washington, D.C. and raised in the upper-middle-class town of New Providence, New Jersey. He was student council president at his high school, and some classmates remembered him as an intelligent person who relied on his winning smile. In contrast, one teacher at his high school remembered him as a slacker who tried to talk him into giving higher grades, and another teacher thought he was not genuine and often used his smile as a tool to get what he wanted. As an undergraduate, he attended Tufts University, where he studied Chinese and economics. He nearly failed Chinese as a freshman, but a semester in Taiwan helped him to improve the next year. Fastow earned his masters of business administration degree at Northwestern University's Kellogg School of Management. Few of his classmates at either university remembered him.

He married Lea Weingarten, whom he met at Tufts. Her family was prominent in Houston, where they had constructed a supermarket and real estate empire. Fastow and his wife raised two sons. In the early 1990s, they worked together in Enron's finance division before she left to concentrate on parenting. At the time Enron collapsed, they were building a multi-million-dollar mansion and Fastow often drove his Porsche around. They were known around town as collectors of modern art and as donors to museums. Fastow was also active at his synagogue.

At Enron, he was much more successful as a number cruncher than as a manager. Colleagues did not like him, and they viewed him as a Skilling crony. While Fastow put on a charming persona for those outside he the company, Enron employees viewed him as a difficult person who would not hesitate to banish someone from his division or publicly lay into someone with an expletive-laced tirade. In 1997, he hired a personal image consultant to assist him about his attire and the image he projected. He wore double-breasted suits and designer ties, which stood in stark contrast to the khakis and polo shirts preferred by most Enron employees. One company executive said he looked like a gangster. He also took other steps to dominate office politics and cow others. Once, he wrote some complex equations on a board near his office, but privately admitted to another executive that he had copied them from a textbook and written them on the board to intimidate others. When the Enron scandal became known, Fastow's friends worried about the enormous amount of time he spent watching news reports and obsessing about the fallout.

Skilling hired him in the 1980s from Continental Illinois, which had collapsed in one of the largest bank failures in history. Skilling was probably attracted to Fastow's experience in asset securitization, a practice that sold off risk by exploiting the special purpose entities that became one of the hallmarks of Enron's malfeasance. Beginning in 1993, Fastow was responsible for engineering the special purpose entities that absorbed Enron's debt and therefore removed it from the company's ledgers. He and colleagues whose support he needed enjoyed enormous returns on their personal investments in those special purpose entities. In 1996, he became managing director of Enron Energy Services but did a poor job, so Skilling had to move him back to finance. In 1997 and 1998, before becoming Enron's chief financial officer, he headed Enron Capital Management. Michael Kopper was Fastow's chief deputy.

In 2000, Fastow set up Chewco, which was a partnership consisting of Enron employees. Chewco hid losses through deceptive listing of assets in their books, which in turn allowed Enron to overstate its earnings by one billion dollars between 2000 and 2001. Richard Buy, Enron's chief risk manager, apparently challenged Fastow's deals, and as a result, Buy was essentially removed from his post.

Fastow was fired on October 24, 2001, as Enron's collapse was attracting publicity. At a congressional committee hearing, he declined to testify and invoked his privilege against self-incrimination. In 2002, he was indicted on seventy-eight federal charges related to fraud. At the time, the government portrayed him as the man who defrauded Enron, rather than a person who worked with other Enron executives to defraud employees and stockholders. In 2004, he pled guilty to two counts and agreed to a sentence of ten years in prison in exchange for cooperation in prosecuting other former Enron employees. His wife also exchanged a plea of guilty to tax fraud for a lenient five-month prison sentence.

Fastow certainly exhibited some psychopathic traits. His grandiose sense of self-worth was reflected in his attire, his treatment of others, and his spending habits. His obsession with the scandal might also have reflected this characteristic. His unempathic personality was clear from his complete lack of compunction about making others feel awful. Outside the Enron setting, where his closeness with Skilling did not make him immune from attack, he attempted to win people over with his charm and smile which some thought was superficial. In a business with many very bright employees, he resorted to artifice to cover up his deficiencies in intelligence. And he also unapologetically defrauded people of millions of dollars through dishonest business maneuvers. He was sentenced to six years in prison.

Cliff Baxter

In the predawn hours of February 25, 2002, former vice chairman of the Enron Corporation, Cliff Baxter, shot and killed himself in his Mercedes Benz just outside his affluent neighborhood in Houston, Texas. Months earlier, Baxter resigned from his position as vice chairman and reentered as a consultant but not before selling Enron stock worth nearly thirty-five million dollars. At the time of his death, Baxter, forty-three years old, was happily married with two young children, all of whom enjoyed a comfortable lifestyle in their mansion. Baxter was described by friends as an outgoing and generous man who donated to charities and cared deeply about what people thought of him. Others noted his qualities as a ruthless negotiator with an air of arrogance around the office. Some suggested that Baxter's frequent mood swings resulted from an undiagnosed case of bipolar disorder, which was manifested as severe depression in the days preceding his suicide.

Baxter came from humble beginnings. He was one of six children born to his police officer father and mother who worked as a planning clerk. The family lived in a small home on Long Island. After graduating from New York University,

Baxter spent several years in the Air Force, followed by matriculation at Columbia Business School. He was a successful student, graduating at the top in his class, and he landed several jobs in finance and investment banking before moving into Enron in 1991. At Enron he quickly befriended Jeff Skilling, the man who would eventually become the president and chief executive officer of Enron. The two men rose through the company's ranks together. Baxter became vice chairman in the fall of 2000.

After Enron's troubles became public knowledge in November 2001, Baxter and several other senior company officials were named as defendants in a lawsuit filed by shareholders in the U.S. District Court in Houston. The lawsuit accused the top executives of conspiring to withhold information about the failing company from the public, as well as with profiting from the company's inflated stock price while concealing the true state of affairs from its shareholders.

Sherron Watkins named Baxter as a key whistleblower in the Enron scandal, stating that Baxter and complained openly about the company's corrupt business practices to Skilling. Baxter was subpoenaed by a Senate subcommittee the week before his death to provide testimony and documents that would possibly flesh out the details of the Enron scandal. It appeared that Baxter would have been a useful witness in the trial; having openly protested against Skilling's financial endeavors, Baxter evidently had a significant amount of knowledge regarding the inside cover-ups.

Baxter ended his life before any of his knowledge made it into court. The suicide note found beside his body testified to the immense guilt and sense of failure that plagued Baxter once the Enron scandal broke. Having dedicated an entire decade of his life building Enron, Baxter was overcome by his role in the demise of the company and the resultant financial and job loss that afflicted thousands. Unlike an ordinary incident of street crime, the events at Enron touched an enormous population. Many said that the weight of his remorse for those individuals is what brought Baxter to take his own life.

However, others insist that Baxter was a man obsessed with reputation. As Skilling would later remark in court, Baxter believed that the accusations against him and the company were comparable to being labeled as a child molester. He believed his image was forever tainted, and Baxter could not live with that possibility.

With Cliff Baxter's death, many questions remain unanswered. For instance, if Baxter had been as vocal with his protests against the corrupt financial behavior of other Enron officials as he had claimed to be, then why was action against Enron not taken sooner? It could be that Baxter was shaped into a martyr by the media following his suicide, and that Baxter was not as disturbed by Enron's misconduct as was claimed by Watkins. Although he had an agenda of his own, Skilling did contend that Watkins' description of Baxter's protests was exaggerated.

As far as a diagnosis of psychopathy, there was nothing to indicate that Baxter behaved in ways consistent with Hare's or Cleckley's descriptions. He may have been arrogant or reputation-obsessed, but he was otherwise a caring and loving husband and father who experienced a range of normal human emotions. However, it does appear that at times Baxter experienced unhealthy extremes of some of these typical emotions. The description of Baxter as having mood swings points to the possibility that he instead suffered from a mood disorder. While it is likely that Baxter suffered from a mental illness, there appears to be no evidence to support a diagnosis of psychopathy.

The smaller players

Many people were responsible for Enron's success as a corporation, as well as its complete failure as an upright company. Brought in and hired by the top executives, it is likely the smaller players were hired for those qualities they shared in common with their bosses. The blame might have been spread in every direction and in varying degrees, but each of these people had a hand in the dishonest business schemes Enron was conducting. In this next section, each man examined individually seemed upstanding to some extent. They came from honest backgrounds, were highly intelligent, and proved themselves to be extremely hardworking individuals. Perhaps the only hint of psychopathy that each man brought to the company was the shallow affect which allowed them to act so irresponsibly. Once the people began earning a living that was difficult to comprehend, it seemed their sense of self-worth and entitlement only escalated with their compensation. Enron's returns propagated their lying and the manipulation, and they became parasites of the company, with no remorse or guilt. In this capacity, these successful, white-collar businessmen were able to carry the Enron Corporation to psychopathic proportions.

Ken Rice

Ken Rice was chief executive officer of Enron Broadband Services, a subsidiary unit of Enron. In this position he used accounting tricks and he deceived investors about the company's financial status. Even when it was known throughout the company that its technology development had stagnated, he claimed they were thriving. He adored Ferraris. In July 2004, he pleaded guilty to securities fraud and agreed to cooperate with prosecutors in the investigation of Lay, Skilling, and Fastow. He had made fifty-three million dollars selling overestimated Enron stock in 2000, fourteen million of which was surrendered to the Justice Department.

Lou Pai

Lou Pai had been called an enigmatic genius by admirers. In 2001, he walked away with over three hundred fifty-three million dollars, bailing out of Enron before the devastation hit. This amounted to more than that of Lay, Skilling, and Fastow combined. He became chief executive officer of Enron Energy Services in 1997. His seventy-seven-thousand-acre ranch in Colorado became a focus of dispute, as local Hispanics claimed the land as their birthright.

Rick Causey

Rick Causey was Enron's executive vice president and chief accounting officer. In this capacity he signed off on many special purpose entities, which were smaller subsidiary companies that absorbed Enron's massive debt. Prosecutors alleged that he oversaw numerous shady contracts to manipulate Enron's reported earnings. More specifically, they claimed that he fraudulently altered Enron's merchant asset portfolio, finessed Enron's business segment reporting to conceal losses, and manipulated reserves. He initially denied any wrongdoing, until finally he pleaded guilty to charges of wire fraud and conspiracy in December of 2005 and received a prison sentence of five to seven years.

Rick Buy

Rick Buy was chief risk officer at Enron until he was fired in February 2002. An internal report released that month to review Enron's failures blamed Buy for failing to review deals that were illegal. Before Congress and in trials, he refused to testify, invoking his Fifth Amendment privilege against self-incrimination.

Michael Kopper

Michael Kopper was originally from Long Island, New York. He majored in economics at Duke University and received a graduate degree at the London School of Economics. He was working for the Toronto Dominion Bank when he was offered a job by Enron in 1994. After joining Enron, Kopper quickly became friends with Fastow and his wife Lea. By 1997, Kopper was in charge of Fastow's special projects group.

Kopper was gay, but Fastow could not have cared less. Within Enron, Kopper was known as a jet setter and a lover of fashion who preferred Prada suits. He was also viewed as greedy. Someone who knew him said all the money in the world was not enough for him. Kopper was not well known in the company but many who knew him disliked him greatly. They said that he did Fastow's bidding and that he was difficult to work with and temperamental. Some believe that it was Kopper, not Fastow, who was the brains behind Enron's faulty balance sheets. Kopper and Fastow also allegedly aided three British bankers in defrauding their employer, National Westminster Bank PLC, out of over seven million dollars. Kopper and his domestic partner, William D. Dodson, made a reported ten and a half million dollars based on a one hundred and twenty-five thousand dollar investment in a partnership called Chewco. Kopper left the company in June 2001.

Kopper pled guilty on August 21, 2002 to federal conspiracy and money laundering charges related to Enron's fall. He then agreed to give up twelve million dollars in illegal profits. Kopper admitted he ran or helped create several partnerships that earned him and others millions of dollars, including kickbacks he funneled to Fastow, while hiding debt and inflating profits at Enron. He cooperated with prosecutors but declined to testify before Congress.

Ben Glisan

Ben Glisan grew up in a working class neighborhood outside of Houston. He majored in finance at the University of Texas and graduated in 1988. He returned to the University of Texas for his masters of business administration degree, maintaining a perfect grade-point average. After graduation he joined Coopers & Lybrand in Dallas, and in January 1995, Glisan accepted a position at the accounting Firm Arthur Andersen in Houston. He was then recruited to work for Enron as an accountant. When he first joined Enron he seemed to get along with everyone. He was not arrogant and did not have an attitude. He seemed much unlike Fastow and Kopper. However, some have said that he was not mature enough to report or try to stop something unethical that was occurring. After some time at Enron, though, his personality changed. He became extremely arrogant and when he did not get his way he would be terrible to those around him.

Glisan became Enron treasurer in March 2000, and earned one million dollars in May of that year on a March investment of five thousand eight hundred twenty-six dollars in Fastow's Southampton Place partnership. Glisan worked with Fastow and Kopper in creating and running LJM2. Glisan also negotiated for Enron in many of their transactions with special purpose entities, which were the subsidiary companies that absorbed Enron's debt. He was fired from Enron in November 2001 and was indicted in April 2003 on charges of money laundering, wire fraud, and conspiracy to commit wire fraud, among others. He tried to make a deal with prosecutors. He pled guilty to one count of conspiracy in September 2003. He was sentenced to prison for five years. He was the first former Enron executive to serve time. He started to cooperate with prosecutors in 2004.

Greg Whalley

Greg Whalley was the former Enron president and chief operating officer of Enron. He became President after Skilling left the company. He resigned on January 28, 2002. Whalley joined Enron in 1992. He attended the United States Military Academy where he received his bachelor's degree in economics in 1984. He then spent six years serving as an Army tank captain in Kentucky and Germany. He left the Army and enrolled in Stanford Graduate School of Business where he received his masters in business administration degree in 1992.

After his graduation from Stanford he joined Enron as an associate. Those who knew him then said that he had intelligence and incredible confidence, which were two of the most important characteristics an Enron employee could be endowed with. Others referred to Whalley as a natural trader. Some of the people who knew him thought he was a jerk: he said whatever came into his head, no matter how terrible or insulting. Those who did not like him said he was immature and arrogant. His job title changed and he rose to a top executive post, where he was known as the man who controlled the traders. His favorite book was *The Fountainhead* by Ayn Rand, which exalts individual achievement and drive over the will of the group. Whalley, much like the traders, was able to strip his decision making of all the emotional content which, in his view, did not contribute to economic growth. Whalley instilled a relentlessly mercenary attitude on the trading floor.

Whalley was described by those he worked with, including Skilling, as incredibly smart. Others describe him as someone people wanted to follow. The traders liked and respected him and many have said they would have done anything for him. Soon after Whalley was promoted to president of Enron, he realized the depth of the company's financial problems. He fired Fastow without formal board approval. Since the collapse of Enron, Whalley has been sued by investors and questioned many times by federal investigators. After leaving Enron in early 2002, he secured a job at Centaurus Energy, a Houston hedge fund founded by John Arnold who worked for Whalley at Enron.

Tim Belden

Tim Belden received a master's degree in public policy from the University of California, Berkeley, and then spent five years working as a researcher at the Lawrence Berkeley National Laboratory, where he coauthored papers on energy markets. He came to Enron in 1997. He did not seem to fit the profile of an Enron trader; his associates called him a tree hugger because of his appearance and because he rode his bike to work. However, Belden was a leading electricity trader. He believed in the beauty of free markets and he had no qualms about exploiting inefficiencies to make money. Those in the industry viewed Belden as very knowledgeable, but he sometimes liked to embarrass and frazzle others. Greg Whalley quickly noticed Belden and within eighteen months he became Enron's vice president. It was Belden's idea to take advantage of the deregulation of California's energy market. He is considered the mastermind of Enron's scheme to drive up California's energy prices. In these schemes Enron bought California power at capped cheap prices, routed it outside the state, and then sold it back into California at inflated prices. He pled guilty to a federal conspiracy charge in October 2002. He admitted to one count of conspiracy to commit wire fraud and promised to cooperate with prosecutors and any non-criminal effort to investigate the energy industry. He stated that he committed these crimes because he wanted to maximize Enron's profits.

The whistleblowers

Whether or not they acted upon it, many of Enron's employees were aware that something within their business was not right. While Sherron Watkins may have stayed and profited from the company longer than she should have, she was one employee who was sure something was wrong, and whom the public came to know as the Enron whistleblower. Bethany McLean, who worked outside the company, was quick to discover that Enron's practice was not adding up to its profits. As a journalist with a background on Wall Street, despite what Enron executives told her, McLean had the facts and knew they needed exposure. Both women in this next section played a large part in unveiling the corrupt explanations for Enron's undeserved success.

Sherron Watkins

Sherron Watkins grew up in the Houston suburb of Tomball. She was the daughter of two middle school teachers. She attended the local Lutheran school through eighth grade then attended public high school, where she was a member of the drill team and a member of the National Honor Society. After high school, Watkins enrolled at the University of Texas, where she took her mother's advice and studied accounting. She graduated in 1981, and received a master's degree the following year, after which she went to work for Arthur Andersen, an accounting firm.

Ms. Watkins was hired through an Enron recruitment program and began work in late 1993, when she managed Enron's portfolio of energy related investments. She transferred to Enron's international group in 1997 where she focused on mergers and acquisition of energy assets. From early 2000 to June of 2001, Watkins worked on Enron's broadband unit then went back to work for Andrew Fastow, aiding again in mergers and acquisitions, this time as Enron's vice president of corporate development. Watkins was not one of the top Enron executives who made millions from the company.

On the surface, Sherron Watkins seemed satisfied enough with her job and content in her comfortable life that it was possible she would close her eyes and not see what was happening at Enron. However, while looking for assets to sell off for the company, she discovered Enron had been covering up significant losses by some of its equity investments. Thus, as the loyal person her brother describes, she decided to speak up.

After nearly a decade of working at Enron, Watkins was fearful of approaching then-chief executive officer Jeffrey Skilling with what she had discovered. Once Skilling resigned on August 14, 2001, Enron Chairman Kenneth Lay invited employees to submit questions. That was when Watkins wrote a now famous six-page anonymous memo to Lay on August 22, 2001, that described the accounting hoax. In her letter, she compared Enron's actions to robbing a bank one year and trying to pay it back two years later. She believed it simply could not be done.

The letter was released in its entirety five months later, on January 15, 2002. Watkins soon found herself cast as the hero in the Enron scandal. Sherron Watkins became a role model as a woman who had stood up to corporate hierarchy and for stockholders' rights. However, it is possible that Watkins was not prepared for what this meant to the company's future or her own.

The term whistleblower originated from the time when someone would spot a criminal robbing a bank and blow a whistle to alert the police. More generally, a whistle blower is someone who alerts the public of illegalities in the work place. However, Watkins merely wrote a memo to the person committing the illegality, Ken Lay, suggesting that he stop before he was caught. If Watkins were a true whistle blower, she would have submitted her detailed memo to someone who would publicize what was going on behind Enron's doors.

Technically, we do not know if Watkins ever intended for her letter to be a public document. One might wonder is why Watkins did not go public with her information. In her letter, Watkins wondered if Enron had become a risky place to work, but she nonetheless kept her job for more than another year until her resignation in November 2002. She even outlasted Lay and the employees at Arthur Andersen.

Watkins' actions actually provided cover for Kenneth Lay and others at Enron. The *New York Times* noted that Watkins' warning to Lay presumed he knew nothing and needed to be warned, which significantly strengthened Lay's legal defense. Even in her testimony, Watkins continued to provide cover for Lay and placed greater blame on Arthur Andersen. Watkins testified that she overheard Fastow telling Lay that he wanted her fired. It is thus possible that Watkins protected Lay because he protected her from losing her job.

Watkins' friends described her as loyal, articulate, and thoughtful, and comment that she always spoke her mind. A friend of Watkins from work, Uhl, said that Watkins was the right person to confront the company because she had the skill and had also worked at Arthur Andersen. Uhl and others agreed that Watkins was a strong female who was acting on her convictions.

Meanwhile, Skilling's lawyer, Ron Woods, painted Sherron Watkins as an opportunist. In 1997, at the age of thirty-seven, Watkins was married and in 1999 she had a baby and bought a new house valued at over half a million dollars. She also bought a Lexus. It is possible that her memo is a manifestation of this opportunism. After Watkins reported her accusations to Lay she moved into a bigger office. Perhaps she expected a raise or other perquisites to keep her quiet. However, the other possibility is that Watkins was truly acting on conscience and was hoping to give Lay a way to resolve Enron's problems quickly and quietly without drawing addition scrutiny to the company.

Watkins resigned from Enron in November 2002. *Time* magazine named Watkins, along with two other female whistleblowers, as its 2002 Persons of the Year. *Time* claimed they deserved the distinction because they not only recognized what was right and true, but also acted on it. Watkins also received numerous other honors for her actions.

Sherron Watkins co-wrote a book, *Power Failure: The Inside Story of the Collapse of Enron*, that was published in 2003. She made a living lecturing around the country on the subject of Enron and the erosion of trust in this country's capitalist system. She charged anywhere from twenty to thirty thousand dollars per speech. In these lectures throughout North America and Europe, Watkins shared her experiences of working at Enron and her opinion of what went wrong. She also discussed the importance of ethics in leadership, the distrust in work settings, and how to recognize corporate problems.

Bethany McLean

Bethany McLean, co-author of *Enron: The Smartest Guys in the Room*, worked as a business journalist for *Fortune* magazine. McLean is best known as the first journalist to raise questions about Enron's business practices. Her article wondering if Enron were overpriced questioned its soaring stock price, and ran prior to further speculation that would lead to the company's eventual bankruptcy and grave legal troubles.

McLean was inundated with questions and spoke on many occasions about the position she takes in her book. She claimed that the outcome of the trial was marginal in the telling of the larger story, which had more to do with the people involved and less with the actual numbers and financial details. McLean certainly did not allow the company's complex financial schemes and transactions to cloud the real people who made conscious decisions to run their business in this manner. Whether Kenneth Lay and Jeffrey Skilling were criminally guilty, their morals failed and they were ethically guilty for cheating others in Enron's brazen manipulation tactics.

Prior to working for *Fortune* magazine, McLean was an investment analyst on Wall Street. She spent three years at Goldman Sachs immediately after college. Jim Chanos, a close friend of McLean, first brought up the idea of covering Enron, suggesting she take a closer look at what the company was doing. At the time, she knew that Enron was an innovative company based purely on its reputation. McLean had no idea she would soon discover how innovative its employees really were.

Upon looking into Enron, McLean first noticed a general unwillingness by its employees to say anything on the record. People described Enron as a black box, for example, but would not comment further on exactly what this meant, or why they feared divulging anything further. Outside sources commented on Enron's business in California, claiming that the company was either losing or gaining a great deal of money, and that whatever the situation was, Enron would find a way to hide it, as the company always did.

A former investment analyst, McLean was almost immediately able to notice the fact that Enron's results did not add up. Their earning per share produced great numbers on Wall Street, but their operations were negative, and the company's return on capital was a mere seven percent.

In a telephone interview with Jeffrey Skilling, McLean raised these very matters. She reported that Skilling became irate, calling her ignorant and unethical for asking such questions. Skilling reportedly told McLean that had she done her homework, she would have realized how silly her questions were, as the company's practices were perfectly clear and understandable.

McLean said that her one reservation was that Skilling's argument might have had merit. Perhaps she did not understand the extent of their business and nothing was wrong. Repeatedly, she was told that nothing was amiss and often grew intimidated when these successful business executives called her ignorant. Their argument, however, was merely that McLean was misinformed, and they explained nothing further. Eventually, McLean began to question herself as well. She figured if the accountants and board directors were signing off on the company's business, how could anything be wrong.

When the company's bankruptcy was finally announced and missteps were accounted for, she believed the rest of the answers would follow easily in her interviews with employees. Instead, she found that no one thought they were doing anything wrong. The higher-ups in the firm were far from remorseful. They would offer explanations saying that they treated others as they wished to be treated themselves, never tolerating abuse or disrespectful behavior. But McLean found that their words did not matter. The actions of those in Enron's upper echelons set the standard for all those below. She described it as a culture in which reported earnings were all that mattered, not economic reality.

Ultimately it was never a case of Enron employees setting out to do bad things. The root of the problem was that everyone in the company had failed to do the right thing. McLean found Kenneth Lay to be an entirely unsympathetic character who was willing to make a great amount of money, but never willing to take professional responsibility for those earnings. McLean believed he was the most extreme example of the self-delusion that plagued Enron. Lay was not alone; everyone blamed someone else.

Questioned on her opinion as to whether Kenneth Lay, Jeffrey Skilling, and Andrew Fastow would act in this same manner were they to come together in a different setting, McLean said their personality characteristics might have made it possible. Between Lay's volatile attitude, Skilling's intelligence and proclivity to gamble, and Fastow's complete aversion to risk, it seemed that given the chance to strike again, with the right amount of power and enough people working under them, these men would not harbor many reservations.

Employees and shareholders

Enron had an interesting arrangement in which most of its employees were shareholders of the company's stock. Its employees can be divided into two groups: the first consisted of a small percentage of employees, namely a handful of top executives and a number of traders, who were heavily involved in illegal trading and therefore profited from the wrongdoings; the second group comprised the rest of the employees who were honest people either oblivious to all the wrongdoings that occurred or uninvolved. This section will explain how Enron's executives and top employees were able to conceal their wrongdoings from the rest of the employees and shareholders, and the effect of Enron's bankruptcy on shareholders. Enron's employees and shareholders contributed to the environment that allowed this fraud to occur. The unethical employees and executives demonstrated many psychopathic tendencies such as lying, cheating, and manipulation that led them to participate in insider trading and other unethical business deals. They had a grandiose sense of self, believing that they were above the law and everyone else. The executives were very charming as well since they were able to create an environment that made employees believe that Enron was garnering huge profits when this was not the fact. Finally, psychopaths cannot commit crimes without victims, and the employees who ended up losing most of their retirement savings exhibited traits of victims of psychopaths, such as gullibility. The psychopathic behavior of executives and a small number of traders combined with the gullibility of the rest of the employees and shareholders created an environment that allowed fraud and unethical behavior to occur without scrutiny.

Enron's employees were required to enter into a retirement 401(k) plan that poured a large portion of their funds into the company's stock. Stocks rose to an all-time high of ninety dollars by August 2000. When allegations surfaced in October 2001 of accounting irregularities, Enron executives issued a complete lock-down on buying and selling stocks for eleven business days in order to change record keepers for their retirement plan. During that period, stocks dropped from thirteen dollars and eighty-one cents to nine dollars and ninety-eight cents a share. It was reported that top Enron executives sold their Enron stocks during this period, even though they publicly encouraged their employees to keep their stocks in Enron; they also promised that their stocks would rebound. When Enron filed for Chapter 11 bankruptcy, its stocks were worth less than a dollar a share. Many employees who were shareholders were left with almost nothing in their retirement plan. Shareholders felt betrayed by Enron executives. Following the bankruptcy, a lawsuit was filed against current and former company executives and directors and against Enron's auditor, Arthur Andersen, on behalf of the shareholders. It was expected that shareholders would receive nothing in return, because Chapter 11 bankruptcy protects businesses that are dissolving from such lawsuits. Even if some funds were recovered, the money would go to Enron's creditors, JPMorgan Chase and Citigroup.

The employees were the unsuspecting victims of Enron executives, who were calling all the shots. The employees were suggestible, and somewhat in denial. One secretary noted that she knew that the company was not making money overall, but she was willing to overlook that because she was caught up in Enron's culture of extravagant spending. Enron executives used this method to keep up the appearance that Enron was doing well. For example, Enron planned to throw a Christmas party costing one and a half million dollars in 2001. At company workshops, executives brought in elephants and horses. Enron executives knew how to keep up appearances while they were defrauding consumers behind their back. Executives obviously knew what they were doing, lied about it, and tried to cover up their wrongdoings. Employees and shareholders trusted in their executives and in the extravagant image that executives were cultivating. This made employees and shareholders more susceptible to exploitation by Enron.

Not all of Enron's employees lost all of their funds. In November 2001, six hundred employees who were considered most critical to Enron's operation received more than one hundred million dollars in bonuses. These employees and shareholders were probably the traders heavily involved in the wrongdoing. Several traders were recorded on tape fully acknowledging what they were doing, that they had agreements with energy companies in California to shut down California's energy in order to raise the prices of energy stock.

Cleckley noted that psychopaths are unreliable, untruthful, and insincere. The Enron executives obviously exhibited these traits when they lied to their employees about the stocks rebounding while they themselves sold their stocks. These executives exhibited superficial charm and intelligence as well. They were very smart to be able to manipulate so many individuals without being caught for a long time, and they must have been quite charming to convince so many people. The employees who were heavily involved in the wrongdoing exhibited psychopathic tendencies as well, since they stole from people remorselessly; one trader was caught on tape viciously stating that he did not mind taking money from people like Grandma Millie. They also exhibited traits that psychopathy expert Dr. Robert Hare considered psychopathic, such as pathological lying, conning, and grandiose sense of self-worth. These individuals thought that they were entitled to taking money from other individuals, demonstrating that they did not value other people.

Financial and legal institutions

Many financial and legal institutions were implicated in the Enron scandal. Without these firms to aid Enron in obtaining funds and to conceal its debt, Enron would not have been able to engage in all its illegal activity. Banks, for example, provided Enron with credit to conceal its debt, law firms approved Enron's transactions when there was much fraudulent activity present, and accounting firms such as Arthur Andersen helped conceal Enron's losses. For the banks and law firms, only few of the individuals who handled Enron's transactions were psychopathic. Even so, these institutions created a culture that implicitly supported such behavior, and therefore one should consider these institutions as a whole when considering their psychopathic dispositions. This section provides an overview of financial and legal institutions involved with Enron, and then focus on Enron's accounting firm, Arthur Andersen, tracing its heavily publicized trial to its dissolution. The last portion attempts to identify psychopathic traits in these institutions.

The banks

Bankers from a large number of prominent banks, including Canadian Imperial Bank of Commerce, Bank America, Barclays Banks, and Deutsche Bank, among others, were involved in insider trading and a variety of deceptive transactions that allowed Enron to disguise its losses as gains. Of these institutions, JPMorgan Chase and Citigroup were Enron's largest creditors. Using a tactic called prepay, the two banks helped Enron cultivate approximately nine billion dollars in the ten years prior to the collapse. Prepay transactions simply allowed Enron to borrow money, which was actually debt, and label it as revenue from its operations. This tool of deception masked the enormous losses Enron was incurring. For their services, Enron paid a combined three hundred million dollars to JPMorgan Chase and Citigroup over the final five years before the collapse.

The government had evidence of this corruption and possessed the ability to end the banks' existences like it had done to Arthur Andersen, but such action would have had significant collateral damage. No only did the government not want to disband more large companies and all their employees and shareholders, but also it did not have a clear-cut case against anybody. Only a few bankers handled the Enron transaction, so prosecuting an entire bank would have been overkill. Furthermore, the specific bankers involved with Enron actually did nothing legally wrong. Their actions were deliberately unethical, but the ground rules allowed for prepays. So instead of spending years battling over ethics and intention, JPMorgan Chase and Citigroup paid a combined two hundred eighty-six million dollars to settle charges for facilitating the Enron fraud. Although the criminal charges were dismissed, civil suits in the aftermath of the collapse may continue to surface for years.

The law firms

Two law firms, Houston's Vinson & Elkins and Chicago's Kirkland & Ellis, were accused of taking part in Enron's fraud. The media paid more attention to Enron's local connection, Vinson & Elkins. The case against the law firm was far from concrete. It was difficult to blame a law firm for financial disasters when banks and other investment institutions were involved, and Vinson & Elkins held that all its dealing with Enron were ethical and professional.

Perhaps most damning for Vinson & Elkins were the opinion letters it wrote. Opinion letters are issued by law firms to certify that business transactions satisfy certain legal criteria. For instance, an opinion letter may attest to the fact that legal business transactions are being made between two separate entities. These letters are commonly used by auditors and rating agencies in order to approve accounting for certain deals or to reassure lenders that the two groups would be treated independently in the case of bankruptcy. In the case of Enron, the company did business with a large number of other entities in which Enron held large stakes, so Vinson & Elkins wrote opinion letters that essentially gave its legal blessings to the transactions.

It was these dealings with a variety of connected institutions that allowed Enron to give a false impression of profit and strength while it lost billions of dollars. Without the opinion letters flowing from the law firms, Enron would not have been able to continue its unethical transactions. If Vinson & Elkins attorneys knew about the fraudulence of the transactions when they authored the opinion letters, they could have been implicated in Enron's criminal and psychopathic behavior.

The Arthur Andersen trial

Arthur Andersen was one of the big five accounting firms from 1998 to 2002. Arthur Andersen was founded in 1913, and some have said that it engaged in fraudulent activity as early as 1950. There was also evidence of scandals having occurred in the 1980s, including accusations involving some of Arthur Andersen's major clients. One client, Sunbeam, artificially boosted revenues by bribing retailers to buy in excess of their demand. Andersen allegedly paid one hundred ten million dollars to prevent its investors from divulging information about fake audits. Andersen also signed off on grossly inaccurate books from Waste Management, Inc. Between 1991 and 1997, in addition to auditing fees of about eight million dollars, Waste Management paid Andersen eighteen million dollars for their services in aiding their accounting fraud. Bad behavior early in life might have made Arthur Andersen a candidate for conduct disorder, the *Diagnostic Manual*'s requisite precondition to psychopathy.

Andersen's relationship with Enron began in 1986. Arthur Andersen had an office at Enron headquarters in Houston, with a staff of about one hundred fifty, making the office about as large as many of Andersen's regional offices. Yet Enron still accounted for very little of Andersen's revenues, less than one percent. In contrast, Enron made up about seven percent of Vinson & Elkins's revenue. Why, then, was Andersen's stake in Enron so high? Despite the low contribution to overall revenue, Enron was Andersen's biggest client, at about forty-nine million dollars. This was, however, only a partial explanation. The other piece of the explanation involves the fact that Andersen began to invest more power in local offices during the 1990s. While Andersen as a whole probably had no unusual interest in the company, Enron was everything to this local office, headed by David Duncan. Perhaps Andersen could make a case for multiple personalities.

The fraudulent activity from here might have pointed to Enron's creation of a series of special-purpose entities, including Chewco, LJM1, LJM2, and Raptor I, II, III, and IV. These entities were technically off-books companies and were used to hide the company's debt. Andersen signed off on accounting reports that included all of these fraudulent entities. One might try to argue that Andersen signed off on reports including such entities without knowing that they were, in fact, fake. Unfortunately for a supporter of such a position, there was Carl Bass, a partner at Andersen's Professional Standards Group. In one LJM2 transaction, known as Fishtail, Bass realized that more than just the name of the deal involved something fishy. For example, JPMorgan Chase was listed as an investor, though it was not actually providing any money. Andersen removed Bass from review of Enron activities. Andersen's signing off on fraudulent activity might have pointed to ignorance or poor accounting. But Andersen's disciplining an employee who uncovered fraudulent activity first-hand pointed to nothing but corruption.

In 2002, Arthur Andersen was charged with obstruction of justice. The charge, surprisingly, did not involve any of the activity mentioned above. Instead, the charges revolved around Andersen's destruction of Enron-related documents during a federal investigation. Despite citing a company policy for general housekeeping and destruction of excess documentation, Andersen was convicted by a jury in Texas District Court. After the trial, the jurors said they agreed that Nancy Temple was the corrupt agent that made their decision easy. Temple was an Andersen attorney who sent an e-mail to executives, conveniently reminding them of company policy about destruction of excess documents. Many prosecutors thought such commentary might have made the success of an Andersen appeal less likely. An appeal to the United States Court of Appeals for the Fifth Circuit indeed upheld the District Court ruling against Andersen.

Andersen finally appealed to the U.S. Supreme Court. The appeal centered on a point of law. Rather than argue whether Andersen actually obstructed justice, the debate revolved around whether instructions to the jury were too vague to accurately determine whether Andersen obstructed justice. Andersen attorneys argued that government attorneys in the original District Court case had conflated persuasion with corruption. They argued that the jury was led to think that persuasion to destroy the documents, even without corrupt intent, constituted grounds for conviction. The statute under which Andersen was charged, however, stipulated that corrupt persuasion to withhold documents, not mere persuasion, was essential to the obstruction of justice charge. Chief Justice William Rehnquist wrote an opinion for a unanimous court that overturned the District Court's ruling. Whether Andersen employees were merely following policy or corruptly persuaded, the Supreme Court ruling emphasized that persuasion was not inherently corrupt, and the definition of corruption presented to the jury was vague enough to include innocent forms of persuasion in conviction.

Nonetheless, the original ruling constituted what many called a fatal blow to Arthur Andersen. Despite a successful appeal, the company was, in essence, executed. All accounting and consulting activities ceased. Twenty-eight thousand people lost their jobs. An appeal could not resurrect a dead company. Assume, though, that Andersen's appeal did not succeed on a legal technicality. Assume the conviction of obstruction of justice was upheld. Is execution a fair punishment for such a crime? Legally, a company on trial is meant to be treated as a person. Surely a person would never be executed for obstruction of justice. It could be argued that Andersen's irresponsibility and leniency toward Enron led to greater scandal, and the job loss that occurred in Enron itself. If Andersen could be held accountable for the death of Enron, the execution of Andersen seems more justifiable by the human analogy. Yet it must again be emphasized, since Andersen was only charged with obstruction of justice, that the size of its penalty is legally questionable.

Despite the successful appeal, the government succeeded in using Andersen as a warning to the corporate world. The death penalty is often defended as a means of warning criminals of the ramifications of their actions. Perhaps the Andersen case was meant to modify the analogy between corporations and people. While only murder may justify use of the death penalty in human cases, even obstruction of justice is grave enough a crime in the corporate world to justify use of the death penalty. But lawsuits seeking lesser penalties continued against institutions. The accounting firm Arthur Andersen and the law firm Kirkland and Ellis, for example, agreed to settlements worth a total of eighty-six million dollars to the University of California.

Psychopathy

How do the various institutions implicated in the Enron collapse relate to psychopathy? As corporations, they can be evaluated as humans as well as entities consisting of humans. Both the corporations themselves and the constituents can potentially be labeled psychopathic. However, regarding the event surrounding Enron, the actions that will potentially be associated with psychopathy were carried out by sectors or multiple levels of the corporations. Rarely did any particular names arise in the media in the way that Enron executives' did. The situation consisted of more than rogue psychopaths within the entities. The financial and legal institutions themselves were functioning to perform those questionable acts and to varying extents exhibited psychopathic qualities in their relationships with Enron.

Although corporations can be treated as human beings, some of the criteria in the Psychopathy Checklist-Revised, or PCL-R, cannot possibly relate to a company. For instance, although companies can be labeled as having a sort of emotion, it is impossible to objectively state that a company has a shallow affect. Furthermore, juvenile delinquency, revocation of conditional release, many short marital relationships, and promiscuous sexual behavior are quite specific to human affairs and, even if an argument could be made for their translation to corporate behavior, assessment of these qualities holds little value.

That being said, the unscrupulous activities of the companies previously mentioned demonstrated psychopathic characteristics. In a very general sense, these companies were all irresponsible, impulsive, and lacked empathy because they did whatever was possible to make the most money in the shortest amount of time, regardless of the law and of how such actions affected stockholders and all employees. The corporations also demonstrated a grandiose sense of self-worth because each thought of itself as above the law and worthy enough to ruin others' lives to improve its own. In such a competitive, success-oriented system, these companies displayed little empathy for the individuals affected by their selfish decisions. Additionally, these banks, firms, and financial institutions were manipulative. They stretched the limits of laws in unethical ways in order to deceive others and make money for themselves. Although not explicitly addressed in the Enron case, many of these corporations had a history of bribery and coercion. Enron proved to have a parasitic lifestyle because it survived by using loans and fraudulent transactions with other companies, but many of these companies performed legitimate services outside of their dealings with Enron and therefore did not rely upon Enron as Enron relied upon them. Also, superficiality is a rather subjective descriptor when attempting to assess psychopathic qualities in corporate behavior. Clearly the inherent deception in the activities of all these entities illustrated that what was visible and public often differed from reality. This could be considered a superficial mask that covered the inner workings of these companies. Finally, the most obvious of all psychopathic criteria regarding all corporations implicated in the Enron scandal was the failure to accept responsibility. This trait was evident in the companies themselves as well as in the individuals who constituted the companies. Nobody admitted guilt willingly. Pointing the finger at someone else was an integral step for all accused in the Enron inquiries.

Except for the solely human attributes of the PCL-R, these companies exhibited a high degree of psychopathy. They satisfied most of the central psychopathic elements and conveyed a general sense of narcissism. The only reason any of these groups were involved in the first place was the lure of enormous profits. They were not helping Enron as friends or partners, but as self-interested entities. That, of course, is a common attribute of any corporation, not just these. Furthermore, it was part of their collective personality to make finding the truth as difficult as possible. Secret meetings, document shredding, faulty corporate branches, and deceptive financial reporting were all in effect for the purposes of deceiving the government and subverting possible whistleblowers. Spearheaded by Arthur Andersen, these companies shirked ethics, laws, and responsible behavior in order to achieve short-term benefits. Only Arthur Andersen, however, received the equivalent of a death sentence. After seeing how disruptive that was to thousands of employees and shareholders, the government was hesitant about doing the same to other implicated corporations. In fact, the banks, law firms, and other financial institutions all ended up benefiting from Enron. The amount of money they made by helping Enron commit its unscrupulous acts was far greater than the amount that they had to pay in fines and lawsuits. Like true psychopaths, these companies used Enron for personal profit, denied responsibility when Enron collapsed, and walked away from the aftermath without remorse and with slightly deeper pockets.

Notes about sources

This case study relied primarily on the film *Enron: The Smartest Guys in the Room*, directed by Alex Gibney, and on the book by Bethany McLean and Peter Elkind on which it is based, *The Smartest Guys in the Room: The Amazing Rise and Scandalous Fall of Enron*. It also benefited from Kurt Eichenwald's book *Conspiracy of Fools: A True Story*, and from news reports in *The New York Times*, the *Boston Globe*, and the *Wall Street Journal*, and on cable news channels.

6

Case Studies

Frank Abagnale, Jr.
Spotlight on an imposter

Abstract

Frank William Abagnale, Jr. spent five years of his young life traveling the world and funding his journeys by being an imposter. Abagnale left home in 1964 at sixteen and was finally caught in France in 1969. By that time he had taken on eight different identities, which included airline pilot, an attorney, a college professor, and a pediatrician. Abagnale had cashed checks worth over two and a half million dollars across twenty-six countries. After his arrest in France, he was sent to Sweden and finally the United States, where he was released after spending approximately five years in prison because the FBI sought his expertise in investigating fraudulent activities. Abagnale's life was featured in an autobiography and a 2002 film, *Catch Me if You Can*, starring Leonardo DiCaprio in the lead role. In 2006, Abagnale was still doing well and had opened his own consulting firm, Abagnale & Associates. Thus, one may ask what made Abagnale commit this series of crimes and what, if any, diagnosis can be placed on this behavior or on the behavior of imposters and conmen in general.

Before sixteen

Frank William Abagnale, Jr., born on April 27, 1948, was one of four children, which included three boys and one girl. His IQ was tested to be one hundred and forty. He began his criminal behavior after his father gave him a credit card for gas when he was fifteen and Abagnale charged three thousand, four hundred dollars on it over a span of three months. He noted that his dad possessed the one necessary trait to be conned: blind trust. Yet, in an interview later with ABC, Abagnale claimed he was too young at the time to think about what he was doing or who would pay the bill. He discussed how he next fell in with the wrong crowd at age fifteen and skipped school in an attempt to get his parents' attention. This landed him in a juvenile detention center.

At the age of sixteen, in 1964, Abagnale ran away to New York after his parents, who were married twenty-two years, got divorced. He claimed that this event spurred his various activities. Abagnale said he ran away because he did not want to have to choose between living with his father or his mother. In fact, he was taken from school, in the middle of class, to go to the court proceedings. After absconding, Abagnale altered his driver's license so that he appeared to be twenty-six years old, which he hoped would improve his employment prospects. He was aided in this by the fact that he was six feet tall and appeared to be about twenty-eight years old. Abagnale's first con job was writing checks on his own overdrawn bank account.

Pan Am

Next, Abagnale pretended to be a Pan Am pilot with the name of Frank Williams. He obtained his pilot uniform by calling up executive corporate offices and pretending to have lost his uniform. He then counterfeited a Pan Am ID after visiting the 3M Company, which produced a mock ID of him in the course of demonstrating how to make an ID using their equipment. They even took his picture. This ID did not have Pan Am written anywhere on it, so he stopped at a hobby shop and purchased a Pan Am model plane for less than three dollars and used the decals for his ID. With this false credential, Abagnale flew on board other airlines in their jump seats. Pan Am claimed that in his two year of getting free flights across the world, Abagnale flew over one million miles. Frank Abagnale stopped at age eighteen after the FBI issued a John Doe warning for interstate transportation of fraudulent checks because they did not know his real name.

Pediatrician

Abagnale next posed as a pediatrician in a community in Atlanta that consisted mostly of single people. He claimed to have obtained his degree from Columbia University and to have spent his residency in Los Angeles. He went to Emory University where he read about medicine and he then discussed the information he learned with a doctor in his community so the doctor would not become suspicious. This doctor later referred Abagnale for an administration job that recently opened at the hospital. This job lasted for a year, during which he had always scribbled his observation on the charts but never practiced medicine and was never questioned about this. He left on his own terms.

Lawyer at large and bank manipulator

Abagnale then moved to Baton Rouge where he heard that the state attorney general's office was looking for a lawyer. He assumed if he could be a doctor, then he could definitely be a lawyer. He passed the bar exam and left shortly thereafter. Then he forged a Columbia University degree and taught sociology at Brigham Young University for a semester. Around this time Abagnale opened a new checking account with one hundred dollars. He began encoding bank deposit slips, using magnetic ink, with his own bank account number so that persons who were depositing money ended up depositing the money into his account. Abagnale collected about forty thousand dollars this way before the bank realized what he was doing. In regard to these bank fraud activities, Abagnale said that he was very much an opportunist. He added that he did not premeditate his crimes. He also posed as a night guard and wrote a sign that said that the night box was out of order, tricking people into leaving money with him.

Arrest in France

Abagnale was eventually arrested in France in 1969 long after his girlfriend, Rosalie, had reported him to the Los Angeles police and sent him on a run across the country. Abagnale spent six months at the French prison Perpignan where he almost died from malnutrition and pneumonia. By the time, Abagnale had been committing crimes for five years, had used eight identities, and had passed bad checks worth over two and a half million dollars in twenty-six countries.

Move to Sweden and to the United States

Abagnale was later extradited to Sweden where he served six months in a low security prison that was substantially more comfortable than Perpignan. Abagnale was next deported to the United States. During this deportation, Abagnale plotted a way to escape from the plane that was en route to the United States. According to his autobiography, Abagnale excused himself to the bathroom in the last ten minutes of the flight. He knew that beneath the toilet was a hatch leading to an open compartment, so he climbed into this and beneath the plane. He was then able to jump from the plane when it reached the ground and escape. Soon thereafter he tried to flee to South America, but was recognized and arrested by Canadian police. Abagnale's ex-girlfriend posed as a journalist and held a mock interview with the prison inspector who believed Abagnale was acting as an undercover agent. Abagnale was able to obtain a business card from the Bureau of Prisons in Washington, D.C. that he then showed to the inspector. The inspector, convinced that Abagnale was undercover, released him. Eventually, Abagnale was caught.

Release by the government and a new job

Interestingly, in 1974, the United States released Abagnale after four years of his term so that he could help the FBI with cases of frauds and scams. He was associated with the FBI for over twenty-five years and lectured at the FBI Academy and field offices. Because Abagnale was unable to find jobs after his release from prison, he went to banks to explain what he done and offered to speak with the bank staff so they would be able to recognize techniques used to defraud banks. In addition to having advised banks, Abagnale founded a company which advised businesses on fraud. It has been said that over fourteen thousand financial institutions, corporations, and law enforcement agencies use Abagnale's suggested fraud prevention techniques. From his consultation job and touring lectures, he became a multimillionaire.

Further headlines

In 2002, *Catch Me if You Can* was released. This movie was based on Abagnale's life, although he claimed to have little to do with the movie. The same year, Abagnale published the book *The Art of the Steal*, which explained ways to avoid fraud, scams, and other forms of theft. As of 2000, Abagnale was living in Tulsa, Oklahoma, with his wife of over twenty-five years and three sons, the youngest having just finished eleventh grade.

DSM-IV: The psychological and legal problems it presents

The diagnoses are hypothetical and based on somewhat limited and definitely slanted information regarding Abagnale's state of mind when he committed his crimes between the ages of sixteen and twenty-one.

It seems that up until the age of about fifteen Abagnale was a loved and basically typical teenager. Around the time his parents began having marital difficulties, Abagnale also started to act up. He got into the wrong crowd because he thought it would get his parents' attention and maybe keep them together. These behaviors landed him in juvenile delinquent centers, from which he was immediately released because his father was forgiving and quick to get him out. However, there is no suggestion that Abagnale would have been considered to have conduct disorder because his behavior was not present prior to ten years of age. Conduct disorder is considered a precursor to antisocial personality disorder.

However, according to the *Diagnostic and Statistical Manual of Mental Disorders,* antisocial personality disorder is only diagnosable after eighteen years of age. Abagnale's criminal activities began when he was sixteen, falling between the two psychological disorders, and seemed to have ended when he was twenty-one. This raises the issue of whether Abagnale can be diagnosed using *Diagnostic Manual* criteria. Even personality disorder criteria suggest that behaviors should be evident in childhood, which was not the case for Abagnale. However, using the *Diagnostic Manual* criteria it may be argued that Abagnale suffered from narcissistic personality disorder, because he sought attention from others, perhaps to make up for the lack of childhood he felt he had, or the desire to have the attention that other children would get from their parents but he felt was lacking. It may also be argued that his autobiography suggested a level of narcissism. He began his autobiography, for example, by saying that a man's alter ego is nothing more than his favorite image of himself. He went on to discuss the personal image he saw in the mirror in his room at the Windsor Hotel in Paris, dark, handsome, smooth-skinned, broad-shouldered, and immaculately groomed. He was proud of what he saw. He admitted that at the time he might not have had virtue on his mind.

Additionally, Abagnale could be considered at least to possess many of the characteristics of a person with antisocial personality disorder. Clearly Abagnale satisfied the first criterion of a person failing to conform to social norms evidenced by his frequent criminal behavior. Additionally, he was deceitful, lying, irresponsible, and impulsive. Though he never knew where his next source of income would come from, he did act on any opportunity that presented itself as when he handed over a cashier's check to a cover girl knowing it was fraudulent. Yet Abagnale did not meet the requirement that the individual must be at least eighteen years of age and show evidence of conduct disorder before age fifteen.

Finally, some may make the extreme argument that Abagnale suffered from multiple personality disorder, now dissociative identity disorder. But this is very unlikely considering Abagnale showed no signs of believing that he was actually the persons he posed as.

Little is known about a psychiatric evaluation Abagnale did undergo. Both in France and Sweden Abagnale signed a confession that resulted in a guilty verdict. He was sentenced to one year in France, six months in Sweden, and ten years in the United States. But it was not until he served time in prison in Virginia that

Abagnale underwent a psychological evaluation that lasted two years and included written and oral tests, polygraph examinations, and the use of truth serum. The only reported finding was that Abagnale had a very low criminal threshold, meaning that he was more willing to commit crimes than most people.

His recollections

Abagnale's criminal record cannot be ignored. Yet he seemed to change dramatically after those five short years as an imposter. In a public speech in 2000, he told the audience he was a gifted child because he had what he called a daddy, a term of endearment. He then told the audience how he cried himself to sleep from age sixteen until he was nineteen because he missed his parents and never shared a relationship with a person his own age or had the life that most high schoolers do because he had to grow up so fast. Abagnale believed that his parents' divorce was so traumatic that he had to run away without ever saying goodbye. Although he avoided his parents by fleeing and may have had persistent disturbances, it seems improbable that the divorce of his parents was the sole cause of his behaviors.

Abagnale also expressed remorse for never being able to tell his father how much he loved him because Abagnale was in the French prison when his father died of an accident at age fifty-five. Abagnale noted how fortunate he was for what the government has done for him and that he was lucky to have met his wife. Additionally, he specifically pointed out that the role of a man is to love and respect his wife and children.

Did Abagnale know what he was doing?

He told his 2000 audience that he always knew he would get caught. He said that only a fool would think one could continually break the law and not get caught. He also stated that although he never felt like a criminal he was one and he was well aware of that fact and never deluded himself. Abagnale knew that he needed to get enough money to live on his own and the only way to do that was to lie. It is unlikely that he would be hired at many places at the age of sixteen and even if he had been hired it was doubtful that he would have made enough money to live on his own. As an intelligent person, Abagnale knew what he had to do to survive and did it. Obviously he took it to the extreme and his methods involved deception, scamming others, and other psychopathic behaviors. At the time he appeared to have no remorse and to consider others as persons to be deceived. While he clearly did not need a Rolls-Royce or to live in a penthouse, his age suggested that he was wrapped up in the moment. It seems that Abagnale was curious as to how far he could go with his schemes, but it is also clear that he knew what he was doing and expected to get caught.

Other imposters

The Abagnale case prompts the question of what other imposters are like and whether they possess similar characteristics, or whether Abagnale is unique in some way. Some may argue that all imposters share similar characteristics. Some people may even employ the following logic to conclude that all serious imposters are psychopaths: Imposters are witty and deceitful. They will pit people against each other and watch others' interactions in order to learn how to use those people's behavior against them. Imposters need to be verbally skilled, creative, charming, and to some extent immoral. These characteristics have been found by many experts to describe the traits found in psychopaths. Fred Waldo Demara, also known as the Great Imposter, was another person who took up multiple identities and was considered a psychopath. But the high profile of this case might indicate that it is atypical of most imposters.

While their behaviors may be similar, different imposters have different motivations for their behavior. Some might hope to obtain money illegally while others pretend to be someone they are not for reasons such as revenge or unhappiness with themselves.

Some scholars have used the word imposter to describe another type of person, who they claim suffers from imposter phenomenon, a term defined as an internal experience of intellectual phoniness in high achievers who are unable to internalize their successful experiences. These individuals are not imposters in the sense that Abagnale was. They have real talent and have achieved success, but are nonetheless insecure about their status. Though research has shown that imposter phenomenon can be particularly harmful to women, it is not more typical in women nor are women used as the defining cases of imposter phenomenon. Those with the disorder displayed generalized anxiety, lack of self-confidence, depression, and frustration due to their inability to meet their own standards of achievement. Despite objective, external evidence of their success and talent, they nevertheless live with a constant dread of being exposed as incompetent, particularly as they enter new roles. They have a persistent belief in their own incompetence, a fear of not being able to duplicate previous success, a belief that they lack skill or intelligence despite clear evidence to the contrary, a belief that they do not deserve their career success and that others have been scammed into believing otherwise, a persistent view that their record of accomplishments is not due to ability but rather to luck, fate, or other factors outside one's control. Obviously

Abagnale was different. He knew from the start that his talent was feigned and that he was merely an imposter. The one real talent he might have been able to question was his talent as an imposter, and his story showed that he had nothing but the utmost confidence in that area. In short, he knew he was an imposter and a successful one at that.

A final noteworthy difference between Abagnale and other imposters is that most imposters stalk their victims for a period of time to gather information about them. Abagnale, however, was much more whimsical in the sense that he saw opportunities and seized them as they came along. The reason was that Abagnale's actions were generally unplanned and unintended to harm others.

Impact of the media

One major difference between this case and other imposter cases is that the life story of Abagnale was documented in a movie in 2002. It is important to consider how accurate this movie was, and then what impact it had on society and the views not only of Abagnale but of the conman in general. Steven Spielberg read Frank Abagnale's biography so that he could make his movie as accurate as possible. For example, the motivations and causes of Abagnale becoming an imposter were accurate: he was deeply troubled by the splitting of his parents and when his father lost his money, Abagnale decided to run away from home. However, as with other Hollywood movies based on reality, *Catch Me if You Can* took some artistic license. Even Steven Spielberg read Abagnale's biography to incorporate detail and nuance into the film. For example, in real life the FBI agent played by Tom Hanks, character Carl Hanratty, did not exist. Rather, a group of FBI agents helped to capture Abagnale, but this reality was seen to be less suspenseful than a story with a single protagonist.

One should also ask how the media attention affected the premises of the case and society's view of the imposter. The most likely answer is that the movie had little or nothing to do in changing any preconceived notions, except to make viewers a little more curious about what it is like to be a conman. Thus, it is possible that the movie gave interested viewers an incentive to read Abagnale's biography in order to better understand what happened and why. It is probable that the only impact this book had on our view of imposters in general was to create more awareness of the problem so that people would be more skeptical and careful when dealing with their finances. It is also possible that the media caused people to be more fearful and paranoid about imposters because the movie made it look so easy.

Legal issues

Several legal issues surround this case. One is the international nature of Abagnale's crimes. Some have suggested that, on the whole, it is more difficult to convict a party in the United States than in Europe, whereas the rights of innocent persons are equally protected.

Another was how Abagnale was able to manipulate the legal system so easily. It seems almost unbelievable that he was able to convince a prison guard that he was posing as an inspector and was thus let free. However, as with any successful imposter, Abagnale had the wit, cunning, and confidence to get anyone to believe what he said. In these instances, people felt that they wanted to help the imposter or generally just felt bad for him. Considering Abagnale's personality and the propriety with which he was brought up, it seemed entirely likely that fooling the legal system would not be such a problem for him. He was able to manipulate the legal system just as he manipulated his peers, coworkers, girlfriends, and patients to believe who or what he was at the time.

A final legal issue was why Abagnale subjected himself to psychiatric evaluation. Perhaps he did think that he was not a criminal and his acts were caused by psychological problems. Or perhaps it was a way of mitigating his guilt. Perhaps his narcissism led him to want to be examined. Unfortunately these answers remained only for speculation as he gave no explanation in his biography. He noted that the forensic psychiatrist spent two years using truth serum injections, polygraph examinations, and various oral and written tests only to conclude that Abagnale had a very low criminal threshold. Others did not believe in this diagnosis and concluded that Abagnale had conned the examiner just as he had conned others. Abagnale's reply was to say that he answered all questions as truthfully and honestly as possible. He said he did not convince the examiner of anything.

Could this happen today?

Abagnale exploited his charm and inside knowledge about the workings of certain systems, such as the different airlines' ability to cash personal checks for workers from other airlines. Additionally, Abagnale was careful not to get caught. For example, he never flew on a Pan Am plane so he would avoid personal questions and specific aircraft knowledge. Additionally, he chose to be a pediatrician in a community of mostly single people because it was much less likely for them to have children and therefore go to Abagnale for advice. Thus, this could probably happen even with today's technology and advancements because Abagnale's success did not depend on taking advantage of technological shortcomings. The increased airplane security following the terrorist attacks of September 11, 2001, however, make it doubtful that Abagnale would have been so easily accepted malingering at an airport or asking for free rides on other airlines.

Concluding remarks

Abagnale has been measured to have an IQ of one hundred and forty, which is far above the average of one hundred. Abagnale moved frequently to keep up his appearances and steer clear of the police. Thus, Abagnale found his way of living both lonely and, in some cases, depressing. As a narcissistic person, Abagnale was seemingly unbothered by his actions. Further, he said that as a child he was always looking for the creative, simple way to do things and has continued that approach. He would look at things with curiosity and wonder if he could beat them. He would try, he said, just for fun, but rewards came with his successes. Even though Abagnale possesses many characteristics of psychopathy, on both the emotional and behavioral factors, he never claimed to have had a malicious intention behind his actions. Nonetheless, Abagnale's actions were no different from most con artists, and his personality characteristics do not differ much from those of other imposters.

Once Abagnale began delivering many speeches on fraud protection, it was possible that his audiences became his new victims. Speeches about his life were often monotone and unremorseful, but such an impersonal approach to intensely personal events might be explained by his dry sense of humor. This author remains skeptical about labeling him because the fact that Abagnale has been living a seemingly normal, happy life with a wife of twenty-five years and has three children who also all seem to be normal is so atypical. Hare has suggested that a psychopath, among other things, would have multiple short-lived marriages, which Abagnale does not, and would continue with his psychopathic behavior which Abagnale apparently has not. Professor Hare described one imposter's wife who thought it was her fault that her husband was the way he was and she wanted to help him as a result. Conmen and imposters charm for a living. Perhaps this author has fallen for Abagnale's wit and charm.

Notes about sources

Cleckley's *The Mask of Sanity* and Robert Hare's *Without Conscience* provided basic background on psychopathic characteristics, tendencies, and examples. The details in this case study were taken from Frank Abagnale's autobiography, from the movie *Catch Me if You Can,* and from a public speech in 2000. Additional biographical information was found online at crimelibrary.com, which provided a chronological account of Abagnale's life. Though specific diagnostic suggestions were unavailable for this case, many studies have been done on imposters and conman in general. The reverse of the true imposter, the imposter phenomenon, resulted from the research of Clance and Imes, who coined the term. Many other studies used that term and their scale to assess persons thought to exemplify that phenomenon.

Marshall Applewhite and Jim Jones
Cults and their leaders

Abstract

Heaven's Gate, a cult led by Marshall Applewhite, culminated with a mass suicide. Thirty-nine people including Applewhite committed suicide in a rented mansion in Rancho Santa Fe, California over several days in late March 1997. When the bodies were found, all the victims were covered in purple blankets and wearing matching Nike shoes at the time of death. Heaven's Gate members believed that their souls would be picked up and taken for a ride by a spaceship that was behind the comet Hale Bopp. The legal issues involved in this case are theft and suicide. The psychological issues of psychopathy, brainwashing, and schizophrenia are implicated in this case.

Somewhat similar to, but yet different from, the Heaven's Gate cult was the Jonestown cult. Jonestown was the name of the town established in 1977 in Guyana by Jim Jones of the People's Temple. By Jones' order, 913 people died, including 236 children. The majority of these people committed suicide, but others were murdered. The legal issues involved in this case are murder, suicide, slavery, and child slavery. The psychological issue of psychopathy is also implicated.

The early years of Marshall Applewhite

Marshall Applewhite was born on May 17, 1931 in Spur, Texas, to a Presbyterian minister father. There is no mention of his mother or a mother-like figure during his upbringing. Applewhite, also known as Herff, was a funny and energetic person, an overachiever and musically talented. During the 1960s Applewhite was a choir director who took part in many musical plays and worked as a music teacher at the University of St. Thomas in Houston, Texas. He lived what many would consider a normal, conventional life. Applewhite, however, was fired from his teaching job for having a sexual affair with a male student. He later married and had two children. In 1970, Marshall entered a psychiatric hospital after hearing voices and sought to cure his sexual urges. It was at this time he felt that his life was falling apart.

Bonnie Nettles

In 1972, Marshall Applewhite was experiencing heart problems and had a near death experience as a result. He met nurse Bonnie Nettles at a psychiatric ward where she worked. She convinced Applewhite that he was having heart problems for a certain reason and that he should join a special group she was involved with. At the time, Nettles' marriage was falling apart. They shared a love for astrology, UFOs and science fiction. Nettles continually talked to Applewhite about her group and how Applewhite could benefit the group and more importantly how they could benefit each other. Eventually Applewhite moved in with Nettles and the two lived together in a nonsexual union. Together they decided that they should preach what they considered the divine truth about life. Applewhite gave public interviews and said how everyone would be killed by their enemies and then rise into a cloud and sail to Heaven.

Their journey

Nettles and Applewhite soon abandoned their families and left Houston to spread their message. Together they formed Human Individual Metamorphosis, referred to as HIM. HIM was dedicated to teaching people that in order to be saved by God they needed to renounce their worldly possessions and follow a strict regimen that included celibacy, privacy, giving up family life, and complete dedication to the group. One member later revealed that scare tactics were used to make members comply with cult rules. Eventually Applewhite became so distraught over his homosexuality that he preached against sex and in favor of nonsexual relationships.

In 1974, the pair was arrested for stealing credit cards and a car. Applewhite served ten months in jail for this. Interestingly, though Applewhite passed a psychiatric test ordered by the judge, the test made him doubt his sanity.

The following year, Nettles and Applewhite convinced twenty people from Waldport, Oregon to leave their homes and journey to Colorado where a spaceship would pick them all up. They even gave nationally televised interviews of their mission and beliefs in which Applewhite and Nettles proclaimed to be space aliens. The spaceship, however, never showed up.

Underground preaching

Some members left the cult while others felt they had invested too much in the cult to leave. Applewhite and Nettles changed their names to Guinea and Pig and then Bo and Peep and later to Do and Ti. They taught members that everyone was related. Members also adopted new names. Applewhite would sometimes refer to himself as father while Nettles was referred to as grandmother. Around this time, two sociologists joined the cult but left after a few months because they figured the cult was so disorganized and so lacked camaraderie that it would probably disband soon anyway. Feeling betrayed and misperceived by the American media, Applewhite and Nettles decided in 1976 to take their preaching underground and avoided all media for seventeen years.

By this time, membership had dwindled to a little more than a dozen members. The cult raised money by charging people four hundred and thirty-three dollars for a spaceship ride. These planned spaceships rides attracted dozens of people. The cult had three hundred thousand dollars in savings at this time. Nettles died of cancer in 1985 and from that point on Applewhite took complete leadership of the cult. Since Nettles was viewed as a sort of immortal leader and her death conflicted with cult teachings, Applewhite altered his preaching and said that Nettles would pilot the spaceship that would come to pick the group up at a later date. It is believed that during this time Applewhite traveled the country trying to gain followers.

Heaven's Gate

In 1993, an advertisement in *USA Today* proclaimed that Earth's civilization was about to be recycled and changed. This thrust the Applewhite-led cult into the spotlight once again but the cult's practices were still secretive. Applewhite now proclaimed to be a messenger from an evolutionary kingdom that was a level above humans. Supposedly, this kingdom sent special messengers to Earth such as Jesus. Applewhite said that like Jesus, he himself was a messenger to Earth. Furthermore, Applewhite claimed to have been inside the body of Jesus. According to Applewhite, the only way to experience this kingdom was to serve and follow him. It is believed that at the height of its membership Applewhite had nearly a thousand members in his cult.

In 1994, several cult members told a news reporter that a spaceship was coming to pick them up at the Santa Monica pier. The spaceship never came. In October 1996, the cult settled in Rancho Santa Fe, California, where it rented a nine thousand square foot mansion. Applewhite renamed the cult Heaven's Gate and continued preaching about a higher level of existence in outer space. Heaven's Gate was a UFO cult that practiced a secret New Age religion. Not much is known about the religion. Membership in Heaven's Gate required giving up all worldly possessions and living simple, secretive, and isolated lives. Sexual abstinence was expected and a few males including Applewhite voluntarily underwent castration. Applewhite most likely underwent castration as a way to cure his homosexual urges. Members were also required to dress androgynously and therefore many female members had short hair. Members were also required to develop nonsexual unions with members of the opposite sex and travel in pairs. To earn money, the cult designed web pages under the name Higher Source. The internet served not only as a way to make money but also as a way to recruit new members. Early in the twenty-first century, the Heaven's Gate website was still running and it was believed that there were only twenty-five members in the cult.

Hale Bopp

One of the most widely observed comets in the twentieth century, Hale Bopp was an important element for New Age religions and cults such as Heaven's Gate. Hale Bopp is a special comet because it is very large in size and far from the Earth compared to ordinary comets, yet it was scheduled to pass close to Earth in March 1997. It was calculated that the last time Hale Bopp had been this close to the sun and to Earth was in 2200 B.C. Historically, comets have been viewed as omens, and many viewed this date as the last time a great prophet had been to Earth.

Heaven's Gate saw the comet as a sign of change and an exciting event. As a result, members of Heaven's Gate watched the movie *Star Wars*, bought a high-powered telescope, and took out insurance against alien abductions and impregnations. The cult even went to a conference on UFOs. Heaven's Gate used the telescope to search for a companion of Hale Bopp's. In actuality, Heaven's Gate was looking for the supposed spaceship behind Hale Bopp that the cult was to take a ride on. That spaceship Hale Bopp was to take them to the higher world. Hale Bopp, along with the spaceship, marked the transition from human level to the above-human level for the members. Furthermore, in January 1997, the outer planets of the solar system aligned in a way that resembled a Jewish star. Since Jesus was Jewish and the last time the outer planets had resembled a Jewish star was during the Renaissance period, Heaven's Gate was convinced that their time to leave the Earth had come. The next month and a half was spent making final preparations for a grand exit from Earth.

Suicide

On March 21, 1997, thirty-nine men and women of Heaven's Gate went into a restaurant and bakery and everyone ordered a salad, potpie, and cheesecake. This is believed to be cult's last meal together. After the meal, Heaven's Gate returned to their rented mansion. The following day Hale Bopp was at its closest point to

Earth. It is on this day that the mass suicide began. All members dressed identically in black pants, black long sleeve shirts and new Nike shoes. On their shirts was a patch that said Heaven's Gate Away Team. All members also packed a bag that contained clothing, lip balm, pens, pencils, and spiral notebooks as if they were going on a short vacation. These bags were placed at the foot of their beds. Each member had three quarters and a five-dollar bill in their shirt pocket that was designated to be used to call and pay for a taxi after the spaceship ride. All of these items symbolized that the members were going on a trip. Fifteen members mixed and ate Phenobarbital, a barbiturate, with pudding or applesauce and then drank some vodka. They then lay down in their beds and put plastic bags over their heads. Some members later placed purple blankets over their bodies. The next day, fifteen more members committed suicide in the same manner and the following day, seven more members similarly committed suicide. The next day, the last two members, both females, committed suicide, exactly as their cultmates had.

The discovery in Rancho Santa Fe

The bodies of Heaven's Gate's members were discovered on March 26, 1997, by a deputy sheriff. The police were alerted by Richard Ford, also known as Rio DiAngelo, a former Heaven's Gate member who left the cult a month earlier out of frustration. Interestingly enough, DiAngelo originally tried to remain anonymous and calmly told the police dispatcher that there was a mass suicide by a religious group and that he was aware of this because he had received an email about the planned suicide. However, his name came up when investigating the case and he was contacted for more information. The eighteen male and twenty-one female members ranged in age from twenty-six to seventy-two years old. It was evident from the scene that everyone had died willingly. It was also discovered that seven males had been castrated including Applewhite. Computers left on in the house displayed the Heaven's Gate website. It was believed that the members of the cult considered themselves to be aliens. It was also rumored that Applewhite had cancer but the autopsy report showed no signs of this.

Although reluctant to be interviewed after the mass suicide, DiAngelo told of how the cult was neatly organized and how everyone had assigned times and positions for eating, bathing, sleeping, and watching television. Members had to email the Individual Needs Department when they needed deodorant and other items. DiAngelo did not elaborate on the cult's practices and beliefs but he did say that Applewhite taught him honesty, awareness, and sensitivity, which improved DiAngelo as a person. A million dollars was offered to DiAngelo to write a tell-all book, but he turned it down. Five years later, he said he would take the money if he were offered the same deal again. He also auctioned off the van used by Heaven's Gate to travel the country. DiAngelo saw himself as the only officer and messenger left in Heaven's Gate but realized that the cult was not all it claimed to be.

Passengers left behind

A week after the mass suicide, Heaven's Gate member Wayne Cooke, also known as Justin, was interviewed. He referred to the mass suicide as graduation. He cried and complained about how he wished he had graduated with the thirty-nine members, one of whom was his wife. A little over a month later, Cooke, along with another member, Chuck Humphrey, followed the same routine as their predecessors and tried to kill themselves in Encinitas, California. Cooke succeeded, but Humphrey failed. Humphrey believed that he failed because he was destined to continue preaching about Heaven's Gate. Humphrey created a website to explain the ideology behind Heaven's Gate. He later committed suicide in 1998 by carbon monoxide poisoning and suffocation. Next to him was a bag filled with the same items as the bags of his predecessors, the exact amount of money that his predecessors died with, a purple shroud and a note that said not to revive him. He too was wearing black clothing and had a patch that said Heaven's Gate Away Team on his shirt.

Jim Jones: The early years

James Warren Jones was born in Crete, Indiana, on May 13, 1931. He lived a seemingly normal childhood and after graduating from high school, became a preacher in the 1950s. He married and had a son they named Stephan Gandhi Jones. He also sold pet monkeys to earn additional money while preaching. Jones founded Wings of Deliverance, which he later renamed the Peoples Temple Full Gospel Church. Jones became an ordained minister in 1964 with the Christian denomination Disciples of Christ despite his lack of formal training. He then moved the Peoples Temple from Indiana to Northern California in 1965.

A few years after settling in Northern California, Jones moved his church to San Francisco in 1972. The Peoples Temple Church was well known for treating African Americans equally with their white counterparts and as a result Jones had numerous African American followers. Jones was appointed to the San Francisco Housing Commission. He often spoke out against the Bible because he claimed it was full of lies and contradictions. He also claimed to be a descendent of Jesus, Buddha, and Vladimir Lenin. Jones was accused of being unfair to church members, practicing sodomy, and performing fake miracles to attract people. Jones began operating a number of care homes for senior citizens and mentally challenged youth while in San Francisco. In December 1973, Jones was arrested for soliciting a man, who turned out to be an undercover police officer, for sex in a bathroom at a park in Los Angeles.

In 1977, Jones and around eight hundred members of the Peoples Temple Church moved to Guyana because the church was being investigated for tax evasion and Jones claimed that in Guyana the church could build an agricultural utopia and live free of racism. Because of his persuasive ability, Jones convinced the government of Guyana to give him three hundred acres to establish Jonestown. But instead of happiness and joy at Jonestown, children and adults worked twelve-hour days and ate very little. Families were split apart and not permitted to see each other, and those who revolted were severely punished. There were always armed guards patrolling Jonestown to make sure no residents left or escaped.

Death at Jonestown

Eventually California congressman Leo Ryan got word of suspicious activity and human rights violations in Jonestown. Ryan decided to go to Guyana to investigate. Ryan went to Jonestown in November 1978 with his staff and media members. After interviewing many displeased Jonestown residents over a few days, Ryan was set to leave early after there had been a failed attempt to slit his throat. While waiting to leave the airport to head back to the United States on November 18, 1978, Ryan was shot and killed by the People's Temple security guards. Three journalists and a Temple member were also killed at this time. Jones then realized that Jonestown was about to be invaded and shut down so he ordered a revolutionary suicide. Many people voluntarily committed suicide by drinking Kool-Aid laced with cyanide and sedatives. Some people resisted and were either shot or injected with cyanide. Jones died from a gunshot wound to the head but it is unknown if it was a self-inflicted gunshot wound or if someone shot him. In all, 913 people died including 276 children.

Jones' son

Stephan Gandhi Jones, the son of Jim Jones, did not participate in the mass suicide. He was nineteen years old at the time of the Jonestown disaster. While the mass suicide and murder was taking place, Stephan was not in Jonestown. He was away representing the Jonestown community in a basketball tournament. He has led a rather anonymous life. As a teenager, he later said, he often questioned his father's behavior and had a hard time understanding everything that his father did. He also has described Jonestown as a concentration camp. Stephan had tried to commit suicide in the early 1970s but failed multiple times. Stephan has called his father a fraud and has said that he was ashamed to be associated with him.

Psychological disorders

It appears that members of Heaven's Gate suffered from many mental problems. But, because they lived secretive lives, they could not be diagnosed individually. Because Applewhite spent time in a mental hospital and was the main spokesman for the group, much more is known about him. A cult expert has noted that many people involved with a cult are intelligent and well-educated people who let their curiosity get the best of them, and they and others may be drawn into the cult by a charismatic and well-spoken leader. Furthermore, because the beliefs of the cult are so extreme their validity cannot be scientifically tested. Eventually, individuals can become so engulfed in this that they follow the leader wholeheartedly without rationally addressing the belief system.

In the recorded footage of Heaven's Gate members, they all had positive things to say about Applewhite. Applewhite and members who were interviewed stated many times that most people thought they were crazy because of their beliefs but that did not matter to them because they knew that Heaven's Gate was on a mission and they truly believed in their leader and the goal of experiencing life on a higher level above humans. Members felt were they part of a complex process that would let them into Heaven and that many people would not understand them.

Those closest to Applewhite before he became involved with cults claimed he was a normal, funny, and charismatic person. His sister noted that Applewhite was not overly religious although he did attend church regularly. She described him as a natural born leader who was always full of charisma. She was certain that Applewhite's near-death experience is what caused him to change his direction in life and eventually start a cult. It has been shown that it is not uncommon for near-death experiences to alter people's lives. Near-death experiences may cause individuals to second-guess their meaning and abilities in life, even their reason for being on Earth. Many times people leave near-death experiences with a better appreciation for life and with the feeling of being awarded a second chance. As a result, they may feel that they have to do some deed or change their lifestyle. It will never be known to what extent having a near-death experience effected Applewhite's behavior.

It is this author's belief that Applewhite was had schizophrenia and was mildly psychopathic, whereas Jim Jones was extremely psychopathic. Applewhite did not hold members hostage or force them to partake in his activities. Members of Heaven's Gate were free to leave at will. Applewhite was also very honest and straightforward with Heaven's Gate members, so they knew what to expect. Nonetheless, the Heaven's Gate belief system can generally be considered bizarre and delusional. The beliefs promoted by Applewhite had no grounding in any rational thought or realistic precedents. Such a delusional network is a key sign that an individual has schizophrenia.

Jones, on the other hand, was cunning, deceitful, and manipulative, among his many other psychopathic characteristics. His ordering members of his cult who would not commit suicide to be murdered highlighted his extreme antisocial actions. Unlike Applewhite, Jones tricked his cult members and promised them a utopia but instead forced them into slavery. They worked long hours, received little food, could not leave, and were subjected to severe punishment for infractions of his rules.

It is somewhat debatable what mental illnesses Jim Jones had. Based on all that is known about him, he appears to be a complete psychopath. Evidence indicated that he tricked and manipulated people into joining his church. He used deceitful practices to take advantage of people. He also showed no mercy or concern for others' welfare. It is hard to judge the mental state of the residents of Jonestown because there were so many of them. However, it is a good assumption that many of them were not happy with the conditions in Jonestown, but nothing could be done because Jones used force to control and monitor the residents. Residents followed him to Guyana because they expected to have better lives. These residents were not planning to fly away on a spaceship or anything drastic, so there was a justified and legitimate reason for people to move to Jonestown. Based on the information available, most of the residents appeared to have no mental illnesses, though he used some as his enforcers and they were caught up in his psychopathic character. Most probably were gullible and naive, and as a group were simply taken advantage of by Jones.

Cults

Factual evidence indicates that most cults are built upon fiction. Heaven's Gate was no different. The patches with the words Heaven's Gate Away Team on it were based on the fictional television series *Star Trek*, where certain members of the spaceship's crew were part of an away team that would travel on missions. Applewhite was a devoted science fiction fan and believed in space aliens and the apocalypse. His cult, and perhaps even to a greater extent Jones' cult, were built, as many cults are, on desperation. Cults solicit people who feel they have little reason or meaning to live and are searching for a deeper meaning in their lives. Not only can cults serve as places to interact; they serve as a family for some people. These people are very susceptible to cults and any of their deceptive practices. Once people begin to indulge in cults' extreme and totalistic beliefs they are entrapped and for many there is no leaving. While Applewhite permitted individuals to leave, Jones, as with totalitarian leaders, prevented his members from escaping his rule in an isolated area. Though many cults begin as warm and caring, they can change once people become immersed in them and give their lives to the cult.

Their leaders

Applewhite had been diagnosed as schizophrenic and a religious mystic by many doctors. He was an unstable person who lacked strength, personality, and morality. During intense times of stress, Applewhite's mind would transform and take over his whole body. Most likely, he had delusions and heard voices in his head.

Although Heaven's Gate had rules, regulations, and practices, it is obvious that many of the cult's rules and restrictions were actually derived from Applewhite's problems or interests. Because of his sexual problems, he insisted that the cult be celibate. He and Nettles had lived in a nonsexual union and Applewhite enforced nonsexual unions upon his followers. Just as UFOs, science fiction, and astrology were all interests to Applewhite, these subjects were made an integral part of Applewhite's delusional network and his cult.

Jones, on the other hand, found that power agreed with him and he increased his power through isolating the members of his cult and imposing his own strict rules on them. He was the psychopathic leader who misled them and used his original status with them, as someone who reached out to them and treated them as equals, to cause them to move to Guyana and to learn later the consequences of that submission to him. Jonestown has become a symbol of the devastation caused by a psychopathic leader who can isolate his followers and manipulate them totally.

Cult leaders and their members often do not die a natural death. Cults may handle death in different ways. Some cults, such as the Branch Davidians, stock up on weapons and prepare for an apocalypse; other cults like Heaven's Gate engage in a mass suicide; and still others, like Jonestown, kill those who come to investigate them, and then end in mass suicide, with the murder of those who refuse to kill themselves or are too young to participate. Though many cults do not end in such fashion, the members of those that do often believe that by facing death in these ways, they will be able to exist on a higher human level. Some have argued that terrorist suicide-homicide bombers are similar to members of these more traditional cults.

Monitoring cults

There has been some debate as to whether the government should have monitored either the Heaven's Gate or Jonestown cults as a result of their secretive behavior. If the government had monitored and known of the planned suicides by Heaven's Gate, or of the murders and suicides organized by Jim Jones, then lives could have been spared. While banning cults is not realistic, the delicate balance between liberty and safety compels the media and others to examine closely the behaviors and personalities of the leaders and their followers.

A final note

While the Heaven's Gate suicide has been the largest mass suicide to occur in the United States, it has also become a popular subject of jokes and has been parodied by many television shows and movies such as *Saturday Night Live*, *The Tonight Show with Jay Leno*, *Dude Where's My Car*, *The Simpsons*, and *Mr. Show with Bob and David*. Many television drama and action shows have created episodes loosely based on Heaven's Gate such as *Star Trek: Deep Space Nine*, *CSI: Crime Scene Investigation*, and *Boy Meets World*, and Jonestown has also occasioned films and reportage. But media attention to Jonestown has always been serious, never light or humorous, whereas Heaven's Gate has produced a mix of reactions. Schizophrenic ideation, it seems, occasions more laughs than does psychopathic violence.

Notes about sources

Much of the information for this case study came from newspaper and journal archives, while transcripts and interviews were taken directly from the sources listed. A few very reliable websites were also used to check and confirm information. Some sources were transcripts from CNN, The History Channel, and *Newsweek*. Articles from the *San Diego Union Tribune* and documents from the U.S. Department of State were also used.

Velma Barfield
A black widow serial killer

Abstract

Velma Barfield was a serial killer of the type often referred to as a black widow. A black widow killer is a woman who establishes a relationship, through affection, sex, perhaps marriage, with her male victims before killing them. Barfield's victims were people close to her such as husbands and employers. Her method of choice was usually a poison like arsenic, though it appears she killed her first husband by setting their house on fire while he slept. In addition to the murders, she was addicted to prescription drugs and often forged checks or stole money from her family and employers to support her habit. Outside of her brushes with the law over the checks, she presented herself as a model individual, a devoted mother and a devout Christian. Barfield was finally caught at age forty-eight after murdering Stuart Taylor, her boyfriend. After her conviction she spent many years on death row. She became the first woman executed after the reinstatement in 1976 of the death penalty.

Barfield's early life

Margie Velma Barfield was born on October 23, 1932, in North Carolina. She was the second of nine children born to Murphy and Lillie Bullard, though only seven of them survived to adulthood. Her family was very poor. Her father was a farmer, but he found it impossible to support his family with the profits from his small farm. To make ends meet, he worked in a series of different factories. Even though farming could not support the family, Murphy still raised some crops in addition to his work in the factory. All the children were responsible for helping to take care of and harvest the crops. Barfield's mother was a housewife. As Barfield was the second oldest, in addition to the farming chores, Lillie required her to help in taking care of her many younger siblings. Barfield's early home life was difficult. Her father drank heavily and often beat Barfield and her siblings with a leather strap. Barfield was resentful towards her mother because Lillie did nothing to protect them from their father's abuse.

Barfield showed some signs of behavioral problems early on. As a child, she stole small amounts of money from her father to buy candy. Her largest theft at this time in her life was taking eighty dollars from a neighbor. She was caught and severely punished when that theft was discovered. Apparently, the beating was an effective deterrent, because there is no sign any other thefts occurred during her childhood after that incident. Barfield was not the most honest of the Bullard children. She developed the habit of complaining about headaches and stomachaches to avoid school and chores. She enjoyed the extra attention she received, but then she stopped when her father forced her to complete her chores regardless of her complaints.

When she was seventeen years old, she dropped out of school and married Thomas Burke. The following fifteen years of her life were relatively uneventful. She gave birth to two children and dedicated herself to being a mother and housewife, partly because Burke did not want her to work. She was very involved in her children's schooling and she was involved in the local religious community, regularly taking her children to Baptist services.

The beginning of the troubles

In 1963, Barfield's simple life began to change. Due to health problems, she had to have a hysterectomy. Following the surgery, her personality shifted. She became irritable and depressed. Her general state of health also deteriorated a bit. Around this time, Barfield's marriage started to suffer. Barfield did not drink, and she started to resent the fact that her husband regularly drank with his friends. In 1965, Thomas Burke had a severe auto accident. Barfield blamed the accident on his drinking, and their arguments started to escalate drastically. In 1967, Burke was caught driving while drunk and lost his license. At the time his job consisted of driving a company truck and making deliveries of soft drinks to various stores. Without a driver's license he could not work, and in addition to the humiliation of having his license revoked he was also unemployed. Though he was able to find another job, his drinking got much worse, and his fights with Barfield became more regular and vicious.

Their fights never escalated to physical violence, but the situation was not good for Barfield. She lost weight and eventually collapsed. Her son forced her to go to the hospital. She was hospitalized for a week and given a prescription for a mild tranquilizer.

This could be seen as the start of her real problems. Shortly after her collapse she started taking more than the prescribed doses of the tranquilizers and started visiting multiple doctors to get additional prescriptions. Around this time, Barfield forced Burke to go in for treatment for his alcohol problem. He was upset by the hypocrisy of the situation and their marriage suffered further.

The first victims

In April 1969, there was a fire in Barfield's home. Her husband was the only one home and died of smoke inhalation. Barfield was apparently doing laundry at the local laundromat when this occurred. It is unclear whether Barfield was actually involved in this incident, but it is possible that she staged the accident. Her drug use got even worse at this point. She was firmly addicted to Valium and had prescriptions for a dozen other assorted tranquilizers, painkillers, and antidepressants. This fire was made more suspicious by the fact that Barfield's house caught fire again, and that fire coincided with Barfield's money problems.

About a year after Burke's death, Barfield decided to marry Jennings Barfield, who had also lost his spouse. It appears they sought comfort from each other. They were married on August 23, 1970, leaving her with the surname by which she became popularly known. Not everyone was happy about the union. Barfield's daughter was reported to be very upset by this perceived betrayal of her father. Soon the marriage developed problems. Barfield overdosed several times, and it was very difficult for Jennings Barfield to deal with the situation as he had severe health problems. Additionally, he caught her forging checks to pay for her prescriptions. It appears that they would have divorced. Jennings Barfield, however, did not live long enough to file divorce papers. On March 21, 1971, he died of what appeared to be heart failure. Much later, Barfield would confess to poisoning him.

Barfield's meltdown

At this point her addiction started to affect her everyday life severely. She was using medications to the point that she could not really function at her job. Adding to her difficulties and anticipating the draft, her son joined the military. Barfield could not stand having her son in the military, and she had a severe emotional breakdown. Her employer was unable to give her any more leeway, and she was fired from her job because of her frequent absences and inability to perform tasks.

Shortly after her son Ronnie told her he had joined the military, her house caught fire for the third time. She had had many people in the community write letters to the military asking that her son be released because his mother needed him. Barfield's doctors, her minister, and various other people in her community were involved in this effort. This third fire apparently started in her son's room, and most of the damage was restricted to that part of the house. It is possible that it really was an accident, but the timing was questionable. Barfield may have staged the fire for sympathy and to try to keep her son from leaving.

Then her father died of lung cancer, and that upset her. She claimed that she had forgiven him for how he raised her because of how well he treated her children. Following this loss her son decided to marry. In theory, this should have been welcome news, but Barfield's reaction to her son's engagement was extremely negative. She complained that she would no longer be the only woman in her son's life. Her son was surprised by how selfish her response was. She eventually lost her house and moved in with her mother.

Barfield's murders escalate

Barfield's behavior continued to get worse. In 1972, she was arrested for the first time for forging a prescription. She started to fight with her mother regularly. In 1974, Barfield may have poisoned her mother for the first time. Her mother suffered from extreme stomach pains and diarrhea. She was hospitalized but improved quickly. Barfield tended to her mother and benefited from the resulting praise for her devotion. Then, during the holidays, one of Barfield's larger acts of fraud came to light. Barfield had taken out a loan using her mother's name. Her mother received a letter from the bank stating that payments on the loan were overdue and that her car would be repossessed if she did not pay promptly. Barfield committed her second confirmed murder shortly thereafter. She poisoned her mother. She confessed to this murder, but during her trial she claimed she only meant to make her mother sick to distract her until she could pay off the loan.

In 1975 she was arrested for writing bad checks, and imprisoned for three months. In 1976, she took a job as a caregiver for an elderly couple. She began to regularly quarrel with her employers. The husband died of apparently natural causes, and there was no evidence Barfield contributed to his death. The wife on the other hand developed symptoms consistent with arsenic poisoning in 1977 and died shortly thereafter. Barfield then found employment with another couple. She apparently began to forge checks on their account to pay for her addiction. She apparently poisoned the husband after the first forged check was discovered in order to hide her theft. She poisoned him repeatedly over a three-month period, making him progressively sicker, and finally killed him in June 1977.

After his death, Barfield moved in with Stuart Taylor. Taylor decided not to marry Barfield because of her history of fraud. She had apparently been forging checks on his account to pay for her medications, and repeated her pattern of poisoning to hide her activities. Taylor died on February 4, 1978. Taylor's children were suspicious, and demanded an autopsy. The cause of death was arsenic poisoning.

The trial and her death

Barfield was arrested, and confessed to three other murders, those of her mother, Jennings Barfield, and one of those she cared for. She was also suspected in the death of another she cared for, and it is possible she was responsible for the fire that killed her first husband. The door to their house was apparently locked when the firefighters arrived, and it was unusual for that to be the case. Regardless of the other crimes she was thought to have committed, she was officially tried for Taylor's murder.

Barfield's behavior during her trial was terrible. She remained on her medications throughout the trial. She repeatedly allowed the prosecutor to provoke her into giving callous and inappropriate answers, and she applauded after the prosecutor's closing statement. Even though murder convictions for women were rare, and it seemed unlikely that any jury would be willing to sentence a grandmother to death, she was convicted for murder in the first degree and sentenced to death. During her time in prison she was able to end her addiction to prescription medications, and reportedly became very religious. She was liked by most of the guards, and many of the other inmates sought her advice. Many people believed she was truly sorry for her crimes. Her lawyer made appeals, and the public protested her execution, but all these efforts proved futile. She was executed by lethal injection in 1984. She was the first woman executed since the death penalty had been reinstated in 1976.

Barfield as psychopathic serial killer

Many aspects of Barfield's life can support the argument that she was a psychopath. Barfield had many of the characteristics commonly found in psychopaths. She had early behavioral problems. She was skilled at manipulation. She repeated the same crimes regardless of the consequences. She lived the parasitic lifestyle typical of psychopaths as described in many of psychopathy expert Hervey Cleckley's cases. Though she expressed grief over the deaths of her victims, it is difficult to believe she actually felt remorse as she continued to kill, and she did so in a particularly cruel way. Her drug problem and the thefts she committed to support her habit showed irresponsibility and a lack of impulse control. She regularly displayed the shallow emotional range characteristic of psychopathy. The immaturity of her emotions was evident in her reaction to her son's engagement, her callous disregard for the stress she placed on her children's marriages, and her repeated inappropriate responses to the prosecutor during her trial.

In many ways, Velma Barfield seems to be a classic example of the female psychopathic serial killer. Like most other female killers, she chose people close to her as her victims, unlike male serial killers who tend to choose strangers. Male serial killers tend towards violent, face-to-face attacks, and their motivation appears to be for power or sex. Female serial killers tend to kill using more distant methods such as poison or faked domestic accidents, and their motivation is often financial gain. This was definitely the case for Velma Barfield. She killed her husbands and boyfriend, her mother, and some of her employers.

While Barfield often benefited financially from these deaths, there was at least one instance where she did not gain anything from the murder. There may have been an element of revenge behind some of her killings, and the desire for revenge is also often found in many psychopathic, female serial killers.

Certain aspects of her case, however, are inconsistent with a diagnosis of psychopathy. Barfield's rearing of her children, and her behavior after her addiction was finally cured, are contrary to the behavior one would expect from a psychopath. Other female serial murderers with patterns similar to Barfield's tend to prey on their children. Barfield was, by all accounts, an excellent and very caring mother. In prison, she claimed to repent and seemed to become very religious. It appears that she was a model prisoner, and she was highly respected by the other prisoners. How much of this turnaround was genuine is impossible to say, but many people seem to believe that she did in fact regret her past actions. So if she genuinely came to feel remorse that perhaps lessens her later psychopathy as one of the defining characteristics of psychopathy is an inability to really feel emotions like regret.

This case was atypical in that among female psychopaths, serial killers are exceedingly rare. She was a very loving mother, which is not a common trait among female serial killers. In fact, many female serial killers victimize their children. Also, her behavior in prison seemed to run counter to what one would expect from a psychopath. While many psychopaths do present themselves as reformed, most psychopaths cannot maintain their good behavior for any significant length of time. Barfield's behavior throughout her entire incarceration following her recovery from her addiction was exemplary.

Other possible diagnoses

Psychopathy is not the only possible diagnosis for Barfield. From the available information on Barfield's childhood, it does not appear that she had conduct disorder as a child, so she could not be given a diagnosis of antisocial personality disorder, even though she met the other criteria for that diagnosis. Barfield appeared to have met the criteria for borderline personality disorder, a condition that shares many traits with psychopathy and antisocial personality disorder, but where the underlying motivation appears to be a desire for attention and nurturance rather than material gain. Borderline personality disorder could be a better diagnosis for Barfield than psychopathy, because it would be a better explanation for her obsession with her children and for her repeated suicide attempts. Narcissistic personality disorder also shares many traits with psychopathy, but individuals with this disorder do not tend to be impulsive and aggressive. In addition to a possible diagnosis of psychopathy or borderline personality disorder, Barfield definitely qualified for a diagnosis of substance dependence. And as her substance abuse escalated so did her murderous behavior.

Some legal issues

Legally, there are several points of interest in her case. Barfield was sentenced to death, and she was actually executed. Considering her gender, her age, and the fact that she was a grandmother when she was convicted, this was highly unusual. Also, Barfield was still taking medications during her trial. Part of the reason for her conviction was her behavior during the trial. Doctors testified that she was competent to stand trial, but Barfield took heavier doses than prescribed and she had a habit of mixing medications that were never meant to be taken together. Many of the medications she took had psychotropic effects. As a result, she may not have been competent to stand trial. If more attention had been paid to her use of various substances, she may not have been considered completely responsible for her actions and thus escaped the death penalty. Subsequent research found more lasting negative effects on behavior from some of the medications she took than were known at the time of her trial.

A closer look at Barfield's treatment of her children

As noted earlier, most psychopathic killers of this type tend to kill their children. In fact, children are often their preferred victims because they cannot really fight back in any way. Until her addiction took hold, by all accounts, Barfield was an excellent mother.

This is a difficult problem. This is the largest departure from the usual pattern found in cases of black widows. Velma Barfield truly appeared to love her children. She doted on her children. She volunteered to help at their grade school. When she was given the opportunity to have a belated honeymoon with her first husband she ended the vacation early because she could not stand to be away from her son. She attended every one of her daughter's basketball games. She was devastated when her son became a soldier.

One possible explanation would be that she was a woman suffering from other sorts of mental problems, such as borderline personality disorder, who stumbled across an immoral but effective solution to her problems. Both her marriages were unhappy, and there is quite a bit of evidence that a difficult environment combined with a feeling of powerlessness has driven otherwise normal women to kill their spouses. Perhaps her first killing was an accident as she later claimed, and her mind, already wracked with other problems and altered by prescription medications, latched onto a solution. It is possible that her string of killings was set off by desperation and then got out of hand. Her children may have been safe because she was more of a normal woman who ended up in an untenable situation. This is of course entirely speculation, but it must be considered.

On the other hand there is plentiful evidence that Barfield was not innocent in any sense of the term. Her method insured that her victims died very painful deaths. Often she nursed these individuals so she witnessed the effects of her actions first hand. That was not enough to stop her. Being arrested repeatedly for fraud was not enough to make her end her addiction. Her addiction showed her impulsivity.

It is possible that her love for her children was not real, and they provided her with something that she wanted more than the possible monetary reward their deaths might win her. For example, when her son married she was enormously jealous. It seemed she had a desire to be the most important person in her children's worlds. Her need to be so involved, particularly with her son, could be seen as pathological. As she might have needed them for another purpose, she could not just kill them. The fact was she was not always motivated by the desire for money. It is quite possible that they were saved by some secondary motive of hers.

It is also important to note that while there was no real evidence that she ever harmed her children physically, she caused them other kinds of problems. At different times she caused difficulties in both her children's marriages, and it can be argued that she did so willfully. Both of her children feared that she would end up destroying their marriages. She forged checks on an account belonging to her daughter's husband. She regularly borrowed money from her children even when they could not really afford to lend it to her. She imposed on them regularly. At different times she damaged their cars by driving them recklessly or while under the influence of medications.

There is also one incident of a possible poisoning of her daughter Pam. Of her two children, Barfield was much closer to her son than her daughter. On one occasion, Barfield asked to borrow her daughter's car. When her daughter refused to let her drive the car, they fought. That night, Pam and her husband developed symptoms consistent with a non-lethal dosage of arsenic. At the time it was diagnosed in the emergency room as the flu, but Pam believed it must have been something else. She thought the pain was too great for it to be the flu, and she did not think it felt like the previous time she had had the flu. It is impossible to say for sure whether or not Barfield poisoned her daughter and son-in-law, but Barfield had killed one of her employers for no apparent financial gain. It is possible that in her anger she chose to cause pain to her child, and Pam believed Barfield poisoned her.

Barfield's treatment of her children can be looked at as evidence for both arguments. It really is difficult to determine whether this was a case of a loving mother becoming mentally disturbed, or if Barfield's tender care served a selfish obsession. As far as her children are concerned, they believe the former, and they did know her best.

A closer look at Barfield's addiction

At one point Barfield blamed her crimes on her addiction to prescription tranquilizers. One must question the role of her addiction in the crimes she committed. It is possible she would not have become a black widow if her addiction had not been present, as most of her killings seemed to result from attempts to hide fraud committed to pay for prescription medications.

Barfield did once blame her actions on the drugs. Research has shown that addictive drugs do affect the physical makeup of the brain, and addiction has been shown to radically alter priorities in individuals. Barfield might have never killed if she had not been addicted to the drugs. She allegedly killed her mother accidentally while trying to keep her from finding out about a loan application Barfield had filled out using her name. Also, apparently her motivation for killing one of her employers was to keep him from finding out about checks she wrote on his account that she was unable to cover. The evidence for Barfield's possible psychopathy comes primarily from her callous disregard for her victims, and from the repeated instances of fraud. Without the drug use to motivate these actions, it is possible she would have never been more than a normal, if unhappy, wife and mother. Again this is impossible to determine, but it is possible that instead of a case of psychopathy or another personality disorder, this was just a case of an addict turning to crime to support her habit.

Alternatively, her addiction could be taken as evidence of psychopathy. Her first husband was hospitalized for alcohol dependence. Barfield was aware of the damage done by substance abuse, and she did not seek out an effective treatment for her problem. This caused a great deal of friction with her first husband and set in motion the chain of events. It could be argued that her impulsivity was high, a characteristic found in many psychopaths, and that her desire for her own self-gratification outweighed all other concerns. If she had not been addicted to the prescription drugs, she very well might have killed for other reasons. It appeared that at least one of her murders was not motivated by financial gain. Whether she would still have killed for revenge the mother she greatly resented, or perhaps killed a lover who did not wish to marry her remains unclear.

One thing is certain: Barfield's addiction was a serious problem. The role it actually played in her crimes is uncertain, but it does appear unlikely that she would have started killing without it. One factor that has to be considered is the effect of the medications on her behavior. Due to the amount of medication she took it is impossible to know exactly what was in her system at any given moment, but it appears that her primary dependency was on Valium. The combined effects of Valium with her other medications are unknown, but Valium alone has been shown in experimental studies to increase aggression to others and towards the self. Valium appears to reduce inhibitions on aggressive behaviors, and individuals on Valium do at times act in ways they might not when off the drug. Valium has also been shown to have some negative long-term effects on behavior, and recovery from Valium addiction has been shown to be as difficult as recovery from heroin addiction.

Barfield had a history of petty theft and lying. The medications may have been more than a motivating factor for her actions. They may have made her more likely to break laws and increased the aggressive level of her responses. Barfield off the medication might not have been capable of murder.

The doctors

The role her doctors played in all this remains a question as well. Doctors continued to prescribe the medications instead of treating the addiction. The doctors may have contributed to Barfield's actions.

Several doctors testified that Barfield was competent to stand trial. Barfield had a history of getting multiple doctors to fill prescriptions for her, so that if one doctor refused to continue treating her, she always had another. She should not have been able to get away with this. Her doctors might have refused to continue prescribing medications, but none of them suggested sending her for treatment at a drug rehabilitation clinic. Addictive medications can cause major changes in an individual's priorities. While Barfield did hold the responsibility for her actions, the medicines and the doctors who prescribed them without looking more carefully at the matter contributed as well, and in some instances have been sued either for damages or malpractice.

Yet it can also be argued that doctors prescribe these drugs to very large numbers of people, and even though some of them develop addictions, cases like Barfield's are rare. Also, it is impossible to know if an intervention could have altered Barfield's behavior after she started her criminal behavior.

It is also important to consider certain facts about Barfield's drug use. Barfield was taken to the emergency room for treatment many times when she overdosed and mixed medicines that were never meant to be taken in conjunction with each other. Barfield would combine painkillers like Tylenol and codeine, with tranquilizers like Valium, and sedative antidepressant medications like Elavil. The interactions of the different medication were not clear, and many of the medications she took have been shown to have different effects than the intended ones when mixed with other drugs. Even though Barfield's children repeatedly explained the situation to her physicians, doctors continued to prescribe the medications and Barfield often left the hospital after treatment for drug overdose with new prescriptions.

A woman who repeatedly proved incapable of following dosage limits and who regularly overdosed continued to be given prescriptions instead of being forced into a drug rehabilitation program. A woman who started to commit crimes to support her habit was not forced into treatment by the court system. Barfield definitely had a degree of responsibility for her own actions, but once addiction has set in, an individual's ability to self-govern is severely impaired. Her children tried to intervene with the doctors, did not seek to use coercive measures. It is possible that Barfield may have slipped through a system not set up to deal with her particular problem.

Tried and found guilty

Another woman, Diana Lumbrera, was a killer active towards the end of Barfield's criminal career. She murdered six of her children by suffocating them. Unlike Barfield, she was sentenced to life imprisonment. Waneta E. Hoyt, also active around the same period, murdered five of her children by suffocation, and was sentenced to seventy-five years in prison. Tillie Gbrurek, active in the early 1900s, killed four husbands and one of her neighbors, and was sentenced to life imprisonment. Barfield was the first woman executed after the reinstatement of the death penalty. Other women committed similar crimes, but avoided the death sentence. One must wonder why society chose to execute this particular murderess.

Something about Velma Barfield made her different enough from these three other killers to earn her the death penalty. Something about her made the jury vote for the death penalty, even though most juries tend to be unwilling to sentence women to death, and even more unwilling to do so to a grandmother. Hoyt might have suffered from Munchausen's syndrome by proxy, a condition where an individual harms another person in order to gain sympathy from others, but the other two were entirely motivated by profit. One of the other two women harmed children.

Many factors might have contributed to the differing perceptions of these women that may have led to the differences in sentencing. One of the key points was Velma Barfield's behavior in her trial. She attempted to contest the charges, and at several points in the trial the prosecutor was able to elicit a sarcastic reaction from her. At critical moments she was made to seem callous and uncaring, and this could have been what earned her the death penalty, while Lumbrera avoided it by confessing once she was caught. Barfield's reactions to the events of the trial were seemed abnormal. She was not concerned about the outcome. She was argumentative when she should not have been. Afterward, she was upset, but not about the death penalty. She was upset that she would not be able to see her grandchildren and that she was not allowed to get all her possessions from the jail before being transported. Reading about the trial seems to support the idea that Barfield was a psychopath, as that could be the best explanation for her shallow and inappropriate emotional responses during her trial.

However, those same inappropriate reactions that likely sealed her fate could also support the idea that she was not entirely rational. Even during the trial she was still taking her medications. She did not react when the death sentence was announced. She did not really seem to understand the seriousness of what was happening.

The fact that she did not victimize her children might have made it more difficult for her to seem like someone suffering from some sort of mental disorder. Most individuals still have trouble believing that a mother could rationally kill her children. As she was more selective in choosing her victims, it made her seem more rational. Through the course of the trial, her attorney attempted to use her addiction as a defense, while the prosecutor tried to make her appear more deliberate in her actions. A rational person would not have reacted the way she did during the trial. She responded to the prosecutor's taunting the way a child would, instead of as a rational older woman unfairly accused of murder. These actions, however, were apparently insufficient to supersede her history of rational, calculating behavior.

There were, of course, other factors. The prosecutor was set on the death penalty from the beginning of the case, and he had a reputation for winning capital cases, while Barfield's attorney was much less experienced and had never handled a capital case before. The prosecutor also made certain that every member of the jury was at least open to considering the death penalty.

The fact remains that Barfield went to her trial drugged on an unspecified cocktail of prescription medications. She received the death sentence partially because of her callous responses to the prosecutor. It is possible that she truly felt no remorse for her actions, but because she was so medicated during the trial her responses might not have been the same if she had not been under the influence of the medication. We will never know for certain, but it is important to note that she was taking medications which may have a negative effect on behavior.

On the other hand, Barfield chose to commit crimes. While she might have never killed without the drugs, the classic psychopath's response to being caught is to shift the blame onto some outside source. Her claims that she only meant to make her victims sick were ridiculous. This may have been an example of the psychopath's ability to rewrite reality to suit them. Psychopaths regularly have trouble with impulse control. From the beginning, Barfield had difficulty controlling her intake of prescription tranquilizers. She was unable to keep herself from reacting when the prosecutor provoked her during her trial. Even knowing that her life depended on presenting a certain image was not enough to make her control herself. She showed signs of the vicious temper and egocentricity that characterized her father. She lacked the grandiosity that is common among psychopaths, but her need to be the center of her son's life bordered on the pathological. This may have been a different manifestation of the psychopath's inflated self-worth. Barfield claimed to have repented, but none of the records of her life show any sign of true remorse for her actions. It is quite possible she was just saying what people wanted to hear without really understanding it. Barfield showed many signs of the shallow and immature emotions that characterize psychopaths.

The question of motive

Killing Dollie Edwards did not appear to bring her any monetary gain. Black widows generally only kill for money. Barfield may have had some other motivation driving her killing. She did not fully fit the expected pattern of the profit-seeking black widow.

Barfield's motivations are definitely unclear. In her autobiography, she blamed the medications and the circumstances of her life. She claimed the drugs had blocked out many of the memories of her actions. There are several possible interpretations. She may have been a psychopath placed in circumstances where she felt murder was the simplest option, or a victim of drug addiction who lost her ability to fully reason. Maybe she just used the drugs as an excuse to eliminate people who irritated her, and monetary gain was a secondary benefit.

If the drugs truly were to blame, then at least four people would not have died if she had not become addicted. However, her reasons for killing her mother were in question, and at least one other death occurred for non-financial reasons. If she had some other underlying motive, then she may have become a black widow regardless of her addiction.

Her motive is additionally important, because it is unclear if Barfield suffered from psychopathy or from some other personality disorder. Some black widows have murdered for jealousy or revenge. Barfield's callous behavior may have been a result of the medications, not a sign of inherent psychopathy. However, it is difficult to reconcile the image of a loving mother with that of a woman who remorselessly killed her husbands. Barfield had to have had some form of psychopathology beyond substance dependence to account for her actions.

On labeling

During her trial, the prosecutor characterized Barfield as a monster. Her defense attorney attempted to use the insanity defense. Her children were shocked that the woman they knew as a loving mother could commit such crimes. In the end her children still could not see her as evil. While she was imprisoned she claimed to have truly found her faith and repented for her actions. Some people have claimed she is proof that individuals who have committed terrible crimes can be redeemed. The suffering she inflicted on her victims and her apparent lack of remorse for her actions makes her appear to be a psychopath. Some people have cited greed as her motivation. The frequent arguments she had with her victims could also point to revenge as a motivation for her crimes.

Before evidence of poisoning was found, Taylor's children had thought she was a good Christian. The Edwardses used the same label when they found a forged check. They would not believe that Barfield, a good Christian, could have done it. Barfield found work in a nursing home while she was dating Taylor. Her boss called her a conscientious and dependable worker. It is unclear what to make of these two conflicting images.

Conclusions

It really is impossible to say for certain whether or not Barfield was a psychopath. There is evidence that she was a victim of circumstance, and there is equally compelling evidence that she was an active agent who chose to commit atrocities. Psychopathy is not a simple disorder. It exists on a continuum. In this author's opinion, Barfield was a psychopath, but not at the extreme of the condition. If it had not been for the drugs she took, the full extent of the damage she did would have been restricted to a series of unhappy relationships instead of to fraud and murder.

Notes about sources

Most of the material on Barfield's life came from Bledsoe's biography, *Death Sentence*. Information on female serial killers came primarily from Kelleher and Kelleher's *Murder Most Rare* and Jones's *Women Who Kill*. Additional information on this case was found on crimelibrary.com. Information on drug effects and addiction was found primarily through journal articles and from drugs.com. Information concerning psychopathy was drawn primarily from books by Cleckley and Hare.

Patrick Bateman, Bret Easton Ellis, and *American Psycho*
Psychopathic literary elements in a novel

Abstract

This case study investigates the depiction of psychopathic literary elements in the novel *American Psycho*. The primary character, Patrick Bateman, and the secondary characters are assessed for psychopathy and other relevant disorders as if they were real humans in order to determine probable clinical diagnoses. The conclusion drawn is that Bateman was a psychopath and clearly exhibited narcissistic personality disorder as well. His peers were partial psychopaths and also fit the narcissistic personality disorder criteria. On the other hand, Bateman's account might not be entirely unbiased. In fact, he may have had a psychotic disorder such as schizophrenia, which causes the reader to question the reality of the book's events. If Bateman's self-described homicidal activity were merely in his imagination, he still would qualify as a partial psychopath. The author, Bret Easton Ellis, is also analyzed for creating intensely graphic scenes in the book. The conclusion drawn is that having the skill to put oneself in the mindset of a psychopathic killer is a mental skill separate from possessing the actual personality traits of a psychopath.

Background

Published in 1991, *American Psycho* is a fictional novel written by Bret Easton Ellis. Before this case study explores the content of the book for its contribution to the understanding of psychopathy, it is important to describe the context of the book itself. Fraught with controversy since its conception, *American Psycho* nearly lost its opportunity for publication. The prominent publishing company Simon & Schuster was originally slated to publish the book. They understood that the book contained graphic scenes of sex and violence, but they also foresaw that the book would most likely earn them a significant profit. Unfortunately, before the book was released, some exceedingly gory excerpts from the novel were printed in both *Time* and *Spy* magazines. These excerpts were read by a wide range of social action and women's groups such as the National Organization for Women. The scenes that they and countless other Americans read depicted what many literary critics described as horrific and vile scenes of violence against women. Feminist organizations were outraged to see such objectification and outright destruction of women promoted in a book to be published by a well-known company. Rumors also surfaced that the female employees of Simon & Schuster refused to do any work regarding *American Psycho*. All of a sudden, the media began to cover the unfolding drama, capturing the essence of the shocking new book and the fury of the offended groups. This firestorm escalated into such harsh criticism of all parties involved with the book that Simon & Schuster decided to cut their losses by putting an end the publication of *American Psycho*, despite having paid Ellis an advance of three hundred thousand dollars before reading the book. Vintage Books disregarded the negative attention surrounding the novel and picked up the rejected work for publication.

The novel sold very well despite media such as the *The New York Times* publishing articles condemning the book. In 2000, a movie version of *American Psycho*, adapted and directed by Mary Harron, was released. By the time the movie hit the screens, the air of disgust had long dissipated. In the interim between the novel and movie, the famous work *The Silence of the Lambs* became extremely popular in book and movie form. Although the scenes in both stories were comparably graphic, *The Silence of the Lambs* drew much less attention for its depiction of mutilated and tortured women. In fact, it received more protests for its portrayal of the homosexuality of the central killer. Perhaps *American Psycho* had already shocked the public with detailed descriptions of intense violence so that people were subsequently desensitized to similar works. It could also simply be the perspective from which *American Psycho* was written. The novel is unique because it is a first-person narrative from the killer's point of view, an outlook no contemporary author had attempted to portray accurately. The experience is more frightening and disturbing when one reads how a killer thinks about his prey than when one reads the same experience from third-person or another character's first-person perspective. It would have been different and probably much more palatable to read Ellis's novel from another viewpoint, but the work would not have had the desired effect or distinctiveness that the author hoped to achieve. Regardless, the social atmosphere transformed dramatically in the nine years between the book and the movie. Many critics and reviewers who wrote about the novel post-release tended to discount the criticism from the offended parties and defend the right to create art that contains a message and embodies creativity. Retrospectively, most agree that it is a work of fiction that is not indicative of the author's ideas. Since the initial uproar, it has been appropriately critiqued for its literary merit and content, not its potentially offensive scenes.

The story of Patrick Bateman

American Psycho took place in New York City in the late 1980s. It was written in the first-person perspective from Patrick Bateman's point of view. In its serious tone, the story manages to be very witty at times and has a substantial amount of social commentary. Bateman was a very wealthy, young businessman who worked on Wall Street for Pierce and Pierce, which seemed to be a brokerage firm, though he never described the actual work he did. Most of his wealth was inherited from his family, but his salary gave him ample funding for going out to the most popular New York restaurants and clubs and vacationing in the Hamptons. He mentioned that he did not really need to work, but he wanted to fit in. He went to Phillips Exeter Academy for high school and graduated from Harvard College in 1984, further showcasing his privileged background.

The novel began with Bateman and his closest acquaintance, Timothy Price, in a taxi going to work. Price, who later went to rehabilitation for a drug addiction, read a newspaper and prattled on about all the bad things that plague society while making derogatory remarks about homeless beggars along the street and continually telling the cab driver to turn the radio volume up. The topic of conversation switched rapidly from food to girls to work to clothing. These topics pervaded every conversation throughout the entire book. Because it was written from Bateman's point of view, the author rightfully had him dwell on the things that matter to him most. The novel is not just a narrative of the events that occur; Bateman focused upon his interests and glossed over the areas that did not matter to him.

Bateman was part of a circle of yuppies, all intent on making money, being noticed, looking attractive, and generally being rich. They constantly obsessed over how they appeared. On a regular basis, Bateman listed in great detail to the reader the clothing ensembles that men he saw were wearing as if he were reciting a clothing article from *GQ*. He usually spent several hours every day working out, deciding upon the proper clothing to wear, and using various male cosmetic products to improve his face, teeth, and hair. He was especially sensitive about how his hair looked. This extensive regimen was facilitated by his easy job, for which he often showed up late and left early. He and his coworkers all shared this obsession with themselves and a total disregard for the wellbeing of each other. In fact, each was simply a tool for the next to use in his never-ending upward quest for wealth and fame.

Some, including Bateman, had long-term girlfriends. However, Bateman did not really care a bit about his girlfriend Evelyn. To him, she was annoying, fickle, and unintelligent. He frequently had sex with his other friends' girlfriends as well as with prostitutes. This worked the other way as well; Evelyn had affairs with Bateman's acquaintances, and although he guessed that she did, he did not care. Bateman constantly sized up random women, also known as hardbodies, in order to find potential sexual partners. Despite the worries about AIDS and other diseases, sexual promiscuity abounded.

The most common discussion among Bateman's peers was about which restaurant to attend for dinner and drinks that night. It took them seemingly hours to figure out which was the most chic, popular restaurant and what was the best thing on each menu. This process inevitably consisted of recitations from Zagat ratings. Once at restaurants, the conversation was equally meaningless. They once chatted about business card design, each flaunting his own as a symbol of superiority. They spent hundreds of dollars on champagne, wine, appetizers, and eventually the main course. All tried to trump the next by offering to pay with their platinum credit cards while secretly hoping someone else would foot the bill.

Finding drugs, primarily cocaine, was also a significant issue in the daily life of Bateman and his peers. It is actually a point of humor in the novel because Bateman and his coworkers regularly went to what they hoped were the most popular clubs and attempted to acquire cocaine from various dealers that someone in the group vaguely heard about from unreliable sources. Usually, they managed to procure only a small amount of cocaine that was not very powerful because the dealers added sugar in order to cheat buyers and make more money. It is humorous how much effort repeatedly went into trying to get high from cocaine. They failed every time and usually ended up buying forty-dollar martinis instead. Often, Bateman grew tired of the monotony and attempted to escape, always using the excuse that he had videotapes he needed to return. That excuse was just one of many instances that comprised his compulsive lying that was evident throughout the book.

Diagnosis

Such was the superficial life of Patrick Bateman and his peers. Occasionally, someone would host a party at a flat on the upper west side or the company would take them and clients to a concert that they cared nothing about, but there was no depth. Bateman needed constant stimulation from a variety of sources and never truly appreciated his life and his personal interactions. He was very removed from any internal connection with himself or others. Using this description as a general outline for the thought and behavior patterns of Bateman and his peers, several of them fit most of the Factor 1 criteria of the Psychopathy

Checklist-Revised. To clarify, the checklist consists of two nine-item categories of criteria, deemed factors. Factor 1 describes the emotional and personality-related aspects of psychopathy and Factor 2 describes the behavioral and interpersonal aspects of psychopathy.

Because the book does not delve into the lives of the secondary characters, their behavioral aspects cannot be accurately interpreted in regards to Factor 2 of the PCL-R. However, enough of the personalities of Bateman's peers were evident in order to label them collectively as having narcissistic personality disorder. They shared sufficient traits that directly relate to the *Diagnostic and Statistical Manual* criteria for this personality disorder. Only five of nine criteria must be met, but these characters satisfied all measures of narcissism. They had a grandiose sense of self-importance, a preoccupation with fantasies of success or power, and a belief that they were special and should only associate with other high-status people or groups; they required excessive admiration, had a sense of entitlement, and were interpersonally exploitative; they lacked empathy; they envied others or believed that others were envious of them; and they engaged in arrogant, haughty behavior. These traits were present in all contexts throughout the book. The other secondary characters unequivocally exhibited narcissistic qualities. These one-dimensional individuals are not the prime focus of diagnosis and examination, though. They simply created the backdrop for the main character's life. The story told from Patrick Bateman's perspective allowed the reader to have an extensive look into his thoughts and actions. If everything he told the reader was at least somewhat true, then there is no question that he was a psychopath. The author clearly designed Bateman to present himself as an unambiguous, frightening model of a rare and exciting killer.

Unbeknown to his peers, Patrick Bateman was a serial killer. He often discussed the admirable qualities of famous serial killers with his peers, but nobody paid too much attention to his obsession. Bateman frequently spent his nights torturing and killing innocent humans. Some victims he knew personally and others he had never met before. Among many others, he murdered homeless men, prostitutes, coworkers, and even a young boy. If he did not feel like going through the hassle of finding a human victim, he bought an animal from the pet store and killed it instead. He did not simply kill these people, though; he destroyed them in the most torturous, gruesome manners. And because the reader received the story told from his point of view, no gory detail was spared. He celebrated his sadistic tendencies and basked in his power over the lives and bodies of others. He found it fun and exciting to create new ways to inflict pain upon what he considered stupid, inferior individuals. For the purpose of this study, Bateman's details of the crimes need not be dwelled upon any further. The essential fact is that Bateman obtained pleasure from killing living things on a fairly regular basis.

Apparently Bateman had been acting antisocially for a large portion of his life. At one point he briefly mentioned the first murder he ever committed. During his years at Harvard he beheaded a girl near the Charles River. That in mind, he probably committed other antisocial acts prior to that first murder, although he never explicitly gave any other references to his past. This aspect of his past likely satisfied the conduct disorder criteria for antisocial personality disorder and the checklist item of early behavioral problems.

In fact, the only PCL-R items that Patrick Bateman did not fit were many short-term marital relationships because he never married and the revocation of conditional release because he was never convicted of any crimes. That second point is worth discussing. Bateman, despite the number of murders he committed and the messy manner in which he performed them, was never apprehended. Interestingly enough, he was simultaneously careful and careless about the murders he committed. Sometimes he left dead bodies lying around his room for a couple of days, but at one point in the book he described how he disposed of them. He owned a low-profile storage space in which he kept a large tub for pouring lime over bodies for decomposition. There was no trace of the body left behind as evidence. His careful cover-up, however, ended there. The rest of the reason for his escaping suspicion was based on social factors. Ellis's social commentary of 1980s New York City consisted of creating a place in which getting away with murder could not be easier. Bateman left bloodstained carpets and fluids of all sorts for his maid to clean up. She returned the apartment to a spotless state without a single comment. Bateman evidently paid her well. Furthermore, he took bloodied sheets to an Asian-owned laundry service and on one occasion, traveled around town in a bloody raincoat after killing someone, but nobody ever paid attention. Ellis evidently wanted to express the message that a naïve society contributed to a psychopath's success just as much as the psychopath himself.

Bateman further expressed his arrogance and grandiosity by keeping parts of bodies that he dismembered. For instance, in one scene he kept female genitals in his gym locker so he could admire his successes. He became so wrapped up in his obsession to kill that he could hardly keep it a secret. In fact, he told people relatively close to him that he had problem and that he had killed a lot of people, but no one took him seriously. One scene that exemplified this murder-friendly social environment was when Bateman sat at dinner with his girlfriend Evelyn. He took a urinal cake from a bathroom, coated it in chocolate, wrapped it up in a Godiva chocolate box, and gave it to her as a gift. She ate it in obvious anguish but made herself enjoy it because the name Godiva meant that what was inside the box must be very good. The evening continued with Bateman telling Evelyn that his need to commit mass homicide could not be corrected. She answered by saying she did not want to get breast implants. This type of semi-humorous social commentary pervaded the novel and jabbed at the inability of people to identify a psychopath when they see one. After another killing episode, Bateman actually left a message on a coworker's answering machine, saying that he killed a man who had gone missing among many others. Later, the man who received the message laughed and told Bateman that that was a really funny joke. Ellis painted this world of the 1980s as a superficial landscape designed for any one of many psychopaths to emerge as a successful murderer without detection. Patrick Bateman was not incredibly skilled at covering up evidence. It was simply a society of people who were obsessed with themselves that allowed Bateman to continue doing whatever pleased him. Society could not take the entire blame for making Bateman the way he was, but it could be held responsible for promoting his lifestyle.

Possible comorbid disorders

Although the book's main character may be proved psychopathic with little ambiguity, this does not exclude the possibility that other disorders were present and often dominated his personality. Throughout the book, Ellis gave the reader occasional glimpses of the possible constellation of mental disorders that may have afflicted Patrick Bateman. Various chapters highlighted the peculiar habits and mental states of Bateman from his interesting vantage point as the storyteller. It was as if Ellis attempted to design a puzzle. He provided the reader with bits and pieces, forcing one to figure out what Bateman's life would be like from a more objective standpoint.

It was hinted at earlier that Bateman could quite clearly be labeled as having antisocial personality disorder. As a broader construct than psychopathy, Bateman easily met the criteria. He broke laws with reckless abandon, deceived, was impulsive and irritable, and lacked responsibility and remorse. There was not a single episode in which Bateman failed to exhibit antisocial behavior.

Also addressed previously, Bateman and his companions fit the criteria for narcissistic personality disorder. This obsession with oneself seemed particularly integral to the understanding of Bateman's mental abnormalities. For instance, it was clear that Bateman had an interesting anxiety problem, but it was difficult to gauge how severe it was. He seemed to become very unnerved if his appearance was not impeccable. His hair, especially, was a very sensitive attribute of his. If he thought his hair was not sitting perfectly or had been messed up, he would break into a cold sweat and not be able to focus on anything else. Bateman reacted similarly if his social interactions were not going as planned. For instance, he mentioned to the reader that he almost ripped a Zagat handbook apart when his friends could not decide on which restaurant to attend for dinner. Combined with his impulsivity and strange interpersonal relationships, this personal instability and difficulty grasping self-image overlapped considerably with criteria for borderline personality disorder. Bateman likely did not fit enough of the criteria for a full diagnosis, but many of the qualities were similar.

Bateman also shared some qualities with obsessive compulsive disorder. This disorder consists of two parts, obsessions, which are intrusive thoughts or mental images that are usually distressing, and compulsions, which are acts that one carries out in order to alleviate or satisfy the obsessions. It is often difficult to distinguish obsession from compulsion when an individual does not clearly explain his thought process. Such was the case with Patrick Bateman when he listed the style and designer name of every visible article of clothing worn by every person he noticed. It is unclear whether he truly enjoyed fashion or had some intrusive anxieties causing him to focus upon the clothing. Somewhat more apparent is how obsessive compulsive disorder might relate to his killings. He occasionally felt overwhelming anxiety and needed to torture and kill someone in order to assuage these impulses and feel at ease. This might not be a clear example of the obsession-compulsion relationship, but a few of Bateman's murders seemed to have stemmed from some internal need to abate desires to kill or find pleasure. In other words, it often mattered more that he killed than whom he killed. Regardless of whether or not Bateman truly had obsessive compulsive disorder, this framework offers a view of why Bateman killed on some occasions.

Bateman's instability became infinitely more obvious during a particular chapter in which Bateman highlighted the middle portion of a day in an almost stream-of-consciousness style. The episode was dizzying. He frantically ran around the city streets panicking, sweating, and acting quite strangely. In his delirium, he searched for Valium, Xanax, or Halcion, any of which usually abated such a situation, but he could only find Nuprin. Nuprin is merely a nonsteroidal anti-inflammatory similar to ibuprofen, so that might have eased the headache Bateman experienced, but it would not have helped the other symptoms. Valium, Xanax, and Halcion are all benzodiazepines, which are used to treat anxiety disorders such as panic disorder. At this point in the description, it seemed that panic disorder was a reasonably well-supported diagnosis for Bateman. His set of symptoms illustrated a panic attack rather well. It was an unexpected, overwhelming activity of Bateman's sympathetic nervous system, his fight-or-flight mechanism. Also, a doctor must have agreed with that diagnosis at some point in order for Bateman to obtain all those prescription drugs. Regardless, he took the Nuprin, but it did not alter his erratic behavior or thought process.

As a matter of fact, Bateman seemed to slip into more and more bizarre and disorganized behavior as the day continued. Among a litany of sudden, confused actions, he tossed his walkman into the trash, shoplifted a canned ham and ate it with his fingers, gave a description of himself baring his fangs like a vampire at a stranger, bought crack from a dealer, consumed the crack on the spot, and wandered into a cheap sandwich shop and said he made reservations with the maitre d' while yelling obscenities at the owner. This scene depicted what seemed to be more a psychotic than a panic episode. He exhibited very disorganized thoughts and behaviors, combined with some possible delusions and hallucinations. Those are the primary attributes of psychosis, which is essentially a distortion in the perception of reality. What seemed like an incapacitating panic attack turned out to be a signal that more severe mental abnormalities might have been present in Patrick Bateman. However, a psychotic episode did not necessarily mean that Bateman had schizophrenia. Psychosis could occur in manic or brief psychotic episodes independent of schizophrenia.

Is it all real?

Until this point, it seemed pretty clear that everything Bateman described from his perspective was quite serious and realistic. Remember that there was only a possibility, not an assurance, that Bateman had a psychotic disorder. One must keep in mind that this avenue of analysis is not necessarily accurate; it is only a prospect to be explored. That being said, if Bateman's story were potentially laced with a psychotic bias, a host of new interpretations of Bateman and the novel become available. In fact, during an interview, Bret Easton Ellis volunteered the idea that everything in the book might not actually have happened. He did not expand on that idea, but the author did mention it as a possibility, a hint for how readers should think about the novel.

Bateman told the story of *American Psycho* from his point of view. If he did have schizophrenia, then his bouts of psychosis might be reflected in his narrative. He might not have related the story as objectively as the terse, straightforward writing style suggests. Whatever may have seemed corporeal and obvious to Bateman may not be what was truly real. Because there was no moderating voice, no narrator but Bateman, there were no checks on the passage between reality and fantasy. So if this hypothesis were true, how much of the story was a delusion and how much was actually real? Some gruesome acts seemed unambiguously real, such as when Bateman stabbed the eyes of a homeless man and then stumbled over the blind man later in the novel, or when a man claiming Bateman killed his friend robbed him at gunpoint, although that could have been a simple case of mistaken identity. However, other scenes are more difficult to comprehend.

One of the extended storylines within the book dealt with Paul Owen, an extremely successful and wealthy coworker in Bateman's firm. Bateman and his peers were envious of Owen because he was in charge of handling a very high-paying secret account that Bateman constantly inquired about. Bateman's jealousy of Owen highlighted the competitive measure of success, compared to internal motivation that seemed to dominate the '80s culture. Nevertheless, Bateman managed to get Owen drunk and alone where he brutally murdered him with an ax. He took Owen's keys, let himself into his luxurious apartment, and changed Owen's answering machine message, explaining that he went away to England. Days later, a detective arrived at Bateman's office, trying to find information on the disappearance of Paul Owen. Bateman became very nervous, but managed to slide through the interrogation without eliciting any suspicion. Evidently, the detective believed the answering machine, but Owen's girlfriend did not. Someone in England said he saw Owen, but it turned out to be a mistaken identity, which happened frequently with all characters. In fact, for the remainder of the book, people mentioned hearing about or seeing Owen in England. Finally, Bateman returned to Owen's apartment one day to find it up for sale by the real estate agent, who was giving tours to prospective buyers. The agent did not admit to knowing about Paul Owen, but seemed to have some hidden knowledge that frightened Bateman, leaving both him and the reader confused.

There are a couple possible explanations for the Owen storyline. First, Bateman could have actually killed him and gotten away with it by deceiving everyone. The remade apartment was simply to eliminate any memory of a murder to future residents. Second, Bateman could have imagined following through with his fantasy of killing the obnoxious Owen when in fact, Owen decided to move to England without giving prior notice except on his answering machine. Bateman could have been unnecessarily nervous when talking to the detective because he was paranoid and actually believed that he killed Owen and recorded the message on the machine. And he was even more paranoid when interacting with the real estate agent, construing every glance and inflection in her voice as a hint that she was on to Bateman when, in fact, she was probably illegally selling his apartment to new wealthy buyers and wanted Bateman to leave because he seemed to know about Paul Owen and could have jeopardized her business. The first scenario is straightforward and plausible, but given the circumstances, the second interpretation might better explain Bateman's awkward encounter with the real estate agent. That portion of the novel is broken into several pieces and is quite difficult to follow, so it will remain ambiguous at this level of analysis.

However, other scenes seemed somewhat unrealistic as well. For instance, Bateman shot a dog and its owner on a sidewalk, but unfortunately a police patrol car was cruising nearby and an officer heard the gunshot. Bateman ran, but was eventually cornered in a standoff with several squad cars full of officers. This was one of the few encounters with law enforcement in the entire novel. Bateman managed to shoot the gas tank of a squad car, causing a giant explosion that killed or decommissioned all the officers. He then ran to his office building, shot the security guard, and went to his office where he called a coworker and confessed to all his murders on an answering machine. This was all very exciting at the time, but there was no subsequent follow-up of the events by the police. No one seemed to recall the incident. Additionally, his acquaintance thought that the message he left on the machine was a hilarious joke and brushed it aside. Besides, he said he had seen Paul Owen in England. Was this another case of people simply not caring about events unrelated to themselves or was Bateman unaware of the distinction between reality and his imagination?

Ellis gave no definitive answer regarding the degree of reality, only the hint that the story might be fantasy. The entire novel might even have been the dreams of an otherwise healthy yuppie on Wall Street. Was he simply playing out his sick desires in his mind and relating them to the reader as if they were real? It is possible, but it seems that he truly was the shallow, pleasure-seeking yuppie portrayed throughout most of the book regardless of the accurate body count from his murders. Despite this ambiguity, one question remains relevant in this context. Even if all the murders that Bateman committed throughout the story were fictional, could Patrick Bateman still have been psychopathic?

First of all, schizophrenia and psychopathy are not mutually exclusive disorders. It is not uncommon for psychopathic deviants also to be psychotic. As was mentioned earlier, Bateman clearly fit the Factor 1 traits of psychopathy, and that would not change with the idea that his murders are imaginary. He remained grandiose, charming, unempathic, deceitful, sexually promiscuous, and shallow. The question was whether or not he satisfied enough Factor 2 characteristics without actually committing murders. The short answer is that the murders were only the most severe expression of Bateman's personality. Bateman still obsessed over murders, even if he only carried them out in his mind. In nonhomicidal interactions with others, he still exhibited irresponsibility, impulsivity, a great need for stimulation, and a lack of realistic, long-term goals. Ellis designed this character to be a frightening, distasteful figure whether or not he committed murders. However, if the murders were a fantasy, might not Bateman's portrayal of himself also be skewed toward his ideal serial killer personality? Through this lens, one cannot accurately distinguish reality from falsehood, and psychopathy would be nearly impossible to diagnose. It is obvious that the novel leaves much for interpretation and personal opinion. That being said, this analysis concludes that Patrick Bateman most likely was a psychopath regardless of the reality of his murders and the existence of any comorbid disorders.

Bret Easton Ellis

The author of *American Psycho* is an intriguing character himself. Bret Easton Ellis was only twenty-seven when his third book, *American Psycho*, was published in 1991. He received good sales and a great deal of publicity from his works that include *Less Than Zero*, *The Rules of Attraction*, *Lunar Park*, and *The Informers*. All his work tended to focus on morbid, twisted plots with mentally estranged characters. Most critics agreed that his prose was not beautiful, but the books made up for those shortcomings through originality and edginess.

The writing process of *American Psycho* is a rather interesting subject. How does one go about making a novel like *American Psycho*? In an interview, Ellis mentioned briefly that the book was autobiographical in nature. He obviously did not mean that his life consisted of lying, murdering, and spending great sums of money in New York, but rather that the mood and the style are indicative of how he was feeling at the time. He said the book would have been much different had he been happier at the time. So although there is a great deal of humor in the novel, it is very dark and subtle.

Furthermore, Ellis noted that the writing process itself was quite rigorous. In order to write the detailed sections of music reviews and clothing descriptions, he had to study a plethora of *Rolling Stone* and *GQ* magazines. He said that in order to write most of the story, he had to assume the role of Patrick Bateman because he was writing in first-person. It was essential to describe and dwell upon things that would be prominent in a psychopath's mind in order to create a psychologically realistic story. Bateman was sadistic, so Ellis had to spend a great deal of time discussing the disgusting details of death. That was what Bateman's character was interested in, so that was what Ellis wrote about. The sex scenes were explicit because those details were what excited Bateman. At times, Ellis had described the emotionally draining process with noticeable agitation while at other times, he seemed to brush the graphic portions off and say that the discussion of music in the book took more effort. No one may ever know exactly how he feels about his own work, but he did emphasize that he did not care about what critics said because authors should write books for personal reasons, not for a reaction.

The relevant issue here is what it means to be able to put oneself in the mindset of a serial killer. In writing this entire novel from the perspective of Patrick Bateman, Ellis demonstrated a skill of great imagination. Does this ability to think and write as a deranged psychopath mean that Ellis is a psychopath or has psychopathic qualities? In other words, does pretending to be someone else connote that one possesses those traits either permanently or temporarily? This is not a heavily studied area of psychology, but it is nevertheless possible to address this question. First of all, the definition of acting or pretending is to put oneself in others' positions and behave or think as they would. Most humans can act with varying degrees of skill, but the only prerequisite for acting like someone else is that one understands the character to be acted. No actor must actually be like the person they pretend to be. Kind, loving people can pretend to be psychopaths and psychopaths can pretend to be kind, loving people. In this sense, it is impossible to determine how psychopathic Bret Easton Ellis may be. Through his literary work, there is no precise manner to psychologically analyze the author without his personal input because he may simply be very talented at pretending to be Patrick Bateman. Ellis might be psychopathic, but he is not psychopathic because he wrote *American Psycho*.

The issue of whether or not one can be temporarily psychopathic is more difficult to determine. Although rare, the legal system allows temporary insanity to be used as a legitimate defense in certain cases. If someone can be temporarily insane, why cannot someone be temporarily psychopathic? This logic may be true, but it must be remembered that psychopathy is a personality disorder, which is defined as a long-term, stable set of attributes. By that definition, someone who acts like a psychopath for a mere moment is simply acting. To actually be a psychopath, one must consistently portray such characteristics for years. Psychosis, on the other hand, can be a temporary disorder. Schizophrenia requires psychosis to be present for at least six months for a full diagnosis, but the actual distortion of reality in the form of delusions, hallucinations, or thought disorder can be a temporary matter. The essential concept is that thinking or acting like someone is different from being like someone. Also, the level of seriousness makes a difference. Even if someone is pretending to be a psychopath, he will stop short of following through with antisocial acts. At least this is the case with

Bret Easton Ellis. He imagined psychopathy and put himself in that frame of mind, but there was a reality check still active that prevented his behavior from expanding beyond his novel and truly mimicking his assumed persona.

Implications and conclusion

Serial killers are not representative of the average psychopath population. Robert Hare estimated that for every psychopathic serial killer, there are tens of thousands of other psychopaths. Some break the law and others do not. Bret Easton Ellis's character, Patrick Bateman, was a rare specimen who represented the most frightening and deplorable human being imaginable. He was the worst of the worst, but that is why he exists. A novel about the average psychopath who roams the street or sits in prison is not exciting or unique. Ellis wrote this book because, as he said, he was going through a strange phase in his life, but also because the book created a glimpse of something that very few people experience closely.

Very rarely is society able to witness the thoughts and actions of an extreme personality so vividly. Although this is a fictional novel and Ellis's portrayal of a possibly psychotic psychopath might be a little more imaginative than realistic, the novel set a precedent for the detailed examination of sensitive and edgy material. As was noted earlier, Thomas Harris's *The Silence of the Lamb* series was released in the years following *American Psycho*, and movie versions of both novels became very successful nationwide. Just as Shakespeare's plays provide an excellent canvas for psychological analysis, Ellis supplies a novel rich with material for psychological interpretation. This is not meant to compare *American Psycho* to *Hamlet* on any literary level, but they are similar in that they contain detailed fictional characters with exposed mental processes rich with interesting abnormalities to analyze.

Diagnosing Patrick Bateman might not be equivalent to diagnosing Ted Bundy, but the portrayal of psychopathy in literature is important as well. *American Psycho* gives the public an image of what a psychopath is like, and because of that image, more people probably believe all psychopaths are irrational serial killers. From the psychopaths Randle McMurphy in *One Flew Over the Cuckoo's Nest* to Alex de Large in *A Clockwork Orange*, literature affects the image of mental disorders, no matter how inaccurate the material may be.

Note about sources

The information involving the storyline and characters was taken directly from *American Psycho*. The background information of the novel was compiled by comparing several book reviews and criticisms, primarily Jackson's *American Psy-*

cho: Sliced. Diced. Back. The same reviews and criticisms, especially Freccero's *Historical Violence, Censorship, and the Serial Killer: The Case of American Psycho*, in addition to an interview with Bret Easton Ellis, were used as starting points for investigating the psychological factors present in the book.

Whitey and Billy Bulger
South Boston's Irish mob and Massachusetts politics

Abstract

For over two decades, James J. Bulger, nicknamed and popularly referred to as Whitey, was the leading figure in South Boston's organized crime ring. His younger brother William Bulger took a drastically different path. Out of Boston College Law School, Billy went on to become president of the Massachusetts State Senate, as well as president of the University of Massachusetts, and was often cited as one of the most superlative politicians of his time. In 1975, Special Agent John Connolly arranged for Whitey to become a top criminal informant for the FBI. Although Whitey had previously served time for bank robbery, during his years as a criminal informant he conspired in at least eighteen murders and escaped charges for each under Connolly's protection. In addition to murder, Whitey remains wanted for racketeering, money laundering, narcotics distribution, extortion, and conspiracy to commit each of these acts. An evasive, detached, and impenitent criminal, it seemed that outside of family, friends, and profitable business interests, there was little to which Whitey was loyal. Billy also remained somewhat obscure, providing little insight under numerous forced testimonies regarding the whereabouts and activities of his brother. Whitey vanished on December 23, 1994, shortly after law enforcement began charging and sentencing his local business associates. The FBI offered a one million dollar reward for his arrest, and Whitey remained high on their list of the Ten Most Wanted Fugitives well into the twenty-first century.

The early years

James Whitey Bulger was born into an average South Boston family on September 3, 1929. James Bulger, Sr. and his wife Jean raised six children who grew up poor, attended church regularly, and were no different from most of the Irish families who populated South Boston prior to World War II. There was a seventh child, born after Whitey and just before Billy in 1934. However, the child died shortly after birth and the Bulgers kept quiet about the existence of this seventh sibling. It was one of the many secrets the Bulger family would eventually harbor.

Whitey and Billy grew up very close and would remain extremely loyal to one another even as they pursued divergent paths through life. Billy joined Massachusetts politics, Whitey, organized crime. However, their respective professions shared a common denominator in that the stakes were high, the players were impassioned, and almost everything was personal. Growing up, neither Whitey nor Billy were satisfied with what opportunities lay ahead for the average, Irish, poor South Boston youth, which included little beyond the level of clerk. This initial proclivity to reject what was standard would evolve into a lifetime of breaking rules for both of the Bulger brothers.

While the brothers may have rejected the constraints of growing up in South Boston, they embraced the community wholeheartedly. The sense of loyalty that pervaded the small peninsula was strong, and within the Old Colony Harbor housing project where the Bulgers lived, this brotherhood was even stronger. The us-versus-them mentality which Whitey carried into organized crime and Billy into politics derived from this unflinching sense of loyalty. Outsiders would always have to prove themselves, and even as the brothers' influence spread outside their small community, they would remain loyal to South Boston for life.

Although the first mark on Whitey's police record came at thirteen, even some of his youthful pranks were inspired by a devotion to those close to him. One such incident occurred while Whitey was driving home from the beach his brother and his longtime friend Will McDonough, who were themselves about thirteen at the time. After Billy spotted a boy his age passing on a bicycle and mentioned never having liked him, Whitey promptly pulled the car up behind the bicycle and tapped the bike's back tire with his front bumper. Billy protested as Whitey continued menacingly, but Whitey simply assured his brother that he would not kill the bicyclist though someone else probably would. Even in his youth, Whitey found ways for others to carry out his business.

Irresistible charm and an ineffectual prison sentence

Just as Billy was a passenger to Whitey's mischievous antics in the Cadillac, there was nothing Billy could do about what future associations would be made between the two of them. By virtue of being his brother, Billy was along for the ride. Although he has passively avoided offering information regarding Whitey the criminal, he has always actively supported Whitey his brother. Even when Billy separated himself by choosing scholarship over athletics, he was as private about his accomplishments as he was about his family. He attended Boston College High School, Boston College, and Boston College Law School, providing him ample preparation for a career in Massachusetts politics. Although he had resigned from the boys on the streets to pursue to classical scholarship, friends say he developed self-deprecating tendencies that kept him on the level of others, and could charm anyone with his wit. However, he never abandoned the hard-nosed mentality learned within the neighborhoods of South Boston. This was the persona with which he achieved great success as a politician: exuding charm along with the message that he was not one to be crossed.

Whitey, too, relied on personal charm as well as astute tactics of manipulation to get what he wanted. It seemed that while Billy charmed his way into positions of power, Whitey charmed his way out of trouble. The ease with which Whitey found exoneration for his actions followed him in his first trip outside of South Boston. In 1948, Whitey joined the Air Force, but soon ran into trouble for his behavior. True to his nature, however, Whitey found a way to escape not only the Air Force, but a dishonorable discharge as well.

Upon returning from the Air Force, rather than reevaluating his goals, Whitey contemplated only the manner in which he would increase his clout and his cash flow. He often spent time in the company of homosexuals, and had made a habit of profiting from these encounters. However, he eventually devoted more of his leisure time to bank robbing. In 1956, he was caught for armed robbery and would spend the next nine years in prison. Punishment did nothing to alter his outlook, and he persisted in rebellion to the point where his conduct earned him a spot in Alcatraz. While first serving time in the Atlanta penitentiary, he became part of several of the prison's LSD studies. Often taking extreme doses of the drug, certain prisoners had to be transferred to a ward for the criminally insane. Whitey explained how the drug triggered not only temporary insanity, but periods of severe depression, suicidal thoughts, and interrupted sleep. Years later, he still reported suffering problems from the LSD.

While Whitey spent the years between 1956 and 1965 in prison, the Irish Gang War began in 1961 between the Winter Hill Gang of Somerville and the McLaughlins of Charlestown. While prison did nothing to reform Whitey's behavior, the nine-year sentence proved to help his criminal career. Not only would he become more sensible in dealing with authority, but during this time, many hoodlums who would have eventually become Whitey's competition were taken out by the opposing gang. During this same period, the FBI appeared as the new force on the underworld scene intending to eliminate organized crime in Boston, with the Mafia as their primary target. Achieving their goal, however, meant many unethical compromises on behalf of the agents, evolving from petty bribery into outright murder.

The Federal Bureau of Investigation's influence

Though Whitey Bulger led a life of mischief from his early youth, it was actually FBI Special Agent John Connolly who helped Whitey become a leader of organized crime in Boston. The two grew up in the same neighborhood and Bulger first befriended Connolly as a young boy, when, feeling beneficent, he walked into an ice cream shop and offered to treat Connolly and his friends. Connolly developed a close relationship with not only Whitey, but Billy as well. As a close friend, Billy Bulger helped Connolly to get into Boston College Law School, the FBI, and a retirement position at Boston Edison.

From the start, Whitey was a curious choice as a top echelon criminal informant for the Bureau. His friend and partner in crime, Stephen Flemmi, was already an informant at the time. Bringing Whitey in seemed to promise little in return, as he had spent most of his time since prison involved in South Boston's rackets and had virtually no information on the Mafia that Flemmi was not already giving them. The main draw was the other Bulger, Billy.

After retirement at fifty, with low federal pensions, former FBI agents often worried about finding jobs. It would be far easier for agent Connolly to find a job if he not only knew someone of influence, but had done a substantial favor for that someone. Taking Whitey in as an informant, Connolly would protect him from the law while benefiting from his criminal ways. Billy had personally warned Connolly to keep his brother Whitey out of trouble, and in turn, Connolly agreed to offer Whitey his protection, as he was greatly indebted to Billy for the favors he had already provided.

By 1975, John Connolly arranged for Whitey to join Stephen Flemmi as a top informant for the FBI. For almost two decades, agent John Connolly, or Zip as he was affectionately referred to, did an impeccable job of protecting Whitey Bulger. He became somewhat of his guardian angel, tipping him off before law enforcement could catch him, or filing reports to clear his name. Even Whitey's street enforcers were unaware that their boss was an informant, and some would later serve jail time due to information Whitey provided. He was treated as a king, and although he acknowledged this treatment with gifts and money, the information and compensation he offered these agents was very little with respect to what they provided for him.

The Bulger effect

From 1956 until 1978, although Whitey had not stayed out of trouble, his name had gone unmentioned in court. After prison, Whitey fell into race-fixing as a means to bring in large sums of money for himself. Eventually, federal agents arrested the boss of the Winter Hill Gang for fixing races, which would help pave the way for Whitey's rise to becoming the gang's new leader. By January 1979, Whitey was deep in the middle of the race-fixing conspiracy along with the rest of the Winter Hill Gang as well; however, Connolly and Morris stepped in to remedy the situation. The agents went to Jeremiah O'Sullivan, head of the federal organized crime strike force, to persuade him that both Bulger and Flemmi were invaluable sources, needed to pull off the wire-tapping they were planning for Mafia leader Gerry Anguilo's Prince Street garage. This was apparently an easy enough sell, as after their conversation both Bulger and Flemmi were labeled as mere co-conspirators, unindicted in the race-fixing case. This exchange became the norm, and would continue until Whitey's most recent and largely successful evasion of law enforcement through his disappearance in 1994.

Billy Bulger enjoyed his share of good fortune in 1979 as well. Three years earlier in 1976, Massachusetts State Senate Majority Leader Joe DiCarlo was indicted for extortion. Fortunately for Billy Bulger, DiCarlo's lawyer worked for a close friend of his, and was unable to prove his client innocent. On January 23, 1977, DiCarlo was convicted, and on February 28, Billy was appointed the new Senate majority leader. His luck would not end there. DiCarlo filed an appeal and the new evidence presented would reveal that Senate President Kevin Harrington had received a payoff from the same company as DiCarlo. This was the end of his campaign for governor against Michael Dukakis, and once again, Billy reaped the benefits, continuing his ascension through the ranks of Massachusetts politics.

In 1979, Billy was sworn in as Senate president, and in this position, everything had to go through him. Friends and fellow politicians observed that the power quickly went Billy's head. As the new president, it was clear that he felt entitled to certain privileges. Assuming more authority than he apparently held, Billy had promised a longtime friend that he could secure a clerk's position for his son. After Judge George Daher refused to grant him the job, the next budget took Daher out of position as a presiding judge. His pay was also cut twenty-five hundred dollars. Billy certainly held grudges, and in this decisive action, sent a clear message that he would operate on his own terms.

Billy's sense of entitlement shone forth once again after Proposition 2 ½ swept through Boston. The new law capped increases in local property taxes at 2 ½ percent a year, making cities and towns extremely reliant upon financial support from the commonwealth. The budgetary constraints on the city forced cutbacks in various areas, but Billy continued to rule as he pleased. Mayor White proposed shutting down the L Street Bathhouse, which harbored memories and great sentimental value to most children who grew up in South Boston, including Billy. Soon after this proposal, a state agency assumed control of L Street and received two hundred eighty thousand dollars for the next fiscal year. The bathhouse was kept open. Both Whitey and Billy had ascended to what many considered corrupt positions of power.

The elusive and anomalous Whitey Bulger

In 1980, Whitey and Stephen Flemmi decided to base themselves out of Lancaster Foreign Motors, their friend's new garage in West Boston. After several murders had been conspired, several getaway cars arranged outside the garage, and several informant reports on the incidents filed away and forgotten, the State Police finally received a court order allowing them to install bugs within the garage. However, almost immediately thereafter, one-step-ahead Whitey began moving all conversations out of the bugged office, speaking overly favorably about the State Police while they were in the office. With a little more than sinking suspicion, he moved all conversations elsewhere after bugs were placed on a payphone he frequently used behind a local Howard Johnson. While Whitey was elusive when left to his own devices, the FBI agents he worked for were making it near impossible to catch him.

Edward J. Mackenzie, former drug dealer and street enforcer for Whitey, described his boss as being the total package as far as successful gangsters went. People not only respected Whitey, but feared him. In fact a great deal of this respect likely stemmed from others' fear. Mackenzie contended that Whitey rose to the top because he was intelligent and disciplined in the way he ran his organization. Combined with his ruthless nature and willingness to kill when necessary, he manipulated people with ease, led by example without drawing attention to himself, and created an organization of crime that worked for him. In return, he had money, women, and invaluable connections at his disposal. He also had no regrets. Mackenzie recalled Whitey's description of the world of legitimate business, professing his belief that the most successful white-collar executives were thieves in their own respect, who manipulated more people than mobsters and their business associates.

Despite Whitey's enigmatic nature, a reporter named Paul Corsetti eventually learned of his involvement in the murder of bookmaker Louie Litif. While working for Whitey, Litif had taken it upon himself to murder a drug dealer who had crossed him. After this breach in protocol, Whitey decided Litif had to go, for he had not been authorized to kill anyone. Whitey believed that if the people who worked for him started taking it upon themselves to carry out business, murder might become habit, and that would mean anarchy. Though Whitey conducted hits with reckless abandon at times, he liked to be in control. For this one misstep, he took Litif into his makeshift office at Triple O's tavern and murdered him.

When Bulger learned that Corsetti heard about the murder, he once again employed fear tactics to make sure that his name stayed out of the press. Whitey phoned Corsetti at the *Herald American*, anonymously, to suggest meeting at P.J. Clarke's if he wanted more information. Corsetti noted that Whitey was quite garrulous, pulling up a bar stool next to him and making small talk before asking his name. When Corsetti explained he was meeting someone, Whitey lost the smile, explained that he was Jimmy Bulger, and that he killed people. After this encounter, fearing for his life, Corsetti asked Larry Baione for advice. Baione was Mafia leader Gerry Anguilo's top enforcer and owner of the tavern where Litif's body had been left. He told Corsetti that Whitey was crazy, and could do nothing with him.

Though his actions were largely driven by a want of money, power, and freedom, Whitey was far from a one-dimensional mobster. Many Southie residents referred to him as a Robin Hood figure, taking out the bad guys while looking out for women, children, and the elderly. Whitey was rumored to have bought a stolen truckload of Reebok sneakers to hand out to the children in the projects. He delivered turkeys to poor families at Christmas time, once personally evicted a neighborhood drug dealer after a mother complained her child had found a hypodermic needle in the field by their house, and was known to have offered rent money to some of the neighborhood's elderly women living on their own. Whitey was certainly not without conscience, he just seemed to live his life by a different set of rules, as Billy was also reputed to do.

Billy's personal and political agendas

Unfortunately, while Billy had the energy to follow his own path, the public did not always have the energy to look past the media's portrayal of him. He certainly had his opinions and held to them, yet felt he was often unfairly pinned as an old-school politician, with narrow views and little ability to look beyond them. One such political stance was his 1970s opposition to busing. Shortly after the Civil Rights Act of 1965 the Massachusetts legislature passed the Racial Imbalance Act, which dictated that schools with a student population over 50 percent black would be deemed imbalanced. Court-ordered busing was the government's answer in the decade to come, and although Billy believed it placed a burden on

South Boston parents who would have to send their children away to school, many viewed his opposition as racist.

South Boston constituents respected his bold stance, but statewide, his image suffered. This steadfast commitment to what he believed was best for his constituents would come to shape his future legislative agenda, producing bills that proposed state aid for private schools and a proposal for open enrollment in suburban schools. However, it was a commitment the media often spun with largely negative connotations. The image propagated out of his opposition to busing represents the vexatious problems that media portrayal can create.

Those closest to Billy knew him as charming, intelligent, and one of the wittiest politicians to come through Massachusetts. However, many others throughout the state saw him as an autocratic ruler who held grudges. In an act of revenge, he once stalled a bill allowing elderly couples to keep half of their life savings while remaining eligible for state assistance with medical bills. However, Bulger had a rapport with the elderly that was equal to his brother's. He was once reported to have arrived late to an important dinner after stopping to visit a ninety-five year old woman on her birthday. Much like his brother, his personal convictions and political contentions made him something of a paradox, and his refusal to speak to the press made him something of an anomaly among politicians. Whitey did his part during the busing scandal to keep the press and the police away from South Boston. However, his actions were more out of his own self-interest, as he knew that authorities would only create trouble for business.

Kings of Boston

In October 1980, agents Connolly and Morris told Whitey that his role as an informant had become common knowledge, and his life was in jeopardy. The State Police were questioning the FBI, and the FBI's top agents were wondering whether Bulger and Flemmi were worth all the trouble they were causing. To help his case, Connolly included himself in a report filed October 30, citing that State Police had speculated he tipped Whitey off to the garage bugs through his brother, Senate President William Bulger. His intent was to portray Whitey as simply a pawn in a political dispute. To further help their case, the agents sent both Bulger and Flemmi to Gerry Anguilo's Prince Street garage to extract information, as the Mafia was a prime target for the FBI. The information they found was hardly enough. Whitey met with Boston's FBI boss, Lawrence Sarhatt, to try to justify his relationship with the Bureau, but Sarhatt was not charmed as most others were. Once again, it was Jeremiah O'Sullivan who stepped in to save

Whitey's place as an informant, as he had previously done during the race-fixing cases.

For Bulger and Flemmi, 1980 brought another temptation into the world of gambling. The World Jai Alai corporation ran a hand-ball like sport that existed primarily for gambling purposes, and its owner John Callahan brought Bulger and Flemmi in to protect the company's Hartford fronton from Mafia infiltration. In turn, they received ten thousand dollars a week, skimmed from WJA's parking revenues. Eventually, however, Callahan's license was pulled and when the new owner suspected foul play, Whitey decided the best bet was to wipe out everyone even remotely involved, from the previous owners, to a WJA cashier and her boyfriend.

As ruthless as he was business-savvy, once the Jai Alai profits had ceased Whitey was on to another business venture. This time his business partner was another one of his street enforcers, Kevin Weeks. The legitimate business proposition at hand lay in the purchase of Stippo's Liquor Mart. The deal, as Weeks claims, is a classic example of the media's distortion of fact. Although a popularly held account illustrates both Weeks and Bulger threatening the store's owner Stephen Rakes, nicknamed Stippo, the truth according to Weeks is that Stippo's sister Mary approached Whitey. Mary had apparently informed Whitey that Stippo wanted to sell the liquor store, and was wondering if he and Weeks were interested. After several drawn-out negotiations, Bulger and Weeks eventually bought and turned the store into a profitable liquor mart. While the sale of liquor was perhaps the one honest business venture that Whitey could lay claim to, it was entirely hypocritical with respect to his personal opinions regarding alcohol and clean living.

Just as the paradoxical Billy Bulger was an anomaly among politicians, Whitey was anomalous in his own right. While he was a criminal, he was not without principles, and while he was atypical he was not amoral. Weeks described Whitey's sense of morality as being uniquely his own. A sense of entitlement and greed motivated most of his lucrative business decisions, yet he hardly ever flashed his wealth, and certainly not within South Boston where he preferred to remain inconspicuous. He was also extremely generous to those less fortunate and without the means to take proper care of themselves, and his loyalty to friends and especially family was paramount.

The able-bodied who crossed him met a different version of Whitey. One night while living with his elderly mother in Old Harbor, Whitey requested that a group of teenagers quit their basketball game outside her house as it had extended past midnight. When they continued with disregard he marched outside with a knife and stabbed the basketball, eliciting an angry retort from one of the boys. Without hesitation Whitey stabbed the boy as he had done the basketball, opening his stomach, and then put him into his car and drove him to the hospital. When he felt the need to make a point, he was ruthless, but always justified his actions as having their reasons.

Justifying drug sales

Whitey's attitude toward alcohol and illicit drugs was not entirely reasonable. An advocate of clean living, Whitey was healthy, kept himself in great physical shape, and disdained drug use and even moderate drinking. He didn't trust those who drank, viewing it as a sign of weakness. However, he openly boasted that he was the top liquor salesman in South Boston. Similarly, while he loathed drugs, a large portion of his revenue came from controlling all drug dealers who operated on his turf in South Boston.

Freddy Weichel and Billy Shea first approached Whitey in 1980, asking if they could control all of the area's marijuana dealers, who would buy from and work for them. Whitey gave them the go-ahead and would come to profit a large percentage of their earnings as they moved from solely marijuana to copious amounts of cocaine. The only drug Whitey didn't allow the sale of was heroin, as it led to problems with needles and AIDS and rendered users virtually defunct. Eventually Shea himself began misappropriating funds, at which point Whitey called for his associates to take over. Drug dealers all over New England who operated under them would now have to pay Whitey in order to continue business. If they did not comply, he would kill them, and so there wasn't very much choice in the matter.

Though Billy Bulger decorated his brother as a man whose awe-inspiring presence and zero tolerance kept drugs off the street of South Boston, Whitey's threats were instead reserved for dealers who operated independently, a practice that would not be tolerated. He seemed to be able to justify his actions by viewing drug money as something entirely separate from the drugs themselves. Likewise, the money that exchanged hands within his liquor store allowed him a profit, and though he was providing liquor, the customers' consumption habits were something apart, seemingly forgotten as soon as they walked out of his door. However, driving through South Boston, he was once rumored to have gotten out of his car to beat a wino, a slang term for an alcoholic, within an inch of his life for drunken loitering.

Political scandal

To a lesser degree, Billy Bulger evoked something of his brother's ability to reconcile his principles with less than honorable, self-serving practices. The 1980s marked a decade in which Whitey was boss on the streets and Billy was the king of Beacon Hill. He had put his time in during the previous ten years as a member of the House. When he was not rushing home to his family after a hearing ended, it was often straight to court to handle criminal cases that would supplement his legislator's salary. He was never a leader in the House, never hung around for drinks with the boys, but after attaining the Senate Presidency in 1979, the opportunities and prestige added a great deal to his individuality. His office was far plusher than those of fellow politicians, he took lavish vacations, and would often manipulate others in displays of brazen political power. However, he quickly developed questionable financial habits, exemplified in the alleged scandal over 75 State Street which would come to cloud much of Bulger's future political reputation.

Successful Massachusetts landlord Harold Brown had intended to purchase the garage at 75 State Street in order to begin constructing his new skyscraper. He had been advised to protect his interests at City Hall, and so in 1985 Brown signed a deal with lawyer and Massachusetts Convention Center Association board member Tom Finnerty: nearly two million dollars for him to monitor the sale. Finnerty was also a long-time law partner of Billy Bulger's, rumored to have watched closely over the Bulger family's interests. It was reported that both Finnerty and Bulger began splitting enormous fees from Harold Brown, for which Bulger allegedly provided little or no service. On November 15, 1985, Brown was indicted for making payments to public officials. The next day, the first of Billy Bulger's repayment checks was signed to Tom Finnerty, with Bulger citing that he had not known the source responsible for the payments. Billy narrowly escaped detection, but his dubious explanations would not be without future consequences.

Tightened surveillance and media attention

The end of the 1980s saw a change in tides for both brothers. The Drug Enforcement Agency had begun its operation to land drug trafficking charges on Whitey and his associates back in 1983, but remained largely unsuccessful for seven years. Aware of the increased surveillance, Kevin Weeks promptly purchased bug-sweeping equipment to remain one step ahead of bugs that were indeed placed in both Whitey's Chevy and his condo in Quincy. A successful drug bust in 1990, however, nabbed fifty-one dealers in South Boston, and forced Whitey's decision to walk away from the drug business.

As the FBI became more daring, the media did as well, and in September 1988, the *Boston Globe* published a four-part series on the brothers entitled *The Bulger Mystique*. From here on out, nothing would be the same for either one. The series was especially tough on Billy, citing schemes over forgotten bills and personal acts of vengeance over even the most obscure political deals. The series portrayed him, perhaps unfairly, as having dishonest and aggressive tendencies that echoed Whitey's persona, and this public association with his brother the criminal would loom over his career thereafter.

With suspicion creeping in from all sides, and from within the FBI as well, John Connolly decided to retire in 1990. Whitey had been preparing to get out of the crime business since 1987 and when the sentences began raining down upon his various South Boston dealers and associates, he knew he did not have very long before he was next. Connolly warned Kevin Weeks in December of 1994 that their indictments would be imminent, and sure enough, Stephen Flemmi was arrested in 1995, the same year an indictment was issued for Whitey. Smart enough to remain undetected, however, by that time Whitey was gone.

Around the same time that Whitey was making preparations to leave South Boston, Billy was nearing the end of his term as Senate President. He most likely would have preferred an appointment to the Supreme Judicial Court, but considering Whitey and scandals like 75 State Street, such an appointment never would have happened. The presidency of the University of Massachusetts was open, and as the scholar with great political instinct and a genuine concern for education, the role was extremely fitting. Furthermore, with the economic foresight he possessed, Billy knew that a higher salary at the University of Massachusetts would mean a higher pension. Power would also be relatively easy to hold as he could bring everyone over from the State House, and his good friend Governor William Weld would be appointing his board of trustees. In 1995 he was sworn in as the new University of Massachusetts president, with a starting salary of one hundred eighty-nine thousand dollars.

Take the money and run

Whitey's quiet evasion of law enforcement in 1994 was so successful that he had the gall to return for meetings with Weeks, even returning to South Boston on several occasions. In February 1995 he returned to Hingham, dropping off Theresa Stanley and picking up his other girlfriend, Catherine Greig. Whitey traveled all over the country under the alias of Thomas F. Baxter from Selden,

New York and had readily abandoned his identity as a hardened criminal. When investigators tried to warn a Louisiana family he had befriended, the Gautreax family, that Bulger was a dangerous fugitive, they did not believe them. With his charm and generosity, Whitey came across as a benevolent, grandfatherly type. As Weeks had always maintained about Whitey, there was very little between the charm that disarmed and the criminal who terrorized. People either saw him as the Gautreax family did, or as dissenting law officials did.

Weeks saw his friend for the last time in September of 1996, when he returned to pick up new IDs and then departed with Greig on a flight out of O'Hare airport. This was the last confirmed sighting of Whitey Bulger within the United States. The next noteworthy mention of Bulger's name came in 1997, and would grab Weeks' full attention when federal agents confirmed that Whitey had been a criminal informant. Though Weeks had been one of Whitey's closest liaisons, he had never known or suspected that Whitey would have agreed to such a position. As Weeks himself had suggested, those who knew Whitey in one way never suspected he had another side to him. However, it was most likely this paradoxical nature that allowed him to remain so hugely successful as a polished business man and notorious criminal.

While Whitey escaped unscathed, those he left behind in South Boston received the brunt of law enforcement's retaliatory proceedings. Connolly was found guilty on charges of racketeering and obstruction of justice, among others, and will not be eligible for parole until June 15, 2011. Billy Bulger was subpoenaed by the U.S. House Committee on Government Reform and sat under the raised eye of the public while denying any knowledge of his brother's activities. Though he repeatedly invoked his Fifth Amendment privilege against self-incrimination and promptly rushed out of the courtroom, his name would always be mentioned alongside future references to Whitey.

In addition to his family affairs, Billy's image was further tarnished in Boston when the University of Massachusetts payroll was somehow leaked to the press. Those in positions of power were clearly taking care of their friends, through the same means that Billy's own salary had escalated to three hundred and fifty-nine thousand dollars, plus perks. When he resigned as university president in 2003, the deal the trustees negotiated with him reportedly cost Massachusetts taxpayers over nine hundred and sixty thousand dollars. Billy Bulger ended up with the largest public pension in Massachusetts history. The amount of money that Whitey accrued over the years was unknown, as were his whereabouts as of 1995. There was a one million dollar reward for Whitey Bugler's capture, as he remained very high on the FBI's Ten Most Wanted List.

A paradox of psychological issues

The Bulger brothers were a paradoxical pair in every respect. Though the paths they took through life diverged during childhood, they shared many of the same beliefs. Paramount among them was of loyalty as a lifelong virtue. It was perhaps Billy's loyalty to his brother that kept law officials from finding Whitey. In fact, the apparent effortlessness with which they made things happen, avoided explanation, and accomplished virtually whatever they pleased was impressive in one respect and largely unsettling in another.

Though they were each committed to finding a way out of what poverty dictated for many families in Old Harbor, their personalities led them into contradictory professions. Whitey may have fallen into trouble during his youth, but thereafter, it was a conscious decision to involve himself in the business of organized crime. While Whitey's delinquency set him apart from the crowd, Billy chose to do so through hard work and scholarly achievement. He maintained a degree of the street mentality that his brother possessed, but unlike Whitey, he was not consumed by it. He chose politics out of a desire to help those less fortunate than he, people like those he had grown up with, whose difficulties he understood. Though outsiders saw him largely as a tyrant, who took even the pettiest issues personally, those closest to him knew that he preferred diplomatic negotiations to malicious political disputes. However, though he was generally reserved, he would resort to spiteful street tactics in order to get what he wanted. This willingness to sometimes go over the top was part of what made Billy Bulger such a successful conciliator, respected among his constituents as a politician who was as compassionate as he was unmerciful.

Though Bulger's policies often received criticism, politicians who respected his views cited him as being extremely likeable. However, they also said that he had no friends. Relatively shy, he could banter on for hours in front of a microphone, and though his speeches were always intelligent, quoting ancient philosophers and political leaders, the references were usually lost on his audience. It has often seemed as though Billy Bulger was caught between two different worlds, just as South Boston often seemed to be a world apart from the rest of the city. Throughout his career he legislated for many, but outside of this role, kept to himself. His antisocial tendencies, however, were unlike the personality disorder that characterized his brother's behavior.

Behavioral and psychological considerations, legal issues

Antisocial personality disorder is predated by conduct disorder occurring in the individual before eighteen years of age. For Whitey, the first instances of disorderly conduct began at the age of thirteen, when he earned the first mark on his police record for stealing. Whitey's juvenile delinquency, which displayed a blatant disregard for authority, lack of remorse for his actions, irresponsibility, and an overall lack of behavioral control, would later cause his expulsion from the Army and his transfer to Alcatraz, and also lent itself to his life as a murderer, drug dealer, and ruthless criminal informant. Although he justified every murder he arranged or committed, and claimed to have only resorted to violence when necessary, he was said to have been a vicious fighter with a hair-trigger temper. There was a Hollywood flare about his youthful pranks and criminal offenses, and though he was a straightforward criminal he was also rather flamboyant at times.

He was transferred to Alcatraz from the Atlanta penitentiary for being overly violent and problematic. It was there that Whitey befriended inmate Clarence Carnes, and after Carnes died in 1988, Whitey spent a reported ten thousand dollars for the funeral services. It was rumored that Whitey had had sexual relations with Carnes while in prison. It was also rumored that Whitey raped and molested at least two young boys, including the younger brother of Catherine Greig, one of Whitey's more serious girlfriends whom he has been on the run with since 1995. In addition to the young boys, Whitey had a following of young high school girls, some of whom willingly hung out in the locker room at Mackenzie's Gym with him and his friends, and some of whom he reportedly raped. Whitey and friends had installed a secret two-way mirror outside the girls' locker room, and it was a habit of Whitey's to enjoy private peep-shows, and to sometimes engage in sexual activities with the girls on the other side of the mirror.

Aside from his promiscuity, Whitey did have two somewhat normal, somewhat serious heterosexual relationships. However, even though he maintained fairly long-term relationships with Theresa Stanley and Catherine Greig, they were overlapping. He may have only been monogamous since taking Greig on the run in 1995, and if so, the relationship was probably more for practical reasons than for any strong emotional attachment. Practicality was the explanation Whitey used to justify the murders he committed, which he viewed as jobs to protect him and his business associates from problematic individuals who knew too much. Kevin Weeks, who was responsible for burying many of the people Whitey killed, recalled his boss retiring to take a nap after having killed someone, claiming that murder had the effect of Valium for Whitey. While he was aware that his work was seriously criminal, the ramifications of these jobs never registered emotionally.

With his ability to remain in perpetual motion, as elusive to his friends as he was to law officials, it is doubtful that Whitey will ever be found. The only legal proceedings to have landed Whitey in prison date back to 1956 for his string of bank robberies. During his incarceration, an initial psychological evaluation described him as being extremely egocentric, claiming that he had not developed any sense of social responsibility. Having essentially withdrawn from society altogether in 1994 or having never reclaimed any sense of social responsibility after leaving prison in 1965, Whitey exhibited the classic traits of a psychopath in his ambivalence toward social norms, shallow affect, and failure to have learned from punishment. Often repaying victims' families with furniture or money, Whitey clearly felt the need to compensate for certain murders or other offenses. Like the relationships he developed with these families, most were for his personal gain and were largely successful in keeping him out of trouble.

Further contradictions and unanswered questions

While the majority of his relationships were dishonest and corrupt, Whitey was smart about how he conducted his personal affairs. It seemed he always had a strategy. Although he dropped out of high school, Whitey was a voracious reader, and had read a number of war books in prison, from which it seems he extracted offense tactics and defense strategies. He could manipulate anyone, even the Federal Bureau of Investigation. The ease with which he turned many of its agents into pathological liars raises the question of whether his psychopathy had bled into their operation during his time as an informant.

To a different degree, Billy remained a largely influential figure over the years as well. His influence undoubtedly elicited more positive change than his brother's, but the influence he had in maintaining Whitey's mysteriousness made the prospects of ever finding him dubious. When asked about Whitey's involvement with the FBI, his crimes, or his whereabouts, Billy simply maintained that certain pieces of information were difficult to recall. He said he could not remember anything precisely, and was extremely evasive in the questions he did answer. Like his brother, Billy's righteousness and the privacy to which he felt entitled clouded him in a similar veil of obscurity.

Conclusions

Though the Bulgers shared certain similarities as brothers, it would be wrong to characterize them with the same psychological profile. Although Whitey was never evaluated on the basis of Robert Hare's Psychopathy Checklist, he displayed something of every indicator on the list. He indeed exhibited everything from the superficial charm that he used to manipulate whomever he needed, to the high level of criminal versatility that characterized his run as one of Boston's most notorious mobsters. It seems evident that Whitey Bulger was not only a veritable psychopath, but one of the most successful in history.

Although both Whitey and Billy rose to the top of their professions through a great deal of good fortune, Whitey created this fortune by manipulating others along the way. Billy became one of the state's superlative politicians through a blend of intelligence, hard work, and at times, genuine good luck that came from being in the right place at the right time. Though he may have exhibited psychopathic tendencies in the revenge tactics he used or the large sums of money he was able to appropriate for himself, and though he could be as glib, as charming, and as righteous as his brother, one would be wrong to characterize him as a psychopath. Billy Bulger was an intelligent politician who harbored a great deal of power and was willing to use it when he deemed necessary. Although many criticized his practices, his intentions were mostly good. Whitey's good nature on the other hand, was the exception to the rule. His intentions were largely of ill nature and had dangerous repercussions when mixed the degree of power that he also possessed.

While the dynamic between their potentials for good and evil differed greatly, the Bulger brothers were each something of an anomaly in their own right. They were an intelligent politician and a dangerously intelligent criminal, two hard-nosed, street-smart forces to be reckoned with, who also harbored a soft spot for the elderly, the poor, and their community within South Boston. While the attention they received was largely negative, and rightly so with respect to Whitey's history, they stood as prime examples of society's fascination with the psychopath. Certainly, the life of crime that Whitey lived, and went unpunished for, is both fascinating and unsettling. As the psychopath's nature is to resist change, it is unlikely that Whitey Bulger will ever abandon the strategies that have kept him something of a mystery his entire life.

Note about sources

I drew primarily from Howie Carr's book, *The Brothers Bulger*, which provided an in-depth account of each brother's life, with commentary from friends and associates regarding their personal psychology. As both Kevin Weeks and Eddie Mackenzie were enforcers for Whitey Bulger, their accounts in *Brutal* and in *Street soldier* provided invaluable insider knowledge about Whitey's personality. Weeks' book was additionally helpful in clearing up factual errors reported in Carr's. I also referred to several *Boston Globe* articles, including the four-part series *The Bulger Mystique*, which ran on the front page of the *Globe* in 1988, at the height of each brother's reign.

Ted Bundy
The poster boy of psychopathy?

Abstract

Ted Bundy, born November 24, 1946, was convicted and sentenced to death for the murders of Kimberly Diane Leach, Margaret Bowman, and Lisa Levy. However, Bundy admitted to and was suspected of dozens of other such murders. He terrorized college campuses and unsuspecting women in at least six states. Often feigning injury or disability he lured women to his car and strangled or bludgeoned them to death. In other instances he confronted the women in their homes while they slept. His attacks were almost always followed by sexual molestation and mutilation. Bundy officially admitted to the murders of twenty-eight women from 1974 to 1978 in Washington, Oregon, Utah, Colorado, Idaho, and Florida, though he is suspected of committing several more. One report suggested that Bundy might have been responsible for over one hundred murders. Bundy's case is of particular interest because of the vast amount of attention it received. Ted Bundy was a sort of pop-cultural icon, what some viewed as the quintessential psychopath. So great was this perverted reverence that he was called the poster boy for serial killers. In the extensive literature covering him, he has also been termed a textbook example or a classic case of psychopathy. His impact on society's general view of psychopathy is certainly not trivial.

Early life

Ted Bundy was born Theodore Robert Cowell to Louise Cowell on November 24, 1946, at the Elizabeth Lund Home for Unwed Mothers in Burlington, Vermont. His biological father was unknown. Two months after his birth Louise Cowell moved to her parents' home in Philadelphia, Pennsylvania. When Bundy was five, she moved again to Tacoma, Washington where she met and married Johnnie Bundy, a military cook. Some claimed that Bundy believed his mother was his sister and that his grandparents were his parents, but interviews conducted by investigative reporters Michaud and Aynesworth concluded that this was not so.

Bundy did, however, have a rather sour and emotionally disconnected relationship with his stepfather. This bitter relationship coincided with Bundy learning he was born outside wedlock. As an adolescent, Bundy was shy, self-conscious, and uncomfortably awkward in social situations. Bundy later told of his feeling alienated in high school, as he could not seem to comprehend the social interactions associated with adolescence. He did not understand what underlay everyday social exchanges, what made people want to be friends, what made people want to have relationships. Old friends remembered him lacking self-confidence.

College life

Bundy eventually learned ways to circumvent his social shortcomings. He put on a public persona of confidence, took up expensive hobbies like skiing, and sought ways to impress people. After a disappointing freshman year at the University of Puget Sound, Bundy enrolled in an intense and unique Asian summer studies program at Stanford. He sought to set himself apart in the large university setting. He believed learning an exotic language, Chinese, would impress his peers. Ted Bundy had begun to construct a mask of sanity.

With his new attitude and look of self-assurance Bundy won himself a girlfriend, a tall, worldly blonde who others say was far out of his league. Seeing through his false bravado and tired of his childish antics she dropped him, and his world and mask collapsed. Bundy gave up Chinese and subsequently failed at several other majors while attending the University of Washington. As the environment around him turned hostile, Bundy withdrew from the university and took a trip around the country. He took a couple of low wage jobs and rented a small apartment. In Seattle, he found a friend in a small-time thief and drug user who introduced him to the world of crime. Bundy became a clever thief and began to acquire the expensive things he wanted for himself.

After a brief foray into politics, at which he was actually quite adept, Bundy met another woman, Liz Kendall, and reenrolled at the University of Washington. This time he chose to study psychology and performed exceedingly well. He graduated in the spring of 1972 and decided he wanted to attend law school. During this period, Bundy maintained his relationship with Kendall, while having an affair with a coworker. This other woman later reported Bundy's peculiar behaviors, including his seemingly aimless driving and hiking in the hilled areas where it was later learned Bundy had discarded his victims.

Serial killer

Bundy's life until 1974 was marked by minor successes and potential. He had received above-average high school grades, a bachelor's degree in psychology, and a promising future with involvement in politics. Beginning in early 1974, several attractive young women disappeared from college campuses and nearby areas in

Washington State and Oregon. In July 1974 two women were approached by a man named Ted who solicited their help but they were suspicious of him and refused. Two other women, however, followed him to his car and were never seen again. In 1974 Bundy moved to Salt Lake City, Utah for law school. In November, a woman, Carol DaRonch, had an encounter with a man posing as a police officer, but escaped. The man she described approached her in a local shopping mall alleging that he was investigating a car break-in. The man led her outside and after finding nothing wrong with her car asked her to come to the station with him and file a report anyways. Carol complied but soon realized the man's malicious intent. He tried to handcuff her but she managed to escape the car in a fit of panic. Later that evening, a seventeen year old student vanished from a local school.

Bundy was stopped by police for erratic driving in August 1975. Items such as handcuffs, pantyhose cut for eyeholes, and an ice pick were found in the car. DaRonch later identified Bundy as her attacker. He was charged with attempted kidnapping and sentenced to one to fifteen years with the possibility of parole. Interestingly, in this trial Bundy waived his right to a jury.

While he was incarcerated, police who had been investigating Bundy's visits to Colorado presented a warrant for his arrest for the murder of Caryn Campbell, a woman who had been abducted and murdered at a ski resort in Aspen in 1975. In June 1977, Bundy managed to escape, leaping from a courthouse window, but was apprehended again one week later. He escaped again December 30, 1977, through a hole in the ceiling and by January was living in Tallahassee, Florida.

On January 15, 1978, Bundy raped, bludgeoned, and strangled two women to death at Florida State University's Chi Omega sorority house and assaulted two others. On February 9, 1978, Bundy abducted twelve year old Kimberly Diane Leach and brutally murdered her. He was eventually arrested for driving a stolen vehicle. In June 1979, he was tried for the two sorority murders, found guilty, and sentenced to death by electric chair. In 1980 he received the same sentence for the murder of Leach.

Death row

Ted Bundy served time on death row for nearly ten years. It was during this time that Bundy revealed most of the details of the other murders. He often received visits from Special Agent William Hagmaier of the FBI's Behavioral Sciences Unit and provided valuable information to him. In 1984, Bundy offered to help Robert Keppel track Gary Ridgway, the Green River Killer, by providing his own insights into the case. Keppel later said that Bundy was actually little help in the

Green River case but provided new information on unsolved cases in which Bundy was the prime suspect and further insight into his demented mind. After exhausting his appeals, Bundy revealed more information about eight additional unsolved murders. In a TV broadcast interview the afternoon before his execution, Bundy discussed what had influenced his behavior. Ultimately he blamed pornography for his heinous actions. He was executed January 24, 1989.

Ted Bundy as psychopath

Ted Bundy has been considered the prototypical psychopath. However much the media may mislead the untrained public to think otherwise, murder or other extreme violence is not by any means a necessary component of psychopathy. Was Ted Bundy actually the poster boy for psychopaths and serial killers? To effectively characterize a psychopath it is important to assess behavioral evidence of personality traits. There were many indicators of Ted Bundy's psychopathic personality disorder. He easily fit many of the characteristics provided by Robert Hare's Psychopathy Checklist. In interviews and other social interactions Bundy appeared glib, charming, and highly egotistical. His grandiose sense of self-worth was seen in the trial proceedings. He waived his right to a jury and acted as his own attorney on several occasions. When on trial for the Chi Omega murders in Florida, Bundy opted to defend himself, despite completing only two years of law school. He expected to dazzle the courtroom with his brilliance but instead revealed his own perverse yearnings when he made witnesses describe gruesome murder scenes explicitly. Such inappropriateness in the courtroom was reminiscent of the famous H. H. Holmes, who in his trial requested a lunch break after a witness had just completed a description of the acid vats Holmes had used for disposing of bodies in his hotel. Further evidence of Bundy's sense of self-worth included his expensive taste. Bundy often felt entitled to more than he owned or could afford. From an early age he enjoyed expensive hobbies like skiing by stealing equipment. He would later adorn his apartment with stolen merchandise. His remorseless crimes also exemplified his complete disregard for society's rules and standards.

Another characteristic of the psychopath is the need for stimulation and proneness to boredom. Bundy frequently prowled about neighborhoods like a Peeping Tom, looking for women undressing. He also stole appliances and electronics. His boredom was also apparent in how frequently he changed courses of study. For a year he studied Chinese intensively to impress girls, only to give up shortly thereafter. He became very involved in Republican politics but had no stable job when not in election seasons. He eventually earned a degree in psychology and tried his hand at law school, which he also gave up on. He often used drugs and alcohol. He admitted he usually drank before committing a crime.

Countless examples point to his pathological lying. He continually denied his guilt throughout his trials, defiantly declaring innocence though the facts were so clearly against him. He utilized lies and cons to lure his victims, often feigning injury with a fake sling or crutches. He engaged in many promiscuous relationships, having multiple affairs with coworkers and classmates.

Bundy showed no remorse of guilt for his crimes. Even the day before his execution he tried to shirk his responsibility, blaming pornography and alcohol for his actions. He made numerous callous statements about his crimes and explicitly declared that he was free from any guilty feeling. He was likewise callous and showed a lack of empathy when discussing the murder scenes and events. In interviews he seemed to show delight in retelling the story and explaining the details to investigators.

Who is to blame?

Personality disorders like psychopathy are not only difficult to diagnose but difficult to understand in terms of cause. There is still no complete explanation for why some people become psychopaths. Furthermore, even the relative effects of nature and nurture on an individual's propensity to display psychopathic characteristics are not fully understood. In this regard, Ted Bundy presented a particularly perplexing case.

From all accounts, there were no early indications that Bundy might become any sort of criminal, let alone a serial murderer. Though certain accounts referred to an unconventional upbringing, there were no indications that any event or events from his childhood might contribute to his personality disorder. He grew up in a loving family and did well in school. In college he showed great promise with his involvement in politics. Those who knew him best from his adolescent years were most unsettled by his outcome. His troubles and obstacles were no more serious than those that nonpsychopaths experience throughout life.

In an interesting turn of events, Ted Bundy offered the world a revealing glimpse inside his mind as his inevitable sentence drew closer. In a final interview the afternoon before his execution, Ted Bundy spoke with Dr. James Dobson, a conservative Protestant psychologist and host of a daily radio program called *Focus on the Family*. Bundy was asked about what motivated or influenced his heinous crimes. He responded that an early experience and obsession with pornography significantly influenced him and his behaviors.

Given the uncharacteristic nature of this response, its validity was dubious. A diagnosed psychopath is an expert liar and manipulator. One had little reason to believe Bundy's final remarks, as the incarcerated psychopath is most adroit at duping those who will listen. Bundy's remarks about the traumatizing effects of pornography were more likely his last attempt to shift the blame or escape his imminent fate. When he was not trying to escape, or writing letters to serial killer David Berkowitz and to John Hinckley, who attempted to assassinate President Reagan, Bundy did everything he could to obtain stays of execution. When he started running out of legal appeals, he turned to police departments around the country, offering his knowledge and skills. Bundy volunteered a psychological profile of the Green River Killer to investigators. He even held out as a bargaining chip the possibility that he would reveal the locations of his missing victims.

Nevertheless, this was Bundy's final interview the afternoon before his execution. He would have realized that there was little he could do to change his fate. He had nothing to gain by lying at this point. Do we risk a better understanding of his condition by disregarding these statements?

The poster boy of psychopathy?

Such examples of personality and of antisocial behaviors led many experts to conclude that Ted Bundy was indeed a psychopath. The public exposure of this case and the magnitude of the crimes led many to agree. However, when Hare's Psychopathy Checklist is applied to Bundy's case, the results are somewhat surprising. In one study, where anecdotal evidence and case materials were used to generate an analysis of Bundy based on the PCL-R standard, Bundy earned a score just shy of the cutoff for psychopathy. The study attributed the discrepancy to Bundy's lack of juvenile delinquency and early behavioral problems. Most psychopaths have an early history of crime and conduct disorder. This of course did not imply that Bundy did not display psychopathic characteristics, as the scale represents degrees of psychopathy. It did imply that Ted Bundy might not be the prototypical psychopath after all.

In fact, Ted Bundy was a rather unique type of psychopath. The extremely violent nature of Bundy's crimes set him apart from most diagnosed psychopaths. Although many psychopaths find themselves in prison after disregarding society's rules or norms, few become serial killers like Bundy. Typical psychopaths are often characterized by delinquency, manipulation of others, and even crime. Most do not turn to violent crimes. Ted Bundy's reputation was quite remarkable in that respect. He confessed to at least twenty-eight murders and might be responsible up to one hundred.

Why then has he been called the poster boy of psychopathy? Why is Ted Bundy the world's most famous psychopath? There are many possible reasons for all this attention. Many are interested in this case because Bundy appeared so normal on the outside. He was a handsome, successful man bred from a decent Christian family. Who could suspect he would become a notorious serial killer? Because he challenged the public's intuition about mass murderers, his case was both frightening and intriguing.

One author examined how Bundy's tale developed into a modern day myth. When Bundy escaped from custody in Aspen, Colorado, he instantly became a folk hero in the area. Radio hosts and restaurant owners made jokes and soon enough, t-shirts bearing puns about Bundy appeared. From the way the folk tale evolved, the actual details of the case were clouded and embellished in certain areas. Very few people are aware that Bundy was actually quite average looking, not to mention a nail-biter and nose-picker, whose life was riddled with failure. In fact, it was his very average and forgettable face that helped him evade police for so long. Yet, the story of a successful and handsome psychopathic serial killer is far more terrifying and surely far more interesting.

Conclusions

Analysis of Ted Bundy using the Psychopathy Checklist-Revised revealed that he was certainly not the archetypal psychopath that folklore made him out to be. He was not a perfect example of the personality disorder. Nevertheless, he somehow became a cultural icon and poster boy for the condition. That this was true might tell us something about how the public perceives the psychopath or what it is about the psychopath the public finds most compelling and disturbing.

The most disturbing aspect of Ted Bundy's case was the fact that so few expected him to be capable of any crime, let alone murder. The notion that a man responsible for the terrible and heinous murders of at least twenty-eight women looks nothing like a monster completely terrifies the public. Such a man could be a neighbor, a friend, or coworker. This fear has produced the mythical nature of Ted Bundy. He reflects our worst fear about a psychopath, that we too could be fooled by him, and that a shallow empathy and lack of remorse may manifest itself in horrendously violent crime. It is therefore not altogether surprising that society has made Ted Bundy a legend amongst psychopaths. However, it is very important for understanding psychopathy that the distinction between what is rare behavior and what is not is made clear. Very few psychopaths, even those that score very high in the PCL-R, become a serial killer like Ted Bundy. He may rightfully represent our worst fears and concerns about the psychopath, but by no means does he define the disorder. Indeed, he defines the myth of psychopathy.

Notes about sources

General diagnostic information relevant to psychopathy was obtained from Hare's *Without Conscience* and Cleckley's *Mask of Sanity*. Primary sources for the biographical account of Ted Bundy's life were Michaud's *The Only Living Witness* and Rule's *The Stranger Beside Me*. Additional sources, especially regarding the Bundy legal proceedings, include the online resources CrimeLibrary.com and Tedbundy.com.

The Corporation

A price paid for the psychopathic pursuit of profit and power

Abstract

The corporation is an institution whose bottom line is profit. Some argue that profit and power are pathologically pursued at the expense of those around it. Others argue that the corporation is fundamental to our functioning society. Through the eyes of the law, the corporation is viewed as a person, with various rights, privileges, and obligations that natural persons also possess. Through the eyes of psychology, how would the corporation, as a person, be viewed? The corporation, taken holistically as a person, has been given the diagnosis of psychopathy, because of its behavioral and personality characteristics. Other questions to consider in making this assessment involve whether the corporation is sanctioned to act in such a way, who sanctions its behavior, and how the corporation's actions affect society.

Introduction

The case of the corporation is atypical in the study of psychopaths because the corporation is not a real person. It has personhood only in the legal sense. The corporation can be, to some extent, studied as one would study a psychopath through a detailed analysis of family background, life experiences, social misdeeds, and psychological profile. Nevertheless, taken as a whole person, with demonstrable actions and goals, there may be something severely pathological in the psychology of the corporation. Some have argued that the corporation's actions parallel those of the psychopath who lies, cheats, steals, and manipulates his way into achieving his goal.

Dr. Robert Hare, a renowned expert and FBI consultant on psychopathy, estimates that about one percent of the population is psychopathic. This means there are approximately three million psychopaths living in the United States. Pertinent to our case study, however, is not the number of psychopaths in the United States, but the number of corporations in the United States. There are about five million corporations in the country, accounting for seventeen trillion dollars in annual revenue. This figure grows steadily by approximately two percent per year. Thus, the corporation is an extremely important fixture in our economy and culture. It is here to stay.

Recently, strategies such outsourcing, and offshoring in particular, have become important tools in corporate finance. Relocating business processes such as production and distribution to other parts of the world make this a very cost-effective maneuver for corporations. Corporations such as Nike, Gap, and Wal-Mart have outsourced to third-world countries in order to lower their costs of production. Such critics charged that these companies' sweatshops exploit the labor of young girls and women and force them to work fourteen-hour shifts in locked and sweltering factories. In addition to being financially robbed, these laborers were often sexually abused and physically beaten. Charles Kernaghan, Director of the National Labor Committee, said that the factory owners do not want these workers to have any human feelings. When Kernaghan and two factory workers confronted Kathie Lee Gifford, the woman whose popular clothing line was sold by Wal-Mart, Gifford declared that she would do everything in her power to stop these conditions and to pay these laborers decent wages.

However, critics of the corporation remained skeptical regarding such reassuring statements, since there has not been any meaningful corporate reaction to this promise. Critics construed such a strategy to allow for irresponsible and manipulative corporate behavior. They cited, for example, that Nike had to pay a mere eight cents to produce a shirt that it sold in the U.S. for twenty-two dollars and ninety-nine cents.

Critics have also accused General Motors of recklessly disregarding concern for the public safety when it positioned the fuel tank of its 1979 Chevrolet Malibu cars only eleven inches from the rear bumper. It did this even with the knowledge that automobile collisions could lead to fuel-fed fires, posing a very real and dangerous threat to the public safety. The motive behind this corporate decision was the maximization of profits. Patricia Anderson's family, whose car's fuel tank exploded upon impact, suffered terrible second-degree and third-degree burns because of this irresponsible action. In a lawsuit against GM, the Los Angeles Superior Court Judge Ernest G. Williams declared that GM's action was morally reprehensible in putting profit above the safety of the public. The Court awarded Anderson and her children one hundred and seven million dollars in compensatory damages and over one billion dollars in punitive damages.

The newest corporate practice, however, is not offshoring its factories, but secretly advertising to consumers domestically. In what has come to be known as undercover marketing, corporations hire professional actors to pose as one of the many consumer-citizens going about life in the most innocuous manners. However, these actors are adeptly and subtly advertising specific products to many an unsuspecting passersby. For example, imagine going on a mountainous trail and overhearing two hikers talk about the best backpack they have ever used in their years of outdoor adventures. You make a mental note to check out such a backpack. Imagine sitting in a bar and having a gorgeous woman tap you on the shoulder asking if you would buy her a certain drink. You are curious because you have never heard of that drink. By the end of the night, however, the whole bar might be consuming such a drink if corporations send in three or four talented undercover marketers. Jonathan Ressler, CEO of a marketing firm called Big Fat, exclaimed that this practice was a beautiful strategy because consumers are not even aware of its existence and if it works, they will never have known that it happened to them. From a marketing perspective, this is a brilliant tactic. From a psychological standpoint, however, this may be construed as psychological manipulation.

Early life

But if these behaviors are becoming more and more characteristic of the corporation, how did they come to be? Have the corporation's destructive actions developed over time, or was it simply born that way? The corporation was born during the late sixteenth century, a time when many people in business and political circles were wary of its emergence. The corporation was an alternate means through which business could be conducted. Until that time, the partnership was the prevailing business form, in which small numbers of individuals pooled their money and energy into an enterprise that they themselves owned and operated. The corporation, on the other hand, was different in its separation of ownership from management. The innovation and appeal of the corporation was that it was able to unite the economic resources and power of a limitless number of individuals. In response to a world that was rapidly becoming industrialized, the corporation came to replace the partnership as the primary means of organizing and conducting business. In the sixteenth century, corporations were created in order to transport water, exploit mines, and produce and distribute textiles. By the beginning of the eighteenth century, the corporation was increasingly seen as an efficient means of economic operation, allowing for fast acquisition of wealth from operations throughout England and enterprises in colonial America.

However, the corporation was carried to prominence amidst a backdrop of criticism and suspicion. From its very inception, this business form was seen as ripe with the potential for fraud and corruption. The economist Adam Smith warned in *The Wealth of Nations* that the corporation could not be trusted with the responsibility of managing other people's money. This suspicious anticorporate attitude prevailed for much of the eighteenth century, so much so that

England banned this business form in 1720, fifty-six years before *The Wealth of Nations* was published.

Created in 1710, the South Sea Company was one of the first corporations in England and claimed that it had exclusive rights to carry on trade with the Spanish South American colonies. The Company promised fortunes for all those who invested, and as a result, the company's stocks increased six hundred percent in the course of a year. When the public realized that the company's directors were swindlers, the South Sea Company collapsed and devastated many people's lives in the process. The English Parliament passed the Bubble Act in 1720, henceforth prohibiting the creation of corporations.

With the advent of the steam-driven machine and the Industrial Revolution, the corporation once more exploded into public and financial consciousness. The corporation could raise the capital necessary to finance large-scale projects that the partnership was no longer able to do. Post-revolutionary America witnessed a tenfold increase in the number of corporations and England was forced to repeal its Bubble Act in 1825. Opportunity for questionable business transactions was once again rampant on both sides of the Atlantic.

If the corporation committed an illegal act, the question arose as to who was to be held responsible for its behavior. The corporation's actions might result in great financial loss, as well as emotional and physical harm to others. With the advent of the concept of limited liability, shareholders were no longer held accountable for the actions of the corporation. Nevertheless, the law needed a person to possess the legal rights and duties in order for the corporation to efficiently function in society and the economy. Thus, as early as 1793, the law came to define the corporation itself as a person.

Since the end of the nineteenth century, the corporation has enjoyed legal personhood and the court's protection of its rights. The corporate person has many of the same rights and obligations as natural persons. Such rights and obligations include the ability to own property, make contracts, and pay taxes. Additionally, the corporation has constitutional rights and may go to court to defend its rights and actions. In 1886, the Supreme Court ruled that because the corporation is legally defined as a person, it may also enjoy the protection of Fourteenth Amendment, especially the rights to due process and equal protection of the law.

Death and rebirth

When we attempt to consider the corporation in terms of a person, how should we view the corporation's coming of age? Its birth was accompanied by doubtful misgivings because many were concerned about its potential for fiscal mismanagement and social irresponsibility. Eventually, due to its illegal transgressions, even its right to exist had to be questioned. At worst, this would be the equivalent of being sentenced to death as a juvenile. At best, it could be construed as an act of juvenile delinquency, with the diagnosis of conduct disorder not far behind. Conduct disorder is the juvenile precursor to antisocial personality disorder, as outlined in the *Diagnostic and Statistical Manual of Mental Disorders*. The possibility of conduct disorder, at least in the case of the corporation's adolescence, would have involved such acts as violating other people's rights, deceitfulness, theft, and a penchant for breaking laws. As the case of the South Sea Company demonstrated, these behavioral disturbances resulted in so much serious occupational functioning that the government had to kill an entity whose birth it had witnessed.

But this was not the end of the corporation. Following its so-called demise, the corporation once again entered the mainstream business world through the sheer force of its power to mobilize capital. The corporation took advantage of the social and technological atmosphere of its time, gaining in commercial consciousness and economic prominence. Apologists called it shrewd; critics called it manipulative.

Possible psychological mechanisms at play

The corporation is held accountable only to its shareholders. However, the sheer number of these people makes it impossible for them to manage a company efficiently. In a hierarchical world like the large corporation, it is easy to see how responsibility may be shirked or diffused. It is very plausible that a group mentality of diffused responsibility has played a prominent role in corporate life. For the small group in high executive positions, physical distance from the people they may harm creates a mental isolation. This has facilitated the decision to externalize the damages onto other people and other institutions.

In addition, the corporation's identity subsumes that of the individual. Regardless of the small-group or large-group context, this phenomenon has played a prominent role in the interaction of group members. It allows for the diffusion of responsibility, thereby creating a protective anonymity because corporate employees no longer view themselves as distinct individuals. The identity of the individual begins to disintegrate within the large collective consciousness of the group, the corporation. Corporate efforts to personalize itself paradoxically bring about a simultaneous loss and gain of identity. When an individual loses his personal identity, group dynamics may induce greater group cohesiveness and thereby replace this loss self-identity with a powerful group identity.

Thus, the individual working within the corporate framework may come to identify more with the values that personify his work setting. Individuals may come to construe their actions as only minute cogs in a huge, unfathomable machine, going about their tasks with an industrious complacency, unaware of the corporation's effect on the world at large.

Psychological and legal professionals commenting on this case

Dr. Robert Hare argued that the corporation would be diagnosed as a psychopath. He stated that the corporation was interested only in itself and was unable to genuinely care for the environment it inhabited. When Hare applied his Psychopathy Checklist to the corporation, he found remarkable matches. Hare noted that the corporation was irresponsible, manipulative, grandiose, and superficial. In addition, it lacked empathy and remorse, and often refused to accept responsibility for its actions.

Joel Bakan, author of *The Corporation: the Pathological Pursuit of Profit and Power*, agreed. He believed, however, that people who work for corporations were not immoral or psychopathic. They were normal people who had families, who had good intentions, and who ultimately wanted to better the world in which they lived. The problem was that they believed they were improving the world by working for psychopathic employers. In daily corporate life, these individuals managed money that was not their own. Their business and legal mandate was to use this money to increase profit and shareholder value. Thus, while individuals making up the corporation were not themselves psychopathic, the corporation was.

The eco-friendly warrior

After the corporation committed a series of human and environmental rights violations, it spurred a serious backlash from anticorporate activists around the world. Its violations even inspired its own management to reconsider the way the corporation does business. The most popular and most widely acclaimed redemptive value of the corporation was its promotion of, and adherence to, corporate social responsibility programs. Optimists championed the corporation as beneficial to society in creating jobs for the neighborhoods in which it was located, improving the infrastructure of the community, and contributing greatly to the overall national economy.

As an example, Pfizer Inc., the world's largest pharmaceutical company, contributed to many philanthropic efforts. Pfizer helped improve the public safety in Williamsburg, New York, the neighborhood where its chemical plant was originally established. It increased security around the platform of the subway station which most of its employees used to travel to and from work. It installed an emergency box near the platform so that threatened passengers could seek the assistance of guards on duty at the Pfizer plant nearby. In addition, Pfizer opened up an elementary school for children near its headquarters. Its redevelopment program also joined efforts with New York City to organize a housing development project for its residents. In terms of its pharmaceutical products, Pfizer donated its antibiotic Zithromax to African countries in its efforts to end trachoma.

The idea of corporate social responsibility is not a new one, for corporations have a long history of philanthropy. They have given to charities, they have created jobs in poor neighborhoods, and they have built houses for working class residents. However, Milton Friedman, a well-known economist and recipient of the Nobel Prize in economic science, advanced the idea that corporate conscientiousness was only acceptable as long as it was insincere. That is, if the corporation was acting philanthropically to further its end profit, then this sort of strategic philanthropy was tolerable, even encouraged. But if the sole aim of the corporation was to act in the public interest with nothing to gain for itself, then it was acting immorally. Friedman argued that the corporation's responsibility was to its shareholders, not its community.

Henry Ford, founder of Ford Motor Company, deviated from this profit-only worldview. In 1916, Ford decided to pay his workers higher wages and give his customers generous price cuts on his Model T automobiles. The major shareholders of the company, however, were less inclined toward such a philanthropic overture. They sued Henry Ford for diverting shareholders' profits toward price cuts for customers. The landmark decision *Dodge v. Ford* established the principle that corporations have a legal duty to maintain as top priority the financial interest of its shareholders and nothing else. Thus corporate social responsibility, for its own sake, had become illegal. To buttress this principle, the American Bar Association stated that the corporation was allowed to practice social responsibility as long it served the interest of its shareholders in the long run.

In the larger scheme of the corporation's psychology, corporate social responsibility did not necessarily equate to the development of a corporate conscience. However, it did imply that corporations were gaining an awareness of the effects of their actions on society. Some argued that social consciousness had become simply another strategy in the corporate machine in order to further maximize profits. Yet others pointed out that although the corporation has a long way to go, its actions demonstrated that contributing positively to its community became a serious factor in the corporate mission.

Commentators and labels

Dr. Robert Hare, discussing the diagnosis of the corporation as a person, used the term psychopath to describe its values and behaviors. He generalized about corporations. He noted that the corporation's self interest was dominant. It was singularly oriented to pursue profit at the expense of those around it, using manipulation and deception at every step along the way if need be. He remarked that it was also irresponsible and left trails of emotional, physical, and monetary damage in its wake. It never learned from its mistakes and financial impositions have never been able to curtail its destructive behavior. It was grandiose in thinking that it was the best in the world, and whatever positive public image it projected simply fed back into its own megalomaniacal attribution to its own grandness.

An *Economist* article, in reviewing the movie *The Corporation*, described the corporation as a lunatic. The article mentioned that protestors of globalization called the corporation a class oppressor, an imperial conqueror, an environmental destroyer. Other parts of the article characterized the corporation as clinically insane. However, psychiatrists, psychologists, and clinicians have often found the psychopath to be very sane and legally competent. Often intelligent, quick witted, and charming, psychopaths rarely used the insanity defense to plead their cases. The corporation was not clinically insane.

The cover of *The Corporation* featured a generic businessman striding with briefcase in hand, a halo over his head, and a devil's tail snaking its way on the ground as he walked. The obvious connotation was the corporation as a devil, a demon in angelic disguise, out to fool and rule the world. The *Economist* article featured the same image, but with an additional twist. In this image, the businessman's suit had been pierced with a white heart. On closer inspection, it was not a white heart, but an empty space where a heart used to be. The real heart was forlornly cast on the ground beside the devil's tail. The label was clear, the corporation as demonically heartless and ruthless.

The corporation with a conscience

Of course, attempts at vilification resulted in an aggressive counterattack on the part of corporations in an attempt to clear their names. Modern corporations upheld themselves as corporate citizens with a strong sense of social responsibility. They called themselves innovators, manufacturers, global competitors, visionary strategists, and most significant of all, good citizens. Corporations realized how important it was to maintain their reputations, especially in the wake of corporate scandals such as those of Enron, WorldCom, and Parmalat. Corporations were combining the monetary bottom line with doing good for the community, with the knowledge that corporate social responsibility programs would ultimately result in increased profits, increased access to capital, increased efficiency, and increased brand image.

Advocates of these programs noted the importance of gaining and maintaining the public trust. They remarked how after the tsunami disaster that struck Southeast Asia in December 2004, corporations were the first on the scene to offer humanitarian relief. Later, in the United States, corporations were extremely generous in aiding victims of Hurricane Katrina. According to the Center for Corporate Citizenship at Boston College, corporations donated a total of five hundred and forty-seven million dollars to relief efforts for Hurricane Katrina's aftermath. But it was important to keep in mind, as the corporations themselves also acknowledged, that these dollars were not given solely with the intent to be socially conscious or humanely philanthropic. These dollars were given with the ultimate goal of gaining reputational capital.

It was not that the corporation, or the psychopath, was incapable of doing good. Psychopaths, though they suffer from defective consciences, shallow emotion, and irresponsible behavior, nevertheless may still be able to hold respectable positions in society. Dr. Hervey Cleckley observed that there were psychopaths in professions such as law, medicine, business, and government. In his book *The mask of sanity*, Cleckley detailed interesting case examples of the psychopath as businessman, the psychopath as man of the world, the psychopath as gentleman, the psychopath as scientist, the psychopath as physician, and the psychopath as psychiatrist. Cleckley did not include the psychopath as corporation, but it would not be a far stretch to add it to this list.

The debate on degrees of psychopathy: Accusations and rebuttals

Cleckley explained that these various individuals were certainly psychopathic, but only milder in a matter of degree, not category. These psychopaths were able to function satisfactorily in a community just as some people with schizophrenia might be able to function outside of a psychiatric hospital. Examples of mild psychopaths demonstrated that psychopaths were still able to serve their community through their technical services and expertise, but they nevertheless caused harm to others through their pathologic behaviors.

Similarly, though the corporation was capable of doing good, it did not mean that the corporation was freed from the psychopathic diagnosis. At best, it might be considered a mild psychopath from Cleckley's perspective. Moreover, the good they did was a secondary result of their selfish goals rather than their primary aim. In other words, doing good was a nice byproduct of the corporation's objective to make more money. But should this matter? In the end, the result was the same. The question, then, was not whether the corporation was capable of doing good, because it already demonstrated that it was. The question was whether the corporation was capable of doing better.

Certainly, proponents of corporate social responsibility programs would adamantly contend that the corporation's survival was highly contingent on its vision of its future. Corporations everywhere would protest against the argument that they were psychopathic due to a lack of long-term goals. In fact, this range of vision was what made corporate philanthropy possible in the first place. Long-term vision allowed the corporation to enhance its reputation, which led to more corporate benefits. Along the same lines, these proponents would also insist that theirs was a vision full of planning, insight, and sound judgment. Whatever acts the corporation might commit, antisocial or not, they were not motiveless. On the contrary, they seem to be motivated by a strong tendency to accrue monetary gain for the corporation. These proponents' claims were certainly reasonable. Any corporation that failed to integrate long-term goals into its vision of the future would not be able to flourish in the global economy.

However, critics of the corporation continued to emphasize the similarities between the interpersonal defects of the psychopath and the socially irresponsible actions of the corporation. Like the superficial charm of the psychopath, the corporation might project the façade of a caring, concerned neighbor, but the destructive tendencies were nevertheless present and threatened to erupt once profit was at stake. These critics insisted that the corporation was unreliable because it consistently failed to deliver on its promises.

Furthermore, these critics maintained that the corporation's schemes to gain public attention and public trust were manipulative by nature. For example, Bakan described how corporations paid corporate spies to steal company secrets in order to eliminate and surpass the competition. BP, which officially stands for British Petroleum, revamped its image to promote the image of Beyond Petroleum. Toward this end, it marketed itself as an environmentally friendly company with a vision for sustainable energy. In fact, it invested sixty-four billion dollars in its oil and gas products while it invested less than one percent of that amount in solar energy. Phillip Morris, the corporation that manufactured major cigarette brands in the United States and the world, renamed itself Altria. The name was chosen to resemble the sound of the word altruism. Altria's mission was professional integrity and corporate responsibility.

Moreover, critics of corporate social responsibility programs noted that the corporation was remorseless and failed to learn from its mistakes. Government officials questioned whether monetary reparations were ever effective in preventing future violations. More skeptical critics argued that financial deterrents had no impact and were not even a factor in the corporate scheme of cost-benefit analysis. In the world of the corporation, a simple cost-benefit analysis revealed that if the cost incurred from violating a law was less than the benefit to be derived from its violation, then the profit imperative sanctioned such infractions. Critics cited the case of General Motors putting profit before human safety. After all, they argued, the corporation, like the psychopath, was programmed to exploit others for profit.

Corporate apologists brought up valid contentions, but corporate critics also made well-reasoned comparisons to the psychopathic personality. One important distinction should be made, however. Often, the typical psychopath committed crimes for no discernible end than to satiate his need for excitement, but the goal of the corporation was clear and singular. It was profit. The true psychopath might wander around society aimlessly. The corporation, however, knew what it wanted and went for it unreservedly. That the corporation pursued its goal with such single-mindedness attracted the label of a psychopath, but raised the question of how this most important distinction of having goals could simultaneously set the corporation apart and incriminate it with a diagnosis of psychopathy.

Interviews

Overall, the corporation might not be the evil machine guilty of social destruction, but in fact responsible for mass employment and societal stability. Joseph Badaracco, professor of business ethics at Harvard Business School, felt that the analogy to a psychopath of something as complex as the corporation was a bizarre argument. Badaracco noted that to take a concept from psychology and to apply it to the corporation was not useful. He stated that characteristics on the Psychopathy Checklist such as promiscuous sexual behavior, short-term marriages, parasitic lifestyle, and juvenile delinquency did not shed any light on the corporation. He felt that it would be just as useful to compare the corporation to cave formations, for example, and noted that a comparison to psychopathy did not do much to soundly criticize or understand the corporation.

Patricia O'Brien, former dean of a business school, former professor at Harvard Business School, and former deputy dean of Harvard College, responded to Bakan's accusation that some corporations were irresponsible in their use of sweatshop labor. She noted that the issue of sweatshops was very complicated and that Bakan had drastically simplified it. The issue needed to be examined in its context. While she admitted that girls in these factors were subject to deplorable working conditions, she noted that these girls might well be faced with the alternative of prostitution otherwise. She also commented that the factories were responses to the economic condition in particular countries, where workers were paid according to the going wage. On the upside, she noted that these jobs are enabling workers' families to survive by doing work that was dignified compared to the alternative. O'Brien believed that the corporation as a psychopath was too simplistic an argument. The people who worked for the corporation were normal people. They had families, jobs, and led lives of integrity. They were good people, smart people, and they thought they were doing important work, providing jobs for others, enabling their children to go to college, producing goods and services that were helpful to and enjoyed by society.

Both Badaracco and O'Brien felt that corporate social responsibility programs were peripheral to the corporation. They agreed that those programs basically made for good public relations. While the programs' motives were often mixed, and while the programs might have benefited for the community, they suggested that the corporation's contribution to society should not be evaluated through their corporate social responsibility programs. Rather, both Badaracco and O'Brien asserted that the real job of the corporation was to provide reliable service and products for society, which too often are taken for granted.

In order to judge a corporation, Badaracco insisted, society needed to look at the ninety-nine point nine percent of what it was doing, not the tenth of a percent that he termed its philanthropic scraps. In the case of Pfizer, its contribution should be understood as providing useful, affordable drugs to the world. The pharmaceutical company has produced drugs that have saved millions of lives, and granted, it did that to earn profits. However, it has turned around and given most of its profits back to its employees, researchers, salespeople, and students. O'Brien noted that the corporation's bottom line was not profit alone. Continuing with the Pfizer example, if this corporation were solely dedicated to the pursuit of profit, then it would not invest nearly so much into its research and development programs, training programs, and mentor programs. Through this specific world enabled by the corporation, and through the multiplier effect, people were able to live and to live better. O'Brien reiterated that the corporation was not solely a profit-driven machine because otherwise the economy would be full of companies constantly popping up and then disappearing. The corporation was much more stable, and had become very integral to our country's economic well-being.

Barbara Christiansen has worked for both a for-profit strategic consulting company, Monitor Group, and a nonprofit consulting company, Bridgespan. When asked about her thoughts on the psychopath analogy, she commented that there was some merit to the application. Certainly, she admitted, there was something about how corporate life was structured that took away the issue of accountability that ideally would be there. Sometimes the necessary checks and balances had been removed. She further noted that Bakan's was an interesting argument, and agreed that corporations were structured to give the highest returns to shareholders. There was always the goal of profit, and thus sometimes the motivation for making a certain decision was not always geared toward the wellbeing of the community. Moreover, the fact that shareholders were so dispersed over the world meant that it would hard for them to care about something going on in a different part of the globe.

Christiansen's examples illustrated these ideas. She noted that when she was working for a for-profit consulting firm, one of her clients wanted to offshore its production. The client demanded that the firm take quick action because the client did not want the standard of living in that country to rise any higher, or for the people in that country to realize that the rest of the world was being paid a minimum wage for their labor. In a counterexample, she recalled how a biotechnology company for which she was consulting decided to continue manufacturing a drug for rheumatoid arthritis even though it was not receiving as much profit from it as it was putting into the making of the drug. Despite examples of exploitation, there were examples of innovation and philanthropic efforts to improve the quality of living in the community. Ultimately, she noted, it all depended on the specific corporations themselves. Different corporations had different attitudes. An overarching statement about all corporations seemed too general, and thus too inaccurate, to be taken seriously. Christiansen was optimistic that the corporation was capable of change and she noted that in the next twenty years, there would be an upsurge in the demand for leaders in the nonprofit world.

Conclusion

The corporation as an institution has permeated every segment of society. It has influenced our daily lives by telling us what to wear, what to eat, and whom to like. It has influenced our intellectual lives by telling us what, how, and when to think. In addition, the actions of the corporation have had strong repercussions for its immediate environment in particular as well as for society in general, and have raised an important question. What has needed to be done regarding the increasing power of the corporation over the lives of society's citizens?

In recent decades, the corporation has risen to a status as the most prominent institution in contemporary society. It has also caused harm to society. Its acts included, but were not limited to, exploitation of labor through third-world sweatshops, devaluation of human life and the denunciation of public safety through industrial accidents like oil spills and automobile fires, disregard for environmental conservation through continual deforestation and investment in non-renewable sources of energy. On the other hand, the corporation has also contributed billions of dollars to charitable foundations and philanthropic efforts around the world, and has made products and provided services that have raised standards of living and made progress possible. The corporation has seemed to be battling a war against what it considered malicious name-callers and constructing for itself a new image as an eco-friendly warrior. In the process, some psychopathic labels have remained, and countering them, redemptive messages of corporate consciousness have emerged. The corporation was, and has continued to be, backed by a formidable reputation and has become a stronghold of economic, social, and political power.

Given its prominence in the structure of the world's economy, what can be done to end corporate abuse and remediate the institution that society has created? First, Bakan argued that corporate self-governance was absurd. If real people were not expected to govern themselves, then how could the corporation, whose psychopathy had been institutionalized, be expected to do so? Laws against crime, theft, and murder existed because people did not act morally or responsibly. If this were so, then the corporation should not be expected to behave in a socially responsible way. Hence, government regulation was crucial in curbing the power wielded by corporations. Next, there was an urgent imperative to educate the public and have formal government sanctions in order to end corporate illegality. It was not enough for laws to exist in theory. They needed to be enforced by government agencies.

The corporation was created to serve the public good. When it failed to achieve this end, it could be dissolved. This would be, effectively, a death sentence for the corporation. Known as charter revocation laws, they could be invoked if a corporation egregiously violated the public interest. Nevertheless, these laws were rarely invoked against big corporations, not even during the

Enron scandal in 2001. Instead, the tools at the public's disposal were consumer education and government regulation backed by enforceability.

The corporation may not be a psychopath in the full sense of the diagnosis, because it was clearly capable of functioning in society and thriving at what it does for a living. All corporations are profit-driven to some degree, but the more socially responsible ones are less psychopathic while the less socially conscious ones are more psychopathic. However, the corporation is undeniably goal-oriented, value-driven, and sharply aware of its power. The corporation is also starting to develop an awareness of its place in society and effects on the world at large, which for a psychopath would be a ludicrous. Psychopaths are notorious for being very resistant to treatment, both in terms of initial attitude and eventual outcome. Corporate social responsibility programs, on the other hand, have paved the way for the business leaders to take a stance on the vision of sustainability and communal improvement, reorienting their mandates away from singular personal profit. This being said, that the corporation manifests certain psychopathic tendencies seems hard to refute. It has been willing to cheat, lie, steal, and manipulate its way to financial glory and economic superiority. The final question, then, has been not whether the corporation was or was not a psychopath, because this is a matter of degree and not dimension. The question has been whether, even if the corporation were a psychopath, would it be capable of change.

My answer to this is twofold. The corporation's image, as it currently promotes itself, rests on a shield of ecological friendliness. This makes me optimistic. However, although corporate social responsibility programs are a factor in corporate decision-making, they are far from being a core component. If the creators and consumers of the corporation, that is the public and the government, were willing to also reorient their vision toward one of collaboration and more firmly monitor corporate behavior, then I feel that change would not only be possible, but feasible.

Notes about sources

The primary sources of information about the corporation were Joel Bakan's book, *The Corporation: the Pathological Pursuit of Profit and Power*, and Bakan's documentary, *The Corporation*. A joint interview with Joseph Badaracco, professor of business ethics at Harvard Business School and Patricia O'Brien, then deputy dean of Harvard College, and an interview with Barbara Christiansen, a consultant for a nonprofit company, provided further information.

Saddam Hussein
A model for politicians, terrorists, and psychopaths

Abstract

Saddam Hussein, former president of Iraq, was captured by United States forces in December 2003. Investigations by the Iraqi Special Tribunal into twelve charges, including the Kurdish genocide, illegal invasion of Kuwait, and various other mass-killings, began in 2004. The media labeled him a terrorist and a psychopath, among other things. The extent to which these labels are accurate and the impact they had on the Hussein trial is of central importance. Hussein helps provide insight into more nuanced aspects of psychopathy including the relationship between psychopathy and religion, the potential heredity of psychopathy, the psychological character of followers of psychopaths, and the institution of politics in general. The legal situation is unique due to the Iraqi penal code, the international scale of Hussein's allegedly psychopathic actions, and the obvious yet questionable role of the media in the legal process.

The facts

Saddam Hussein was born in Tikrit, Iraq in 1937 to a poor family of Sunni Muslims. Saddam's father, Ibrahim, died before his son's birth. His mother, Sabha, abandoned Saddam shortly after birth, only to reunite with him when he was three years old and to subject him to an abusive stepfather. Saddam was denied even the semblance of self-worth, and simple, fundamental desires, such as gaining an education. It is worth exploring whether the overused diagnosis of a traumatic childhood and poor parenting is not so far fetched in Saddam's case.

At age ten, Saddam left home to live with his uncle Khayrallah, who had an obvious influence on the fragile, malleable Saddam. Khayrallah was known to be an avid supporter of Hitler and the Nazi movement. Khayrallah filled Saddam with ideas of heroic ancestors, Iraqi nationalism, evil foreigners, and Baath ideology. The Baath party called for an Arab revolution for independence and a new socialist order, justified by a history of oppression from the Zionists and the West.

Saddam quickly gained favor with the Baaths. His rapid ascent to power was attributed to his zeal and dedication to the organization, namely his willingness to use violence in service to the party. This power eventually gained Saddam the critical support to lead a successful coup of the Iraqi government in 1968. Flagrant abuses of this power began immediately. One of Saddam's key intelligence agents was executed shortly after the coup; Saddam called it an act of gratitude for his services. Yet Saddam constantly referred to the divine ordination of such acts, naturally leading to the conclusion that Saddam considered his mission noble, holy, messianic.

From here, the story becomes quite familiar. The genocide of the Kurds, which did not come to the forefront of international attention until the invasion of Kuwait and the Gulf War in the early 1990s, had its roots in the early 1970s. The Kurds are a non-Arab, mostly Sunni Muslim, people who live in a mountainous area that straddles the borders of Armenia, Iran, Iraq, Syria, and Turkey. Enraged by their neutrality, Saddam began a massive relocation of the Kurds, mostly into Iran. He simultaneously began to procure weapons from major European powers, and sought chemical weapons manufacturers. Tricked into thinking they were contracted for pesticide and fertilizer plants, major European and American companies contributed to the production of nerve gases like Tabun and Sarin. On this point, it is not unreasonable to compare Saddam to Hitler, who was known to use Tabun in concentration camps. Estimates counted up to two hundred thousand Kurds killed in 1988 alone due to Saddam's razing of villages and use of chemical warfare.

Through it all, Saddam never seemed to have trouble justifying his actions and convincing others of their merit. The examples were endless. Saddam rebuffed United Nations weapons inspections, calling them a mere tool of the United States' stranglehold on international policy. Following the Gulf War, Saddam manipulatively rebuilt relations with Syria, Jordan, Iran, Saudi Arabia, and Egypt. He improved relations with the Arab community in general by abandoning his secular image and beginning a campaign heralding Iraq's, and his own, return to Islam and strong Islamic values.

Despite his attempts to bolster his image in the early 1990s, Hussein was still most widely known as the madman of the Middle East. The terms psychopath and sociopath were excessively and carelessly used in news reports. A cursory glance over various articles floods one with references to Saddam as insane, psychotic, megalomaniac, tyrannical. Osama Bin Laden even called Saddam an infidel, citing his highly secular government. As is obvious from the factual material, parallels to Hitler became quite prominent. Nonetheless, as far as he was concerned, Saddam was Iraq and Iraq was Saddam, and many of his followers agreed.

Is Hussein a psychopath?

How do all these historical facts and media labels relate to the psychological truth? Labels of psychosis are clearly misguided because Saddam was a rationally calculating, shrewd political figure. Instead, almost all of the hallmarks of psychopathy can be taken directly from Dr. Robert Hare's Psychopathy Checklist, or PCL-R, and applied to Saddam. His aggressive acts are well documented and instantly satisfy one of the major criteria for diagnosis of psychopathy. His self-proclaimed messianic mission and pursuit of this mission without regard for human life support another factor: the ability to rationalize his aggression and act without conscience. The ability to indict the Zionist movement and the United States as the cause of Hussein's violence expand upon the rationalization factor, and reached into yet another: the reluctance to accept responsibility for actions, blaming another as the cause. The list continues: the pathological lying, manipulative behavior, lack of remorse, unrealistic long-term plans, and diverse criminality were all noticeably present in Hussein's personality.

There is, however, confusion regarding Hussein's emotional state. Saddam seemed to act and speak with fervor and deep emotional investment. One of Dr. Hare's main diagnostic criteria, though, is shallow emotional affect. Psychologist Walter Weintraub's work was helpful on this issue. He conducted a speech content analysis of Saddam, categorizing the use of various verbal forms. The most relevant here are the low counts of creative expressions and feelings used in Saddam's speech, at 1.3 and .5 references per thousand words respectively. These are astounding compared to the number of nonpersonal references, recorded at 793.6 references per thousand words. Saddam's apparently emphatic and impassioned speech would naturally lead to the assumption that his nationalism had deep personal meaning. Weintraub's analysis helps to rectify the contradiction between such impassioned speech and emotional deficiency. Based on his data, one could deduce that Saddam's apparent zeal was in fact superficial, merely a façade for a cold and detached speaker. Going beyond shallow emotional affect, the analysis also supports the PCL-R factor of displaying false emotions, emotions that are not really felt but used as manipulative tools.

With this final piece of the puzzle, one can legitimately conclude that Saddam possessed all the major psychopathic traits. There are, though, a few important practical matters to keep in mind. In psychological practice, psychopathy is usually associated with antisocial personality disorder, as defined in the *Diagnostic and Statistical Manual of Mental Disorders*. Most of the behavioral characteristics overlap, and psychopaths are assumed to have more specific emotional and personal traits. However, the *Diagnostic and Statistical Manual* stipulates that antisocial personality disorder be preceded by conduct disorder. Conduct disorder, usually diagnosed for children under the age of eighteen, involves a history of violence, bullying, cruelty toward persons or animals, theft, disturbance of occupational functions, and general violation of rules and societal norms. Even though Saddam began his messianic quest around age ten, his childhood was relatively innocuous by *Diagnostic and Statistical Manual* standards, and it would be presumptuous at best to diagnose young Saddam with conduct disorder. More detailed information about his childhood would be required to make a confident diagnosis.

This idea of the messianic quest, however, lends itself naturally to consideration of narcissistic personality disorder. The defining elements of narcissistic personality disorder and antisocial personality disorder largely overlap, including characterizations as glib, superficial, exploitative, and unempathic. Saddam's grand vision for himself and Iraq, however, is not often associated with antisocial personality disorder. Narcissistic personality disorder better captures Saddam's grandiosity, arrogance, and sense of entitlement over Iraq. As the term antisocial would intimate, antisocial personality disorder does not tend toward the need for admiration and envy involved in narcissistic personality disorder. Yet it is also unclear, at least as far as has been shown, whether Saddam displayed such envy and need. Antisocial personality disorder and narcissistic personality disorder are not mutually exclusive; Saddam could be diagnosed with both disorders.

Note, though, that merely one personality trait, the grandiose sense of self-worth, raises very difficult questions about the integrity of the diagnosis. While the absence of conduct disorder and presence of pomposity may put a diagnosis of antisocial personality disorder in question, a diagnosis of psychopathy is unaffected, if not strengthened. This is crucial evidence in support of parsing psychopathy from antisocial personality disorder. One can comfortably diagnose Hussein psychopathic and leave the gritty details of the antisocial personality disorder—narcissistic personality disorder debate behind. It will be useful to keep these subtleties in mind as the more nuanced aspects of Saddam's psychology are examined. Let us take the information above and apply it to questions about the role of fervently nationalist and fanatical religion in psychopathy, the psychological character of those who follow psychopaths, and the institution of politics in general.

Nationalism, religious fanaticism, and psychopathy

There seems to be a trend of associating religious fanatics or fervent nationalists with psychopathy. Do these characteristics cause psychopathy, stem from psychopathy, or coincidentally coexist with psychopathy? Saddam's example seems to illustrate that religious fanaticism and nationalism work in both the formative and derivative directions. The early presence of strong nationalist and religious ideas was clearly a strong developmental force on Saddam. They shaped his approach to life, power, and politics.

Saddam is also useful in breaking down stereotypical representations of terrorists as religious fanatics. While it may be naïve to think that the apparently high ratio of religious fanatics and nationalists to psychopaths is coincidental, the explanation need not be such a rudimentary causal process. In this case, religious and nationalist ideals seem to have been mere tools for Saddam's psychopathic rule. The Baath call for Arab independence certainly crafted a revolutionary spirit and defiant figure. Actual investment in Arab life, however, served only as a façade, a political tool to gain favor and support among the Arab community. Thus one might claim the stereotype that fervent nationalists and religious fanatics are all psychopaths is misguided; these groups may merely be more susceptible targets of psychopathic manipulation. Psychopaths are adept at exploiting the sensitivities and hot-button issues in people's lives. Those with strong religious and nationalist ideals have an obvious vulnerability to the psychopath's manipulative capabilities.

Looking at nationalism and religious fanaticism in this light suggests there remains a more general question to be answered about psychopathy. If nationalism and religion are, at least sometimes, tools of psychopathy, must the followers who listen to these ideas always be psychopaths as well?

Psychopathic allegiances

On first impression, it may seem reasonable to claim that all followers of psychopaths are psychopaths. People may be charmed and deceived by psychopaths in passing, but broader knowledge of their life tends to cause repulsion among common people. Hussein's followers continued to follow despite such a broad knowledge. One could argue they must, therefore, have shared in his impulsivity, aggression, and lack of conscience. Such a response seems most likely in the case of Hussein's closest colleagues. Taha Yasin Ramadan, Hussein's Vice President from 1991 to 2003, was known to be as cunning, ruthless, and deceptive as Hussein himself.

It was estimated, though, that twenty percent of Iraq's twenty-six million people supported Saddam. It would be astonishing to conclude that five million Iraqis were psychopathic solely in virtue of the fact that they are supporters and followers of Hussein. A more reasonable conclusion is, obviously, that followers of psychopaths are not necessarily psychopaths. One could, however, point to extenuating circumstances related to the leader and followers.

An obvious historical trend is the manner in which leaders can manipulate crises to gain support and to exploit the followers' psychological vulnerabilities. In the twelfth century B.C., Agamemnon gained support for the Trojan War by construing the capture of Helen to be a major crisis. Oliver Cromwell accumulated power in seventeenth century Britain by emphasizing the threat of a returning monarchy. In the early twenty-first century, George W. Bush launched a war, tortured prisoners, and spied on American citizens, using the September 11 crisis as justification. Saddam Hussein employed chemical warfare, torture, and invaded Iran and Kuwait, justified by the imposing Zionist movement. The obvious distinction between the cases of Agamemnon, Cromwell, Bush, and the Hussein case should be apparent. Despite any hyperbole or overstepping of bounds in the Trojan War, dictatorship over the English Commonwealth, or the War on Terror, the events that rallied their support were clearly tangible events: Helen was stolen, absolute monarchs ruled Britain for 600 years, and jet liners destroyed the Twin Towers.

The Zionist movement may be no less real than the aforementioned events, but the effort needed to prove it is much more extensive. Hussein was certainly ready to face the challenge. He used typical terrorist modes of rationalization to justify his actions and gain support. He was skilled at embedding in his follows a mentality of us versus them. He possessed the deceptive capacity and the media control to have his message, and only his message, heard throughout Iraq by even the youngest of citizens. Such a system requires no psychopathology to turn listeners into followers. With a strong message and strong media control, this transformation from listener to follower is a useful framework for evaluating the psychology of the follower. An important factor in the transformation is the exorbitant influence of group mentality. Social norms come from society, one's group. In much of Iraq, groups were defining morality based on limited filtered information, which was, obviously, provided by Hussein. An outsider, such as the United States, might have considered an Iraqi group's norms to be corrupt. A member of the group, however, cannot be diagnosed with a personality disorder for obeying norms because antisocial personality disorder and narcissistic personality disorder are defined as deviation from social norms.

The question returns: were many of Hussein's followers aware of the atrocities and that they were wrong? No doubt some did, but a diagnosis of psychopathy may remain unjustified. Group pressure sounds like a childish excuse, but Saddam was infamous for making people disappear if they did not conform, as has been noted. On a psychological level, many of the followers probably also felt deep affiliative needs within the group. Laden with internal and external insecurities, it is likely many followers felt the need to latch on to a charismatic leader, who had been idealized during the time of crisis, even if the leader himself had invented the crisis. It was reported that Taha Yasin Ramadan lost twenty-seven kilograms, about sixty pounds, when Saddam criticized his ministerial panel for gaining weight. It is irrelevant to ask whether Taha Yasin Ramadan's actions were conducted out of fear, vanity, a copycat mentality, or outright reverence for Saddam's words. The crucial point is that these are all reasonable explanations that should be examined before the label of psychopath is carelessly applied.

A final possibility that has not yet been explored is that followers of psychopaths are not psychopaths, and there are no extenuating circumstances. They are sane, normal people, living an ordinary life. This, however, seems to devolve into some form of psychopathy, or more likely psychosis. One must be delusional to have absolutely no grasp on someone like Hussein's actions. If one has not fallen subject to a psychopath due to priming or deception, undoubtedly the mind is deceiving oneself.

Followers with a special connection

Two particularly interesting cases of Saddam's followers are his sons, Uday and Qusay. Do they provide any insight into the heredity of psychopathy? Uday's media labels were as extreme as Saddam's. He was often labeled psychopathic or insane. He also, as son of the madman of the Middle East, received the apropos nickname of bad boy of Iraq. He was known to have a hot temper and a taste for alcohol. His aggression included, and was not limited to, killing one of his father's aides with a carving knife, beating a valet to death at a party, and orchestrating the murder of his cousin, Hussein Kamal, whom Uday felt jeopardized his relationship with his father. Such a rationale was odd, because Qusay had always been in higher favor with Saddam anyway. Qusay served for Saddam as part of the Special Republican Guard, Regional Leadership, and the Revolutionary Command Council. Had it not been for the American military action, which killed both Uday and Qusay in 2003, Qusay would have succeeded Saddam as president of Iraq.

So, again, what information do Uday and Qusay provide about the heritability of psychopathy? Noting the similarity of their behavior to their father's, one might claim it is relatively clear they were psychopaths and inherited the trait from Hussein. However, psychopathic behavior by Saddam's sons might merely have been result of growing up in Saddam's world; they could have been a classic case of nurture over nature. Uday and Qusay's diagnoses are further complicated by the consideration that Saddam might not be a psychopath. This diagnosis would emphasize social factors in development because Uday seems to have been a fairly obvious example of a psychopath. His early aggressive and impulsive behavior indicates that Uday might have had conduct disorder, which would allow for a diagnosis of antisocial personality disorder. The mature characteristics of deceitfulness, shallow emotions, and rationalizing were obviously present. Hussein's pomposity, however, stands in stark contrast to Uday's insecurity and struggle for recognition. Uday's jealousy toward his brother is more characteristic of narcissistic personality disorder. Nonetheless, the central aspects of antisocial personality disorder and psychopathy were prominent features of Uday's personality and actions.

It may be the differences in the brothers' personalities in general that is the most convincing evidence that psychopathy is not, at least not fully, hereditary. Uday's more prominent aggressive tendencies might be attributed to the envy and self-esteem issues derived from the obvious favoring of his brother. The trends leading to Qusay's psychopathic traits look much more like those of a follower than a genetic copy of the original psychopath. Qusay, as a high ranking officer, was clearly subject to a group mentality closely regulated by Saddam. He undoubtedly faced the pressures and threats, to both his psyche and his life, that would have led to apparently psychopathic behavior. The external influences seemed to weigh heavily and diversely upon the sons' psychological characters. At the very least, scientists have not compared Hussein and his sons' genetic inheritance and brain structures in order to make any sort of assumptions about heritability of psychopathy. And even if scientists could conduct such a study, they would likely not even know for what they were looking.

The legal questions

The legal questions at hand are particularly unique because Saddam was tried under the Special Iraqi Tribunal. Some of the basic relevant elements are quite similar to United States law. Chapter four, section one of the Iraq penal code protects those who, at the time of the crime, had lost their reason or volition due to insanity or infirmity of mind. As has been explained, though, Saddam was undoubtedly rationally calculating and did not suffer from psychosis. Under the American precedent, Saddam would be treated as sane. This has become fairly standard legal treatment of psychopaths, and would apply even if Saddam were merely diagnosed with antisocial personality disorder or narcissistic personality disorder.

Some of the more interesting questions deal with Saddam's followers and co-defendants. The Iraqi Penal Code protects those who commit crimes out of compulsion or necessity to protect themselves. Based on the aforementioned dynamics between Saddam and some of his colleagues, exemption might be made. Saddam's Minister of Defense, Hashem Ahmed, turned himself in to American forces, indicating someone who was not a psychopath, unable to escape during Saddam's rule, and a candidate for leniency.

If the Nuremberg trials are any precedent, though, Hussein's cohorts may not be in as hopeful a position as the above paragraph suggests. The concept of a defense by claiming that one was just following orders was not a new idea. In anticipation of such a defense, the Allies created the London Charter in August 1945, which explicitly stated that the Nuremberg defense, as it is now called, is an illegitimate defense. Robert Jackson, chief prosecutor for the United States, emphasized in his closing statements that the role of each defendant in the conspiracy as a whole, the operating mechanism, was certainly grounds for conviction. The defendants' positions were only worsened when Hans Frank, governor-general of Nazi-occupied Poland, adamantly insisted that those who plead ignorance to the atrocities of the Nazi regime were blatantly lying. Eleven of the twenty-four defendants at the original trial of major war criminals were hanged; only three were acquitted. Given this evidence, coercion and ignorance seem unlikely escapes for Saddam's closest colleagues.

The psychopathy of politics

The characteristics and tools that have been used to characterize Saddam Hussein as a psychopath seem very common among politicians. How similar is Saddam to other prominent political figures? Is psychopathy perhaps inherent to the institution of politics?

All politicians rely upon the media to some extent. Hussein clearly used the media to stabilize his regime. He continued to use the media to his advantage even while on trial. On March 15, 2006, Judge Abdel-Rahman suspended television and radio broadcasting of the trial and asked reporters to leave the courtroom while Saddam urged supporters to continue their resistance against American and Zionist forces. His statements were made in lieu of providing a defense against his charges. Even under normal circumstances, it seems psychopathic leaders might be capable of manipulating the media to mask their psychopathy. The media becomes, in many ways, another one of the psychopath's many tools.

Relevant modern examples include George W. Bush, Bill Clinton, and Kim Jong Il. Bill Clinton, despite explicitly lying to his followers, was never labeled a psychopath even by his adversaries. Bush, however, was often referred to as psychopath, as was Kim Jong Il. Hussein was not considered psychopathic by his followers, but commonly labeled a psychopath throughout the rest of the world. It is perhaps too soon to explain why these dichotomies existed. One possibility is that we are in many ways still trapped within a media curtain that skews our judgments on these issues. The media, in this respect, ranges from television to history books.

Since such biases may be present, a historical perspective is helpful. How was Hussein, or any leader named above, similar to a figure like Adolph Hitler? The Nazi propaganda campaign was surely one of the most psychopathic systems in history. Yet it is shocking to compare some of the psychopathic highlights of the Nazi regime to modern politics. The Nazi party mastered the system of mass politics, perhaps the prerequisite for survival in a modern political climate. The Nazis co-opted German nationalism for their own purposes, and the similarity to Hussein's use of Arab pride and Bush's use of September 11 has been noted above. The German Socialist Democratic Party, or SPD, labeled as the status quo, was blamed for Germany's economic crisis due to war reparations, hyperinflation, and the Great Depression. As is obvious, the Nazis were superb at crafting the aforementioned us versus them mentality. Us, the Nazis, promised a glorious German future, while them, the SPD, was denounced as the route to conservatism and economic failure. And of course, the Nazis had a shrewd, charismatic leader in Hitler. Just as much has been seen in Hussein's pitting of Iraq against the Zionists, and Bush's pitting of America against terror. Moreover, the Nazis, via intensely personal and local methods, could preach different promises to different social groups in order to most effectively turn them away from the SPD. Here is a notable difference. Hussein joined the aggressive, threatening ranks of persuasion, whereas Bush and many other supposed run-of-the-mill politicians employ their methods more subtly. Yet it has been made particularly clear throughout this volume that psychopaths come in many different flavors and degrees. The noticeable extremes of self-proclaimed violence and aggression should not mask the equally dangerous middle that still contains the classic psychopathic traits of pathological lying, shallow affect, pomposity, redirection of responsibility, and diverse criminality, which may include more illegitimate violence than meets the eye.

Many recent psychological analyses have concluded that Hitler was not psychopathic, but rather was afflicted with some Axis I disorder like schizophrenia. A salient point remains, though, similar to one made about Hussein and his allegedly psychopathic followers: undoubtedly the thirteen million Germans who voted for Hitler in 1932 did not all share his psychological disorder. This number is also useful in pointing out that the scope of Hitler's media dominance is probably of deeper semblance to Bush's than Hussein's. The question lingers as to how people discern appropriate applications of the psychopathic label. Media influence, cited above as a psychopathic tool, might also be a key diagnostic tool used by populations to evaluate their leaders. Perhaps someone like Clinton never reached psychopathic status because his media influence was never seen as comprehensive. Or perhaps he was excused because his manipulation of the media dealt with personal rather than political matters. Nonetheless, some accounts show that even Julius Caesar used the *Acta Diurna*, arguably the first newspaper, as a propaganda machine. Co-opting the media was a precedent set extraordinarily early in the history of political life. Obviously use of the media alone does not prove anyone to be a psychopath. But as has been shown, a certain use of media can be taken to implicate a vast number of psychopathic traits. It appears, then, some degree of psychopathy might be inherent to the very institution of politics and political life, not just obvious or extreme cases like Saddam Hussein.

Conclusions

In this author's opinion, Hussein was a psychopath. While there are indications of co-morbidity with narcissistic personality disorder, the hallmarks of psychopathy are undoubtedly present and prominent in Hussein's personality. Nonetheless, an anecdote from Dr. Jerrold Post, political psychologist, provides the best approach to these cursory, long-distance analyses. Dr. Post created an extensive psychological profile of Hussein. Putting that profile to use, Post predicted that Hussein would withdraw from Kuwait to avoid confrontation with the United States. Hussein, obviously, did not withdraw from Kuwait, sparking the first Gulf War. This unfortunate and embarrassing event for Dr. Post should be sufficient warning to take all of the above conclusions with a grain of salt. No psychological profile is perfect, especially when conducted with a great deal of cursory information. The topics of religion, nationalism, genetics, and group dynamics are related areas of psychopathy still ripe for exploration. The best we can do is watch, learn, and continue to refine our position as the psychopathic political landscape continues to unfold before our eyes.

Notes about sources

Biographical information about Saddam, his sons, and affiliates is from Con Coughlin's *Saddam: The Secret Life* and Shiva Balaghi's *Saddam Hussein: A Biography*. Information about personality disorders is from the DSM-IV. Content analysis of Saddam's speech is from Jerrold Post's *The Psychological Assessment of Political Leaders*. Information on terrorist psychology is from Jerrold Post's *Leaders and Their Followers in a Dangerous World*. Brief history of the Nazi propaganda movement is from Allen's *The Nazi Seizure of Power*.

Ted Kaczynski and Henry Murray
Psychopathy at Harvard and beyond

Abstract

Henry Alexander Murray, Harvard College class of 1915, was one of the most respected and admired psychologists of all time. He pioneered the study of personality, using a variety of creative and unconventional techniques. His laboratory at Harvard, called the Annex, was for many years an epicenter for psychological research in America. With the help of Christiana Morgan, he invented the Thematic Apperception Test, or TAT, which detects interpersonal relations and subconscious cultural biases that both normal and abnormal people possess. In his personal life, he maintained a forty-year relationship with Morgan, an affair that would foreshadow the free love movement of the sixties. In his spare time, he was an influential scholar of Herman Melville.

Theodore John Kaczynski, Harvard College class of 1962, is one of the most notorious American terrorists in history. Known as the Unabomber to denote his preference for bombing universities and airlines, he was responsible for twenty-eight injuries and three deaths. For nearly eighteen years he eluded capture, until his brother David recognized his writing style in the so-called Unabomber Manifesto, which was published in the Washington Post and the New York Times, and turned him in. He is now serving a life sentence in prison after trying unsuccessfully to hang himself with his underwear.

Kaczynski seems a logical enough candidate for a diagnosis of psychopathy, but one might wonder why Murray, a noble and aristocratic gentleman, is being included in this collection of case studies. The reason is that he may have been responsible for instigating psychopathy in Kaczynski when the two crossed paths at Harvard in the early sixties, as philosopher Alston Chase also '62 has speculated. In this study we will investigate the lives and works of Murray and Kaczynski to determine their relation to one another and to mental disorders.

Background

Henry Murray was born into a wealthy, well-connected New York family. He studied history at Harvard and medicine at Columbia. He was handsome and athletic, beloved by the ladies, known for his charm and charisma. He went on to teach physiology at Harvard for several years until he encountered psychology in the form of Carl Jung's book *Personality Types*. In Switzerland he met Jung, whom he would consider one of his greatest mentors. After returning to the United States he was appointed director of the Harvard Psychological Clinic in 1937 and a year later he published his famous *Explorations in Personality*, which outlined his newly developed TAT. During the war he served as a lieutenant colonel in the Office of Strategic Services, or OSS, a forerunner to the Central Intelligence Agency. His psychological profile of Adolph Hitler concluded that the Fuhrer was a sexual deviant and deeply insecure. After the war he returned to Harvard and his work at the Annex. Some of his most grandiose research and theories were initiated in this postwar period, including one study in which Kaczynski served as a subject. Towards the end of his career Murray was at the forefront of LSD research and may have been responsible for dosing many unsuspecting students with the drug. He died of pneumonia at the age of ninety-five.

Ted Kaczynski was born to working-class Polish immigrants. At the unusually young age of sixteen he began his studies of mathematics at Harvard. Like Murray, he received poor grades. Unlike Murray, he was not able to compensate with his looks or athletic abilities. Insecure and alienated, he began to increasingly fantasize about breaking away from society. At this crucial juncture in his life, Kaczynski met Henry Murray. According to Chase, this meeting determined many of Kaczynski's notions about psychology, which would be a central focus to his later ideology of terrorism.

Several years after Harvard, while working as a graduate student in mathematics at the University of Michigan, Kaczynski decided that he wanted to become a woman. In the initial interview with a psychiatrist, he changed his mind at the last minute and left, bitterly vowing revenge against the psychiatrist. Humiliated and ashamed, Kaczynski then concluded that not only was he capable of murder, but he was bound by duty to kill.

By this time his worldview was more or less fully developed. As he would later reveal in his Manifesto, he felt that the Industrial Revolution had been a disaster for the human race. He found the system oppressive and technology unbearable. Most relevant to our concerns here, he believed that mind control by the government was becoming increasingly powerful. As a solution, he proposed violent revolution.

The Dyad

From 1960 to 1962, Kaczynski was a subject in one of Murray's largest psychology experiments, later titled *Multiform Assessments of Personality Development Among Gifted College Students*. In this study approximately fifty Harvard students were extensively evaluated using a variety of different measures. To protect identities, each participant received a code name. Ironically, Kaczynski was dubbed Lawful. All subjects wrote essays, answered questionnaires, endured interviews, and so on for hundreds of hours, all in an effort to gain an accurate picture of their personalities. Murray called this process Personology.

The centerpiece of Murray's study was what he called the Dyad. This referred to a carefully staged confrontation between the subject and an agent of the experimenter. One by one, the subjects were brought into a small room with a single chair. They were strapped into the chair, which faced an enormous one-way mirror and a multitude of bright lights and cameras. Instruments monitoring blood pressure, heart rate, other vital statistics were attached to the subjects. Next, they were introduced to a debate opponent, whom they were told was an undergraduate just like them. In actuality, the debate opponent was a well-trained law student and a cohort of Murray's. He had been told beforehand the subject of the debate, and was given ample time to prepare his argument. Most importantly, he was instructed by Murray to be as abusive, demeaning, and confrontational as possible. The law student cohort was to attack the very foundation of the subjects' personalities.

The Dyad as a concept appears repeatedly in Murray's writing. In the most general sense, a dyad is a group of two. For Murray, it has many other more specific meanings. For example, the Dyad could refer to his relationship with Christiana, Ahab and the whale, or the altercation between subject and cohort in the *Multiform Assessments* study.

What must it have been like to be on the losing end of Murray's Dyadic relationship? In correspondence from prison Kaczynski has described it as an extremely unpleasant experience. Murray would later recount with great relish how the subjects were reduced to a state of stammering, quivering impotence when confronted with a superior personality.

Deception

The key to Murray's Harvard experiment was a simple deception. The subjects thought they were to be treated to a friendly discussion with a fellow student on the nature of love, or justice. Instead they were mercilessly attacked, ridiculed, and insulted by an experienced debater. In general, deception is a crucial technique for many social psychologists. It is a very useful skill for the experimental social psychologist, who supposedly must deceive his subjects in order to obtain unbiased data.

As Cleckley and Hare have pointed out, one of the major hallmarks of a psychopath is an outstanding ability and willingness to deceive others. The psychopath has no compunction about lying to his victims, and does so with great facility. Councilman Morgan, the son of Christiana Morgan, would later describe Murray as a master manipulator.

A psychopathic psychologist

Broadly speaking, psychology is the scientific study of the human mind. Murray was a psychologist par excellence. He knew that science demanded a dispassionate technique, a detached observer. Although he had always been an outspoken critic of what he called scientism, or the excessive application of scientific criteria to a humanistic discipline, Murray was also devoted to the objectivity of science. This method puts a premium on quantitative knowledge. Accordingly, Murray sought to express personality traits such as emotionality and aggression in terms of discrete variables. In this way the subjective experience of emotion can be removed from the equation.

Cleckley and Hare frequently write about the psychopath's emotional poverty. The psychopath is often only capable of shallow imitations of emotional affect, rather than genuine feelings of identification with another individual. This cognitive defect is frequently coupled with a grandiose, narcissistic sense of self. As a result, the psychopath tends to regard emotionality in others with puzzlement, or outright derision.

Like a psychopath, the experimental psychologist does not personally identify with the emotions of others. Modern psychology encourages use of the scientific method to investigate emotional phenomena, because subjectivity contaminates results. Murray's psychological technique may have reflected a mind that could not process emotions in an ordinary way. He built his career evaluating the personalities of his experimental subjects in terms of his own theories, reducing complex human characteristics to numerical values. In this way, Murray's psychopathic tendencies may have been of some benefit to his success.

However, all this experimentation was before research proposals had to be evaluated and approved by an institutional review board. Researchers were free at that time to use whatever techniques they wished. Researchers Stanley Mailgram and Philip Zimbardo also took advantage of this freedom with their legendary experiments on obedience to authority and prison behavior, respectively.

In his personal life, Murray had serious emotional deficiencies as well. Initially charming and effusive upon meeting a new person, Murray would quickly cool on him if they did not express deference toward the master. Acquaintances would relate that Murray frequently left friends and coworkers cut and bleeding, figuratively speaking, if they crossed him in any way.

Furthermore, there was the matter of his romantic life. Although married, Murray made only superficial attempts to conceal his forty-year affair with Morgan. In sex he demanded submission, frequently making use of bondage and the whip to subjugate his partner. And when Morgan began to decline emotionally in her later years, increasingly turning to alcohol and drugs, Murray abandoned her. She died under rather suspicious circumstances with no one around, drowning in a few inches of water while Murray supposedly slept on the beach several yards away. In Murray's last statement to Morgan before her death, he called her disgusting.

Strong vs. weak

Another characteristic of the psychopath is the tendency to target vulnerable individuals. This was one of Murray's strong points. His time in the OSS honed this skill, for his task was to determine which recruits were fit for combat, and which combatants would hold up under interrogation and torture by the enemy. Experimental subjects endured brutal treatment and merciless deception. The intention was to weed out the weak. As World War Two waned and the Cold War waxed, Murray made a smooth transition. Establishing ties with the CIA, he continued the research begun with the OSS. In Kaczynski, who already considered himself an outcast, he found an ideal subject for his experiments. Young Ted was weak and vulnerable.

The Second World War was a formative time for Murray and psychology in general. Known as sykewarriors, psychologists in the service of the military believed they were fighting for the very survival of mankind. Mind scientists like Murray sought techniques with which to mold and craft personality. In this battle for the mind of man, only the strong would survive.

Education of a psychopath

When Kaczynski arrived at Harvard for his freshman year, he was housed at Eight Prescott Street. At the time this was a special residence for exceptionally bright yet socially maladjusted students. Some questioned the wisdom of putting all such socially inept freshmen in one place. For Kaczynski, it further supported his status as an outcast.

The General Education curriculum, required of all Harvard undergraduates, introduced Kaczynski to many of the concepts that he would appropriate into his philosophy. Formerly a classmate of Kaczynski's at Harvard, Alston Chase claimed in his book that the Gen Ed program promoted a culture of despair. Undergraduates read Dostoevsky, Camus, and Nietzsche and accordingly absorbed the notion that man is alone in the universe. The absurdity of life, the omnipresence of suffering, and the disintegration of Western civilization were central themes in the General Education curriculum. Lewis Mumford declared that the achievements of modern technology were part of a culture whose central theme was the seizure and exploitation of power. Jacques Ellul wrote that man now serves technology, not vice versa. Kaczynski took these ideas to heart; they formed the central argument of his manifesto.

Logical positivism, the theory that only empirically verifiable statements are meaningful, also influenced Kaczynski to a high degree. In positivism, science offers the only true insight. As science progressed, so too did technology. Kaczynski was both fascinated and repulsed by this idea. He considered himself a scientist, and constructed his bombs according to his own rigorous scientific method. Yet he also feared that science would lead to the demise of humanity. He sympathized with Ellul's fear of technology, yet rejected his pacifist humanism.

Mind control

Around the time of Kaczynski's Dyadic encounter with Murray, he was becoming anxious that science and technology were developing increasingly sophisticated techniques of mind control. Kaczynski felt that psychology was at the heart of this process.

Some experts, including Dr. Sally Johnson, the prison psychiatrist who interviewed Kaczynski to determine if he was fit to stand trial, felt that these beliefs were evidence of psychosis. In other words, they felt that Kaczynski's beliefs were absurdly unrealistic. If this was in fact true, then his status as a psychopath must be questioned because, according to Cleckley, the genuine psychopath is not delusional. However, Dr. Johnson may not have been aware that Kaczynski's first encounter with mind science was in the form of Henry Murray, whose avowed professional goal was the creation of a new World Man, crafted according to the science of Personology. Mind control was Murray's greatest ambition.

Non-psychopathic qualities

It could be argued that Murray and Kaczynski exhibited incomplete manifestations of psychopathy, for several reasons. For one, it could be argued that they possessed real and insightful intelligence that was not entirely malicious. In Murray's case, it is conceivable that the advancement of science sufficiently promoted the good of humanity, such that the harm done to individuals like Kaczynski was relatively minor.

The clinical counterpart to psychopathy is called antisocial personality disorder. A clinical diagnosis of antisocial personality disorder appears probable for Kaczynski, considering his stable and persistent attempts to violate the rights of others. This diagnosis, however, requires evidence of a conduct disorder before the age of sixteen, and Kaczynski did not exhibit this type of behavior. For the same reason, antisocial personality disorder seems unlikely for Murray as well.

Legal issues

The cases of Murray and Kaczynski raise a number of legal issues. One issue is the ethics of human experimentation. The Nuremburg Code of 1947 was formulated in response to the inhumane human experimentation conducted by Nazis such as Dr. Josef Mengele in the concentration camps. The code demanded that experiments on humans be non-coercive, non-deceptive, and must be of lasting benefit to humanity. If Murray's experiments violated this code, then it is possible that he could have shared some indirect responsibility for Kaczynski's later bombings, as Chase claimed.

Another issue is the sanity of Ted Kaczynski. If he is determined to be psychotic, he could employ the insanity defense; if successful, then by law he would not be held responsible for his actions. Psychopathy, on the other hand, is not a legally viable defense. On the contrary, a diagnosis of psychopathy tends to work to the defendant's detriment. In actuality, Kaczynski was diagnosed with schizophrenia by Dr. Johnson; despite this, he was declared competent to stand trial. However, no trial ever occurred, for Kaczynski made a plea bargain. As a consequence, the question of psychopathy was never formally addressed in court. Kaczynski, for his part, ardently did not want to be considered psychotic. Thus he wanted no insanity defense. Furthermore, there is nothing in the modern psychological definitions that would prevent a diagnosis of both psychopathy and schizophrenia. In fact, they are comorbid disorders on occasion. Kaczynski would most likely have fit criteria for both conditions. But once again, the issues never arose in court.

A third issue involves the consequences of Harvard's allegedly nihilistic curriculum. If Harvard did in fact supply Kaczynski with his ideological ammunition, then it might well share indirect responsibility for his crimes, just as Murray's experimentation may have. Thousands of students graduate from Harvard annually and during their lives never commit violent crimes even resembling Kaczynski's. One student is far from a pattern of systematic training of mentally disordered thinking. It would be difficult to provide evidence compelling enough in a court of law to indict Harvard University for the psychopathy of one of its students, just as it would be difficult to indict Murray for the psychopathy of one of his subjects. It is probable that Harvard and Murray had a negative impact on Kaczynski, but it must remain an individual case and not be expanded farther than this one man's life.

Notes about sources

Information about the *Multiform Assessments* experiments, which involved the Dyadic interaction study, was culled from the original article provided by the Murray Research Archive. Murray's life and work was discussed at some length in Robinson's laudatory biography and in Schneidman's comprehensive compilation. Many of the insights into the dark side of Kaczynski's and Dr. Murray's characters were provided by Alston Chase's *Harvard and the Unabomber*. Information about psychopaths and psychopathy was gathered from the works of Cleckley and Hare. Kaczynski's ideas are passionately and repetitively presented in his own Manifesto.

Devin Moore and Grand Theft Auto
Are video games breeding a generation of psychopaths?

Abstract

Devin Moore, an eighteen-year-old youth from Alabama, went on a shooting rampage through a police station after officers attempted to book him on charges of grand theft auto. After killing three officers in the station, Moore stole a police cruiser and fled. Moore was convicted on three counts of homicide in his criminal trial. Family members of the officers filed a civil suit against the makers and distributors of the video game Grand Theft Auto, claiming that Moore had been conditioned to murder the officers by role-playing the psychopathic main character in the game. This case raises psychological issues about how media violence affects the psyche of youths, and whether or not youths identify with these psychopathic characters while playing the game. These games also work using a reward system. Perhaps these games are teaching youths that antisocial behavior will be rewarded. In terms of legal issues, this case raises issues of censorship of violent media for youths. Initiatives have also been implemented in order to pressure the video gaming industry to tone down violence and sex in their games.

Facts of the case

During one afternoon in Fayette, Alabama in June 2003, Officer Arnold Strickland brought Devin Moore in to the Fayette police station for a routine booking on suspicion of driving a stolen car. Moore, an eighteen year old black male, had recently graduated from high school and was about to join the Air Force. While he was being booked, Moore allegedly lunged at Officer Strickland, grabbed the officer's .40-Glock automatic and shot him twice, once in the head. Another officer, Officer James Crump, was in the building and ran towards the gunshots. Moore met Crump in the hallway and shot him three times, again once in the head. Moore continued to walk down the hallway towards the door, where he encountered Ace Mealer, the station's 911 emergency dispatcher. Moore pumped five bullets into Mealer, grabbed a set of keys, and fled in a police cruiser. The entire incident took less than a minute.

Officers captured Moore four hours after the incident, twelve miles from the Alabama state line in Mississippi. When police officers apprehended him, Moore allegedly stated that life was similar to video games in that all people eventually die.

Criminal charges were immediately brought against Moore for the homicide of the three officers. Jim Stanridge, his defense attorney, argued that Moore had mental defects caused by childhood physical and mental abuse. Stanridge also argued that Moore had played violent video games as an adolescent and that these games had influenced his criminal actions. The games that were noted were Grand Theft Auto III and Grand Theft Auto: Vice City.

Grand Theft Auto

Grand Theft Auto is a popular computer and video game series notable because the protagonist's activity and objective are entirely illegal, criminal, and antisocial, unlike most other role-playing games in which the protagonist aims to achieve some heroic aim. The Grand Theft Auto series consists of seven standalone games and two expansion packs for the original game. The series has been divided into three eras. In the first era, the first Grand Theft Auto was released in 1998 and was available on personal computers and the PlayStation game console. Two expansion packs, Grand Theft Auto: London, were both released in 1999. The second era, with the release of Grand Theft Auto 2 in 1999, featured improved graphics and different gameplay that centered on the player's preference for various criminal organizations. The third era, from 2001 through 2005, included Grand Theft Autos III, Vice City, San Andreas, Advance, and Liberty City Stories. The games in the third era shifted from a top-down aerial view of the player to a third-person view, in which the perspective comes from behind the player. Graphics and voice-overs improved substantially, and III became the first blockbuster game of the series, paving the way for subsequent Grand Theft Auto games to be bestsellers. It also set the precedent of heavy violent content for later games.

Was Grand Theft Auto the cause of Moore's shooting rampage?

Moore had apparently bought versions III and Vice City as a minor, and had played these games for hundreds of hours in the months prior to the incident. His defense attempted to argue that the responsibility of Moore's criminal actions rested with the makers of the video games, since their games had psychologically altered their client by conditioning Moore to commit these criminal acts in certain scenarios, one of which was how to respond when arrested by the police. They noted that Moore's action exactly paralleled how the protagonist of Grand Theft Auto would have responded if he were in the same situation. They believed that Moore would not have committed these violent acts if he had not played these games.

Even though the judge barred testimony linking Moore's action to his extensive experience with video games, Moore's defense attorney managed to sneak in Moore's statement about how life was like a video game during his closing argument to demonstrate Moore's affinity towards video games and how that might have influenced his violent behavior. The prosecutors rejected all claims that Moore's behavior was influenced in any way by video games, and argued that Moore knew what he was doing at the time of the crime.

Articles written about the case have focused predominantly on the possible effects of the video games on Moore's behavior, and have mentioned childhood abuse in passing. Therefore, it is difficult to assess whether such abuse actually did occur or whether this was a defense strategy concocted by the defense attorney. Moore's father did state that he had had difficulties disciplining his son in the past couple of years. He believed that his son deserved capital punishment for his crimes.

The jury did not believe that the games played a large factor in influencing Moore's actions. In August 2005, the jury in the criminal suit against Moore found him guilty of triple homicide and recommended the death penalty. Moore was sentenced to death by lethal injection in October 2005, though he has appealed his conviction.

The civil suit against Grand Theft Auto

Attorney Jack Thompson, an activist against violence in media who had on several occasions sued the video game industry in the past, led the victims' family in filing a civil suit against the publishers, makers, and distributors of Grand Theft Auto. Family members of two of the victims believed that these games transformed and programmed Moore to kill police officers; they noted that his killing spree was comparable to one of the scenarios he would have encountered as he played the video games. The family members filed a civil suit against Take Two Interactive, the publisher of Grand Theft Auto and parent company of Rockstar Games, the maker of the game; Sony, the maker of the game console that runs the game; and GameStop and Wal-Mart, distributors of the game. Thompson represented the plaintiffs in the case, *Strickland v. Sony*. Thompson withdrew from the case, however, in November 2005. The game makers' defense claimed that Thompson had been threatening and assaulting their defense attorneys. Since Thompson did not want the case to be dismissed because of his conduct, he withdrew from the case.

Thompson had been involved in numerous cases against the gaming industry in wrongful death suits prior to his involvement in *Strickland v. Sony*. Thompson had been involved with a case in 2003 involving a youth named Dustin Lynch, who was charged with the murder of Jolynn Mishne. Lynch had apparently been obsessed with Grand Theft Auto III. Thompson petitioned to file an amicus curiae brief explaining the effect of video games on violent behavior, and at one point asked to be recognized as Lynch's lawyer. In the end, Lynch's mother, Jerrilyn Thomas, decided not to have Thompson as her son's lawyer because she believed that her son was not a murderer, and that the crime was not caused by video games. In October 2003, Thompson went to Tennessee to defend two teenage stepbrothers who had pled guilty to reckless homicide, endangerment, and assault, and had claimed that they were influenced by Grand Theft Auto III. Thompson filed a suit for two hundred and forty-six million dollars against Take-Two Interactive, Sony, and Wal-Mart, arguing that they should have anticipated that their game would lead to copycat behavior in players. In another case in California, Thompson argued that one particular gang had used the game to train their members in shooting simulations.

In these cases, Thompson typically argued that youths had been influenced by the violent media presented in video games and that these games were training youths to be violent criminals. Playing these games, he alleged, caused youths to commit violent criminal acts, including engaging in school rampages and homicides. Thompson, a well-known activist against media violence, has received recognition for his advocacy efforts to implement a stricter video game rating system.

Psychopaths in Grand Theft Auto

Attorney Jack Thompson has called Grand Theft Auto a murder simulator. As mentioned before, Thompson had prosecuted a case in California in which he claimed that a gang was using the game to train its members to shoot and target police officers. Some researchers have argued that when individuals play these first-person role-playing games, players assume the identity of the character, and thus experience the violent graphics and actions first hand.

If players are to assume the identities of these characters, then the question is what type of individual these games are training players to become. By looking at Cleckley's psychopath characteristics and by reading his typologies of a psychopath, one can see that the main character of Grand Theft Auto fits the typology of a criminal psychopath. Cleckley stated that a criminal psychopath commits criminal acts not for the sake of his own personal gain or out of passion; he commits crimes, particularly violent crimes, for no specific reason. Though Carl Johnson, the main character of Grand Theft Auto: San Andreas certainly kills police officers in order to flee them, he oftentimes kills prostitutes after he has sex with them, presumably because he does not want to pay them. However, killing them is excessive, as he could achieve the same result by injuring them slightly or by fleeing. Johnson exercises excessive force and is a threat to the people around him, though he does not believe so as he does not have the capacity to empathize with their fear.

The main characters of these games are usually young, lower-class males who attempt to gain control and overtake particular cities through organizational crime. The characters commit a wide array of criminal acts, including grand theft auto; homicide of prostitutes, rival gang members, police officers, and innocent civilians; drug and arms trade and use; store and home robberies; assault; and other criminal and antisocial activities.

The main character of Grand Theft Auto: San Andreas engages in other psychopathic behavior; he steals whatever car catches his eyes and robs stores and homes. In the Grand Theft Auto games, the main character's objective is to take over the city, and the character reaches his objective by committing these antisocial activities. The characters do not seem to feel any remorse, and neither do they seem to empathize with their victims as they kill them swiftly and violently. The characters possess other psychopathic qualities, such as need for excitement and stimulation, and an emotional deficit for negative emotions such as fear. The main characters of Grand Theft Auto thus fit several criteria for psychopathy.

Training a generation of psychopaths

Opponents of these violent games argue that youths such as Devin Moore who play first-person role-playing games such as Grand Theft Auto are engaging in psychopathic behaviors through these video game characters. These games are simulations, and youths are training to lie, cheat, and kill through these games. In a sense, these ultra-violent games are breeding a population of psychopathic youths who are desensitized to violence, and encouraging them to engage in ultra-violent antisocial behaviors. Furthermore, role-playing games are so appealing because players are able to adopt the role of the protagonist. Players become the individual wielding the gun, running through the streets and murdering police officers. This is the reason why players are so involved in these games, when spectators standing next to them tend not to see the appeal.

One study noted how engaging in violent behavior can lead an individual to commit violent acts in other aspects of his life. The study found that fifty-two percent of rampage murderers have had military experience compared to thirty percent of typical murders who have military experience. From this study, we can extrapolate that living the life associated with the military, situations with high stress in which the individual is required to kill other human beings, in a sense trains and predisposes the individual to rampage killing behavior. Therefore, as the individual plays Grand Theft Auto, he is undergoing virtual training for the behavior depicted in the game, which is defying the law and killing police officers.

At the same time, perhaps there is only a correlation between rampage tendency and joining the military. It is likely that those who seek to join the military are seeking exciting, high-risk situations, as well as the ones who have the tendency to go berserk, a possible manifestation of psychopathic behavior. Regarding violent video games, perhaps many individuals who are most likely to murder are also attracted to violent video games. This is a correlation, but does not prove causation. In other words, attraction to violent video games may just be a sign, not a cause, of personality traits that predispose violence.

One study that examined role-identification in role-playing games found that behavior and attitude in games are not congruent with behavior and attitude in real life. This particular study looked at selfish or group-oriented behavior in a game in which the player was a part of a community, and his actions affected the wellbeing of the entire community. Researchers compared behavior in these games to these subjects' attitudes towards carpooling. Again, there was a lack of congruency in real-life and gaming attitudes. In a gaming condition, individuals often exhausted all possibilities, often acting in immoral or selfish ways just because it was an option, but eventually normalized to group-oriented behavior that was beneficial to the community as a whole. In real life, all these individuals tended toward group-oriented behavior in regards to carpooling. Therefore, players do not adopt their role-playing characters into their identity.

Psychological issues

There is no question that these violent video games do affect individuals in some way, just as educational children's programs are aimed to stimulate youths' cognition. Some argue that these games affect the psychology of youths by lowering human empathy and sympathy in individuals. In games such as Grand Theft Auto, players are exposed to a high level of deviant behavior, such as grand theft auto, killing of police officers, prostitution, and other forms of violence. After long-term exposure, individuals become desensitized to violence, and thus their tolerance for experiencing and inflicting damage is higher. These games also have a reward system, such that players progress through the game if they participate in deviant behavior. Some fear that individuals are subconsciously learning that deviant behavior is acceptable and that it is rewarded, leading them to commit deviant acts in reality.

Some have compared Devin Moore's shooting rampage behavior to that of Eric Harris and Dylan Klebold, the two students who went on a shooting rampage through Columbine High School, killing fifteen and wounding twenty-three students. They also compared Moore's behavior to that of postal workers who have gone on revenge rampages at their workplace after they were laid off. Researchers suggested that these individuals are exhibiting berserk responses. A berserk response occurs when an individual experiences extreme stress, especially in a situation when he feels very near death. Traditionally, this term has been used to describe soldiers near death, who under their frenzied berserk state have acted recklessly, sometimes leading to their own demise or to valorous and heroic results. Berserk individuals experience a combination of terror, grief, and rage, and it is both a psychosomatic and psychological response of coping with death. They feel that they are completely removed from reality, and thus act with cold indifference in their hyperaroused state. Some have suggested that individuals can experience berserk as a result of social death. In the 1980s, in the midst of economic unrest and a lack of job security, many postal workers lost their job, and there was a string of incidents in which these workers returned to their workplace and shot their employers. According to this theory, these individuals were not acting out of revenge. It is their psychological and bodily response to a situation of extreme stress. In cases of Devin and the main character of Grand Theft Auto, perhaps they were reacting from a lifetime of stress, which resulted from living in a disadvantaged community with little opportunities and high crime rate, as well as discrimination since they are both young, black males.

On the other hand, many individuals undergo the same stressful environmental situations but they do not exhibit the same berserk response. Perhaps some individuals are more susceptible to this response, and these individuals might be the ones who have inborn psychopathic tendencies. These games are exposing these individuals to stressful situations, provoking the berserk response.

Further issues

Senator Hillary Clinton has attacked violent games such as Grand Theft Auto, calling them a silent epidemic. This was in response to the discovery of one of Grand Theft Auto's special feature that removed censorship of pornographic material in the game. For example, makers of Grand Theft Auto had deactivated its pornographic elements, such that when the main character visited his girlfriend's house for a cup of coffee, the image would zoom to outside of the home and the player would only hear suggestive sounds. However, with a special modification to the program, players can see the player having sex with his girlfriend. The problem is that Grand Theft Auto had received an M rating, meaning that it was not suitable for youths under seventeen years of age. However, with the pornographic material, the game should technically receive an Adults Only rating. Senator Clinton pushed for the Federal Trade Commission to review the game and to revoke its M rating. Clinton has been a vocal activist against violent media.

Conclusions

It is unfair to characterize the makers of Grand Theft Auto as psychopaths. To them, violent media is merely entertainment. It is possible that the main characters of the Grand Theft Auto games are psychopaths, as they exhibit the characteristics of psychopaths. However, they have also been pushed to the edge by their environment, growing up in a neighborhood of despair where criminality is rampant and opportunities are few. The youths who play these games and imitate their behavior have been thought to exhibit copy-cat behavior. At the same time, not all youths are susceptible to influence by these games. Perhaps the youths who do imitate their behavior are more open to suggestion. Or perhaps it is a self-selecting process, and only youths with psychopathic tendencies would abide by the behaviors of the psychopaths portrayed in video games.

There has been a recent wave of ultra-violent crimes committed by youths, and some argue that this is because youths are playing violent games such as Grand Theft Auto, which in effect act as killing simulators. However, there are other factors that have contributed to the current wave of violence, including the introduction of firearms into street culture and increased violence caused by the drug market. Violence in media is possibly a reflection and result of the crack epidemic and introduction of firearms. Video games do affect the psyche of youths that play the game, just as many educational programs are supposed to positively influence children. Violent media cause youth tolerance for violent media to increase. There have also been studies showing that youths do imitate what they see and experience. With that said, youths of a young age should probably not play ultra-violent video games such as Grand Theft Auto. The Entertainment Rating System should be implemented more strictly, so that games that are rated suitable for mature audiences should not be sold to minors. We have to anticipate that these games will get into the reaches of minors either through older peers or even parents. But it is unfair to place the blame on the video game industry and to force them to restrict or censor their product. Parents should be the mediators, either by not allowing their children to play these games, or by speaking to their youths about violent media, making sure to emphasize that the image on videos is fake and that real life is not similar. In summary, video games cannot be held solely responsible for youths' violent actions because most youths who play violent games never commit violent crimes, but the games do seem to be one social factor in violence that can be potentially mitigated.

Notes about sources

The author utilized several articles from online gaming websites, including GameStop and xbox.com. She also used a journal article from *Cultural Critique* for her discussion on how youths can undergo berserk under stressful conditions. Articles from Sixty Minutes, Fox news, and *USA Today* were used to inform the author about Devin Moore's case.

Scott Peterson
Issues in his killing his pregnant wife

Abstract

In Redwood City, California on December 13, 2004, twelve jurors, who had convicted Scott Peterson of murdering his wife and unborn son, recommended that Peterson receive the death penalty. The verdict came nearly two years after Laci Peterson, a twenty-seven year old woman who was eight months pregnant, was reported missing from her Modesto, California home. Even before Laci and her unborn son's bodies washed up onto the San Francisco Bay shore in April 2003, the police and media began to suspect Scott Peterson. After the discovery of the bodies Peterson was arrested and charged with murder. The evidence against Peterson was mostly circumstantial, with suspicions growing from Peterson's odd behavior, which many felt was out of line with how a grieving husband and expecting father should act. Adding to the distrust of Peterson, Peterson had been seeing another woman, Amber Frey, before the time of Laci's disappearance and during the investigation. Police had Frey tape conversations she had with Peterson. The conversations did not, however, lead to a confession. The case was discussed and followed in the national media and questions of whether Scott Peterson was a psychopath were common discourse. Psychological issues include whether Scott Peterson was a psychopath, how cases and jurors are affected by intense media attention and why husbands kill their wives and children. Legal issues include the role of the death penalty and whether a fetus is considered a person.

Scott Peterson's early life

Scott Lee Peterson was born October 24, 1972 in San Diego, California. Peterson's father, Lee, worked for a trucking company, and later owned a packaging business. His mother, Jackie, was owner of a boutique. Scott's parents both had children from previous marriages and Scott was their only child together. Scott's mother called him the golden boy and he was doted on and carried around so much by his family that some were worried he would never actually learn to walk. Scott was not a violent child.

Scott enjoyed golf as a boy and was on the golf team at the University of San Diego High School and worked as a caddy at a near by golf course. While in high school he had a girlfriend who found out that he had been cheating on her with another girl. This unfaithfulness in intimate relationships would continue throughout his life.

Scott first attended Arizona State University where he was on the golf team with the now famous golfer Phil Mickelson. Interestingly, Mickelson said he could not remember him since he said Peterson was not in his league. Peterson was not happy at Arizona State University, perhaps because he felt he could not be admired for his superior golf skills, and left to attend Cuesta Junior College in San Luis Obispo where he was on the golf team and made the Dean's List. Peterson stayed at Cuesta for about eighteen months. His friends from Cuesta said Scott dated several people while attending Cuesta but was not seriously involved with anyone since they said he liked things his own way.

In 1994 Scott then transferred schools again, to California Polytechnic Institute, or Cal Poly, also in San Luis Obispo. He graduated from Cal Poly with a degree in science of agriculture. While at Cal Poly Scott began dating a waitress, whom he worked with at the Pacific Café, named Michelle. They had been dating for eighteen months when Scott began talking about marriage. Michelle said that Scott became overbearing and jealous and that she then broke off the relationship. Michelle has said that Scott did not want to take no for an answer and that he had what appeared to be an emotional breakdown: crying and begging Michelle to take him back. It was not clear whether these emotions were genuine or simply an act. Regardless, it is clear that Scott was not happy when he did not get what he wanted. Even after Michelle broke up with Scott he continued to show up at her apartment and attempt to win her back.

Scott and Laci's early years

Only a few weeks after his breakup with Michelle, Scott met his future wife, Laci Rocha, while he was working as a waiter in the Pacific Café. After her first date with Scott, which was a deep-sea fishing expedition, Laci told her mother that she had found her future husband. However, even as Laci was thrilled with her new boyfriend, Scott was still begging Michelle to take him back. Scott was bringing Laci to the café while Michelle was working in an attempt to make her jealous. Not long after this, though, Michelle moved away and never saw or spoke to Scott again.

By the end of 1995 Laci had moved into Scott's apartment. Scott and Laci married on August 9, 1997. Several guests at the wedding reported that Scott was heavily drunk on his wedding night and the general manager of the resort where the wedding was held told police that Scott also hit on the waitresses at the bar. During the early months of marriage Scott began an extramarital affair with Janet

Ilse, a Cal Poly student who had no idea that Scott was married. The relationship grew strong and the couple even spoke about moving in together after dating for less than five months. Janet once decided to surprise Scott at his apartment but it was she who was most surprised. She found Scott in bed with Laci. Janet became incredibly angry that Scott had cheated on her. One of Scott's roommates told Janet that Scott had been cheating with, not on, her.

Also during the early part of his marriage Scott dated another Cal Poly student named Katy for nearly three months. Scott told Katy of his aspirations to travel the world and to be mayor of Fillmore, California. Katy actually asked Scott whether he had ever been married or engaged and he told her no, but then called the next day to say he had lied: he was married in the past but was now single. Katy only realized Scott was involved with someone else when she saw Laci kiss him passionately at his graduation from Cal Poly. Scott never explained the situation or offered an apology to Katy, but later sent her a dozen roses with an odd note. She never spoke to Scott again. It was not clear how aware Laci was about these affairs. Soon after graduation Laci and Scott moved to Modesto primarily to be closer to Laci's family.

Scott's infidelity was clearly a pattern, and from these affairs, it was apparent that Scott did not care who suffered from his lies and he seemingly had no empathy. He also showed signs that he was a pathological liar. One commentator said that there were two Scotts: one was a responsible, gentle, and faithful husband; the other was someone who was having affairs and displaying emotional mood swings. The one thing that was clear about Scott was that he took great pride in his public image. All the women he had affairs with described him as being incredibly charming when wooing them but then instantly he would turn cold and uncaring and would drop them with no feelings whatsoever.

Laci and Scott moved into their own home in Modesto in 1999 and in October 2000, they purchased a larger home. Scott and Laci lived what appeared to be a happy and normal married life. They had a full social calendar. Scott made improvements to their home such as adding a swimming pool and retiling a bathroom. Scott was working at Tradecorp and often traveled to see customers. In the spring of 2002 Laci discovered she was pregnant after much trying. Laci was overjoyed that she was pregnant, but although Scott seemed happy as well, he told Laci's sister-in-law that he had been hoping for infertility. Also when friends would congratulate him that he was having a boy by saying he could play catch he allegedly told them he had friends he could do that with. Outwardly, however, he doted on Laci and seemed excited about the birth of his son, Conner.

The disappearance

On December 24, 2002 Scott reported Laci missing from their Modesto home. At the time of her disappearance Laci was nearly eight months pregnant. Scott said he came home from a fishing trip to Berkeley Marina and his wife could not be found anywhere. Before contacting the police, however, he called Laci's mother, Sharon, to ask if she was there. Laci was not at her parents' home and Sharon began to panic, since Laci was having some problems related to her pregnancy. After calling hospitals and friends Laci was not located and Ron Grantski, Laci's stepfather, called 911. Although police typically wait at least twenty-four hours to investigate when adults go missing, the police quickly took her disappearance seriously due to Laci's advanced pregnancy.

The investigation

By six p.m. on December 24, 2002 the investigation in Laci's disappearance had begun. The Modesto Police were on their way to the Peterson home. Sharon called Scott and arranged to meet him to start searching for Laci. Sharon Rocha had commented on how she was surprised at how calm Scott seemed. Detectives began to question Peterson. Although Scott told investigators that he had been fishing his equipment did not appear to be used and he could not answer what he was fishing for. There were many things that seemed suspicious to the police as they interviewed Peterson and investigated his home. Searches for Laci continued for months by the police and by volunteers. The police were contacted by Amber Frey. She told them that she had been having an affair with Peterson, beginning before Laci's disappearance. Frey agreed to tap her conversations with Peterson. Although these recordings did not contain a confession for the murder of his wife his personality and psychology were made apparent through these taped conversations. In these conversations, Peterson was above all shown to be a pathological liar. Finally on April 14 and 15, 2003, Conner and Laci's bodies were found washed up on the shore of the San Francisco Bay. On April 18, Scott was arrested in La Jolla, California. When Scott was arrested he had died his hair blond and grown a goatee. He had the driver's license of his brother, John Edward Peterson, fifteen thousand dollars in cash, four cell phones, a gun, a dagger, the directions to Amber Frey's workplace, and Viagra among many other things. Many involved in the case speculated that Peterson may have planned to flee to Mexico, or knowing that he was being followed by police and had in fact confronted them earlier that day, was on his way to murder Amber Frey. With Peterson arrested these theories remained unverified. Scott was then taken into custody.

The Amber Frey conversations

Amber Frey and Scott Peterson had a six-week relationship which was notable because Frey taped her conversations with Peterson to aid in the investigation and prosecution of him. The taped conversations with Amber Frey, while not giving direct evidence to the murders of his wife and unborn son, did give evidence that showed Peterson as egocentric, glib, manipulative, lacking responsibility, as having no remorse, and as being a pathological liar and promiscuous. Scott met Shawn Sibley, Amber Frey's best friend at the time, at a business conference in Anaheim, California in October 2002. Sibley has said that Scott told her he was single and that he wanted to meet someone to have a long-term relationship with. Sibley told Amber about Scott and Amber agreed to let Sibley give Scott her number. Scott called Amber in early November and they made a date to meet on November 20, 2002. The couple went to dinner, went dancing and ended up spending the night together in a hotel. When asked if Peterson was married or had ever been married, at first he denied it, he then told Frey that he had been married but that he lost his wife, before she actually went missing. While Scott was attending a vigil for Laci and supposedly searching for her he told Frey that he was traveling around Europe. On New Years Eve, he told Frey he was partying and watching fireworks at the Eiffel Tower with friends including Francois from France and Pasqual from Spain. From these kinds of statements to Frey, the depth of his lies and deceit appeared immense. Scott told grandiose lies, not just simple ones, and experts have said this is because they helped to boost his ego. Peterson also continually asked Frey whether she thought he was intelligent. He also continually told Amber that he was confident that their relationship would grow. Never did he seem sad about the disappearance of his wife.

The trial

Since there was intense media attention and hostility toward Peterson in Modesto, on January 20, 2004 the trial was moved to Redwood City, California. The trial proceeding began in June 2004. The lead prosecutor for the case was Rick Distaso and Peterson was represented by Mark Geragos. The defense argued that there was no direct evidence linking Peterson to the crime. The defense also made sure to downplay the circumstantial evidence including Peterson's behavior, which did not seem to many the behavior of a grieving husband. The prosecution in his case presented three possible motives for his killing Conner and Laci: he did not want to be tied down to having a son; he wanted to collect on Laci's two hundred and fifty thousand dollar life insurance policy, which he suggested she get; and because he was in debt and he wanted to be able to have affairs and sexual relationships with no interference. All of these possible motives were extremely selfish and appeared to be the motives of a psychopath. Peterson's sexual promiscuity, which did not necessarily point to psychopathy, was yet another factor in his psychopathic profile. During the trial Scott appeared stoic or laughing as Geragos joked with him. Witnesses of the trial said that he never appeared anguished, sad, or fearful. Experts said that this is because Peterson did not have the feelings others in his situation would have. He appeared calm, easygoing, and relaxed which was very odd in light of his predicament.

After a five month trial the case went to the jury. There were some problems among jurors: one juror had to be removed because of juror misconduct, and the jury foreman then asked to be removed because of threats he allegedly received. Regardless of these problems the jury did reach a verdict on November 12, 2004. They found Scott guilty of first degree murder with special circumstances for the murder of Laci and second degree murder for killing his unborn son, Conner. The fact that Peterson was convicted of second degree murder for the murder of his unborn son is important, because in California a fetus over seven weeks can be considered a person, or in this case, a murder victim. Because Conner was considered a person Peterson was convicted of double homicide and was then eligible to receive the death penalty. The jury returned on December 13, and did recommend that Peterson receive the death penalty. On March 16, 2005 Judge Alfred A. Delucchi formally sentenced Scott Peterson to death. Delucchi called the murder of Laci uncaring, cruel, heartless, and callous.

Media involvement

The media played a significant role in this case. Supporters of Scott's innocence say it was unfair from the beginning because the media rushed to judgment and these people believed the legal proceedings were affected by this bias. Scott was certainly not innocent until proven guilty in the media's eyes. The media flocked to this case because it was so heart wrenching as well as sensational to the general public. A charming woman who was about to give birth goes missing; meanwhile her husband had been cheating on her and acting in an atypical manner. The taped conversations with Amber Frey were leaked to the media and the general public heard Scott's lies to Amber. He told her he was in Europe while he was actually searching for his wife. While attending a vigil for Laci on New Years Eve, he told Frey he was in Paris at the Eiffel Tower with his so-called friends Francois from France and Pasqual from Spain. The media was speculating on his psychological state, including whether he was a psychopath, sociopath, narcissist, or, perhaps and, pathological liar.

The media used the evidence presented to them including Peterson's own behaviors in interviews, his personal history, and his taped conversations with Amber Frey. In several interviews Scott participated in, he seemed to be emotionally flat when discussing his wife and yet also seemed to have crocodile tears when interviewed about Laci. He never once mentioned his unborn son Conner by name. Scott sold Laci's car and belongings before anyone knew what actually happened to her. The transcripts of his taped conversations with Amber Frey painted him even more as a pathological liar and man with no feelings of sadness that his pregnant wife was gone. He lied so easily that he even made up names of imaginary friends and travel partners. Although the media is not in a position to diagnose someone as a psychopath, it does not seem off base that many media outlets and individuals on talk shows were declaring that he was a psychopath. These rushes to judgment that Scott was a psychopath might have influenced the way the public viewed the case and perhaps how the jury saw the case.

Labeling of Scott Peterson

Scott Peterson was the center of much media attention and many individuals speculated on his mental state. Many commentators, including psychiatrists and forensic psychologists, mentioned on air and in articles that he exhibited many of the characteristics of a psychopath or sociopath. Others mentioned that he was the perfect example of a narcissistic individual. One such expert is Dr. Keith Ablow, a forensic psychiatrist who had been an expert witness for many highly-publicized trials. He wrote *The New York Times'* bestselling novel *Inside the Mind of Scott Peterson* and appeared on the Oprah Winfrey Show where he spoke about Scott Peterson's mind and personality. Ablow said that from what he had witnessed of the case, Peterson was a perfect example of a psychopath. Ablow wrote that Peterson had no true self and had been able to go through life imitating others and their emotions without feeling them himself. Ablow wrote how Scott Peterson used lines from movies and television when describing his feelings. Ablow wrote that there were early signs that Peterson was losing his ability to empathize with others, if he ever could. Also, Ablow said that Peterson had a sex addiction and that he believed if Peterson were released he could kill again.

Catherine Crier, a former judge and well-known television legal analyst on Court TV, covered the Peterson case from the beginning. In her book *A Deadly Game*, she detailed Peterson's life before the murders and during the investigation and trial. She came to the conclusion many times that Peterson displayed many textbook qualities of a psychopath. She details many occasions in his life where he displays odd or out of place emotions. She saw Scott as a person able to morph into different personalities based on the person he was with at the time. With one girlfriend, who was a health nut, he did not drink. With another girlfriend, who was a vegetarian, he said he was too. With Laci, he became a suburban father and entrepreneur who did work around the house just as Laci desired. Although never religious before, with Amber Frey, Peterson told her he wished he could get out of prison to do God's work. Crier used these examples to show that Peterson had no real self, which is one telltale sign of psychopathy. Crier said Peterson showed absolutely no normal signs of grief. At the vigil for his wife he was repeatedly photographed grinning. Crier states many times in her book that Scott Peterson was a psychopath. Crier says that Peterson reminds her immensely of Ted Bundy. Both seemed charming and handsome on the outside but completely different under the surface. Both men had a mix of charm and callous and emotionless calculation.

Those close to Scott Peterson who knew him personally, such as his half sister Anne Bird, described Peterson's personality and through their depictions it can be inferred that he exhibited many of the characteristics of a psychopath. Anne Bird described Peterson as vacant, without emotion and without a true core self. She also described him as a pathological liar. Bird went on to say outright that Scott had no conscience and because of this, along with other factors, she believed he was a psychopath.

Signs before the murders

Interestingly, there did not seem to be a major indication, besides his lies, that Peterson was a psychopath before he killed Laci. There were clues that he was not quite right but nothing so great that anyone would have thought that he was a psychopath. People in his life looked back on his behaviors while the trial was going on and said in retrospect he had acted odd in his life but these people had not noticed his off kilter behaviors before this. Some described him as glib and perhaps insincere. His girlfriends' friends and family viewed him as a smooth operator and a person whom they should be slow to trust. Laci's mother Sharon Rocha thought he was a good man and defended him directly after Laci went missing and the media began accusing Scott. The major indication that Scott was perhaps psychopathic was his sexual promiscuity. He had various affairs while married to Laci and was an incredibly fanciful and inventive liar in order to keep these affairs going while continuing to make others believe his marriage to Laci was going perfectly. No one really realized he was a pathological liar and a person with no emotions or feelings for others until the facts of his life were scrutinized for the murder case against him. Scott simply kept up his mask of normalcy so well that no one seemed to notice his psychopathic personality. Certainly it was clear that Scott was a well-behaved child and that he did not appear to have any of the symptoms of conduct disorder. Because he did not have conduct disorder, he could not officially be diagnosed with antisocial personality disorder. However, he could still be diagnosed with psychopathy because juvenile delinquency is one item on a psychopathy checklist, but it is not necessary for a diagnosis.

Similar cases

There have been many other men who have killed their wives and children. Some have then killed or attempted to kill themselves. Charles Stuart is one example of a husband who killed his pregnant wife and, later, himself. In 1989 he shot and killed his wife, Carol, and shot himself. He told the police, however, it was a black man who shot them. Stuart, like Peterson, was having an affair and he, like Peterson, was having financial problems. The police became increasingly suspicious of him and he killed himself. The recent Entwistle case is another example. Neil Entwistle was arrested for the murder of his wife and daughter. Entwistle was thought to have murdered his wife and daughter at their home and then was about to kill himself but could not go through with it. Entwistle, like Peterson and Stuart, was also having financial problems. Financial problems are often a catalyst of these crimes. There were many possible motives for Scott to murder Laci and Conner that the prosecution brought up at trial. One motive was that he was in financial debt and he did not want to have to pay for a child. He also thought he would get Laci's two hundred and fifty thousand dollar life insurance policy. Perhaps he was worried with the baby coming that he would no longer get the attention he believed he deserved. Another motive, which fits with his psychopathy, is that he felt tied down and wanted to go back to the bachelor life. A difference between the Peterson case and others is that he showed no remorse or worry and he showed no signs that he would try to commit suicide. As Hare has pointed out, psychopaths rarely, if ever, commit suicide. Commentators said that Peterson was certain he would not be found guilty of the crime and that he would then be free to live his life as he pleased.

What is Scott Peterson's diagnosis?

Scott Peterson exhibited many of the characteristics of psychopathy as well as narcissistic personality disorder. Regarding psychopathy he seemed to exhibit all of the emotional and interpersonal symptoms. He was glib and superficial; he was charming and articulate; he was egocentric; he had a lack of remorse or guilt over the death of his wife; he seemed to lack empathy; he was manipulative and deceitful when it came to his extramarital affairs; he appeared to have shallow emotions when he spoke on television about the disappearance of his wife. He seemed to exhibit fewer antisocial traits. He did have a need for excitement and a lack of responsibility but the other symptoms do not seem to define him clearly. He was also sexually promiscuous, which is a trait not directly associated with either factor. Peterson also seemed to embody the characteristics and symptoms of narcissistic personality disorder, which makes sense since he embodied nearly every characteristic in the emotional and interpersonal area, Factor 1 of psychopathy, also known as aggressive narcissism. He seemed to be the model for narcissistic personality disorder. He had a grandiose sense of self-importance; he was preoccupied with fantasies of unlimited success, power, brilliance, beauty, and especially ideal love; he believed that he is unique and special; he required intense and excessive admiration; he was interpersonally exploitative and used others to achieve his own ends; he seemed to lack empathy; and he showed arrogant behaviors. It is unclear whether he was envious of others or that he believed others were envious of him. It appears from these criteria that Scott Peterson suffered from narcissistic personality disorder and it seems that he would score highly on the Hare Psychopathy Checklist. It seems from this evidence that Scott Peterson was a psychopath who also had a narcissistic personality disorder. This seems to correlate with the research that male psychopaths exhibit many narcissistic traits whereas female psychopaths exhibit traits of Histrionic Personality Disorder.

Scott Peterson had many affairs while he was married to Laci, beginning at the earliest stages of their marriage. Although Scott's incredible ease in lying to his wife and his mistresses pointed perhaps to his psychopathy, the affairs themselves do not necessarily point in that direction. Many men and women cheat on their significant others and the majority of them are not psychopaths. More pointed than his actual affairs is the lack of actual feelings he had for the women with whom he had relationships, including his wife. While Scott bought the women in his life lavish gifts and told them deep declarations of his love, it is clear that he never really felt or meant what he said and was completely selfish in these relationships.

Concluding thoughts

Without actually meeting with Scott Peterson for a psychological interview, one cannot know for sure what his pathology is. It is clear, however, that from the information available to the general public Scott Peterson fits the criteria for narcissistic personality disorder nearly perfectly. He also meets many of the criteria for psychopathy, especially the emotional and interpersonal symptoms on the Psychopathy Checklist. Until the murder of Laci and Conner, no one seemed too aware of Scott's pathology. He was able to keep his mask on and fool individuals around him. Only after the murders did people really realize the full extent of Scott's lies, callousness and reckless behavior. However, the fact that Peterson turned to violence, something he had never done before, made him score higher on the Psychopathy Checklist than he would have earlier. If his behavior and personality was thoroughly investigated before Laci's and Conner's murder it seems he would have been diagnosed with narcissistic personality disorder. After the murder of his wife and unborn child, his true colors came out. The murders showed that he was capable of ending the lives of those close to him, and also displayed just how devoid of emotions and remorse he really was.

Notes about sources

The CourtTV website was an especially helpful and comprehensive resource in researching the case. The book *A Deadly Game* by Catherine Crier was detailed and informative. *Blood Brother* by Anne Bird, Scott Peterson's half sister, gave an inside and personal view of the case. For psychological information on Scott Peterson I found *Inside the Mind of Scott Peterson* by Dr. K. Ablow to be particularly salient.

Gary Ridgway
The Green River killer

Abstract

On November 5, 2003, Gary Leon Ridgway was convicted of fatally strangling forty-eight women who lived near the Seattle/Tacoma area. His confession and eventual conviction was the final note in the longest and largest manhunt the United States has ever seen, one that spanned over two decades and cost the state of Washington tens of millions of dollars and countless hours of manpower. Although Ridgway was officially convicted for murdering forty-eight women, it is widely believed that the number of his victims tallies well over sixty, making Gary Ridgway the deadliest known serial killer in U.S. history. Astonishingly, nearly all of his murders, with the exception of two victims, took place within a two and a half year period between 1982 and 1985 along a ten-mile strip of highway in Seattle. His eventual capture was made possible by advances in DNA technology, which connected a sample of his saliva to traces of semen taken decades earlier from several of his victims' bodies. Ridgway escaped the death penalty by entering a plea bargain with King County prosecutors and is currently serving forty-eight consecutive life sentences.

Ridgway's early life

Gary Leon Ridgway was born February 18, 1949 to Mary and Tom Ridgway in Salt Lake City, Utah. He was the eldest of three brothers born into the Ridgway family. His family was marked by the dichotomy of his parents' personalities. His mother was a domineering and controlling woman whose insistence on maintaining a clean and orderly home bordered on pathological. Mary Ridgway kept tight reins on her family, and would continue to be a controlling force in Gary's life well into his married adulthood. In contrast, his father was a very meek man who lacked the confidence and ability to defend himself against his physically and emotionally abusive wife.

In retrospect, it is easy to identify the early signs of the psychopath growing within the young Ridgway. He had a penchant for destruction. He compulsively broke windows, set fires, and eventually turned to torturing and murdering animals and pets. Gary was also a bed-wetter, a trait that persisted throughout his youth and into his early teenage years. His childhood bed-wetting and fondness for abusing animals are two characteristics that are well-documented as common traits among serial killers. As a punishment for his bed-wetting, Ridgway's mother would parade him naked in front of his brothers and force him to take cold baths during which she would scrub his body, focusing much of her energy on cleaning his genitals. Eventually this behavior led Ridgway to develop elaborate sexual fantasies about his mother that ultimately evolved into a strong desire to rape and kill her.

In several instances, the young Ridgway was able to find human victims to serve as conduits for his sadistic desires. When he was fourteen years old, he convinced his six year old cousin to follow him into the woods and allow him to touch her genitals in exchange for a penny. The traumatized cousin immediately recounted the interaction to her parents and Ridgway was punished with a beating. At sixteen, Ridgway stumbled upon a nine year old boy dressed in a cowboy outfit playing outside. Again, he convinced the boy to accompany him into the woods where Ridgway stabbed him through his side and wiped the blood off the knife with the boy's shirt. When the boy, clutching his bleeding side, asked Ridgway why he stabbed him, Ridgway laughed and responded that he simply did it out of the desire to know what it was like to kill someone. Many years later, the young boy, then a grown man, recounted that the injury was near fatal and his liver had to be stitched back together in order to save his life. By examining instances from Ridgway's childhood, it is interesting to notice the red flags signaling the psychopath that was budding within him.

The violent behavior that riddled his childhood generates suspicion that the young Ridgway suffered from conduct disorder. According to the *Diagnostic and Statistical Manual of Mental Disorders*, conduct disorder is a mental illness that afflicts adolescent and pre-adolescent youth, defined by violent and antisocial acts. Conduct disorder is a prerequisite for and precursor to antisocial personality disorder, for which Ridgway most likely meets the criteria.

Personal life

Ridgway was an exceptionally poor student. His dyslexia and low IQ made it difficult for him to focus in his classes, and he had to be held back for two years before graduating high school at age twenty. Ridgway also faced sexual frustrations during this period. Because his mother taught him that masturbation was the ultimate sin and because most girls were unwilling to date the awkward Ridgway, he found it difficult to relieve his sexual appetite. Eventually he turned to voyeurism, exhibitionism, and frotteurism in order to receive sexual gratification.

Once out of high school, Ridgway married his steady girlfriend, joined the Navy, and became part of the Vietnam War. He was shipped out to sea and began frequenting Filipina prostitutes. Within a few months, Ridgway contracted gonorrhea. The self-consciousness and rage that detailed his early life grew stronger. When he returned home to his wife after being discharged by the Navy, he learned that she had also been unfaithful and the marriage abruptly ended. However, Ridgway's need for female companionship persisted, and he continued to date women and solicit prostitutes.

Although Ridgway lacked academic capacity, he had a knack for working with tools and machines. Immediately after high school, Ridgway was hired as a truck painter for Kenworth, a job he held for thirty years until his arrest in 2001. Coworkers described Ridgway primarily as a loner. He was nice enough, but there was something about him that put many ill at ease. Sexual harassment charges were brought against him multiple times and his dyslexia sometimes created problems with his work. However, he was dependable and rarely took sick days. The days he did not come in were later shown to correspond with the dates of his murders.

Shortly after the divorce with his first wife, Ridgway met and married another woman, Marcia, with whom he fathered a son. Close friends of the couple described Ridgway as charismatic and eager to please; they thought of him as someone who went out of his way to charm people into liking him. He also became deeply involved in his church.

Despite a relatively pleasant relationship, the couple did experience several difficulties. Marcia experienced some displeasure in the control her mother in law exerted over Gary. Mary Ridgway insisted on buying all of her son's clothes and often criticized his wife for her inability to keep a house that met her standards of cleanliness. Mary also demanded that Ridgway hand over his paycheck every month and would give the couple spending money with the stipulation that she be told exactly where the money was going. Within the marriage, Marcia also faced the demands of a husband with an insatiable sexual appetite. He insisted on having sex multiple times a day, generally outdoors and in locations that would eventually be identified as dumpsites for the bodies of his victims. The marriage eventually ended in 1981 due to Ridgway's temper and infidelity on the part of both Gary and Marcia. Some wonder if this divorce was the spark that ignited Ridgway's murderous rampage.

The murders

Over the course of twenty years, Ridgway is known to have killed forty-eight women and it is suspected that his death count is actually much higher, making him the deadliest known serial killer in American history. Most of these murders took place within a two and half year period from 1982 to 1984 along a ten-mile strip of highway in Seattle. Two aspects of his career as a murder stand out as being particularly unusual when compared to other notorious serial killers: his ability to evade capture for twenty years, and his apparent fifteen-year hiatus from murdering between the mid-1980s and late 1990s. An important question stems from these two phenomena: Was Ridgway's psychopathy the driving factor or were the murders the result of some external forces?

On July 15, 1982, the clothed and strangled body of sixteen year old Wendy Lee Coffield was found floating in the Green River of Seattle, Washington. Coffield was eventually identified as the first victim in the series of Green River murders. A month later four more bodies were found nude and strangled in the Green River. The police determined that all five women were linked to prostitution. With such striking similarities between the death and backgrounds of the victims, police began to recognize that they were dealing with a serial killer. This came during a time when the term serial killer had only recently been coined following the Ted Bundy case several years earlier. A task force composed of King County detectives, known as the Green River Task Force, was established to investigate the murders. It was the largest police task force since the Bundy murders and the detectives drew from their experience with collecting and analyzing evidence during the Bundy years to help them make sense of the murders they were facing eight years later. Over the next twenty years, the task force would grow considerably as more and more girls were reported missing and the body count continued to rise.

Interestingly, Ridgway was never far from the top of the Task Force's suspect list. Ridgway was a viable suspect for a number of reasons. He was well known for soliciting prostitutes and was not ashamed to talk about it openly with detectives who came to question him multiple times throughout the manhunt. He was arrested several times for hiring prostitutes, several of whom were undercover cops. He was also known to have solicited many of the victims for sex prior to their disappearance, which he also readily admitted to detectives during the investigation. Ridgway's complete lack of any outward signs of anxiety consistently led police to believe in his innocence. He simply did not act like a guilty man. He easily admitted to behavior to which a guilty man would never confess.

However, there remained elements of his history, particularly his record of violence against women, which kept Ridgway high on the list of possible suspects. His second wife accused him of strangling her during a fight, which resulted in charges that she later dropped. Several prostitutes claimed that he attempted to strangle them, and one of them gave a very detailed account to police. When Ridgway was confronted with the claim, he admitted to strangling her but retorted that the prostitute had bit his penis during oral sex and the violence against her was a reflex that any man would have had. The police evidently agreed and the charges were dropped. Furthermore, the boyfriend of one of the victims had witnessed his girlfriend get into Ridgway's truck and tracked the vehicle to Ridgway's house. Once his girlfriend failed to return home he led police back to Ridgway's residence. When confronted by police, Ridgway remained calm and told police he did hire the girl but knew nothing about her disappearance.

Although the bodies of Ridgway's victims continued to be found for decades, the disappearances and killing eventually died down in 1984. Ridgway married, and although he continued to solicit prostitutes, it appears for the most part that he stopped murdering them. Several bodies were discovered during the 1990s that would not be linked to the Green River killings until after Ridgway was in custody.

In 2001, almost twenty years after the first body was discovered, a saliva sample taken from Ridgway during a search of his house that had been conducted years earlier was linked to DNA found on several of the victims' bodies. Later, microscopic bits of paint found on many more victims were found to be identical matches to the paint Ridgway used at the Kenworth factory. In 2002, Ridgway entered a plea bargain with prosecutors stipulating that Ridgway would not face the death penalty in exchange for the locations of the bodies of his other victims. Ridgway agreed and was sentenced to serve 48 consecutive life sentences, one for each woman he confessed to murdering.

Psychological issue

What factors of Ridgway's personality allowed him to operate below the radar of police? With so much evidence against him including eyewitness testimony and a penchant for strangling women that perfectly matched the modus operandi of the killer, how is it that Ridgway managed to escape the law for two decades? In part, Ridgway's success as a serial killer was a result of his psychopathic qualities.

Ridgway was able to evade capture through his amazing attention to detail. For a man who appeared to struggle through his academic career, Ridgway had an incredible innate grasp of forensic science. His targeting of prostitutes was deliberate. He knew that these women were drifters and that their absence would go undetected for extensive periods of time. Ridgway also recognized correctly that identifying their remains would be a difficult task for police. He even went so far as to pose one of his victims in an attempt to mislead police into thinking a different murderer had committed the crime. He often scattered the remains of his victims between Washington and Oregon to throw of police pursuits. His killings were systematic and his clean-ups were thorough. This was not the work of an insane man; Ridgway knew exactly what he was doing and did it with great attention to detail.

Ridgway's ability to lie without any expression of guilt or anxiety aided him in his evasion of arrest. Ridgway was taken to Task Force headquarters on several occasions to undergo questioning and polygraph tests. Ridgway consistently passed the polygraphs and those who interviewed him described Ridgway as calm, collected, and always able to provide reasonable answers for the accusations against him. This unusual ability to lie undetected is common among psychopaths, who experience anxiety, guilt, and a fear of being caught differently from normal individuals.

Ridgway's childhood: A budding psychopath

Ridgway's childhood misconduct is another interesting area of his life that may bear some relevance in understanding the man he eventually became. Children who aggressively disregard social norms and rules generally meet the *Diagnostic and Statistical Manual* criteria for conduct disorder. An individual must have had conduct disorder as a child in order to be diagnosed with antisocial personality disorder. Many psychopaths engaged in extreme acts of childhood antisocial behavior and are diagnosed with conduct disorder. Ridgway's torture of animals, violence against other children, obsession with setting fires, and instance of coercing sexual favors from his cousin all suggest that Ridgway suffered from conduct disorder as a child.

An important question that arises from examining Ridgway's childhood is whether Ridgway's unhealthy home environment and relationship with his mother contributed to the behavior in which Ridgway would late engage as an adult. The nurture versus nature question is one that is common among literature about psychopathy. Many argue that Ridgway grew up in an incredibly unhealthy family environment that produced the monster he eventually became. His mother's inappropriate touching and bathing of her child combined with her controlling nature and penchant for spousal abuse had an extremely unhealthy impact on his mind. Many other serial killers and psychopaths have come from similar family backgrounds, suggesting that this style of development is conducive to the production of psychopathy in children.

Others argue that psychopathy is rooted in genetics, citing the fact that many children come from broken homes with abusive parents and do not become psychopathic serial killers. Also, Ridgway's psychopathic tendencies were evident at a very young age. By the age of six he was torturing and killing family pets and other animals. This early age of onset of psychopathic behavior suggests that Ridgway would have become the man he did no matter who raised him. Congruent with most current theories of psychopathy, it appears that the combination of innate qualities and a detrimental childhood environment led to Ridgway's psychopathic characteristics.

Psychopath in the personality

Ridgway's narcissistic notion that his murders were acts of service to society speaks to his apparent psychopathy. Ridgway acknowledges that he preyed on prostitutes and young runaways because he saw them as ills of society. He often claimed that he should be thanked for the work he did and expressed confusion over the notion that he should be punished for his actions. Ridgway noted that he selected prostitutes as his victims because he believed in their status as subhuman.

Ridgway also had difficulties with impulse control. He developed a list of rules by which to abide when choosing targets and disposing of the bodies. Several of the rules restricted him from killing girls he picked girls up who were with a pimp or another prostitute who would witness the victim getting into his car. Ridgway, however, occasionally failed to respect these self-imposed rules, which often resulted in a positive identification of his truck. His description of his relationship with prostitutes as similar to a junkie's relationship to their drugs also indicates his inability to control himself. This type of behavior is consistent with Hare's description of the psychopath as having difficulty controlling his impulses.

While some neighbors claimed Ridgway was a nice guy, much of his behavior was extremely unusual and he had a tendency to put people ill at ease. Sexual harassment charges were filed against him multiple times at work. Coworkers described Ridgway as going through religious fanatical periods during which he would give drawn out speeches during lunch hour about the evils of prostitution. In addition to his tendency toward antisocial behavior, Ridgway had a ferocious sexual appetite. He demanded sex from his wives and girlfriends multiple times a day, which led many of them to believe he was a faithful partner. On the contrary, Ridgway saw prostitutes throughout his life, apparently unable to have his sexual needs fulfilled. Promiscuity and antisocial behavior are two central elements of psychopathy.

Ridgway's chronic narcissism combined with his utter void of remorse, anxiety and other basic human emotions contribute to the argument that he is a psychopath. When faced by the families of his victims in court, Ridgway's expression of sorrow and remorse were limited to the infrequent times when a family member told Ridgway that they had forgiven him for what they had done to their family. Otherwise, Ridgway sat emotionless and appeared completely unaffected by the stricken families addressing him. During rounds of questioning with detectives Ridgway's expressions of regret and remorse were again reserved for himself. As interviewers reported, the tears he shed were tears of self-pity. The acts of narcissism that were reported of Ridgway are consistent with the profile of psychopathy that was developed by Hare and Cleckley. As both authors noted, narcissism is an essential feature of psychopathy. Like Ridgway, psychopaths care for nobody but themselves and typically reserve displays of emotion for times when they perceive themselves to be the victim of the situation.

Plea bargain

Ridgway entered a plea bargain with prosecutors which guaranteed that he would be spared the death penalty under the condition that he honestly answer detectives' questions and locate the bodies of his remaining victims. Despite the threat of a death sentence if he failed to cooperate, it was extremely difficult for detectives to get consistent answers out of Ridgway. He often told several inaccurate versions of the same story and sent police teams on wild goose chases, hunting down non-existent bodies throughout the greater Seattle area. While detectives were able to uncover four additional victims with Ridgway's help, the discussions with Ridgway that preceded the discoveries were tedious due to Ridgway's unwillingness to be forthcoming with details of his crimes. Many believe that there are more Green River victims that Ridgway did not confess to murdering. Several times Ridgway remarked that he killed over eighty women only to retract that statement the following day.

There were several theories explaining why Ridgway refused to be forthcoming with the truth. Many suggested it was a product of his personality. Ridgway was a self-proclaimed chronic liar. And while he played dumb when asked certain questions, he often provided information after persistent interrogation. Ridgway refused to admit to having sex with the bodies of his victims, but he eventually admitted to necrophilia and claimed that he would occasionally bury bodies to keep himself from returning and having intercourse with them. Ridgway was capable of recalling details of his crimes as minor as the exact time he arrived at work the day after a murder and the type of debris that littered the areas in which he killed his victims, but he had extreme difficulty remembering physical features of his victims. This highly selective memory suggested that Ridgway was intentionally keeping information from detectives despite the dire consequences he faced if he was caught lying.

Others argued that his failure to answer questions was due to his low intelligence and poor memory. While it seemed implausible that Ridgway could forget the names, faces, and locations of the bodies, most of his known crimes were committed over twenty years earlier. So much time had passed that it could be difficult to recall the details of bodies that he spent no more than an hour or two with. Also, the sheer number of women he killed may have added to the difficulty of remembering their individual features and locations.

Legal issue

The Green River case sparked an enormous amount of controversy and criticism at the efforts of the Task Force responsible for tracking down the killer. Some argued that the depraved backgrounds of most of the victims weakened police motivation to work as vigorously as they would have if the women had led more socially acceptable lives. In mid-March of 1984, a march through Seattle was led by a group called the Women's Coalition to Stop the Green River Murders and joined by a San Francisco group called U.S. Prostitutes Collective. The group leaders announced that their mission was to end the farce that was the Green River murders investigation. Many women's rights and domestic abuse groups supported the movement. Women were still being murdered and they were frustrated by the lack of progress in solving the case.

On the other hand, the Task Force was ill equipped to provide the time, money, and energy that a case like the Green River killings demanded of them. In the early 1980s, computer technology was in its early stages of development. Records and notes were not kept in online databases, making it extremely difficult for detectives to organize the incredible volume of information they were gathering about their cases. Detectives were dealing with hundreds of thousands of pages of notes and everyday they were accumulating more. The Task Force argued that the lack of apparent progress was not due to any weakness in their motivation to find the killer. Instead, the vast amount of information and insufficient resources to analyze it were preventing them from making more headway.

The sophistication of forensic technology, such as fingerprinting and DNA profiling, was primitive during the early '80s. Fingerprints were matched through a meticulous, manual process and DNA matches could only be made by comparing blood types. Police were scientifically ill-equipped to solve this case during the 1980s. It was not until several years later that they would have a computer system to input all of their leads and notes. However, they did have the foresight to collective DNA samples from the crime scenes, including pubic hairs, semen stains, and articles of clothing left at the sites. They also thought to take a saliva sample from Ridgway during a search of his house 1987 that was conducted after they were able recognize how many times Ridgway's name had been brought to their attention with the help of their new computer system. Ultimately this DNA evidence material would be the most vital evidence implicating Ridgway in the murders.

Despite the celebration that occurred after detectives arrested Ridgway, criticism continued to be raised against the Task Force. DNA experts were outraged that detectives waited until 2001 to submit their DNA evidence for testing. By 1996, DNA profiling was finally able to determine if two DNA samples were taken from the same individual. The delay in the Task Force's move to action cost them lives.

The plea bargain that saved the life of Gary Ridgway also generated public outcry and caused debate in Washington courts whether a precedent has been set to exclude the death penalty as a punishment for murderers. While many victims' families understood the decision of the King County Prosecutor to provide Ridgway a life in prison in exchange for the locations of more bodies, others did not agree. Again, the argument was presented that Ridgway was spared the death penalty because of the nature of the backgrounds of his victims. Less than five years before Ridgway's first murders, his victims' families saw Ted Bundy sentenced to death. Many then posed the question: If Gary Ridgway, like Ted Bundy, had murdered college women rather than prostitutes, would the outcome have been different? The incongruence bothered many.

In 2003, the Washington State Supreme Court was forced to review their decision in the Ridgway case. Another man was found guilty of murdering his wife and two daughters and faced the possibility of a death sentence. His lawyers presented the argument that if the state's most prolific killer could avoid the death penalty, the state could not justify sentencing anyone else to death. Essentially, the court was faced with deciding whether the death penalty should be eliminated from Washington State law. In a five to four ruling, the court defended the state's right to preserve the death penalty, citing the specifics of Ridgway's plea bargain as a just reason to have spared him death. However, the question does reflect the controversy that arose from the legal decisions that were made in Gary Ridgway's case.

Conclusion

In this author's opinion, Gary Ridgway is a unique example of a psychopathic serial killer. Nothing in his behavior or personality profile indicated that he suffered from any type of insanity. His murders did not appear to be motivated by psychotic states or any type of mental disease that could have altered his ability to reason. He understood what he did and could offer no real reason other than the pleasure he received in satisfying his own compulsion to kill. Videos of interviews with him attest to his utter lack of emotion and remorse for the crimes he committed. He impressively passed polygraph tests and lied without fear or hesitation when confronted by police. By all accounts, Ridgway easily fits all descriptors of a psychopath. His ability to evade arrest for two decades speaks both to the value of forensic technology and also to the slippery nature of the psychopath. Multiple times police discounted Ridgway as a suspect because he appeared to be a regular mild-mannered person, both physically and intellectually incapable of committing heinous murders. The psychopath's ability to blend into the crowd and wear their mask of sanity is precisely what allows them to commit their crimes undetected.

Notes about sources

Most of the factual content about Ridgway's life and the specifics of his crimes were provided by Ann Rule's *Green River, Running Red* and the summary of evidence written by Norm Maleng, the King County prosecutor who oversaw the case. The references to the behavior and personality of the psychopath were based on Hare's book *Without Conscience*. Finally, the information I gathered about the legal debate regarding the death penalty in Washington State came from various Seattle newspapers including *The Seattle Post-Intelligencer* and *The Seattle Times*.

Martha Stewart
Corporate executive and white-collar criminal

Abstract

Martha Stewart, a well-known television and magazine personality, became famous for marketing hobbies in cooking, gardening, etiquette, and arts and crafts. As a successful American businesswoman, she became an international icon for homemakers by the 1990s. In 2002, Stewart became involved in a scandal involving the sales of her shares in a biotechnology pharmaceutical company, ImClone, just before an application for a new drug was denied. She and her stockbroker, Peter Bacanovic, were indicted for conspiracy, perjury, securities fraud, and obstruction of investigation. In 2004, she was sentenced to prison. She was released on March 4, 2005. She returned to promoting her career and hosted her own show modeled on The Apprentice. Various sources have made public claims and allegations that Stewart could exhibit some psychopathic predispositions similar to many corporate or white-collar psychopaths. In fact, she has been labeled a sociopath.

Background

Martha Stewart was born Martha Helen Kostyra on August 3, 1941 in Jersey City, New Jersey. She grew up with four siblings as the oldest daughter in a large middle class Polish-American family in Nutley, New Jersey. Her parents, Eddie and Martha Kostyra, raised Martha with a strong work ethic and taught her to master the arts of homemaking as a child, which eventually led her into defining a successful career. Her father, Eddie, was particularly stern and rather demanding in his efforts to instill an attitude of achieving excellence and perfection in all his children, particularly young Martha.

As a young girl, Stewart perfected household skills such as gardening, cooking, baking, and sewing. She was a very ambitious and determined student and excelled in her schoolwork and extracurricular activities. She began a modeling career, appearing in television commercials and magazines and was determined to expose herself as much as possible to the city in neighboring New York, which she found exciting compared to her New Jersey suburb. Stewart was not a particularly popular figure in high school and students recall her as an ambitious girl whose lofty aspirations were matched by her outward confidence. As a straight-A student in high school, she enrolled in New York City's Barnard College on a partial scholarship. Shortly, after the start of her sophomore year, she married a law student named Andrew Stewart. She graduated with a degree in history of art and architecture and pursued modeling while her husband received a law degree at Yale Law School. In 1965, her daughter Alexis Stewart was born and Stewart quit modeling to raise her daughter.

In 1967, Stewart became a stockbroker, which was her father-in-law's profession. Her successful career as a stockbroker ended when she decided to leave the brokerage due to the recession that affected Wall Street in 1973. She and her husband moved to Westport, Connecticut to restore a nineteenth century farmhouse where they raised Alexis and later filmed her television show.

In 1976, Stewart started her first business, a catering enterprise, in the basement of her Connecticut home with a college friend and fellow model, Norma Collier. After ten years, the business was valued at one million dollars and Stewart opened a retail store in the neighborhood to sell home entertainment kits to the local community. Stewart became well known in the area, providing cooking classes and homemaking tips to the local women. She also wrote articles for *The New York Times* and was an editor and columnist for the magazine *House Beautiful*. In 1982, Andy used his networking connections with Crown Publishing Company and Martha convinced their executives to publish a book about home catering and entertainment. Her biggest break into the public eye occurred when *Entertaining*, co-written with Elizabeth Hawes, was published and immediately hit the bestseller list. Despite a divorce with her husband in 1988, Stewart continued to reap the success of her first published project by producing popular videotapes, CDs, books, and television specials on home entertainment planning and house restoration and decoration.

Scandal and the media

Following the success from *Entertaining*, Martha Stewart quickly rose to fame as a popular icon for giving tips on event planning and home development. She was featured on The Oprah Winfrey Show and became a spokesperson for K-Mart, which featured her own line of home products. After working as a contributing editor for *Family Circle*, she founded her own magazine named *Martha Stewart Living*, which was also the title of her own television program that started in 1991. Martha Stewart Living became a popular television show featuring guests and tips on cooking, gardening, flower arrangement, interior design, and homemade decorations. By 1997, her project developed into a company named Martha Stewart Living Omnimedia, with Stewart as the primary shareholder.

Martha Stewart continued her success by publishing popular books, making public appearances, continuing her television show, and expanding her home products line at K-Mart. However, in 2002, Stewart was investigated for selling 3,928 shares ImClone Systems, a biotechnology company co-founded by her friend and Alexis's ex-boyfriend, Samuel Waksal, on December 27, 2001. Prior to this date, ImClone submitted a Biologics Licensing Application for a colon cancer drug, Erbitux. An application is necessary for drug approval by the Food and Drug Administration, which has sixty days to evaluate the application. On December 28, only one day after Stewart's sales, the Food and Drug Administration announced that it would not review ImClone's application for Erbitux. Within the following month, ImClone's stock plummeted by approximately seventy percent.

As a result of the ImClone stock scandal, Stewart was charged with conspiracy, obstruction, lying to investigators, and securities fraud. Stewart's stockbroker, Peter Bacanovic, was also charged with conspiracy, obstruction, and lying to investigators as well as allegations of fabricating documents and perjury. Although Stewart profited fifty-one thousand dollars by selling her shares in advance, she was never charged with insider trading. Waksal was, however.

Prior to the incident, Waksal had already pled guilty to six accounts of insider trading scandals. Less than a year later, Stewart resigned from the board of directors of the New York Stock Exchange and avoided any attention drawn to the ImClone scandal. In June 2003, a federal grand jury in Manhattan indicted Stewart and Bacanovic on nine criminal charges from the U.S. Securities and Exchange Commission. Stewart pled not guilty to the charges and insisted that there was an understanding with Bacanovic to sell her shares if ImClone stock fell to less than sixty dollars. On the same day of her indictment, Stewart resigned as chief executive officer of her company, but remained on the board. A day after, she published a letter in *USA Today* and online assuring her supporters and the rest of the public community that she was innocent of the charges and intended to defend herself until all she was acquitted. Throughout this time, Stewart continued to make public appearances, but avoided interviews as they questioned her involvement with ImClone. The Securities and Exchange Commission soon filed a civil suit against Stewart for insider trading and set a trial for January 2004. The trial was presided by U.S. District Judge Miriam Goldman Cederbaum and during the trial, Stewart continued to insist that she was not guilty. One month later, Judge Cederbaum dismissed the charge of securities fraud. However, in March 2004, a jury found Stewart guilty on all four of the remaining accounts: conspiracy, obstruction of justice, and two counts of false statements.

Prosecutors claimed that Stewart and Bacanovic conspired together to disguise evidence regarding the affair and that Stewart deliberately lied to the public about her involvement in the scandal for the sake of protecting the stock price of her own company, Martha Stewart Omnimedia. Many federal prosecutors argued that Martha Stewart was a liar who intentionally defrauded shareholders in her company

A few days later, her show Martha Stewart Living was taken off the air and Stewart resigned from the board position of her company. K-Mart sued Martha Stewart Living Omnimedia with allegations of double-counting royalty payments and advertising spending. In July 2004, Stewart was sentenced to five months in prison, five months of home confinement, two years probation, and a thirty-thousand dollar fine. She served prison time at the Alderson Federal Prison Camp in West Virginia starting on October 8, 2004 and ending on March 4, 2005.

Sociopath?

On the May 1995 cover of *New York* magazine, Martha Stewart was named as the definitive woman of the modern era although later public labels shifted. Only a couple of years later, allegations of Stewart's possible propensity to display a personality disorder became public. Following her ImClone scandal and prison release, those public allegations did not decrease. Later feuds with Donald Trump stemmed from the competition over their respective Apprentice reality television series. According to Trump, Stewart blamed poor viewer turnout and low ratings of her Apprentice series on the existence of Trump's version, which was more popular and widely viewed. Trump called her a liar, indirectly highlighting her behavior during the insider trading scandal, and insulted her intellect in reaction to her allegations.

During the time Martha Stewart started her career as a model and developed into a successful businesswoman, she appealed to her supporters and audience as an intelligent, independent, and charming woman. She served as a distinguished role model for modern women by demonstrating how to balance a successful occupation and the role of a homemaker. As a host of her own daytime show and a primetime reality show, she portrayed eloquence and poise in her mannerisms and speech. Audience members and fans often commented on her graceful and charismatic air when walking into a room. Yet, there were allegations of another side to her. Some critics suggested that Stewart's publicly charming persona was not an accurate reflection of her everyday self. Colleagues, ex-coworkers, and family members accused her of being as domineering and controlling as her father. Some said her friendships tended to be short-lived perhaps due to her propensity to form relationships based on personal advantage. Her marriage with her first husband eventually failed as she began to achieve major success, while her relationship with her daughter, Alexis, also began to suffer. It was also rumored that she had an affair with Alexis's ex-boyfriend, Waksal.

The 1988 *Stewart v. Stewart* case file traced the allegations and claims that the Stewarts made against each other throughout the process of their divorce. The case file stated that Stewart, as the plaintiff, threatened to break her husband's eleventh floor office window multiple times, physically and verbally assaulted him in public regularly, sent letters to his personal colleagues filled with derogatory remarks, and interrupted his business affairs by coming into his office and insulting him publicly with emotional outbursts. Stewart's counterclaim read that her husband committed adultery, also physically assaulted her, and neglected and deserted her. Martha and her husband both ceased to treat each other respectfully as their marriage continued, Martha's behavior was often inappropriate and violent.

One close source, Norma Collier, Stewart's former colleague and catering business partner, accused her of being a sociopath and difficult to trust and cooperate with. She claimed that during their business venture, Stewart constantly lied and used Collier for personal gain and abandoned their friendship once Stewart achieved the success she wanted. Collier commented that Stewart was overbearing and domineering during the business endeavor. When Collier discovered that Stewart was booking jobs alone and banking all the profits while insisting that she was splitting the profits fifty-fifty, Collier immediately quit the business. Collier recalled Stewart harshly criticizing and insulting her in public, both in front of and away from Collier. Although Collier's specific accusation of Stewart's sociopathy might not have been made with educated speculation and were not directly supported by details, it was one of the first publicly made allegations that suggested Martha Stewart's potential psychopathic behavior. Many members of the public often used the terms sociopathic and psychopathic interchangeably, which was something Collier may have done. According to Collier's descriptions, Stewart exhibited many of psychopathic traits including pathological lying, lack of empathy, and parasitic and manipulative behavior.

In 1997, the *National Enquirer* tabloid ran an article with a title that called Stewart mentally ill. Stewart filed a ten million dollar lawsuit against the *National Enquirer* and claimed that the story falsely portrayed her as mentally unbalanced. At around the same time, Jerry Oppenheimer wrote *Martha Stewart: Just Desserts*. Oppenheimer recounted stories of her apparent abusive treatment of coworkers and friends, her terrible temper, episodes of severe depression and suicidal threats, her frequent use of foul language, and her mistreatment of past reporters and interviewers she had worked with. In the same year, the Associated Press published an article that reported an incident where Stewart injured her neighbor's landscaper by backing her car into him, which she claimed was an accident. Suddenly, Stewart's reputation began to plummet as interviewers, such as Larry King, inquired about the truth behind these allegations. She often immediately changed the subject to a topic related to her career, which made the public more suspicious.

Christopher Byron's *Martha, Inc.* reported incidents of marriage difficulty between Martha and her husband. He is portrayed as docile and agreeable whereas she appears to be a carbon copy of her father, domineering and manipulative. Byron traced occasions where Martha was cursing and yelling at her husband during public events. He suggested that she began to isolate herself from her husband, daughter, business partners and colleagues as she achieved social reputation. Kathy Tatlock, a long friend of Martha Stewart who often worked and traveled with her, commented that Stewart's relationship with her husband and daughter were distant and emotionally vapid. *Martha, Inc.* highlighted an incident in which Stewart told the public that the reason she and her ex-husband Andy only had one daughter was due to her husband's impotence resulting from cancer. At the time Steward made this claim, though, his current wife was five months pregnant with his twins. Stewart had actually undergone a hysterectomy during their marriage to prevent pregnancy again after the birth of her daughter. In *Martha Stewart: Just Desserts* sources claimed that Stewart's intent for the fabrication was to mortify her ex-husband publicly and attack his masculinity.

Analysis

Martha Stewart's father, Eddie Kostyra, was reportedly domineering and authoritarian. He had high ambitions for his family and was very strict in raising his children, particularly with young Martha who learned to adopt his mannerisms. Sources portrayed him as an alcoholic who managed his relationships impersonally and often engaged in violent verbal outbursts over minimal matters. Stewart's older brother commented that Martha shared many similar qualities as their father. Although Stewart's father might not have been psychopathic, Stewart might have inherited certain traits of psychopathy such as authoritarianism, controlling behavior, and a determination to succeed at any cost.

As the oldest daughter from a family of five children, her parents had demanding expectations for her and she was determined to follow them. As a child, Stewart may have felt a pressure to succeed and excel. With her father's expectations, young Stewart could have easily learned to do anything to reach success regardless of its morality. Her determination to become successful carried all the way throughout her adulthood.

According to the *Diagnostic and Statistical Manual* criteria, antisocial personality disorder includes many of the same characteristics as psychopathy. Both disorders feature deceitfulness and manipulation, lying, irritability and aggressiveness, and lack of remorse or empathy. However, the *Diagnostic and Statistical Manual* states that there must be indication of conduct disorder, which is socially delinquent behavior as a youth, before the age of fifteen years to be diagnosed with antisocial personality disorder. Although Stewart exhibited many characteristics similar to antisocial personality disorder, her past did not give signs of having conduct disorder as a young girl. This requirement was listed as one of several shortcomings with the application of antisocial personality disorder criteria to her.

Also, in understanding Martha Stewart, it is important to distinguish manic episodes from antisocial personality disorder. Stewart appeared to exhibit many features of manic episodes, including grandiosity and inflated self-esteem, decreased need for sleep, foolish business endeavors, and flight of ideas. She often claimed that she had little sleep every night and functioned every day on a few hours of rest. She wrote in her high school yearbook that she could succeed with ease in anything she desired to. Her attitude never changed and as she grew older and into a successful businesswoman, she continued to believe and to insist that she was capable of anything she wanted to achieve. Yet, her stock scandal with ImClone was a clear example of a foolish business endeavor. Stewart's coworkers for her television program commented that she would often make hasty changes to the script, which were indicative of her having flight of ideas and of impulsive decision-making.

Stewart was rumored to suffer from severe depressive episodes, often making suicidal threats and attempts. Her depression seemed to grow worse in times when her husband and daughter seemed distant from her and would avoid her during the holidays. In addition, her coworkers commented that Stewart arrived on set of her television show in either a great mood or a highly irritable one. Such drastic changes appeared to suggest that she was exhibiting bipolar disorder, a cycle of manic and depressive episodes.

On the other hand, while a key component of psychopathy is glibness, which Stewart conveyed well to the public, she perhaps used her charm for personal advantage to form relationships with socially distinguished people and to use close friends for selfish ambitions. She was accused of lying, particularly regarding the ImClone scandal. In addition to abusing her relationships and lying to the public, sources accused Stewart of being unremorseful. In *Without Conscience*, Hare suggested that white-collar psychopaths typically painted others as culprits and portrayed themselves as victims in any failed endeavors, which Stewart often did with her ex-husband in the context of their failed marriage.

Several publications profiled Martha Stewart, describing her either as a successful figure who fell under a negative public light due to a mistake or as a manipulative woman who used her networking connections and charisma to achieve personal success at the expense of others. The latter concluded she was psychopathic. Others concluded from her history of depression and of manic episodes that she exhibited symptoms of bipolar disorder. Still others suggested that she had both conditions. But it was difficult to assess the validity of such diagnoses without a professional evaluation. Most likely, the many stories of Stewart's behavior as evidenced by close encounters of hers suggest that she had an abnormality in personality closely mirroring descriptors of psychopathy. Although not likely to be diagnosed as a full psychopath because of a lack of severe antisocial actions, Stewart appeared to be someone who would register relatively high on the psychopathy checklist due to her interpersonal abuse and self-centered nature. Those who termed her a sociopath evidently wanted to label her personality and behaviors as highly psychopathic without giving to her that more negative-sounding diagnosis.

Notes about sources

Sources include biographies written by Christopher Byron, author of *Martha, Inc.* and Lloyd Allen, a friend of Stewart's and author of *Being Martha: The Inside Story of Martha Stewart and Her Amazing Life*. Articles from online sources, such as *Forbes*, CNN, and Court TV, were also used to research facts and timeline of the ImClone case.

Bibliography

Abagnale, F. (1980). *Catch me if you can*. New York: Grosset and Dunlap.

Ablow, K. (2005). *Inside the mind of Scott Peterson*. New York: St Martin's.

Ackerman, D. (2002), October 3. Andrew Fastow, fall guy. *Forbes*. Retrieved August 30, 2006. <http://www.forbes.com/2002/10/03/1003topnews.html>

Ackman, D. (2004, March 5). Martha Stewart found guilty. *Forbes.com*. Retrieved August 21, 2006. <http://www.forbes.com/business/2004/03/05/cx_da_0305marthafinal.html>

Acton, G. (1998). Sensitive responding. *Great ideas in personality*. Retrieved August 21, 2006. <http://www.personalityresearch.org/attachment/sensitive.html>

Acton, G. (2002). Attachment theory. *Great ideas in personality*. Retrieved August 21, 2006. <http://www.personalityresearch.org/attachment.html>

Adam, S. (2005, April 4). Left behind: Man lives painful life in shadow of brother's crime. *Lawrence Journal-World*. Retrieved August 27, 2006. <http://www2.ljworld.com/news/2005/apr/04/left_behind_man/>

Aigner, T. and Balster, R. (1978). Choice behavior in rhesus monkeys: Cocaine versus food. *Science, 201,* 534-535.

Allen, L. (2006). *Being Martha: The inside story of Martha Stewart and her amazing life*. New York: Wiley.

Allen, W. (1984). *The Nazi seizure of power*. Danbury, CT: Franklin Watts.

American Psychiatric Association (1985). *Statement on the insanity defense*. Washington, D.C.: American Psychiatric Association.

American Psychiatric Association (2000). *Diagnostic and statistical manual of mental disorders* (4th Ed., text revision). DSM-IV-TR. Washington, D.C.: American Psychiatric Association.

Amerika, M. and Laurence, A. (1994). Interview with Bret Easton Ellis. *The Write Stuff.* Retrieved August 20, 2006.
<http://www.altx.com/interviews/bret.easton.ellis.html>

Anderson, S., Bechara, A., Damasio, H., Tranel, D., and Damasio, A. (1999). Impairment of social and moral behavior related to early damage in human prefrontal cortex. *Nature Neuroscience, 2,* 1032-1037.

Associated Press (2005), February 16. Lawsuit: Grand Theft Auto led teen to kill. *FOXNews.com.* Retrieved August 21, 2006.
<http://www.foxnews.com/story/0,2933,147722,00.html>

Associated Press (2005), June 14. Clinton seeks 'Grand Theft Auto' probe. *USA Today.* Retrieved August 21, 2006.
<http://www.usatoday.com/news/washington/2005-07-14-clinton-game_x.htm>

Bakan, J. (2004). *The corporation: The pathological pursuit of profit and power.* New York: Free Press.

Balaghi, S. (2006). *Saddam Hussein: A biography.* Wesport, CT: Greenwood.

Barfield, V. (1985). *Woman on death row.* Nashville: Oliver-Nelson.

Baron, C. (Producer) and Miller, B. (Director). (2005). *Capote* [Motion picture]. United States: United Artists.

Barrionuevo, A. (2006), March 29. Enron prosecutors drop some charges and rest case. *The New York Times,* C4.

Beard, A. (1996). Boyhood gender non-conformity and narcissism in gay and bisexual men: The influence of parental behavior on the development of narcissistic issues. Doctoral dissertation. Georgia State University.

Bell, R. (2005). Frank Abagnale, the great con artist and imposter. *Crime Library.* Court TV. Retrieved August 20, 2006.

<http://www.crimelibrary.com/criminal_mind/scams/frank_abagnale/index.html>

Bell, R. (2005). Ted Bundy, notorious serial killer. *Crime Library*. Court TV. Retrieved August 20, 2006. <http://www.crimelibrary.com/serial_killers/notorious/bundy/2.html>

Ben-Porath, D. and Taylor, S. (2002). The effects of diazepam (Valium) and aggressive disposition on human aggression: An experimental investigation. *Addictive Behaviors, 27,* 167-177.

Berry, J. (1991). *American psycho* is not the problem. *Library Journal, 116,* 6.

Bird, A. (2005). *Blood brother: 33 reasons my brother Scott Peterson is guilty.* New York: HarperCollins.

Bird, H. (2001). Psychoanalytic perspectives on theories regarding the development of antisocial behavior. *Journal of the American Academy of Psychoanalysis and Dynamic Psychology, 29*(1), 55-71.

Blackburn, R., Logan, C., and Donnelly, J. (2003). Personality disorders, psychopathy and other mental disorders: Co-morbidity among patients at English and Scottish high-security hospitals. *Journal of Forensic Psychiatry and Psychology, 14,* 111-137

Blair, R. (1995). A cognitive developmental approach to morality: investigating the psychopath. *Cognition, 57,* 1-29.

Bledsoe, J. (1998). *Death sentence.* New York: Penguin Putnam.

Block, L. (2004). *Gangsters, swindlers, killers, and thieves: the lives and crimes of fifty American villains.* New York: Oxford University Press.

Briggs, W. and Verma, A. (2006). Sharing the wealth. *Communication World, 23*(1), 25-28.

Brooks, R., dir. (1967). *In cold blood.* [Motion picture]. United States: Columbia Pictures.

Brottman, M. (2005), September 16. Nutty professors. *Chronicle of Higher Education*. Retrieved August 21, 2006.
<http://chronicle.com/free/v52/i04/04b00701.htm>

Brown, P. (2005). The real serial killer. *Crime Library*. Court TV. Retrieved August 22, 2006.
<http://www.crimelibrary.com/criminal_mind/profiling/s_k_myths/index.html>

Bruno, A. (2005). Hannibal Lecter: Fact and fiction. *Crime Library*. Court TV. Retrieved August 22, 2006.
<http://www.crimelibrary.com/serial_killers/weird/lecter/1.html>

Bruntz, M. (2005), April 5. Witness to execution: Prison director Charles McAtee recalls killers. *Lawrence Journal-World*. Retrieved August 27, 2006.
<http://www2.ljworld.com/news/2005/apr/05/witness_to_execution/>

Butterfield, F. (2002, August 21). Father steals best: Crime in an American family. *The New York Times*, A1.

Byrnes, N. (2005), November 28. Smarter corporate giving. *Business Week*. Retrieved August 20, 2006.
<http://www.businessweek.com/print/magazine/content/05_48/b3961607.htm?%20chan=gl>

Byron, C. (2002). *Martha, inc.* New York: Wiley.

Can a video game lead to murder? (2005), June 19. CBS. Retrieved August 21, 2006.
<http://wwjtv.com/rooney/sixtyminutes_story_170194936.html>

Capote, T. (1966). *In cold blood*. New York: Random House.

Caputi, J. (1993). American psychos: The serial killer in contemporary fiction. *Journal of American Culture, 16,* 101-12.

Carey, B. (2005, February 8). For the worst of us, the diagnosis may be evil. *The New York Times*, D1.

Carr, H. (2006). *The brothers Bulger: How they terrorized and corrupted Boston for a quarter century*. New York: Warner.

Chae, J., Piedmont, R., Estadt, B., and Wicks, R. (1995). Personological evaluation of Clance's impostor phenomenon scale in a Korean sample. *Journal of Personality Assessment, 65,* 468-485.

Chase, A. (2000, June). Harvard and the making of the Unabomber. *The Atlantic.*

Chase, A. (2003). *Harvard and the Unabomber.* New York: W.W. Norton.

Christianson, S. (2003, February 8). Bad seed or bad science: On reflection, a family long seen as congenital misfits were victims of skewed data. *The New York Times,* Arts section, 1.

Christianson, S., Forth, A., Hare, R., Strachan, C., Lidberg, L., and Thorell, L. (1996). Remembering details of emotional events: a comparison between psychopathic and nonpsychopathic offenders. *Personality and Individual Differences, 20,* 437-443.

Clance, P. and Imes, S. (1978). The impostor phenomenon in high-achieving women: Dynamics and therapeutic intervention. *Psychotherapy: Theory, Research & Practice, 15,* 241–247.

Clarke, G. (1988). *Capote: A biography.* New York: Linden.

Cleckley, H. (1988). *The mask of sanity.* Augusta, GA: E.S. Cleckley.

Cloninger, C., ed. (1999). *Personality and psychopathology.* Washington, D.C.: American Psychiatric Publishing.

Connelly, C. and Williams, S. (2000). A review of the research literature on serious violent and sexual offenders. Scottish Executive Central Research Unit. Retrieved August 21, 2006.
<http://www.scotland.gov.uk/cru/kd01/green/s-off-01.htm>

Correctional Services of Canada (2006). Can criminal psychopaths be identified? Retrieved August 21, 2006.
<http://www.csc-scc.gc.ca/text/pblct/forum/e012/e012l_e.shtml>

Coughlin, C. (2002). *Saddam: The secret life.* London: Macmillan.

Crier, C. (2005) *Deadly game: The untold story of the Scott Peterson investigation.* New York: HarperCollins.

Cults (1996). *Twentieth Century with Mike Wallace.* History Channel.

Davis, I. (2005), May 28. The biggest contract. *Economist,* 69-71.

Dillon, L. (2005). *Stone cold guilty: The people v. Scott Lee Peterson.* Napa, CA: LuLu.

Dodge v. Ford Motor Company (1919). 204 Mich. 459.

Dolan, M. and Anderson, I. (2003). The relationship between serotonergic function and the Psychopathy Checklist: Screening Version. *Journal of Psychopharmacology, 17,* 216-222.

D'Silva, K., Duggan, C., and McCarthy, L. (2004). Does treatment really make psychopaths worse? A review of the evidence. *Journal of Personality Disorders, 18,* 163-177.

Edens, J., Desforges, D., Fernandez, K., and Palac, C. (2004). Effects of psychopathy and violence risk testimony on mock juror perceptions of dangerousness in a capital murder trial. *Psychology, Crime and Law, 10*(4), 393-412.

Eichenwald, K. (2005). *Conspiracy of fools.* New York: Broadway.

Eichenwald, K. and Henriques, D. (2002, February 10). Enron's many strands: The company unravels; Enron buffed image to a shine even as it rotted from within. *The New York Times,* 1.

Elavil (2003). Drugs.com. Retrieved August 20, 2006. <http://www.drugs.com/elavil.html>

Elavil (2006). *Health Square.* Retrieved August 20, 2006. <http://www.healthsquare.com/newrx/ela1155.htm>

Ellis, B. (1991). *American psycho.* New York: Vintage.

Ellul, J. (1964). *The technological society.* New York: Vintage.

Enron employees ride stock to bottom (2002), January 14. *CNN.com*. Retrieved August 26, 2006.
<http://archives.cnn.com/2002/LAW/01/14/enron.employees/>

Enron's J Clifford Baxter: A profile (2002), January 27. *BBC News*. Retrieved August 24, 2006.
<http://news.bbc.co.uk/1/hi/business/1784945.stm>

Enron traders caught on tape (2004), June 1. *CBS News*. Retrieved 26 April, 2006 from
<http://www.cbsnews.com/stories/2004/06/01/eveningnews/main620626.shtml>.

Explaining the Enron bankruptcy (2002), January 13, 2002. *CNN.com*. Retrieved August 26, 2006.
<http://archives.cnn.com/2002/US/01/12/enron.qanda.focus/>.

Eysenck, H. (1993). Creativity and personality: Suggestions for a theory. *Psychological Inquiry, 4,* 147-178.

Farrell, K. (2000). The berserk style in American culture. *Cultural Critique, 46,* 179-209.

FDCH e-Media (2004), July 1. Transcript: Saddam Hussein court hearing. *Washington Post*. Retrieved August 21, 2006.
<http://www.washingtonpost.com/wp-dyn/articles/A20462-2004Jul1.html>

Fersch, E. (1970). The relation between students' experience with restricted-access erotic materials and their behaviors and attitudes. In *Report of the President's Commission on Obscenity and Pornography*, 153-156, 167. Washington, D.C.: U.S. Government Printing Office.

Fersch, E. (1971). Don't ask. *Yale Alumni Magazine, 34,* 28-29.

Fersch, E. (1974). Court clinic treatment in Massachusetts: Mental health care v. civil rights. *International Journal of Offender Therapy and Comparative Criminology, 18,* 275-282.

Fersch, E. (1975). When to punish, when to rehabilitate. *American Bar Association Journal, 61,* 1235-1237.

Fersch, E. (1979). *Law, psychology, and the courts.* Springfield, IL: Charles C Thomas.

Fersch, E. (1980). *Ethical issues for psychologists in court settings.* In Monahan, J. (Ed.) *Who is the client?*, 43-62. Washington, D.C.: American Psychological Association.

Fersch, E. (1982, September 26). The insanity plea on trial. *The New York Times Magazine.*

Fersch, E. (1982, November 22). Guilty but mentally ill. *The Harvard Crimson.*

Fersch, E. (1982). Law and psychiatry. *International Journal of Offender Therapy and Comparative Criminology, 26,* 157-175.

Fersch, E. (Ed.) (2005). *Thinking about the insanity defense: Answers to frequently asked questions with case examples.* New York: iUniverse.

Fersch, E. (Ed.) (2006). *Thinking about the sexually dangerous: Answers to frequently asked questions with case examples.* New York: iUniverse.

Fersch, E. (2006, August 3). Yates beats justice. *Boston Herald,* 28.

Fine, C. and Kennett, J. (2004). Mental impairment, moral understanding and criminal responsibility: psychopathy and the purposes of punishment. *International Journal of Law and Psychiatry, 25,* 425-443.

Former Enron exec dies in apparent suicide (2002), January 26. *CNN.com.* Retrieved August 24, 2006.
<http://archives.cnn.com/2002/US/01/25/enron.suicide/>

Forth, A., Brown, S., Hart, S., and Hare, R. (1996). The assessment of psychopathy in male and female noncriminals: reliability and validity. *Personality and Individual Differences, 20,* 531-543.

Fracher, J. (2004). Review: The clinical and forensic assessment of psychopathy: A practitioner's guide. *Journal of Psychiatry & Law, 32*(1), 97-99.

Freccero, C. (1997). Historical violence, censorship, and the serial killer: The case of 'American psycho.' *Diacritics, 27,* 44-58.

Frodi, A., Dernevik, M., Sepa, A., Philipson, J., and Bragesjo, M. (2001). Current attachment representations of incarcerated offenders varying in degree of psychopathy. *Attachment & Human Development, 3*, 269-283.

Fujii, D., Tokioka, A., and Lichton, A. (2005). Ethnic differences in prediction of violence risk with the HCR-20 among psychiatric inpatients. *Psychiatric Services, 56*, 711-716.

Fullam, R. and Dolan, M. (2006). Emotional information processing in violent patients with schizophrenia: Association with psychopathy and symptomatology. *Psychiatry Research, 141*, 29-37.

Funk, J. (2005). Children's exposure to violent video games and desensitization to violence. *Child and Adolescent Psychiatric Clinics of North America, 14*, 387-404.

Ghebrial, M. (2005). Hormone-behavior correlates among male and female psychopathic participants: Relationship to Gray's model of behavioral inhibition and activation systems. Doctoral dissertation. Pennsylvania State University. Retrieved August 22, 2006.
<http://etda.libraries.psu.edu/theses/approved/WorldWideFiles/ETD-1097/Grad_School.pdf>

Gibney, A., dir. (2005). *Enron: The smartest guys in the room.* [Motion Picture]. United States: Sony Pictures.

Gretton, H., Hare, R., and Catchpole, R. (2004). Psychopathy and offending from adolescence to adulthood: A 10-year follow-up. *Journal of Consulting and Clinical Psychology. 72*, 636-645.

Grixti, J. (1995). Consuming cannibals: Psychopathic killers as archetypes and cultural icons. *Journal of American Culture, 18*, 87-96.

Grossman, W. (2006), April 28. Shaking Ken Lay's cool. *Time.* Retrieved August 24, 2006.
<http://www.time.com/time/nation/article/0,8599,1188701,00.html>

Guttridge, L. (2004), October 14. Thompson's GTA hunt continues. (14 Oct., 2004). Ferrago Ltd. Retrieved August 21, 2006.
< http://www.ferrago.com/story/4589>

Hare, R. (1999). *Without conscience: The disturbing world of the psychopaths among us*. New York: Guilford.

Hare, R., Hart, S., and Harpur, T. (1991). Psychopathy and the DSM-IV criteria for antisocial personality disorder. *Journal of Abnormal Psychology, 100*, 391-398.

Harris, G., Rice, M., and Cormier, C. (1994). Psychopaths: is a therapeutic community therapeutic?. *Therapeutic Communities: International Journal for Therapeutic and Supportive Organizations, 15*, 283-299.

Harris, G., Rice, M., and Quinsey, V. (1994). Psychopathy as a taxon: Evidence that psychopaths are a discrete class. *Journal of Consulting and Clinical Psychology, 62*, 387-397.

Hatfield, L. (1998), November 8. Utopian nightmare. *San Francisco Examiner*. Retrieved August 20, 2006.
<http://www.sfgate.com/cgi-bin/article.cgi?file=/examiner/archive/1998/11/08/NEWS4041.dtl>

Haysom, N., Strous, M., and Vogelman, L. (1990). The mad Mrs. Rochester revisited: The involuntary confinement of the mentally ill in South Africa. *South African Journal on Human Rights, 6*(3), 341-362.

Heaven's Gate website. Retrieved August 20, 2006.
<http://www.heavensgate.com/>

Herpertz, S. and Sass, H. (2000). Emotional deficiency and psychopathy. *Behavioral Sciences and the Law, 18*, 567-580.

Herrling, P. (2006), March 30. Experiments in social responsibility. *Nature, 439* (7074), 267-268.

Hoffman, M. and Morse, S. (2006, July 30). The insanity defense goes back on trial. *The New York Times*, 13.

Hogue, I., Heineman Jr., B. and Smith Jr., F. (2006, January 9). Corporate social responsibility: good citizenship or investor rip-off? *Wall Street Journal*, R6.

Holden, C. (2005). Sex and suffering brain. *Science, 308*, 1574-1577.

Holtzman, M., Venuti, E., and Fonfeder, R. (2006). Enron and the raptors. *CPA Journal.* Retrieved August 24, 2006.
<http://www.nysscpa.org/cpajournal/2003/0403/features/f042403.htm>

Horwitz, M. (1987). Santa Clara revisted. In Samuels, W. and Miller, A. *Corporations and society: Power and responsibility.* New York: Greenwood.

Hyman, S. and Nestler, E. (1996). Initiation and adaptation : A paradigm for understanding psychotropic drug action. *American Journal of Psychiatry, 152,* 65-75.

Iraq Ministry of Justice (1980). The penal-code with amendments. *Court TV.* Retrieved March 15, 2006.
<http://www.courttv.com/trials/saddam/docs/iraqpenalcode.pdf>

Iraqi Special Tribunal (2006). Revised version of the Iraqi special tribunal rules of procedure and evidence. *Court TV.* Retrieved March 15, 2006.
<http://www.courttv.com/trials/saddam/docs/tribunalrules.pdf>

Johnson, A. (1949). Sanctions for superego lacunae of adolescents. In Esman, A. (1975). *The psychology of adolescence.* New York: International Universities Press.

Jackson, B. (1991, April 9). *American psycho*: more than it seems. *The Tech.* Retrieved August 20, 2006.
<http://www-tech.mit.edu/V111/N18/jackso.18o.html>

Johnson, T. (2006, March 31). Death sentence affirmed: Court rules inmate can be executed despite life for Ridgway. *Seattle Post-Intelligencer,* A1.

Jones, A. (1996). *Women who kill.* Boston: Beacon.

Kaczynski, T. (1995). *Industrial society and its future.* Retrieved August 21, 2006.
<http://www.unabombertrial.com/manifesto/index.html>

Kelleher, M. and Kelleher, C. (1998). *Murder most rare: The female serial killer.* Westport: Praeger.

Keppel, R. (1995). *The riverman.* London: Constable.

Kimura, D. (2002), May 13. Sex differences in the brain. *Scientific American.* Retrieved August 22, 2006.

<http://www.sciam.com/article.cfm?articleID=00018E9D-879D-1D06-8E49809EC588EEDF>

Koski, C. (1999). The non-fiction novel as psychiatric casebook: Truman Capote's *In Cold Blood*. *Journal of Technical Writing and Communication, 29,* 289-303.

Kramer, P. (1993). *Listening to prozac.* New York: Penguin.

Krueger, A, and Gembrowski, S. (1997), April 13. Strange odyssey of Heaven's Gate. *San Diego Union-Tribune*, A1.

The Laci Peterson case. *Court TV.* Retrieved August 21, 2006.
<http://www.courttv.com/trials/peterson/>

Laci Peterson case information (2006), January 5. Lifeboat Party. Retrieved August 21, 2006.
<http://www.crimenews2000.com/lacipeterson/index.htm>

Lalich, J. (2004). Bounded choice: True believers and charismatic cults. Berkeley, CA: University of California Press.

Lamotte, G. (1997), April 18. Heaven's Gate 911 call eerily calm. *CNN.com.* Retrieved August 20, 2006.
<http://www.cnn.com/US/9704/18/cult.911>

The lunatic you work for (2004, May 6). *Economist.*

Lykken, D. (1995). *The antisocial personalities.* Hillsdale: Erlbaum.

Mackenzie, E. (2003). *Street soldier: My life as an enforcer for Whitey Bulger and the Boston Irish mob.* South Royalton, VT: Steerforth.

Maleng, N. (2001). Prosecutor's summary of evidence. *State of Washington v. Gary Leon Ridgway.* Superior Court of Washington for King County.

Maloney, J. (2006). In cold blood: A dishonest book. *Crime Magazine.* Retrieved August 27, 2006.
<http://crimemagazine.com/CrimeBooks/incold.htm>

Marin, R. (2000), April 9. *American psycho*: sliced. diced. back. *The New York Times*, ST1.

Martens, W. (1997). Psychopathy and maturation. Doctoral dissertation. Tilburg University, the Netherlands.

Martens, W. (1999). Marcel—A case report of a violent sexual psychopath in remission. *International Journal of Offender Therapy and Comparative Criminology, 43*, 391-399.

Martens, W. (2000). Antisocial and psychopathic personality disorders: causes, course and remission: A review article. *International Journal of Offender Therapy and Comparative Criminology, 44*, 406-430.

Martens, W. (2001). Effects of antisocial or social attitudes on neurobiological functions. *Medical Hypotheses, 56*(6), 664-671.

Martens, W. (2002, January). The hidden suffering of the psychopath. *Psychiatric Times*. Retrieved August 21, 2006.
<http://psychiatrictimes.com/p020128.html>

Martha indicted. (2003, June 5). *CNN Money*. Retrieved August 21, 2006.
<http://money.cnn.com/2003/06/04/news/companies/martha>

Martha Stewart living (2006). Retrieved August 21, 2006.
<www.marthastewart.com>

Martha Stewart stock scandal (2006). *Court TV*. Retrieved August 21, 2006.
<http://www.courttv.com/trials/stewart/index.html>

McGrath, D. (2006), dir. *Infamous*. [Motion Picture]. United States: Warner Independent Pictures.

McLean, B. (2001), March 5. Is Enron overpriced?. *Fortune*. Retrieved August 25, 2006.
<http://money.cnn.com/2006/01/13/news/companies/enronoriginal_fortune/index.htm>

McLean, B. and Elkind, P. (2004). *The smartest guys in the room: The amazing rise and scandalous fall of Enron*. New York: Portfolio.

Michaud, S. (1983). *The only living witness.* New York: Linden.

Michaud, S. and Aynesworth, H. (2000). *Ted Bundy: Conversations with a killer.* New York: Authorlink.

Miller, B., dir. (2005). *Capote.* [Motion Picture]. United States: Sony Pictures.

Millon, T., Simonsen, E., Birket-Smith, M., and Davis, R. (1998). *Psychopathy: Antisocial, criminal, and violent behavior.* London: Guilford.

Mitchell, M. and Blair, J. (2000). State of the art: psychopathy. *The Psychologist, 13*, 356-360.

Moffitt, T. (2005). The new look of behavioral genetics in developmental psychopathology: Gene-environment interplay in antisocial behaviors. *Psychological Bulletin, 131*, 533-554.

Moffitt, T., Caspi, A., Rutter, M., and Silva, P. (2001). *Sex differences in antisocial behaviour: Conduct disorder, delinquency, and violence in the Dunedin longitudinal study.* New York: Cambridge University Press.

Moran, S. (1999). *The secret world of cults.* Surrey, England: CLB International.

Mulder, R. (1996). Antisocial personality disorder: Current drug treatment recommendations. *CNS Drugs, 5*, 257-263.

Murphy, B. (2002, October 3). A study in contrasts: Described as a charmer with a winning smile, Andrew Fastow's ferocious tirades to intimidate colleagues displayed his dark side. *Houston Chronicle*, 1.

Murphy, S. (1998, January 4). Whitey Bulger's life on the run: Fugitive's trail crisscrosses U.S. *Boston Globe*, A1.

Murphy, S. (2006, March 13). For weeks, life of crime is all over: Says book helps close the chapter on Bulger. *Boston Globe*, B1.

Murray, H. (1938). *Explorations in personality.* New York: Oxford University Press.

Murray, H. (1975). *Multiform assessments of personality development among gifted Harvard students.* Henry A. Murray Research Archive, Harvard University.

The mysterious death of an Enron exec (2002, April 10). *CBS News.* Retrieved August 24, 2006.
<http://www.cbsnews.com/stories/2002/04/10/eveningnews/main505845.shtml>

Nader, R. (2005, October 10). How to curb corporate power. *Nation.* Retrieved August 20, 2006.
<http://www.thenation.com/doc/20051010/nader>

New Yates verdict points to reform (2006, July 29). *Boston Herald*, 20.

Noe, D. (2005). Velma Barfield. *Crime Library.* Court TV. Retrieved August 20, 2006.
<http://www.crimelibrary.com/notorious_murders/women/velma_barfield/1.html>

Ogloff, J. and Wong, S. (1990). Treating criminal psychopaths in a therapeutic community program. *Behavioral Sciences and the Law, 8,* 181-190.

O'Neill, G.. (1988), September 18-21. The Bulger mystique: Parts 1-4. *Boston Globe.* Retrieved August 20, 2006.
<http://www.boston.com/news/packages/whitey/globe_stories/1988_the_bulger_mystique_part_1.htm >

O'Neill, G., Lehr, D., and Cullin, K. (1995), March 5. New team, tactics hastened Whitey Bulger's fall. *Boston Globe.* Retrieved August 20, 2006.
<http://www.boston.com/news/packages/whitey/globe_stories/1995/0305_new_team_tactics_hastened_whitey_bulger_s_fall.htm>

OxyContin (2005). Simmons Cooper. Retrieved August 20, 2006.
<http://www.simmonscooper.com/CM/FSDP/PracticeCenter/Personal-Injury/OxyContin.asp?focus=topic&id=3>

Paredes, J. and Purdum, E. (1990), April. "Bye-bye Ted…": Community response in Florida to the execution of Theodore Bundy." *Anthropology Today, 6,* 9-11.

Patrick, C., Hicks, B., Krueger, R., and Lang, A. (2005). Relations between psychopathy facets and externalizing in criminal offender sample. *Journal of Personality Disorders, 19,* 339-356.

Pitchford, I. (2001). The origins of violence: Is psychopathy an adaptation? *Human Nature Review, 1,* 28-36.

Pitofsky, R. (1999, June 25). The influence of violent entertainment material on kids: What is to be done?. Speech to the National Association of Attorneys General. Retrieved August 21, 2006.
<http://www.ftc.gov/speeches/pitofsky/naag99.htm>.

Plimpton, G. (1966, January 16). The story behind a nonfiction novel. *The New York Times.* Retrieved August 27, 2006.
<http://www.nytimes.com/books/97/12/28/home/capote-interview.html>

Plimpton, G. (1997). *Truman Capote: In which various friends, enemies, acquaintances, and detractors recall his turbulent career.* New York: Doubleday.

Post, J. (2003). *The psychological evaluation of political leaders.* New York: Cornell University Press.

Post, J. (2004). *Leaders and their followers in a dangerous world.* New York: Cornell University Press.

Profit and the public good (2005, January 22). *Economist,* 15-19.

The proper role of the state's death penalty (2006, April 3). *Seattle Times,* B4.

Raine, A. (1996, September 20). Autonomic nervous system factors underlying disinhibited, antisocial, and violent behavior. *Annals of the New York Academy of Science 794,* 46-59.

Raine, A., Lencz, T., Bihrle S., LaCasse, L., and Colletti, P. (2000, February). Reduced prefrontal gray matter volume and reduced autonomic activity in antisocial personality disorder. *Archives of General Psychiatry, 57,* 119-129.

Ramsland, K. (2005). The childhood psychopath: Bad seed or bad parents?. *Crime Library.* Court TV. Retrieved August 21, 2006.
<http://www.crimelibrary.com/criminal_mind/psychology/psychopath/1.html>

Ramsland, K. (2005). Heaven's Gate. *Crime Library.* Court TV. Retrieved August 20, 2006.
<http://www.crimelibrary.com/notorious_murders/mass/heavens_gate/1.html>

Rapoport, N. (2006, September 27). Don't outsource your conscience: Lessons in corporate truth. *Jurist*.

Reichert, D. (2004). *Chasing the devil: My twenty-year quest to capture the Green River killer*. New York: Little, Brown.

Rice, M., Harris, G., and Cormier, C. (1992). An evaluation of a maximum security therapeutic community for psychopaths and other mentally disordered offenders. *Law and Human Behavior, 16*, 399-412.

Richards, H., Casey, J., and Lucente, S. (2003). Psychopathy and treatment response in incarcerated female substance abusers. *Criminal Justice and Behavior, 30*, 251-236.

Robinson, B. (2006), May 7. Heaven's Gate: Christian/UFO believers. *Religious-Tolerance.org*. Retrieved August 20, 2006.
<http://www.religioustolerance.org/dc_highe.htm>

Robinson, F. (1992). *Love's story told: A life of Henry Murray*. Cambridge, MA: Harvard University Press.

Robinson, S. (2006, March 31). Justices uphold death penalty despite Ridgway. *News Tribune* (Tacoma, WA), B1.

Robinson, W. (1997), December. Heaven's Gate: The end?. *Journal of Computer and Mediated Communication*. Retrieved August 20, 2006.
<http://jcmc.indiana.edu/vol3/issue3/robinson.html>

Ross, R. (1999). Heaven's Gate. Retrieved August 20, 2006.
<http://www.rickross.com/groups/heavensgate.html>

Rule, A. (1980). *The stranger beside me*. New York. Norton.

Rule, A. (2004). *Green River, running red: The real story of the Green River killer: America's deadliest serial murderer*. New York: Pocket Star.

Sabbatini, R. (1997). Are there differences between the brains of males and females? *Brain & Mind*. Retrieved August 22, 2006.
<http://www.cerebromente.org.br/n11/mente/eisntein/cerebro-homens.html>

Salekin, R. (2002). Psychopathy and therapeutic pessimism: Clinical lore or clinical reality? *Clinical Psychology Review, 22*, 79-112.

Salekin, R., Leistico, A., and Neumann, C. (2004). Psychopathy and comorbidity in a young offender sample: Taking a closer look at psychopathy's potential importance over disruptive behavior disorders. *Journal of Abnormal Psychology, 113*, 416-427.

Samenow, S. (2004). *Inside the criminal mind* (Revised and updated). New York: Crown.

Samples, K. (1994). *Prophets of the apocalypse: David Koresh & other American messiahs.* Grand Rapids, MI: Baker.

Saporito, B. (2002), February 10. How Fastow helped Enron fall. *Time.* Retrieved August 30, 2006.
<http://www.time.com/time/business/article/0,8599,201871-1,00.html>

Schneidman, E., ed. (1981). *Endeavors in psychology: Selections from the personology of Henry A. Murray.* New York: Harper and Row.

Schwellnus, I. (2004). Psychopathic traits in a group of Basotho students. Master's thesis. University of the Free State, South Africa.

Skeem, J., Edens, J., and Camp, J. (2004). Are there ethnic differences in levels of psychopathy? A meta-analysis. *Law and Human Behavior, 28*, 505-527.

Skeem, J., Monahan, J. and Mulvey, E. (2002). Psychopathy, treatment involvement, and subsequent violence among civil psychiatric patients. *Law and Human Behavior, 26*, 577-603.

Smith, A. (1776). *An inquiry into the nature and causes of the wealth of nations.* London: Methuen and Co.

Springer, J. (2006). Psychopath or abused child? A judge hears arguments about Cody Posey. *Court TV News.* Retrieved August 21, 2006.
<http://www.courttv.com/trials/posey/022106_ctv.html>

Stanley v. Litscher (2000). *213 F.3d 340.*

Steel, W. (2005, November 8). Jack Thompson withdraws from GTA case: Controversial attorney recuses himself amid ethics allegations. *IGN.com*. Retrieved August 21, 2006.
<http://xbox.ign.com/articles/665/665357p1.html>

Storey, M. (2005). "And as things fell apart": the crisis of postmodern masculinity in Bret Easton Ellis's *American psycho* and Dennis Cooper's *frisk*. *Critique, 47*, 57-72.

Stout, M. (2005). *The sociopath next door*. New York: Broadway.

Strand, S. and Belfrage, H. (2005). Gender differences in psychopathy in a Swedish offender sample. *Behavioral Sciences & the Law, 23*(6), 837-850.

Sutton, S., Vitale, J., and Newman, J. (2002). Emotion among women with psychopathy during picture perception. *Journal of Abnormal Psychology, 111*(4), 610-619.

Swan, N. (2000), March 17. Frank Abagnale: new life. *Life Matters*. Australian Broadcasting Corporation. Retrieved August 17, 2006.
<http://www.abc.net.au/rn/talks/lm/stories/s111098.htm>

TedBundy.com. Retrieved August 20, 2006.
<http://www.tedbundy.com>

Thomas, E. (1997, April 7). The next level. *Newsweek*, 28.

Torsen, T. (2005, February 15). Grand Theft Auto sparks another lawsuit. *Gamespot News*. Retrieved August 21, 2006.
<http://www.gamespot.com/news/6118699.html>

Valium. PsyWeb Mental Health Site. Retrieved August 20, 2006.
<http://www.psyweb.com/Drughtm/jsp/valium.jsp>

Vitacco, M., Neumann, C., and Jackson, R. (2005). Testing a four-factor model of psychopathy and its association with ethnicity, gender, intelligence, and violence. *Journal of Consulting and Clinical Psychology, 73*, 466-476.

Vogel, D. (2005). *The market for virtue: The potential and limits of corporate social responsibility*. Washington, D.C.: Brookings Institution Press.

Weeks, K. (2006). *Brutal: The untold story of my life inside Whitey Bulger's Irish mob.* New York: HarperCollins.

Wessinger, C. (2000) *How the millennium comes violently.* New York: Seven Bridges.

Wick, S. (1997). The imposter phenomenon. 1997 WICB/Career Strategy Columns. Retrieved August 20, 2006. <http://www.ascb.org/index.cfm?navid=112&id=1545&tcode=nws3>

Wilkinson, C. (1985). Effects of diazepam (Valium) and trait anxiety on human physical aggression and emotional state. *Journal of Behavioral Medicine, 8,* 101-114.

William, H. (1997). *The keepers of Heaven's Gate: The millennial madness.* Anchorage, AK: Earthpulse.

Will the corporation survive? (2001, November 3). *Economist,* 14-18.

Wilson, J. (1985). *Thinking about crime* (Revised). New York: Vintage.

Wong, E. (2006, March 15). Hussein's testimony prompts closure of court to public. *The New York Times.* Retrieved August 21, 2006. <http://www.nytimes.com/2006/03/15/international/middleeast/15cnd-hussein.html>

Wong, S. and Hare, R. (2005). *Guidelines for a psychopathy treatment program.* Toronto: Multi-health Systems.

Wrangham, R. and Peterson, D. (1997). *Demonic males: Apes and the origins of human violence.* New York: Mariner.

Wyatt, E. (2005, August 7). The man in the mirror. *New York Times,* sec. 2, 1.

978-0-595-41544-1
0-595-41544-X

Printed in the United Kingdom by
Lightning Source UK Ltd., Milton Keynes
137101UK00001B/105/A